Fundamentals of Government Information

Mining, Finding, Evaluating, and Using Government Resources

Eric J. Forte,
Cassandra J. Hartnett, and
Andrea L. Sevetson

Neal-Schuman Publishers, Inc.
New York   London

Published by Neal-Schuman Publishers, Inc.
100 William St., Suite 2004
New York, NY 10038

Printed and bound in the United States of America.

The paper used in this publication meets the minimum requirements of American National Standard for Information Sciences—Permanence of Paper for Printed Library Materials, ANSI Z39.48-1992.

Library of Congress Cataloging-in-Publication Data

Forte, Eric J., 1967-
  Fundamentals of government information : mining, finding, evaluating, and using government resources / Eric J. Forte, Cassandra J. Hartnett, Andrea L. Sevetson.
      p. cm.
  Includes bibliographical references and indexes.
  ISBN 978-1-55570-737-8 (alk. paper)
  1. Government information—United States. 2. Government publications—United States. 3. Electronic government information—United States. 4. Libraries—Special collections—Government publications. 5. Government publications—Bibliography—Methodology. I. Hartnett, Cassandra J., 1964- II. Sevetson, Andrea. III. Title.

ZA5055.U6F67 2011
025.17'34—dc22

                                                          2011009275

To Francesca Hartnett for teaching her children
the value of civic involvement

Contents

Part I: Overview of Key Government Information Resources

PART II: Government Information in Focus

List of Figures

Preface

For decades, librarians in all settings have known that government information is an integral part of their work. Examples include public librarians who assist users with consumer questions, job seeking, special queries at tax and election time, or applying for government benefits; community college librarians who discover that the Congressional Research Service offers the best concise overviews of controversial topics; academic librarians who are often amazed that a high percentage of their grand collections are in fact government holdings; law librarians who help users find government cases, legislation, and regulations; and medical librarians who have built an entire intellectual framework around the government-produced PubMed database.

Our ardent belief is that greater knowledge of government resources can strengthen the skills of any librarian. *Fundamentals of Government Information: Mining, Finding, Evaluating, and Using Government Resources* introduces librarians, library and information science students, educators, and information seekers of all kinds to the world of government material. Far from dry, dusty "documents," today's government offerings are deep, far-reaching, and ultimately essential to an informed citizenry, a true democracy, and outstanding library collections and services. For most of the examples in the book, we assume a context of online government communication, but we frequently refer back to resources in print as well. It will be not the container, but rather the content, that will guide our journey through government resources.

Earlier government documents overviews and texts have not adequately addressed the fundamental changes in the means of producing, distributing, and accessing government information that have occurred over the past ten years. Since we believe it is time for some new basics, we have designed *Fundamentals of Government Information: Mining, Finding, Evaluating, and Using Government Resources* as the first government information text to be conceived, written, and published in the twenty-first century. The book provides the reader with the following:

- Models and techniques for discovery of government information
- Insight into the popular and research value of government publications
- Experience acquiring new skills in a simple, sequential manner, reinforced by exercises

Above all else, we aim to help you, the reader, become comfortable with the "everydayness" of government information. Rather than worrying about not being conversant in all things governmental, we will encourage you to look for basic evidence of government in your daily life. Breathing clean air? Think of the U.S. Environmental Protection Agency. Watching a television set that does not explode? Give a nod to the Consumer Product Safety Commission. Looking forward to a nip of alcohol after work on Friday night? Your state's liquor authority will greatly influence your ability to do so. Throughout the book, we encourage you to observe the world around you with an eye to government agencies and policies. You will be pleasantly surprised at how quickly your skill level grows at this game. Do not worry about mastering this art, which takes a lifetime of applied work; in truth, mastery never occurs in the government information world, because governments are ever changing. Still, our goal is to define the new fundamentals of government publications for any non–government documents librarian or student.

Government information should be considered a *genre* of public literature. Whether one is perusing a congressional hearing, a NASA technical document, an FDA advisory, or a historic War Department pamphlet, this literature stands apart because of its provenance and official nature, concepts that become complicated in the era of easily modified online publications, as we will explore in Chapter 1. Although government information exists at the state and local levels (city, county, and in some cases neighborhood), this book focuses primarily on the U.S. federal government. We intersperse examples from state and local governments, but we generally do not explore international or foreign government literature in depth, except for a few instances in which this content is essential to the information at hand. The U.S. federal government is vast enough on its own and provides a good working model for other levels of government. One could argue that state and local governments do most of the actual governing, but the federal government certainly is the most prolific publisher. If one can appreciate the basic structure and function of the mammoth United States federal government, other government models may be relatively easy to understand.

How the Book Is Structured

Fundamentals of Government Information is divided into two main parts.

Part I, "Overview of Key Government Information Resources," provides an overarching view of government resources that sets the context for the more specific information to come. Chapter 1 looks at the nature of government information. Why do governments publish, after all? What types of literature do they distribute, and how is this accomplished? It reviews the history of government publishing, the concept of designated "depository" libraries, and the rapid evolution to nearly exclusive digital publishing—and the issues that followed that change. Chapter 2 delves into general tools and strategies for describing and identifying government information, including reference books and textbooks about government information, comprehensive catalogs and indexes, databases, and online search tools. It is natural to follow with a chapter on Congress and laws, as most librarians appreciate an overview of the legislative process and the information created along the way. Chapter 3 aims to stoke readers' enthusiasm for some of the most valued public affairs literature in the world: congressional publications (such as hearings, reports, and research studies). We explore the array of documents that contribute to the making and codifying of our laws, focusing on freely available sources but including some discussion of private sources and their value. In government documents, the difference between what is free and what is fee can be an important distinction: some government output, like the bills from a single session of Congress, is so voluminous that the materials may be overwhelming to use without the extra value added by commercial publishers.

Chapter 4 explores government rules, also known as regulations. Most Americans know little about the process of creating administrative law (regulatory materials). Readers learn the difference between regulations and laws passed by Congress; the draft and comment process; final regulations; codification; and the Reginfo.gov, Regulations.gov, and FederalRegister.gov projects. Strategies are offered for tracking the same processes at the state level. The next logical step is an introduction to the legal system and both statutory and judicial law, found in Chapter 5. Readers discover what legislatures and courts publish and how decisions and other court materials are accessed. Much legal material is privately published, due to the rather unusual evolution of legal publishing in this country, but it is important to highlight some of the growing free, government-produced court publications at both the federal and the state level. Chapter 6 addresses some of the most classic reading in government publications: the information output of the U.S. president. The chapter examines the way presidential papers have been compiled over the years, as well as executive orders, proclamations, decisions, press conferences, WhiteHouse.gov, and bill signing statements.

Part II, "Government Information in Focus," begins with a 360-degree sweep through the rest of the executive branch (Chapter 7), exploring the incredible array of agencies and their publications found online and in libraries nationwide. The following chapters in Part 2 are arranged by broad topic area, starting with Statistical Information (Chapter 8), and the simple becomes multifaceted as we show the many ways in which government documents librarians utilize their most essential reference work, the *Statistical Abstract of the United States*. Readers are coached to think like the government officials responsible for collecting and distributing statistics. Chapter 9 (Health Information) examines PubMed and its prominent role in the movement toward open access to scholarly, medical, and scientific literature, along with a review of consumer and statistical health information and the vital role played by local health departments across the country. In Chapter 10, the focus shifts to resources from the U.S. Department of Education, such as enrollment and performance data, directories, school information, curricular materials, and laws like No Child Left Behind.

Chapter 11's treatment of Scientific and Technical Information adds coverage of cross-disciplinary government tools (the National Technical Information Service, Science.gov) and other major government scientific publishing agencies, such as the National Aeronautics and Space Administration (NASA) and the United States Geologic Survey (USGS). Chapter 12 focuses on environmental and energy resources from agencies like the Environmental Protection Agency and the Department of Energy, but also covers other related material, such as weather data from the National Oceanic and Atmospheric Administration.

Next, in Chapter 13, readers learn that government sources have everything to do with the financial machinery that keeps our nation's economy running. Included is a close look at information from agencies as wide-ranging as the Federal Reserve Board, the Treasury, and the Bureau of Labor Statistics as we consider business, economic, and financial sources.

Chapter 14 brings readers to a full exploration of census data, truly the mother lode of federal statistics, with not only the decennial census but the myriad other surveys conducted by the Census Bureau on topics ranging from childcare to marriage to immigration. The book concludes with Chapter 15, a journey through historical and archival information, which is the type of government record most familiar to many people. The convergence of libraries, archives, and museums is a central focus. After considering the expanding field of genealogy and its intersection with government information, the chapter concludes with a review of the Freedom of Information Act and the public's right to request release of unpublished government materials.

We have included over 50 exercises, allowing readers to assess their understanding of government information and have a little fun playing with a wide variety of real government documents. These exercises are designed to (1) be useful in a library science classroom, (2) clarify some of the more challenging concepts in government information, and (3) give readers a chance to use a particular information resource to answer a question and evaluate its effectiveness step by step. For example, in Chapter 6, readers are asked to think about where a president's letters would be found and weigh the importance of different signing statements cited in an article.

We hope all our readers find this journey through Congress, the courts, the president, federal agencies, statistics, regulations and more . . . to be a rewarding and memorable adventure.

Acknowledgments

Eric Forte wishes to thank Brenda Burton and Mary Whisner, as well as Cass and Andrea for all their support. Cass Hartnett thanks the University of Washington Libraries for the time grant to work on this project; her coworkers for filling in so many hours; and Sandy Wood, Linda Whitaker, Terry Jankowski, and especially Marianne G. Taylor. All three authors thank our families and friends for sticking with us over the past year, and the community of government documents librarians for educating us.

Part I

Overview of Key Government Information Resources

Chapter 1

Introduction: The People's Information

Government information provides a window to current society and its history, documenting and informing the communities and citizens it governs. With the emergence of representative governments such as those of the United States, its states, cities, and counties, and an increasing number of the world's nations, government information is truly the people's information. Although sometimes considered a unique skill set requiring specialized knowledge and access tools, finding government information is a fundamental information competency. The ability and need to find and use government information ranges from necessity to responsibility, from inquiry to curiosity. And what one finds in government information is endlessly fascinating and often surprising.

Government information may cover nearly any topic, can be used by any citizen, and encompasses almost every type of information:

- Tax forms
- Voting records of senators and representatives
- The laws about educational standards that influence school curriculum
- The latest research on health and medicine, geology, physics, and more
- Information about the flu and other infectious diseases
- Trade agreements affecting the import of consumer electronics
- Pollution readings for your city
- Weather records
- Data on unemployment and prices
- Brochures for national parks
- The personal papers of former presidents
- The wisdom of Smokey Bear, Woodsy Owl, and Sprocket Man (Figure 1.1)

Government information comprises a broad array of types of material:

- Historical documents
- Legal treatises
- Posters
- Maps
- Statistics and datasets
- Scientific papers
- Satellite imagery
- Databases and web services

- Transcripts of press conferences and speeches by presidents, governors, members of Congress, and government officials
- Supreme Court decisions

The closest thing to an official definition of a government publication is "informational matter which is published as an individual document at Government expense, or as required by law" (44 U.S.C. §1901). This broad definition fits, as in the course of carrying out their missions, governments produce nearly every type of information product short of poetry and novels, a diversity of output that fits the diversity of its citizenry.

Figure 1.1. Sprocket Man

Relatively early in United States history, governments and libraries formed a special relationship to provide government information to citizens. This was especially true at the federal level, although it applied generally to most states, too. Libraries became the repositories for government information, the conduits delivering government information to its people. Citizens needing access to any of this information trekked to a local library designated, through agreement between the government and the library, to house government materials amongst its collections. Once there, citizens could not only access government information, but also be served by librarians who were experts in locating sometimes obscure, and frequently specialized and arcane, government information. These so-called depository libraries house the information of our democracy.

Largely because most federal government documents are free of copyright and because they are, by nature, designed to serve the public, government information has taken full advantage of the web era, making a rapid and early transition to providing all types of information almost exclusively via web access. While this rapid change has brought government information ever closer to the public and to reference librarians, government information still encompasses countless unique resources and characteristics requiring special expertise, information skills, and strategies. This book, with the aid of a knowledge of civics and general reference skills, provides the foundations of government information.

Introduction

Public government information and depository libraries are a domain of information that is sometimes misunderstood by the outsider, but can be endlessly valuable, rewarding, and fascinating to those in the know. The very existence, production, and management of government information is indicative of the development of our society. The content and types of information the government produces, and how that information is shared, also reflect issues of how we govern ourselves as a nation, interact with our communities, and participate in a worldwide community.

Government documents sometimes top the bestseller lists. National bestsellers have included the *9/11 Commission Report: the Official Report of the 9/11 Commission*; the Warren Commission report (officially known as the *Report of the President's Commission on the Assassination of President John F. Kennedy*); and the Clinton impeachment era's Starr report (officially known as... are you ready... the *Referral from Independent Counsel Kenneth W. Starr in conformity with the requirements of Title 28, United States Code, section 595(c) : communication from Kenneth W. Starr, independent counsel, transmitting a referral to the United States House of Representatives filed in conformity with the requirements of Title 28, United States Code, section 595(c)*) (Figure 1.2).

Figure 1.2. Starr Report Title Page

105th Congress, 2d Session – – – – – – – – – – – – House Document 105–310

REFERRAL FROM INDEPENDENT COUNSEL KENNETH W. STARR IN CONFORMITY WITH THE REQUIREMENTS OF TITLE 28, UNITED STATES CODE, SECTION 595(c)

COMMUNICATION

FROM

KENNETH W. STARR, INDEPENDENT COUNSEL

TRANSMITTING

A REFERRAL TO THE UNITED STATES HOUSE OF REPRESENTATIVES FILED IN CONFORMITY WITH THE REQUIREMENTS OF TITLE 28, UNITED STATES CODE, SECTION 595(c)

SEPTEMBER 11, 1998.—Referred to the Committee on the Judiciary pursuant to H. Res. 525 and ordered to be printed

U.S. GOVERNMENT PRINTING OFFICE

50–800   WASHINGTON : 1998

For sale by the U.S. Government Printing Office
Superintendent of Documents, Mail Stop: SSOP, Washington, DC 20402-9328
ISBN 0-16-057480-3

Other government document gems don't sell any copies, but address very popular issues. The *Munson Report* famously assessed Japanese-American loyalty prior to Pearl Harbor (although these citizens were judged loyal, the report was buried after the attack and only resurfaced later as part of the mammoth set of congressional hearings about Pearl Harbor that took place after the war, and after Japanese-American citizens were detained in camps anyway). Another Munson, the famous 1970s-era New York Yankee baseball player Thurman Munson, who fatally crashed his private jet, is the subject of a report from the National Transportation Safety Board, *Thurman L. Munson, Cessna Citation 501, N15NY, near Canton, Ohio, August 2, 1979*. A more recent plane crash that had a happier ending thanks to pilot Chesley Sullenberger was the subject of *US Airways flight 1549 accident: hearing before the Subcommittee on Aviation of the Committee on Transportation and Infrastructure, House of Representatives, 111th Congress, first session, February 24, 2009*.

One of the most empowering aspects of understanding government information is the ability to conduct one's own fact checking. Not sure what to make of a media or third-party account of a government event or document? Want to investigate an interesting tidbit forwarded to your e-mail, read on a blog, or heard on the radio? Want to find the actual reported statistics of a government agency, or check the veracity of an accusation from an angry political pundit? Depository libraries and government information librarians and specialists can lead patrons to the actual text of a piece of legislation, show details of an actual budget that a president actually proposed or a Congress actually passed, find the actual words that an official said in a press conference, and produce the full text of the real government report. Such direct, rather than secondary, access to government information is the whole reason government information exists, and government documents librarians thrive on empowering the public to understand and research the information and actions of their own governments.

Lest one think that government documents attempt to address just the facts, there's the *Roswell Report: Case Closed* (Figure 1.3) from the U.S. Air Force addressing fictitious (so they say!) government encounters with aliens, and the aforementioned fictional character Smokey Bear, who stars in a whole series of U.S. government documents. Yet sometimes the debate over government truth covers more serious topics than extraterrestrials and talking mammals: in the midst of national recessions that included significant corporate layoff activity, administrations have twice attempted to stop their own reporting of mass layoffs, a statistic tracked in the course of duties by the Bureau of Labor Statistics. Such moves—both times reversed—were nonetheless often believed to be efforts to restrict government information for political gain. Similar concerns have also been aired over government science, such as disputed National Cancer Institute information discussing possible links between abortions and later incidents of breast cancer ("Abortion and Breast Cancer," 2003), and suppression of information in a Environmental Protection Agency report reiterating scientific evidence of human-induced causes of climate change (Revkin, 2003).

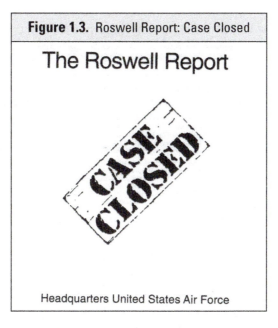

Figure 1.3. Roswell Report: Case Closed

The Roswell Report

Headquarters United States Air Force

Government information, not surprisingly, covers many fascinating and useful historical topics. The massive, 130-volume set *War of the Rebellion* collects firsthand accounts, letters, maps, government reports, and more from both sides of the Civil War, providing a nearly endless source for historians, while World War II–era government posters (available online via Northwestern University at http://www.library.northwestern.edu/govinfo/collections/wwii-posters/index.html) illuminate many aspects of the American war effort. Citizens come to depository libraries seeking official military histories for specific battles, geologic and archaeological reports on antiquities, demographic statistics of colonial America, or information about the specific ships they may have served on in the military as cataloged in the *Dictionary of American Naval Fighting Ships*.

Government information is by no means limited to the federal government, historical topics, or printed reports. One can search state court records to find business bankruptcies in one's town. Government information reveals that vanity license plates such as "ILVTOFU" and "DNASTY" have been rejected by state departments of motor vehicles, and the California Board of Registered Nursing allows the public to access the disciplinary records of nurses (Figure 1.4). The Minnesota Department of Transportation provides access to inspection reports of the state's bridges, while Arizona's Maricopa County provides access to which of the county's speed cameras were activated by location, and how many citations were issued as a result. One popular type of database is produced by state property assessors and includes the sales prices of homes across the nation. Truly, the capabilities, the possibilities, and increasingly, the realities of e-government initiatives—providing government information *and* services online—are nearly limitless. And limitless is the imagination of the

---

Figure 1.4. The California Database of Registered Nurses, One of Hundreds of Databases of Government Information

DEPARTMENT OF CONSUMER AFFAIRS

CA.GOV *Board of Registered Nursing*

| Home | About Us | Applicants | Schools | Licensees | Forms | Enforcement | Diversion | Regulations | Online Services |

BOARD OF REGISTERED NURSING

Licensee Name: DOE, JANE L
License Type: Registered Nurse
License Number: 1234567
License Status: ACTIVE Definition
ACCUSATION FILED Definition
Expiration Date: March 31, 2012
Issue Date: October 7, 2002
County: SAN DIEGO
Actions: Yes

Related Licenses/Registrations/Permits

No records returned

Disciplinary Actions

Public documents relating to this action are available here: http://m.ca.gov/public/dddd.pdf

May 06, 2010 Accusation Filed

---

expert government documents professional who is adept at mastering the many opportunities for government services and information.

The amount of available government information and data is staggering. How did we come to this rich government information environment? The path was sometimes slow and rocky, and reflects steady progress from the founding of the nation through recent efforts to make this type of data available via the web.

Background: History of Government Information

The unique nature of the United States' representative democracy gave government information an importance unprecedented in the history of information, knowledge, and libraries. To make informed decisions, people needed to know about the actions of their representatives in Congress and their nation. To this end, the United States Constitution contains the first mention of U.S. government information, calling on Congress to keep and publish a journal of its proceedings:

> Each House shall keep a Journal of its Proceedings, and from time to time publish the same, excepting such Parts as may in their Judgment require Secrecy; and the Yeas and Nays of the Members of either House on any question shall, at the Desire of one fifth of those Present, be entered on the Journal. (U.S. Constitution, art.1, sect.5)

This line from the Constitution, however, expresses the opposing forces in play in the early days of government information. While it calls for publication of a record of Congress, it also contains provisions to restrict government information, whether because of a need for secrecy or at the simple desire of a large majority.

Seavey argues that "it seems fairly clear that the framers of the Constitution were very concerned that there be a free and easy flow of information in order to make democracy work" (2005: 42). To support this view, Seavey references not only the Constitution but the *Federalist Papers* and their underlying assumption of the need for an informed citizenry with access to government information. Seavey notes a Daniel Webster speech of 1825 in which Webster, discussing this informed citizenry, declares that "under the influence of this rapidly increasing knowledge, the people have begun, in all forms of government, to think, and to reason, on affairs of state...Regarding government as an institution for the public good, they demand a knowledge of its operations, and a participation in its exercise" (43).

President James Madison issued the most famous call for access to government information, writing in an August 4, 1822 letter to W. T. Barry:

> A popular Government, without popular information, or the means of acquiring it, is but a Prologue to a Farce or a Tragedy; or perhaps both. Knowledge will forever govern ignorance: And a people who mean to be their own Governors, must arm themselves with the power which knowledge gives. (Madison, 1822: 103)

This may be true, but a government that *did* little may be expected to have *produced* little government information: Walters argues that for many decades after the nation's founding, the U.S. federal government did not do much and produced a corresponding scarcity of official government information. Discussing the relative dearth of federal government, he writes

> In its first 100 years, American political scientists revered a form of government Thomas Carlyle derisively described as "anarchy plus a street constable"...in accordance with these Jeffersonian tenets, the U.S. government governed very little for much of the nineteenth century. Citizens generally demonstrated a corresponding indifference to politics. (Walters, 2002: 2–3)

As to the government information that did exist, its publishing was largely left to newspapers, which did not necessarily do a very accurate job. Walters quotes Alexis de Tocqueville, who says that "the proceedings of American society leave fewer traces than do events in a private family. Nothing is written"

(2002: 4). Indeed, Quinn notes that the "the idea of public information was a radical concept at the time of the American Revolution" (2003: 283). What the early leaders and political scientists thought about the nature of government information is subject to debate. What is not as open to debate was the relative lack of attention paid to accuracy, quality, or longevity when it came to actually printing government information.

Still, the idea of access to government information did exist and continued to evolve. Building on the mention in the Constitution, federal laws passed in 1795 (1 Stat. 443) and 1813 further addressed distributing laws and printing government information for the benefit of the citizenry. The 1813 resolution (Statute II, 13th Congress) actually called for the printing of 200 extra copies of the journals, and sending a copy to each state legislature, college, and historical society. While this still constituted a small volume of printing—and, as Quinn notes, the quality of this outsourced printing was often poor (2003: 285)—the idea of printing extra copies of government documents and distributing them around the nation is a seminal one in the history of government information, hinting at fulfilling Madison's edict and inspiring the mature depository library system, an idea to which we'll return shortly.

During these early decades of the nation there was still a relatively small output of material to be printed. Beyond what appeared in newspapers, the output of the executive branch, scarce as it was, was often in the form of reports to Congress, and such material was published in a large catchall series called the *United States Congressional Serial Set*. Comprising a mix of congressional publications, executive agency reports, and messages and communications from the president, the *Serial Set* was the primary vehicle for all government information.

The poor and inconsistent quality of government printing was addressed by the creation of the Government Printing Office (GPO) in 1860 (through the Joint Resolution in Relation to the Public Printing, 12 Stat. 117), which aimed to remove competing private printers from government publishing and bring such printing under the umbrella of the government itself. This act also marked the beginning of the printing of executive branch publications as separate reports, although for another 40-plus years, they were also often printed as congressional documents in the *Serial Set*.

The years following began to see some growth in both government itself and government publications, driven largely by government science (specifically the study of agriculture, water, and geology, inspired by the Louisiana Purchase and lands on the frontier, beginning with the work of Lewis and Clark) and by slowly evolving ideas favoring a more active government role in the quality of life (Walters, 2002: 5–13). The federal government was starting to do more, publish more, and pay more attention to the quality of the publishing process.

Acts in the 1850s (11 Stat. 253, 11 Stat. 368, 11 Stat. 379) further advanced the idea of distributing these government documents via the central printing of extra copies and distributing those copies throughout the nation in what was the official creation of depository libraries. The 1813 act had called for copies to be sent to colleges, historical societies, and states. But now, each representative and senator was permitted to designate official depository libraries in his district. These libraries would then receive one of these extra copies of each government document that GPO printed. Depository libraries were spread across the lands of the governed.

In 1895, the General Printing Act advanced the idea of government publications much further: it compiled and updated all of these previous laws regarding the printing and distribution of government documents, streamlined federal printing and publishing, moved the Federal Depository Library Program (FDLP) from the Department of the Interior to the GPO, and mandated free public access in depository libraries (28 Stat. 601). The act also called for the creation of an ongoing bibliographic catalog of government documents (which became the *Monthly Catalog of United States Government Publications*). For the seeker of government documents, this act could scarcely be more important, and lay the foundation for twentieth-century government information. In fact, the work of a depository library went essentially unchanged from the passage of this act in 1895 until the 1970s (Kessler, 1996: 371).

But it was another factor that truly led to the maturity of government information: Franklin Roosevelt and the New Deal. As Shiflett explains, "the actual evolution of the GPO...is largely a product of the expansion of the executive department during the Great Depression and the response of the Roosevelt administration to the social problems that came to be considered in the domain of the federal government" (1982: 118–119). The federal government expanded quickly, and with it the quantity of government publications. As the quantity rose, so did the number of depository libraries. Issues remained, however. Sears (2008) discusses this period, describing how depository library designations did not change with geographic shifts in population (and congressional districts), how depository designations were sometimes political, and how some depositories were ill-equipped to either house or provide public service to their collections of government documents. The Depository Library Act of 1962 (76 Stat. 352) addressed these issues. It formally ingrained requirements for public service at depository libraries, and allowed more depository libraries to be designated, doubling their number relatively quickly from under 600 to 1,200 and truly leading to the modern era of government information and the depository library. Perhaps the most thorough and critical history of government publications is *U.S. Government Publication: Ideological Development and Institutional Politics from the Founding until 1970* (Walters, 2005).

Depository Libraries and Twentieth-Century Government Information before the Web

The expansion of government information continued for decades, only slowing some in the Carter and Reagan eras, which saw first the Paperwork Reduction Act of 1980 and then Reagan's decree to limit spending on information that did not truly serve the public interest (Richardson, 1982). Formats began to evolve as well, with the first government documents on microform shipping in 1977, and the first CD-ROMs coming in the 1980s.

Depository libraries and services shared many characteristics in this mature period leading up to the web era. Since the aforementioned Depository Library Act of 1962, federal depository libraries have come in two types: regionals and selectives. Of the 1,200 to 1,400 libraries that have been depositories in this modern era, some 50 of them are designated as regional depository libraries. These regionals have greater responsibilities: they serve selectives in their regions, providing interlibrary loan, reference, and support for government publication collection development. While regionals are required both to receive all available government documents and to keep them forever, selectives are permitted to select particular classes of government documents and, after a period of time, are allowed to donate older government documents to other depositories, or to discard them, under the direction of their regional.

Selectives choose these classes of government documents for acquisition by working from the *List of Classes*. The *List of Classes* is a listing of over 10,000 categories (called classes) of government documents, and is available from the suite of tools available on the FDLP Desktop, the administrative home on the web for the federal depository library program (Figure 1.5). A class may be a particular publication, a particular series, or a genre of publication within an agency. Examples of classes include 00-C-27, the *Daily Grain Report* from the Department of Agriculture; 0786-T-01, *Metropolitan Area Employment and Unemployment*; 0876, General Publications from the Department of State; 1037-B, Hearings, Prints, and Miscellaneous Publications from the Committee on Homeland Security and Governmental Affairs; and 0159-C-25, *Census of Population and Housing: Population and Housing Unit Counts* (Missouri). A selective chooses some hundreds or thousands of these classes to best serve its local clientele. For instance, a selective generally makes sure it selects government documents of state and local interest, such as local census volumes and local maps. Likewise, a selective within a law library might choose mainly legal materials. A selective located at or near a medical school might select health and human services resources heavily; an Alaskan selective might select many materials from the U.S. Forest Service, the Department of the Interior, and the U.S. Fish and Wildlife Service. Selectives everywhere might select popular materials related to health, education, and social security, while an official *List of Essential Titles* are classes *required* by the FDLP to be selected by all depository libraries and cover many popular and core topics, including laws and regulations.

Depository libraries do not, however, hold all federal government information that exists. As noted above, they hold largely what GPO has produced via its printing operations. It's no secret that a large number of executive agency publications were not printed by GPO and were not funneled through GPO. These so-called fugitive documents have often been collected by depository libraries, but only after focused efforts to contact and procure copies directly from the issuing agencies. Walters (1996) offers a compelling review of the political tensions involved with the legislative branch overseeing functions of the executive branch (Congress's Joint Committee on Printing oversees GPO and federal printing), the result of which was sometimes executive agencies

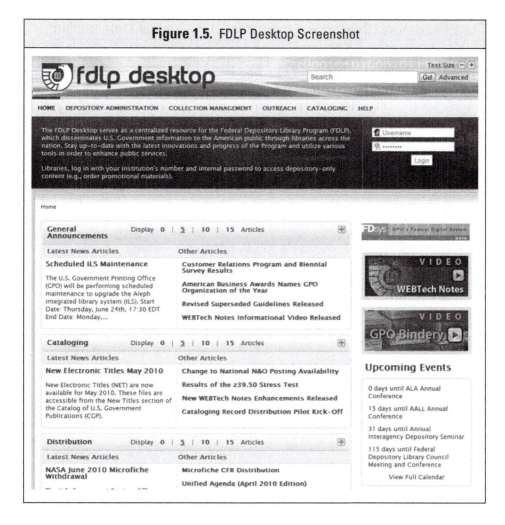

Figure 1.5. FDLP Desktop Screenshot

ignoring GPO and making their own arrangements to print documents. Nonetheless, GPO has a long history of working hard to ensure that important publications are part of the depository library program.

Note that basic records of government are not printed as government documents. Various documents, correspondence, and more ephemeral items not intended for public usage may be found instead in the National Archives (covered in Chapter 15). Further, some scientific and technical reports have not been distributed to depository libraries for various reasons (scientific reports will be covered in Chapter 11).

Meanwhile, as librarians built their government documents collections, service remained at the forefront. Government documents depository libraries answered a myriad of questions and inquiries using the government documents in their collections. It is excellent service to these collections that forms the basis of the remainder of the chapters in this book.

State Depository Libraries and International Government Information

State governments, meanwhile, generally had and continue to have government documents depository programs bearing a resemblance to the federal program, although they were less likely to have the concept of selecting certain classes (that is, a depository for a state typically receives all available publications for that state). While states produce much less material than the federal government, they also usually lack quite so robust a system for distributing and managing state government documents.

These state depository programs feature a lot of variety. Early in their histories, a few states began systems of collecting government information, usually housed in libraries, universities, or museums. Most states, however, have state depository programs that date from the mid- to late twentieth century. Smith et al. (2003) provide a state-by-state summary of documents programs.

Documents and information policies of foreign nations are much more inconsistent. While countries such as Canada have robust depository systems not unlike that of the United States, many nations do not have a tradition of government information or its distribution. Some international organizations, such as the United Nations and the European Union, do have well-established depository systems. Morrison and Mann (2004) summarize programs and information from both foreign countries and international organizations.

Classification of Government Documents

Federal government documents in physical formats use a unique classification system called the Superintendent of Documents (SuDoc) system. This system was developed by Adelaide Hasse, a pioneering and strong-willed librarian who is somewhat of a folk hero in government documents circles. The SuDoc system differs from general classification systems in that class numbers are based on issuing agency, subagency, and publication type.

> **Health, United States, 2005**
> SuDoc HE 20.7042/6: 2005
>
> HE: Department of Health and Human Services
> HE 20: Centers for Disease Control
> HE 20.7042/6: *Health, United States*
> HE 20.7042/6: 2005: *Health, United States*, 2005

SuDoc numbers are devised and assigned by GPO. Some libraries classify and integrate their documents into their regular collections using LC or Dewey, but the SuDoc system is used in most depository libraries and in many standard bibliographies, such as the *Catalog of United States Government Publications*. Most states and some intergovernmental entities (notably the United Nations) and foreign governments also use their own classification systems.

Government Information in the Web Era

Government information quickly took advantage of the Internet era. For quite some time, GPO, at the urging of Congress, had been migrating a few items to electronic formats, usually on floppy disks. This continued through early online access projects such as the Federal Bulletin Board, which was a varied collection of selected government document files available via early Internet protocols such as WAIS, Telnet, and Gopher. But it was the wide adoption of the Internet that led to the significant, profound, and lasting shift to electronic dissemination. Congress—in a visionary or perhaps luckily timed action— passed *The Government Printing Office Electronic Information Access Enhancement Act of 1993* (107 Stat. 112, the GPO Access Act) in January of 1993, mandating that GPO create an electronic public access system to key government publications such as the *Federal Register* and the *Congressional Record*. Just three months later, the graphical web browser Mosaic was released, leading to the explosion of the World Wide Web. The timing, if not the content itself, rendered the GPO Access Act the real kickoff of the era of widespread online government information for the public. Soon thereafter, Congress (via THOMAS, in 1994) and executive agencies, such as early adopters the Bureau of Labor Statistics and Bureau of the Census, led the rapid shift away from government documents printed and distributed via GPO, to agencies transforming and posting their government information directly on the web. As Aldrich et al. wrote in 2000, "Strongly entrenched in print on paper since its origins in the 1890s, the FDLP has undergone a remarkably swift transition toward web-based information delivery, particularly after the launch of GPO Access in 1994" (274) (see Figure 1.6).

The transition has led to a situation where nearly all federal government information is not only available online, but is born digital directly at the agencies. The process of this birth varies by agency, and sometimes resembles processes for creating and sharing earlier printed publications. Often, however, the web era is a more decentralized information dissemination environment characterized by little central control (i.e., from Congress or the president) and inconsistent dissemination policies: one agency may have dozens of offices and individuals posting information from the agency with relatively little oversight, while other agencies have more rigid procedures for controlling website content (Mahler and Regan, 2007). Further, the public's discovery of government information takes place predominantly via commercial search engines rather than via traditional government documents tools (Shuler, 2010).

As Aldrich continues, this fast, dramatic shift from a largely tangible paper collection to a ubiquitous web of government information has had many effects. Formerly distinct documents collections and services began to be a part of every librarian's realm, and the number of paper documents distributed to depository libraries plummeted. As government information moved rapidly and comprehensively online, the collections aspects of selectives and regionals began to blur in many ways. With the abundance of information online, it wasn't just that any library was now effectively a depository library in terms of its collection—any citizen held a depository library on his or her computer. Access did not and does not equate to success, however, and service to the many intricacies and nuances of government information remains as vital as ever.

GPO and the FDLP, which formerly spent much time in printing, distribution, and bibliographic control of government documents, have increasingly attempted to focus on service, preservation, and permanent public access, tasks

---

Figure 1.6. GPO Access circa 1990s Screenshot

Connect to Databases Online via *GPO Access*

List and Descriptions of Online Databases

Access Methods for Online Databases

Specialized Search Pages

Because the content of each database is unique, the databases on the Specialized Search Pages allow you to perform fielded searches to help make the search more specific. These fields make it possible to perform more advanced functions, such as limiting results by date or by section of the *Federal Register,* *Congressional Record* or *Code of Federal Regulations,* for example, but are tailored to the individual databases.

Select databases and enter searches below. Access is also available through Federal Depository Library Gateways or on-site at a Federal Depository Library. Helpful Hints provide instructions for searching the databases.

For simple searches select one **OR MORE** databases from the list below:

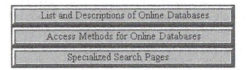

```
Budget of the US, FY1999
Budget of the US, FY1998
Budget of the US, FY1997
Campaign Reform Hearing
Congressional Bills, 103d Congress (1993-1994)
Congressional Bills, 104th Congress (1995-1996)
Congressional Bills, 105th Congress (1997-1998)
```

---

made more difficult by the shifting distribution channels and formats of government information, as well as the concurrent political realities of a government responding to terrorism threats.

Issues in Government Information

This book, through its expert coverage of sources and strategies for finding and using government information, addresses in detail contemporary issues in government information. As mentioned, the ready web availability of much government information potentially brings it much closer to citizens. Yet finding details such as the status of legislation, a statistic, an obscure technical report, or the location of local speed trap cameras requires specific knowledge, skills, and tools beyond a web search engine.

Also of vital importance in contemporary government information are issues related to access and preservation. While in some respects more government data are available than ever before, concerns about what and how much should be public information can—and have—placed limits on access. Meanwhile, the days of the FDLP handling permanent access through copies stored in the depository library program are largely over; born-digital government information suffers from incomplete and shifting efforts at preservation, and the risk of certain government information disappearing before being archived is real.

Access to Government Information Post-9/11

As we have seen, GPO has provided government information to depository libraries and the public for many years via the FDLP. While issues related to printing and fugitive documents have been real impediments to sharing government documents, it is access to government records in general that is the source of greater concerns about government openness.

Over the recent decades of the nation's history, public access to government records (as opposed to published government reports) has received more attention. Until the Freedom of Information Act (FOIA) established procedures whereby government agencies must provide access to government records upon request, the federal government had wide authority to restrict access to perceived sensitive government information. FOIA, passed in 1966, immediately provided a mechanism for opening access to many unreleased government records. Since that time, further efforts to make government more open have frequently been balanced by concurrent efforts to restrict government information, a back-and-forth summarized well by McDermott (2007). Recent years have seen perceived erosion in access to public government records, with national security cited in the need to restrict public access to potentially harmful information. Fowler notes that "since 9/11 there have been many more restrictions on the documents that are being made available to the public," citing an 81 percent increase in classified documents (2007: 20–21). Such information included documents and databases relating to public water supplies, facilities with toxic or potentially toxic chemicals, and energy transmission, all efforts that Hernon (2004) discusses. Hernon generally concludes that any security gained through restricting access to such information is insufficient compared to the need for open government. Nonetheless, as Hogenboom (2008) asserts, agencies have been and will be more cautious. To government agencies, the negative implications in having their information potentially compromise national security outweigh the negative implications of withholding information from citizens.

A bigger issue, however, is the worry that it is not simply national security driving government secrecy. According to Gordon, "the original intent was to protect military secrets, but between 2000 and 2006 the program expanded to include anything embarrassing to the government..." (2007). And in a far-reaching review of the history of government information policy, Jaeger (2007) traces the nearly uninterrupted trend of the federal government becoming increasingly open throughout the nation's history, only to have this trend seemingly reversed in the second Bush administration, even before the 9/11 attacks spurred heightened concerns about enemy access to sensitive information. Website content was removed, and several very public battles about access and secrecy to government records began, with the administration seeking to limit or restrict access altogether. After 9/11, this trend accelerated. Yet as Jaeger continues, "much of the information being classified seems tenuously related to national security, such as information on auto and tire safety, the quality of drinking water supplies, safety violations by airlines, and the amount of money spent by the federal government on information technology" (847–848). Limitations on access to government correspondence with private corporations and contractors such as Halliburton occurred at the same time that the amount of government information collected about citizens increased. The administration was marked by wide-ranging and comprehensive actions to limit and influence information across the board. Jaeger ultimately concludes:

> The perspective of the administration appears based on a belief that access to information, in general, should be very limited and tightly controlled in a centralized manner by the executive branch of the federal government. It also appears to include the belief that information that is made available for access should fit with the administration's opinions, as evidenced by the attempts to influence scientific committees and research studies and reports. Taken together, these policies have significant impacts on the amount and types of information available for access as well as presenting serious questions about the long term impact on democracy in the United States and internationally. (853)

The Obama administration quickly asserted a commitment to return to more open government (see the Open Government Initiative at http://www.whitehouse.gov/open/). This emphasis on increased transparency includes more open FOIA responses. The outcomes of these initiatives on citizen access to the information about and by their government remain to be seen.

Open Access to Government-Funded Research

Another important contemporary issue in government information is the movement toward greater access to federally funded scientific research. Each year, hundreds of millions of dollars of federal money are distributed in the form of grants to scientists in order to conduct research. Medical research may be the most prominent category of this support, but scientists in all genres may receive funding from various federal funding agencies.

Historically, the results of this federally funded research generally are written up and find their final public form in scientific papers submitted to and published in the key research journals in different disciplines, whereby they would be accessible to other scientists, scholars, policymakers, and bureaucrats. These journals—usually published by nonprofit scientific societies, private publishers, or a partnership between the two—were accessible to most researchers in the United States, Europe, and the most developed nations because those who needed to read them either subscribed to the journals themselves, or had access to a research library that subscribed. As most of these scientists were employed in universities and other research centers supported by libraries, access to the results of the research wasn't really a problem.

However, recent decades have seen an accelerating and dramatic inflationary pricing trend for many such journals. While the reasons for the inflation are many, major factors are inelastic demand (a medical researcher cannot simply cancel a subscription to a journal just because the price has risen, not if key findings are there) along with a shift from nonprofit, society-published journals, to for-profit, privately published journals whose incentive to publish is not simply to share knowledge, but also to maximize profits. In many cases, journals that previously cost hundreds of dollars per year quickly began to cost thousands of dollars per year, and both scientists and libraries began having to cancel subscriptions. The effect of this rising cost barrier is simple: often scientists perform research using taxpayer dollars, and the results are given to private publishers, who manage the peer-review process and publishing and then sell the journals back to scientists and libraries at prices increasingly difficult to afford.

Scientists, libraries, and now Congress have begun to act to correct this situation. Librarian and scientist led efforts such as the Alliance for Taxpayer Access (http://www.taxpayeraccess.org/) and the Scholarly Publishing and Academic Resources Coalition (SPARC, http://www.arl.org/sparc/, an effort of the Association of Research Libraries) have taken action toward opening access to such research, with scientists and librarians around the world increasingly working to ensure that the results of taxpayer-supported research are accessible to the public they are meant to serve.

Most importantly, Congress has stepped in and begun mandating that taxpayer-funded research be made available. The National Institutes of Health (NIH) now requires that all scientific papers published with the support of NIH grants be deposited in the freely accessible public archive PubMed Central (http://www.ncbi.nlm.nih.gov/pmc/) within 12 months of publication. Subsequent proposed legislation would expand such requirements to federally funded research beyond NIH, such as that sponsored by NASA, the Environmental Protection Agency, the Department of Education, and any other agency that funds significant research via grants and awards to outside entities. Open access to taxpayer-funded research will be mentioned in several later chapters, such as those on health, education, and scientific information.

Permanent Public Access to Government Information

The formats of government information have transitioned quickly in recent years. The print era evolved to the web era; then HTML and PDF documents became blogs and wikis, which became videos, which became ever-evolving websites including Web 2.0 and social media aspects. Modern government documents may be in flux, each one changing continuously, with countless revisions and versions, making identifying a government document or a single distinct version of a government document—much less preserving it—increasingly complex. The government information professional can keep up with finding the information in changing formats. But figuring out how to catalog, archive, preserve, and access it in perpetuity is extremely difficult, and much is lost as agencies—sometimes on purpose but often simply because they lack a plan or mechanism for preservation—delete documents unthinkingly (Pear, 2008).

GPO and the FDLP have made efforts to adapt. GPO's new Federal Digital System (FDsys) strives to address these concerns by collecting and ingesting government information, verifying versions, providing authenticity, and preserving information in perpetually usable formats, an ambitious, if maddeningly difficult, set of tasks (Priebe, 2008). Concurrently, GPO has planned for massive digitization projects, asserting a goal to digitize all known government documents—some 2.2 million—back to the *Federalist Papers* (GPO, 2004). This project (which as of 2011 had yielded an RFP, but still no actual funding) has yet to truly move forward. In its stead, numerous efforts, both private and nonprofit, aim to make at least some progress toward the idea of permanent public digital access, albeit in a limited and uncoordinated way. GPO maintains a Registry of U.S. Government Publication Digitization Projects (http://registry .fdlp.gov/), linking to some 100 valuable, but often very specific and somewhat limited, digitization projects. Broader organized projects include longtime open public information advocate Carl Malamud's Public.Resource.Org (http:// public.resource.org), which is both an archive and an advocacy effort for open government information, and addresses specific genres of government information, such as law, patents and trademarks, court cases and information, and National Technical Information Service and Government Accountability Office reports, although the organization is interested and involved in government information across the board. The Sunlight Foundation (http://www.sunlight foundation.com/, "Making Government Transparent and Accountable") is a similar advocacy organization, as is OpenTheGovernment.org. These are only three of the most wide-ranging nongovernmental organizations aiming to protect access to our public government information.

The Internet Archive (http://www.archive.org/) does mass-scale scanning and contains thousands of government documents. One looking for a known historical government document can frequently locate a copy in this archive. The largest scanning and digitization project (which includes large collections of government documents likely approaching GPO's vision of 2.2 million historical documents) is the Google Books Library Project. This project, which as of this writing remains mired in a multi-year legal limbo, has scanned and stored a huge number of government documents, yet most remain incompletely accessible as Google treats them as copyrighted books, offering only previews in most cases. A true opening of the documents in the Google Books project would approach GPO's vision, even if there are serious concerns about the quality of the scanning and the legal, economic, and social ramifications of the project in general. An ancillary Google Books project—a partnership between Google and the Committee on Institutional Cooperation (CIC) (http:// www.cic.net/home/projects/Library/BookSearch/GovDocs.aspx)—specifically focuses on federal government documents and promises to open access to these documents. Copies are also stored at the Hathi Trust Digital Library (http://www.hathitrust.org/).

As revolutionary as this electronic migration has been for government information, many aspects of depository libraries and services are less changed. Just because federal regulations are freely available does not mean that very many people know how to access them and understand what they mean. The same is true for many of the unique types of government information. Understanding these fundamentals of government information leads to exemplary service to citizens, and is the goal of this book.

Sources Mentioned in This Chapter

Sources mentioned in this section do not duplicate the References that follow.

Famous Reports

9/11 Commission Report: The Official Report of the 9/11 Commission, http://purl.access.gpo .gov/GPO/LPS51934, SuDoc: Y3.2:T27/2/FINAL.
Dictionary of American Naval Fighting Ships. SuDoc: D 207.10:1/pt.A/991-.
Munson Report (Japanese on the West Coast) found in Joint Committee on Investigation of Pearl Harbor Attack. 1946. *Pearl Harbor Attack* pt 6, pp. 2682-2696, SuDoc: Y4.P31:P31/pt.6.
Referral from Independent Counsel Kenneth W. Starr in conformity with the requirements of Title 28, United States Code, section 595(c) : communication from Kenneth W. Starr, independent counsel, transmitting a referral to the United States House of Representatives filed in conformity with the requirements of Title 28, United States Code, section 595(c), http://purl.access.gpo.gov/GPO/LPS1737, SuDoc: Y 1.1/7:105-310.
Roswell Report: Case Closed, SuDoc: D 301.2:R 73.
Thurman L. Munson, Cessna Citation 501, N15NY, near Canton, Ohio, August 2, 1979.
US Airways flight 1549 accident: hearing before the Subcommittee on Aviation of the Committee on Transportation and Infrastructure, House of Representatives, One Hundred Eleventh Congress, first session, February 24, 2009, http://purl.access.gpo.gov/GPO/FDLP455, SuDoc: Y 4.T 68/2:111-10.
War of the Rebellion (officially known as *The War of the Rebellion: A Compilation of the Official Records of the Union and Confederate Armies*) printed in the U.S. *Congressional Serial Set* over some 20 years, and available online in several locations.
Warren Commission report (officially known as the *Report of the President's Commission on the Assassination of President John F. Kennedy*), http://catalog.hathitrust.org/ Record/000035711, SuDoc: Pr 36.8:K 38/R 29/report.

World War II–era government posters, http://www.library.northwestern.edu/govinfo/collections/wwii-posters/index.html.

GPO Sites

Federal Digital System (FDsys), http://www.fdsys.gov/.

List of Classes, http://purl.access.gpo.gov/GPO/LPS89650/.

List of Essential Titles (*Essential Titles for Public Use in Paper or Other Tangible Format*), http://www.fdlp.gov/collections/building-collections/135-essential-titles-list/.

Monthly Catalog of United States Government Publications (1976–), http://catalog.gpo.gov/.

Registry of U.S. Government Publication Digitization Projects, http://registry.fdlp.gov/.

Superintendent of Documents (SuDoc) Classification System explanation, http://www.access.gpo.gov/su_docs/fdlp/pubs/explain.html.

Legislation (in Chronological Order)

U.S. Constitution, Art.1, Sect.5.

Promulgation of the Laws of the United States (March 3, 1795, 1 Stat. 443 Ch. 50).

Resolution for the Printing and Distribution of an Additional Number of the Journals of Congress, and of the Documents Published under Their Order (December 27, 1813, 3 Stat. 140).

Distribution of Public Documents (January 28, 1857, 11 Stat. 253).

Distribution of Certain Public Documents (March 20, 1858, 11 Stat. 368).

Keeping and Distribution of Public Documents (February 5, 1859, 11 Stat. 379).

Resolution in Relation to the Public Printing (June 23, 1860, 12 Stat. 117).

General Printing Act (January 12, 1895, 28 Stat. 601).

Depository Library Act of 1962 (August 9, 1962, 76 Stat. 352).

Freedom of Information Act (FOIA) (July 4, 1966, P.L. 89-487, 80 Stat. 250).

Paperwork Reduction Act of 1980 (December 11, 1980, P.L. 96-511, 94 Stat. 2812).

The Government Printing Office Electronic Information Access Enhancement Act of 1993, also known as the GPO Access Act (June 8, 1993, P.L. 103-40, 107 Stat. 112).

Other

Alliance for Taxpayer Access, http://www.taxpayeraccess.org/.

Committee on Institutional Cooperation (CIC), http://www.cic.net/home/projects/Library/BookSearch/GovDocs.aspx.

Congressional Record, http://purl.access.gpo.gov/GPO/LPS1671; SuDoc: X 1.1/A.

Federal Register, http://purl.access.gpo.gov/GPO/LPS1756, SuDoc: AE 2.106 (online), AE 2.7, or GS4.107.

Google Books Library Project, http://books.google.com/.

Hathi Trust Digital Library, http://www.hathitrust.org/.

The Internet Archive, http://www.archive.org/.

Open Government Initiative, http://www.whitehouse.gov/Open/.

OpenTheGovernment.org, http://www.openthegovernment.org/.

Public.Resource.Org, http://public.resource.org/.

PubMed Central, http://www.ncbi.nlm.nih.gov/pmc/.

Scholarly Publishing and Academic Resources Coalition (SPARC), http://www.arl.org/sparc/.

The Sunlight Foundation, http://www.sunlightfoundation.com/.

United States Congressional Serial Set, http://purl.access.gpo.gov/GPO/ LPS839, final bound version SuDoc: Y 1.1/2:.

References

"Abortion and Breast Cancer." 2003. Editorial. *New York Times*, January 6. http://www.nytimes.com/2003/01/06/opinion/abortion-and-breast-cancer.html.

Aldrich, Duncan, Gary Cornwell, and Daniel Barkley. 2000. "Changing Partnerships? Government Documents Departments at the Turn of the Millennium." *Government Information Quarterly* 17, no. 3: 273–290.

Beck, Clare. 2006. *The New Woman as Librarian: The Career of Adelaide Hasse*. Lanham, MD: Scarecrow Press.

Fowler, Rhonda E. 2007. "I've Got a Secret: Government Information Availability and Secrecy." *DttP: Documents to the People* 35, no. 2: 18–23.

Gordon, Bennett. 2007. "For Their Eyes Only." *Utne Reader*, January/February. http://www.utne.com/2007-01-01/ForTheirEyesOnly.aspx.

Government Printing Office. 2004. *A Strategic Vision for the 21st Century*. Washington, DC: Government Printing Office.

Hernon, Edward. 2004. "A Post-September 11th Balancing Act: Public Access to U.S. Government Information Versus Protection of Sensitive Data." *Journal of Government Information* 30, no. 1: 42–65.

Hogenboom, Karen. 2008. "Lessons Learned about Access to Government Information after World War II Can Be Applied after September 11." *Government Information Quarterly* 25, no. 1: 90–103.

Jaeger, Paul T. 2007. "Information Policy, Information Access, and Democratic Participation: The National and International Implications of the Bush Administration's Information Politics." *Government Information Quarterly* 24, no. 4: 840–859.

Kessler, Ridley. 1996. "A Brief History of the Federal Depository Library Program: A Personal Perspective." *Journal of Government Information* 23, no. 4: 369–380.

Madison, James. 1910. *The Writings of James Madison, Volume IX, 1819–1836*. Edited by Gaillard Hunt. New York: G. P. Putnam's Sons.

Mahler, Julianne, and Priscilla Regan. 2007. "Crafting the Message: Controlling Content on Agency Web Sites." *Government Information Quarterly* 24, no. 3: 505–521.

McDermott, Patrice. 2007. "Current Government Information Policy and Secrecy." *DttP: Documents to the People* 35, no. 2: 24–29.

Morrison, Andrea M., and Barbara J. Mann. 2004. *International Government Information and Country Information: A Subject Guide*. Westport, CT: Greenwood Press.

Quinn, Aimee. 2003. "Keeping the Citizenry Informed: Early Congressional Printing and 21st Century Information Policy." *Government Information Quarterly* 20, no. 3: 281–293.

Pear, Robert. 2008. "In Digital Age, Federal Files Blip into Oblivion." *New York Times*, September 13. http://www.nytimes.com/2008/09/13/us/13records .html.

Priebe, Ted, Amy Welch, and Marian MacGilvray. 2008. "The U.S. Government Printing Office's Initiatives for the Federal Depository Library Program to Set the Stage for the 21st Century." *Government Information Quarterly* 25, no. 1: 48–56.

Revkin, Andrew, with Katharine Seelye. 2003. "Report by the E.P.A. Leaves out Data on Climate Change." *New York Times*, June 19. http://www.nytimes.com/2003/06/19/politics/19CLIM.html.

Richardson, John. 1982. "The United States Government as Publisher Since the Roosevelt Administration." *Library Research* 4: 211–233.

Sears, Suzanne. 2008. "Connecting Constituents to Government Information: 150 Years of Congressionally Designated Libraries." *DttP: Documents to the People* 36, no. 3: 16–19.

Seavey, Charles. 2005. "Musings on the Past and Future of Government Information." *American Libraries* 36, no. 7: 42–44.

Shiflett, Orvin Lee. 1982. "The Government as Publisher: An Historical Review." *Library Research* 4: 115–135.

Shuler, John, Paul Jaeger, and John Bertot. 2010. "Implications of Harmonizing the Future of the Federal Depository Library Program within e-Government Principles and Policies." *Government Information Quarterly* 27, no. 1: 9–16.

Smith, Lori L., Daniel C. Barkley, Daniel D. Cornwall, Eric W. Johnson, and J. Louise Malcomb. 2003. *Tapping State Government Information Sources*. Westport, CT: Greenwood Press.

Walters, John Spencer. 1996. "The Presuperhighway Politics of U.S. Government Printing and Publishing, 1917–1960." *Journal of Government Information* 23, no. 2: 93–121.

Walters, John Spencer. 2002. "The Ideological Development of U.S. Government Publication, 1820–1920: From Jefferson to Croly." *Journal of Government Information* 29, no. 1: 1–15.

Walters, John Spencer. 2005. *U.S. Government Publication: Ideological Development and Institutional Politics from the Founding to 1970*. Lanham, MD: Scarecrow Press.

Chapter 2

How to Think Like a Government Documents Librarian

Introduction

Government information questions can be among the most challenging and rewarding queries that come across a librarian's actual or virtual desk. And they can also be surprisingly simple. Requests such as "I need the infant mortality rates for South American countries" or "Can I get the hearing from the Committee on Science and Technology on April 1, 2008?" come in as frequently as more involved questions like "I need census data from 1960 to 2010 with education information for my census tract" or "I need figures comparing the economic recovery of the current recession with that of the Great Depression."

A patron may read about a recently released (and unsourced) U.S. Census Bureau publication in the morning's paper or on a favorite website, or need to see FedBizOpps or the *Federal Register* to learn about a grant or business opportunity. Questions may require data or statistics from or about your city or county, the United States, or other countries. There may be a congressional hearing on steroids in sports, a proposed policy on school nutrition, or a controversial nomination for the supreme court in the news, and the patron wants to see who testified and what the witnesses said. Questions come from all directions and can reflect a dinner table bet that needs to be resolved, a school project, a term paper, or even an English 101 paper where pro and con arguments must be made.

Requests may not always make sense without further questioning, but each represents a need on the part of the requester. Developing your sense of the kinds of questions that get asked at your library will set you on a path of lifelong learning and success in your career.

Reference Interview Strategies

Unlike other kinds of librarians, documents librarians are all about where the information came from. This is partly because the SuDocs (Superintendent of Documents) classification system uses agencies as the basis for its organization (both for hard copy and for online publications and databases), but also because most of the finding tools created specifically for government information—indexes, abstracts, and publication lists—classify the information the same way (http://www.access.gpo.gov/su_docs/fdlp/pubs/explain.html). And it goes beyond the U.S. government, as classification systems for different state governments and international organizations such as the United Nations and the European Union also use the authoring agency of the document to catalog publications. Because the materials, in print and online, are organized by authoring agency, librarians must consider where the document originated, and their strategies for talking to patrons revolve around this, as well.

If the patron has asked a question and a source springs to mind, generally only a bit of follow-up is needed to focus the question, so the questions flow easily and generally elicit the desired response. For example, in response to the request for infant mortality rates for South American countries, the question "Do you need recent infant mortality rates or rates for a specific time period?" would help narrow the scope of the question and decide whether to head for materials about or from those countries, or whether tables with international comparisons would suffice. Some questions, for which the right source doesn't come easily to mind, can be more difficult. One old reference saw states that "the patron doesn't know what he wants, and if he did, he wouldn't tell you." While this may sometimes be true, often the patron knows more than he or she lets on in the initial query. In fact, librarians have been known to think of patrons' initial questions as a hook because some patrons believe that if they can interest you in their research, they'll get better assistance—and they may be right.

For the many interactions where we find ourselves floundering, it's good to have a few stock questions to elicit additional information from the patron. Interestingly, while some of these questions might be considered standard for all information queries, questions regarding the information producer are more specific to government information. Consider asking about information already in hand (What information do you already have?) to see if there are any cited sources you might go back to for additional information. Another question (Who would be interested in producing this information?) goes to the mandate of the agency. Often patrons have some background or have done some research that can be helpful in directing you to additional resources. When you know nothing about the information request, a good place to start is to ask the patron to talk about his or her research. Good follow-ups to that include questions about sources already checked as well as the purpose of the research (is it a short paper, a doctoral dissertation, or information for filing a business plan?). Each of these questions can draw out surprisingly useful information that will help steer you to the correct source. In addition, if you still know very little about the question, listening to the answers might give you a bit more time to think about how to proceed or to consult a knowledgeable colleague.

Some government information questions will go beyond the resources in your own library and even on the open web. You'll find it extremely helpful to network (see Other Help: The Network near the end of this chapter) and to get to know the collection and people strengths of the libraries around you.

How long have they been collecting government information? Are they depository libraries for the organization in question? Do they have collection strengths in the subject area under discussion? Are they considered research or subject specialty libraries? Do they have technical reports or patents? What other abstracts and indexes or databases do they subscribe to? Knowing the resources around you can help you connect the patrons with needed material.

With the libraries, Google, and companies scanning and converting materials to be placed on the Internet, an additional helpful question to add to the repertoire might be "Who would be interested in putting that information on the Internet?" That question helps clarify for the patron that while there might be a focus on putting certain kinds of information on the Internet, not all material from pre-Internet days may be there yet; it may also send you to other resources.

Research Strategies

Different strategies abound for answering government information questions and for managing documents collections. A few to keep in mind include the following.

Strategy 1: Read User Guides

There is almost always a user guide. Whew! Of course, some guides are better than others, but there is usually some help available when you click on the browser and go to a website, or when you open an index. Given that most tools are created to fill a specific need, it can be worthwhile to take a short look at the user information—just to see what is available, even if you don't happen to need it at that point in time.

Guides for print material generally include information about the organization of the index, the key to abbreviations, and how to read citations. Online user guides should include information about both the interface and what is on that specific website or database. Using American FactFinder (http://factfinder.census.gov/), for example, the Help section includes information about census geography (tracts, blocks, counties, and county equivalents) and about the data sets that are included in the interface.

A notable fact about government material is that sometimes the necessary user information may not accompany the publication. For example, the questionnaire for the 1880 census may not be in the census volumes themselves, but printed separately. Notably, Census 2000 print volumes included the questionnaire in every single publication.

Strategy 2: Learn Government Structure

This may be called the Civics and Search approach: learn which agency is responsible for what and search there. In searching for government information, there is a certain knowledge base that will give you a head start on all of your reference questions. For the U.S. government, that knowledge has its base in the organization of government (remember your civics class on how government works?) and can also be found, in part, in the *U.S. Government Manual.*

The *U.S. Government Manual* (http://purl.access.gpo.gov/GPO/LPS2410) may not help you answer a lot of questions, but it can tell you if a particular agency's mandate extends into the subject area under question. The *Government Manual* typically includes the following in the agency description: a list of officials heading major operating units; a statement of the agency's purpose and role in the federal government; a brief history of the agency, including its legislative or executive authority; and a description of its programs and activities.

The initial discussion of an agency will tell you its scope of responsibilities. For example:

> The Department of Agriculture works to improve and maintain farm income and to develop and expand markets abroad for agricultural products. The Department helps to curb and cure poverty, hunger, and malnutrition. It works to enhance the environment and to maintain production capacity by helping landowners protect the soil, water, forests, and other natural resources. The Department, through inspection and grading services, safeguards and ensures standards of quality in the daily food supply. (National Archives and Records Administration, 2009: 104)

The agency's mission is followed by the statutory authority: "The Department of Agriculture (USDA) was created by act of May 15, 1862 (7 U.S.C. 2201)." Consulting the statutory authority—the statutes (laws) that created the agency—may seem dry as dust to the casual user, but the statutes will have a wealth of additional material about specifics of the charge and the responsibilities of the agency.

For cabinet-level agencies, there is always a phone number, an organization chart and a URL in the introductory information.

Strategy 3: Consult the *Statistical Abstract*

Another strategy is to use what is on hand to identify resources. While the *Statistical Abstract of the United States* (http://www.census.gov/compendia/statab/) isn't organized by agency, many librarians use it as an index to agency information-gathering activities and publications, as it is organized by broad topic. Annually printed with more than one thousand tables from all aspects of American life (there are more than just federal government statistics here!), it gives great footnotes so that users can track the information back to the source for additional or related information. For example, in the 2010 *Statistical Abstract*, Table 127, "National Health Expenditures—Summary, 1960 to 2007, and Projections, 2008 to 2018," gives the citation "U.S. Centers for Medicare & Medicaid Services, Office of the Actuary, 'National Health Statistics Group'; <http://www.cms.hhs.gov/NationalHealthExpendData/>." So if Table 127 isn't detailed enough, the user now has the information to go back to the source to see if there is more detail, or related information that will answer the question. A note for those who use the older editions on the Census Bureau websites (http://www.census.gov/prod/www/titles.html): before 1987, the number referenced in the index was the page number; 1987 to current volumes' indexes reference the table number. (For more on the *Statistical Abstract* and other strategies for finding statistical information, see Chapter 8).

Similar to the *Statistical Abstract*, many other agencies had annual statistical reports: *Agricultural Statistics, Business Statistics, Condition of Education, Highway Statistics, Sourcebook of Criminal Justice Statistics, Uniform Crime Reports* (also known as *Crime in the U.S.*), *Public Land Statistics, Science and Engineering Indicators, Statistical Yearbook of the Immigration and Naturalization Service, Vital Statistics of the United States,* and the *World Military Expenditures and Arms Transfers,* to name just a handful. If a library had a separate government documents desk, these often sat near that desk for easy access. Each title had certain kinds of information that made it quite valuable. For example, *Agricultural Statistics* provided international comparisons for production, imports, and exports, while *Uniform Crime Reports* and *Science and Engineering Indicators* had data users simply couldn't find anywhere else. Most of these compendia started much later than the *Statistical Abstract* (1878), and, while the Statistical Abstract continues to this day, some of the other titles have completely changed their presentation as a result of being on the Internet, while others have disappeared.

It is also worth mentioning here that most states, governments, and international organizations also have statistical annuals. While many are as well organized and sourced as the *Statistical Abstract of the United States,* some are not as lengthy or do not provide as many links out to other agencies. The *Statistical Abstract of the United States* provides a list of state and foreign statistical annuals in the appendices. So the *Statistical Abstract* may have the answer to a reference question, the source notes from a table may lead you to the answer, or the list of other websites may lead you to a site with the answer!

Strategy 4: Learn about Government Processes

Learn the processes behind the publications. For instance, a bill is not just a bill: it represents part of the legislative process (bills, reports, hearings, and more—see Chapter 3) and so may be revised multiple times or simply incorporated into other legislation. Or it may be referred to committee and never see the light of day again. Users often ask about a bill and are dismayed to learn it was referred to a committee and never came out—but that is a hard fact of life for the majority of bills, and one that a librarian will explain repeatedly to users.

There are also processes for rulemaking (Chapter 4), environmental impact assessments (Chapter 12), censuses and surveys (Chapter 14), and more. Being familiar with the processes—which may include the questionnaires, strategies, or public input—will help you be aware of the agencies, or players, involved. It's understandable that you may have more of a familiarity with some processes, as questions related to these come to you (over the desk or through the myriad other ways our users have of communicating with us) more often than others, but it's good to remember that many publications, either online or in hard copy, represent part of a process.

Strategy 5: Skim a Few Textbooks

Government documents textbooks are quite valuable for reference use. Looking at a current or historical textbook for information on government agencies and publishing patterns may be useful, and when working with intergovernmental organizations or state publications, there may be books written that detail publishing patterns, key documents, and legislative or parliamentary processes and the publications.

Older, Treasured Texts

The first and second editions (1931 and 1941, respectively) of *United States Government Publications* were written by Anne Morris Boyd, an associate professor of library science at the University of Illinois. For the 1949 third edition, Boyd was joined by Rae Elizabeth Rips of the Detroit Public Library to create a classic text. Popularly known as **Boyd and Rips**, this text has extensive indexes and is almost encyclopedic in its approach, covering the history, organization, duties, and major publications of each agency. Need to find immigration statistics from the 1900s? The section on the Immigration and Naturalization Service tells you the predecessor organizations and the dates for each.

Government Publications and Their Use has undergone many revisions, as well. The original edition, from 1936, and the first revision in 1939 were written by Laurence F. **Schmeckebier**. The 1961 and 1969 editions were coauthored by Roy B. **Eastin**, Superintendent of Documents from 1949 to 1953. Schmeckebier was a member of the Brookings Institution's Institute for Government Research and wrote a number of monographs on different government agencies; he was working on the revisions for what would be the 1961 text at the time of his death. The Schmeckebier texts are shorter than that of Boyd and Rips; however, they bring readers into the 1960s in their texts and capture changes in the evolving government information environment and the depository library program.

One of Schmeckebier's early texts was the seminal *The Statistical Work of the National Government*. This 1925 text has the distinction of being possibly the best explanation and index of federal government statistics up to the 1920s. He goes into detail about the different questionnaires, or lack thereof, and the resulting impact on the statistics. This text is a must-have for any library that works with statistics from the nineteenth and early twentieth centuries.

More recently, Joe **Morehead** has written *Introduction to United States Government Information Sources*. The first edition was printed in 1975; updates followed in 1978, 1983, 1992 (with Mary Fetzer), 1996, and 1999. The fourth edition with Mary Fetzer may be considered an update to the 1949 Boyd and Rips text, as the executive branch publications are covered more extensively than in the other editions. Morehead uses lots of examples of documents but doesn't discuss the processes (legislation, rulemaking, etc.) in as much depth as Boyd and Rips does.

The three editions of *Tapping the Government Grapevine* (first published in 1988, and most recently updated in 1998), by Judith Schiek **Robinson**, have been lauded by teachers of government documents classes as much more engaging reading and a briefer text than any of the other titles in this list. Robinson is an associate professor at the School of Information and Library Studies, State University of New York at Buffalo.

In their three editions of *Using Government Information Sources* (1985–1986, 1994, 2001), **Sears and Moody** approached government information very differently than all of the other texts to date, organizing the material around the most effective kinds of searches: subject searches, agency searches, statistical searches, and special techniques. This volume probably would have become a standard text for library school classes, replacing both Morehead and Robinson, had it not been for the prohibitive price tag. Used copies are now available for those who want their own. Jean Sears, now retired, was the head of the Government Documents Department at Miami University Libraries in Oxford, Ohio. Marilyn Moody is the Dean of the Albertsons Library at Boise State University.

Supplemental Materials: Be on the lookout for news and journal articles that supplement your knowledge of frequently used materials. If, for example, you are looking for materials on Congress, in addition to Chapter 3, you'll want to look at the newspaper (e.g., your local news sources, the *Washington Post*, or the *New York Times*) for good, current examples of legislation and how it proceeds through Congress. If you live in the West, for example, you might look for materials about public lands and land usage and articles that highlight the issues between ranchers and wildlife advocates. Good examples will both inform your use of the materials and allow you to create interesting presentations.

Some of these books are extremely detailed in their approach and may be found through bibliographies posted on library websites. Many documents librarians have their favorite textbooks at their desks or cataloged as part of the reference collection to ensure quick and easy access. Names like Schmeckebier and Eastin, Morehead, Robinson, and Boyd and Rips are common in discussions among documents librarians, as the actual titles of the texts are somewhat interchangeable.

Classic Texts on Government Documents

Boyd, Anne Morris, and Rae Elizabeth Rips. 1949. *United States Government Publications.* 3rd ed. New York: H. W. Wilson.

Morehead, Joe, and Mary K. Fetzer. 1992. *Introduction to United States Government Information Sources.* 4th ed. Englewood, CO: Libraries Unlimited.

Robinson, Judith Schiek. 1998. *Tapping the Government Grapevine.* 3rd ed. Phoenix: Greenwood.

Schmeckebier, Laurence F. 1925. *The Statistical Work of the National Government.* Baltimore: Johns Hopkins.

Schmeckebier, Laurence F., and Roy B. Eastin. 1969. *Government Publications and Their Use.* 4th ed. Washington, DC: Brookings Institution.

Sears, Jean L., and Marilyn K. Moody. 2001. *Using Government Information Sources: Electronic and Print.* 3rd ed. Phoenix: Greenwood.

Strategy 6: Note the Most-Loved Print-on-Paper Sources

Look on the reference shelves to see the worn and rebound publications. Libraries will often have many of the favorite paper tools at their fingertips, though increasingly, some reference collections have moved the older tools to the stacks. Most of the older textbooks will have good overviews of staples such as the 1909 *Checklist* and titles commonly known as Ames and Poore (see texts in sidebar—especially Boyd and Rips, Chapter 3—for information on these classic indexes). Certain libraries will use these tools more than other libraries do, chiefly for budgetary reasons: they haven't cataloged older publications, or they don't have the resources to purchase online equivalents or other sources that might render these obsolete.

Strategy 7: Check Library Webpages and Links

As a corollary to strategy 6, the online equivalent of seeing the most-loved print volumes is checking out what other libraries have linked to for specific topics. If you need a guide on California legislation or New York legislation, for example, consult a guide from an institution in that state. The guides should point you to online resources, as well as libraries with good collections of, for example, historical bills if you need to borrow the material (see the Guides section later in this chapter).

Strategy 8: Read about It

One of the best ways to see how things actually work is to read books about different aspects of government. You may not always agree with the political point of view, but getting the insider perspective can give you additional insight into how it actually works inside the hallowed halls of government.

Books by Peggy Noonan, a former speech writer for Presidents Reagan and George H.W. Bush, gives an insight into the inner workings in the cabinet, while books such as *The Brethren*, about the Supreme Court, talk about how the justices communicate, who gets along and who doesn't, how decisions are made, who circulates the opinions (and the effect of that first draft), and how much power and authority is given to clerks. And of course books such as *The Best and the Brightest* and *All the President's Men* can give you insight into the personalities and egos at work in the White House.

The book reviews in the *Washington Post* can give you a good idea of what is being read by those in power at any given time, and can serve to give you an overview of what may be worth your time and reading energy.

Strategy 9: Keep Up-to-Date!

With journals, the Internet, and web-based training, it's easier than ever to keep up on issues and to both renew skills and acquire new ones. Web-based training is a boon for those who don't have the time, or whose libraries don't have the budget to support attendance at conferences or other training events—and it makes it easier to try out new groups without ever leaving the comfort of your office!

One of the cheapest and easiest things to do is join the relevant electronic discussion lists. It doesn't matter if you get them directly in your e-mail account or use a blog reader; they are invaluable for getting the latest information to your desktop. While most professional organizations (see Other Help: The Network later in this chapter) restrict their lists to members, there are a number of open discussion lists such as GOVDOC-L, INTL-DOC, and more that are valuable not only for bringing information to you, but also for allowing you to query your colleagues when you get a tough question.

For those with government information as part of their responsibilities, there are a few tips for staying in the know. First, check out the professional literature. *DttP: Documents to the People* is the quarterly journal of the Government Documents Round Table (GODORT) of ALA. If you're not an ALA member, you can subscribe to the journal for $35 per year; however, ALA members can join GODORT for $20 per year and receive *DttP* as a membership benefit. The journal is written for practitioners and has relatively short articles, columns, reviews, and conference wrap-ups. Watch GOVDOC-L and the GODORT wiki (http://wikis.ala.org/godort/) for announcements of new issues and to peruse the contents of back issues.

Another journal, *Government Information Quarterly*, is written at a more scholarly level and describes itself as "a cross-disciplinary and refereed journal that covers information and telecommunications policy, information management, information technology planning and management, and e-government practices, policies and issues relevant to all levels of government within the United States and abroad"(Elsevier, 2011). The subscription price, currently $186 per year, is steep; however, the journal's website allows you to view tables of contents for each issue, read abstracts of many articles, and purchase individual articles.

Another journal to subscribe to includes *Government Computer News* (GCN), available free in print or online at http://www.gcn.com/. Articles from GCN are often noted in blogs such as FGI (http://www.freegovinfo .info/); several free e-mail newsletters, including the "GCN Daily" update, help you to stay on top of the issues.

Web-based training is now offered by professional associations, vendors, and GPO (through OPAL: Online Programming for All Libraries). Watch the various electronic discussion lists for announcements and attend a training that interests you. The beauty of online training is that, if it turns out to be not quite what you expected, you can always quit the program, or just monitor it while working on other items on your to do list.

And don't forget publications and social networking from your favorite agencies. Many agencies (federal, state, local, and international) have easy ways to keep up on new publications, data releases, and more. These can be especially important if questions in your job may be focused more in certain areas. It can be quite useful to stay ahead of the curve!

The Internet

Search Engines

While an Internet search using a favorite search engine will often bring up the desired results, it may just as easily bring an avalanche of information that doesn't answer the question. Before turning to the Internet, it is important to understand what will and won't show up from a search engine. Many government agencies have databases on their sites. As an example, two well-known databases are FDsys (GPO) and American FactFinder (Census Bureau). FDsys contains bills, laws, and congressional and agency publications on it (FDsys is sometimes referred to as GPO Access, the name of its predecessor system, but the two work very differently). American FactFinder has census information including population breakouts for each state county and place in the United States. However if you search Google, Bing, or Yahoo!, you will not be retrieving the full complement of GPO-published bills and hearings, or the depth of census population statistics for your city, because the search engines don't generally search into the databases, often known as the deep web. You will often find census information posted on city or county websites, but it may not provide the breakdown of data needed. Likewise, you may find a bill or a government report located on another site; however, with government information it may be important to know that the information has not been changed or redacted in some way, so looking at the URL to make sure the document is from the official site is an important safety check for the information.

To obtain results more focused on government entities, there are several government-specific search tools that may help winnow out the chaff of the rest of the Internet and help you focus on government-produced information. Two of these are USA.gov, brought to you by the federal government, and Google U.S. Government Search (http://www.google.com/unclesam/). Google U.S. Government Search, formerly known as Google Uncle Sam, was one of the early search engines to specialize in government information and so got a lot of early press. It was followed, on September 22, 2000, by USA.gov (then called Firstgov.gov), administered by the General Services Administration's Office of Citizen Services and Communications. USA.gov focuses on searching government information and, in addition to the search engine, has links to the following lists of resources: Get Services, Explore Topics, Find Government Agencies and Contact Government Officials.

For a different kind of search engine, don't forget WorldCat (http://www.worldcat.org/). WorldCat contains more than 500,000 catalog records from the Government Printing Office, starting in 1976. Cataloging records will include classification information and URLs for both print and online-only material. These records are duplicated in the Catalog of Government Publications, or CGP (http://catalog.gpo.gov/), but librarians may find it easier to use World-Cat for several reasons. First, it's a tool used for other material too, so there is no need to learn a new search engine. Second, using WorldCat will give users more than one chance to come across material, since catalogers may enhance records for local needs or even post records faster than GPO because of a user request. Finally, for pre-1976 publications, there is a growing body of libraries that have cataloged, or are in the process of cataloging, their retrospective collections, and these records may be loaded into WorldCat. One fly in the ointment for the pre-1976 publications: because cataloging standards have evolved, some libraries have decently cataloged pre-1976 materials that aren't compatible with WorldCat, so talk to your colleagues and find out where these treasure troves may be!

Online Collections

There are many websites inside and outside of the federal government with government information collections. Some may give excerpts and some may have collections of materials digitized from older documents.

The biggest collection of publications across agencies is FDsys (http://www.fdsys.gov/). FDsys is the new system that houses the material that was previously found on GPO Access. The legislation enabling GPO Access is discussed in Chapter 1; however, the initial collections effort was focused on providing electronic access to congressional publications, and it expanded to host publications from the Supreme Court and other, generally smaller, agency websites. In 2010, all GPO Access content was migrated to FDsys, the largest cross-agency effort to provide and maintain access to federal government information.

The functions of FDsys include

- Publishing: The U.S. Congress and federal agencies can submit files and orders electronically to GPO for printing and publishing services, electronic distribution, and inclusion in the Federal Depository Library Program.
- Searching for information: Government information will reach a wider audience by providing authentic, published government information to the public through an Internet-based system.
- Preserving information: The preservation function of FDsys ensures public access to government information even as technology changes.
- Version control: Multiple versions of published information are common; FDsys provides version control for government information. (Government Printing Office, FDsys)

Outside of government, the other projects to know about include the Hathi Trust (http://www.hathitrust.org/), the Internet Archive (http://www.archive.org/), and the Google Books Library Project (see Chapter 1 for more background on each of these projects). Each of these is a large-scale project scanning thousands, if not hundreds of thousands, of government documents.

For specific projects, look at the GPO Registry of U.S. Government Publication Digitization Projects (http://registry.fdlp.gov/). Libraries provide these listings, so while it's a good starting place and probably the most inclusive listing available, it isn't necessarily comprehensive.

What Is Version Control (and Why Should I Care)?

In the paper world, ideally documents were date stamped in some way, giving readers the knowledge that they could refer to a text from a specific time. Congressional bills have versions (see Definitions of Common Versions of Bills at http://www.gpo.gov/help/index.html #about_congressional_bills.htm) both to indicate which stage of the legislative process the bill has reached, and also to facilitate discussion of a particular edition of a bill. Insert the phrase *version control for government information* in your favorite search engine and you'll see discussions about why this is such an important concept: first so that you can see when and by whom changes were made (if we're talking about a process, such as creating legislation or making regulations), but also to have the assurance that, if you're looking at a document or a webpage, you're looking at the edition from the relevant time—be it the most current, or, in the case of a lawsuit, the edition of the document that was available at a particular point in time relating to the litigation.

Interestingly, in what could be another type of version control, the *Federal Register* and *Code of Federal Regulations* came about because of confusion about whether or not a regulation was still in effect. "The U.S. Department of Justice itself had a difficult time determining the status of regulations as became embarrassingly apparent when the Department had to acknowledge before the Supreme Court that an Executive order it was trying to enforce had been inadvertently revoked" (McKinney, 2010). If the Department of Justice had the correct version of the regulations available, it wouldn't have ended up in front of the Supreme Court!

With electronic documents becoming the norm, having version control will become ever more important—not just for determining the status of bills, laws, and regulations, but also for something as simple as knowing which version of a webpage is being reviewed.

Agency Websites

Most, if not all, federal agencies have large and well-developed websites. If you don't know the URL for the agency you need, USA.gov (http://www.usa.gov/) provides links to federal and state agencies by agency name or governmental structure. Once found, these sites can be a virtual treasure trove of information. The content can range from data sets, maps, and publications to consumer-oriented publications and discovery tools. For example, the home page of the Environmental Protection Agency (EPA) provides an interactive tool for retrieving local environmental information under My Environment discussed in Chapter 12. A search by ZIP code brings up an extensive array of local information, interactive maps, and more.

Online Indexes

In addition to the websites already discussed, and the resources covered in the other chapters of this book, there are several indexes worth noting here.

The Monthly Catalog

The *Monthly Catalog of United States Government Publications* is the granddaddy of government documents indexes, starting in 1895. The paper version was

Tips for Navigating Agency Websites

Because of their sheer size, some agency websites can be intimidating or confusing. Look for a site map—when available, these tools provide a good overview of information available at the site.

In addition, look for:

- **An index**. This can be much more effective than searching the site unless you know exactly what you are looking for. For example, the EPA website has a list of popular topics that are further subdivided into narrower subtopics. The U.S. Geological Survey site features a similar breakdown of science topics.

- **About pages**. When available, these pages often provide a good overview of the agency's mission.

- **An Ask Us or Contact Us link**. Most agencies are eager to provide information about their services.

- **Information arranged by interest group**. Fact sheets and other introductory material are sometimes available under headings such as Information for Citizens or Just for Teens. Many sites include an Education section with information designed to educate the general public at various levels, including primary and secondary school students, and college undergraduates.

- **A Publications or Library menu**. Many agencies have an extensive array of publications online. These may be centrally located or divided by topic, but take a moment to see if what is there is what you think should be there. If expectations don't match reality, take a moment to look at a site map or other navigational aids to see if the additional material can be located.

organized by SuDocs classification (agency) and the quality of the indexing has increased greatly since the index began in 1895. There are several online versions of this, of which two are publicly available. A free version of the *Monthly Catalog* (1976–current) is offered as the Catalog of Government Publications (CGP) by GPO (http://catalog.gpo.gov/). OCLC's WorldCat (http://www.worldcat.org/) also offers CGP as part of the catalog (so documents results are mixed in with other materials) and as a separate database in its fee-based First-Search offerings (OCLC, 2010).

ProQuest is one of two vendors offering the online version of the *Monthly Catalog of United States Government Publications*, 1895–1976 (http://monthlycatalog.chadwyck.com/marketing/about.jsp). The other vendor, **Paratext**, offers the Public Documents Masterfile, which includes not only the Monthly Catalog, but a variety of other government documents:

- Post-1976 GPO documents
- GPO monthly catalog indexes 1895–1976 with page/entry numbers and depository status
- Cumulative title index 1789–1976 with SuDocs numbers
- Pre-1900 United States public documents
- Department of Energy Records, 1930–present
- ERIC documents
- Non-GPO public documents held by the Library of Congress

In addition to this federal material, the website mentions that indexing of non–U.S. documents is available, and that indexing for state and provincial public documents is forthcoming (Paratext, 2010).

1909 *Checklist*

An additional publication, now online, for those who need indexing to older materials is the *Checklist of United States Public Documents, 1789–1909, Third Edition Revised and Enlarged, Volume 1, Lists of Congressional and Departmental Publications*, better known as the 1909 *Checklist*. While the subject index was never produced (though the CIS Index to U.S. Executive Branch Documents, 1789–1909, discussed in the following section, fills this void), this is a well-worn reference tool for many, listing all congressional and executive branch publications up to 1909. The 1909 *Checklist* is notable because it provides not just the SuDocs classification number for a publication, but also background information on various series (see Figure 2.1). While there are other scanned copies of the 1909 *Checklist* available, the UNT Digital Library has a searchable and browsable version at http://digital.library.unt.edu/ark:/67531/metadc1029/.

Print Tools

When considering tools, it's important to note the scope. Unless you have knowledge of a specific title that will help answer the question at hand, a broader index is often the best choice. A federal government resource that cuts across agency lines is the Government Printing Office's *Monthly Catalog of U.S. Government Publications*, long known as MoCat. The online versions of the MoCat are discussed earlier in this chapter. The MoCat has undergone multiple title changes, but started in 1895 as the *Catalogue of publications issued by the Government of the United States during the month of . . .* and was organized by SuDocs classification (agency), with indexes for each monthly issue, and, usually, an annual index. The quality of the indexing varied over time.

There were also several commercial indexes to the MoCat that covered large spans of time, making research easier because the user didn't have to definitively know when something had been printed or indexed:

- *Cumulative Subject Index to the Monthly Catalog of U.S. Government Publications, 1895–1899*. 1977. Arlington, VA: Carrolton.
- *Cumulative Subject Index to the Monthly Catalog of U.S. Government Publications, 1900–1971*. 1973–1975. Arlington, VA: Carrolton.
- *Cumulative Title Index to United States Public Documents, 1789–1976*. 1979–1982. Arlington, VA: United States Historical Documents Institute.

The watershed date for the MoCat is July 1976, when the catalogers at the Government Printing Office started using Library of Congress subject headings and the records were accepted by OCLC. Because of the standardization of the

Figure 2.1. 1909 *Checklist* Detail

874

P18. SUPPLIES DIVISION

[Act approved June 8, 1872, authorized the establishment of a blank agency for Post-Office Department which afterward became Division of Post-Office Supplies, the work being carried on by a superintendent under control of 1st assistant Postmaster-General

Placed under supervision of 4th assistant Postmaster-General, Dec. 1, 1905, since when it has been known as Supplies Division.]

Classification
no.

P18.1:	**Annual Reports**
(date)	[Note issues.]
P18.2:	**General publications**
P84[1]	Postal supplies. List of postal supplies furnished presidential offices, post-office inspectors, and Railway Mail Service by 4th assistant Postmaster-General. July 1, 1909.
P84[2]	Postal supplies. List of postal supplies furnished post-offices of 4th class by 4th assistant Postmaster-General. July 1, 1909.
P18.3:	**Bulletins**
(nos.)	[None issues.]
P18.4:	**Circulars**
(nos.)	[None issues.]

PR. PRESIDENT OF UNITED STATES
(APR. 30, 1789–DEC. 31, 1909)

[As complete lists can not be made of all original prints of official papers of the Presidents, references are given below to such compilations of presidential papers as are public documents. The most complete collection is Richardson's Compilation of messages and papers of Presidents, 1789–1897, in 10 volumes (Y4.P93[1]:3[1–10]). This set also appears as a Congressional document of the 53rd Congress, serial no. 3265[1–10]. It contains all the presidential papers through Cleveland's 2nd administration, ending Mar. 4, 1897. For later administrations these papers are generally accessible in separate form. The 10th volume of Richardson's set includes, besides the index containing "a large number of encyclopedic articles," the papers of President McKinley relating to War with Spain, and many papers of the earlier Presidents which had been omitted from their proper places.

The separate issues of the Presidents' papers from Washington through Madison are listed under Early Congress papers (Z4.1:). The list of Early Congress papers will appear later in separate form.

Annual messages, besides being found in the publications as indicated under the name of each President (Pr1.1:–Pr27.1:), are also found in the Senate and House journals; 1848–92, in Messages and documents (Y8.); 1859–1909, in Abridgment of messages and documents (Y4.P93[1]:2); and in Congressional record in its predecessors as tabulated below, in every case being in that part which contains the proceedings at the opening of each regular session of Congress:

> 1790–1823, in Annals of Congress (X1.–X42.)
> 1824–1836, in Register of debates in Congress (X43.–X71.)
> 1833–1872, in Congressional globe (X72.–X180.)
> 1873–1909, in Congressional record (X181.–X439.)

It may be mentioned here that until the removal of the seat of Government to Washington, the annual messages are referred to as "speeches" because those of George Washington and John Adams were delivered orally before the two legislative branches in general assembly. Thomas Jefferson established the custom, which has ever since been followed, of sending his annual statement in the form of a message.

Executive orders prior to Oct. 1905, were sometimes printed as presidential papers, but were more frequently issued in printed form only by those Departments immediately concerned in their promulgation. Since Oct. 1905, it has been customary for the President to send all Executive orders to the Bureau of Rolls and Library, State Dept., to be printed on foolscap paper for limited distribution on demand.

Inaugural addresses, besides being issued separately, are found in the Senate journals and in the Congressional record.

catalog records, that date is also the date that the online MoCat (the CGP) starts, and of course, also the date that GPO records show up in WorldCat. The sole exclusion to MoCat's domain is technical reports, which are indexed elsewhere (and covered in Chapter 11). While you may find some technical reports in the CGP, they would be the exception.

In addition to the MoCat, it is important to remember that many agencies have, or had, their own lists of publications. These may have been published annually, or compiled to cover longer time periods. Research libraries will often have these in their collections. Though they are used less and less, they are still valuable tools to use when hunting to verify the existence of a document. Remember though, that a list of publications from, for example, the U.S. Department of Commerce may not include all of the subagencies, so you may want to start at the bottom of the organization chart, rather than at the top.

Also remember that, up until the early 1900s, many important agency publications were also included in the U.S. *Congressional Serial Set* (see Chapter 3 for a discussion) that was distributed to libraries. The Public Printing and Binding Act (March 1, 1907, P.L. 59-153) changed the distribution to allow certain libraries (for example, the libraries of the House and the Senate, sometimes referred to as posterity libraries) to continue to receive the more complete *Serial Set* with the executive branch materials. As a cost cutting measure, P.L. 59-153 changed the rules so that depository libraries received a version that did not include much of that material, since they may have received an agency (or departmental) version of the publication printed outside of the *Serial Set*.

While the overlap between the *Serial Set* and the agency publications may have decreased with P.L. 59-153 in 1907, it is still possible that a library may have two or more copies of the major reports—one in the *Serial Set* and one that was issued separately. Wooster College has a wonderful website, the U. S. Congressional Serial Set Finding List (http://www3.wooster.edu/library/ Gov/serialset/main.htm), that highlights executive branch material in the *Serial Set* (see Chapter 3 for a complete description of the *Serial Set* and the Wooster College site).

Finally, there are commercial compilations of materials from the executive branch, such as the *CIS Index to U.S. Executive Branch Documents, 1789–1909* with an accompanying microfiche collection. This collection, based on the 1909 *Checklist*, includes the location, organization, and description of approximately 200,000 documents issued by federal agencies before 1909. A second iteration, the *CIS Index to Executive Branch Documents, 1910–1932*, also has an accompanying microfiche collection and provides indexing of, and access to, the vast body of material issued by federal departments and agencies, including annual reports, general publications, serials, instructions, rules, circulars, decisions, and registers as identified by the Government Printing Office.

Another collection found in many libraries is the Readex non-depository collection. For many decades of the *Monthly Catalog*'s run, the presence of a black dot in a bibliographic entry denoted that the document in question had been sent to depository libraries; thousands of titles per year were listed but not distributed. Starting in 1953, Readex began harvesting those publications listed in the *Monthly Catalog* but not distributed to libraries, reproducing the publications in microform, and selling them to interested libraries. The original format was microcard, and later switched to microfiche in the 1980s. The company began selling depository materials this same way (in a microfiche set). The collection ceased in 2008.

Citation Manuals and Style Manuals

One of the hardest moments for many scholars isn't actually writing the paper, it's the time when they have to put their bibliographies or endnotes together. Did they remember to make notes of everything they needed, or do they need to go back and find something typed on a computer or jotted on paper? While faculty choose from between the varieties of MLA, APA, Chicago, Turabian, and the Bluebook, few government document librarians will disagree with the statement that most of these manuals leave room for improvement in providing decent examples of how to cite government documents.

The golden rule of citations is that *a citation must include enough information for readers to (relatively) easily find their way back to the item cited*. Librarians often have researchers coming to the desk to assist in figuring out bad citations, as well as helping users create good citations. The goal here is good scholarship.

Before starting to write—ideally, when the research is started—it is quite helpful to find the style manual required. Different faculty and different disciplines demand different citations styles, and they don't appreciate it (and may even downgrade the work!) when writers make their own choices. If the work is being done with publication in mind, often manuscripts will not even be considered if the citations are not done in the appropriate style as it will take the editors much too long to make revisions. Do it right the first time and life will be easier.

Next, while style manuals are on the whole correct, they don't always make all of the most sensible decisions regarding government information sources. For example, section 17.309 of *The Chicago Manual of Style* (15th edition) seems to indicate that when citing a congressional bill, one should cite the *Congressional Record*. This creates extra work for the student to see if the bill was read into the *Record*, and a small crisis if the bill isn't found (as many are not). Often, erroneously, writers will try to force material into one style and create problems for readers trying to look at the cited material. It is incumbent on the writer to be aware of errors and omissions in the style manuals before the last minute so that editors or faculty can be consulted about potential problems.

While the 16th edition of *The Chicago Manual of Style* has fixed the problem with the congressional bills (see section 14.295) the important take-away is that you need to get the reader back to the items you are looking at. Be it bills, technical report numbers, or draft environmental impact statements, when in doubt, consult!

Citing Government Documents

The only manual specifically about citing government information is Debora Cheney's *The Complete Guide to Citing Government Information Resources*, though there are other citation manuals that cover government information in addition to other types of material. In addition to this book, many websites discuss citing government information and compare different style manuals (see sidebar). More than just the differences in how government information may be cited, there are specific challenges facing users of government information. These challenges are outlined in this section.

Citing Online Materials

Online government information is the norm now, and so of course URLs are to be included in citations. Some of the challenges facing citations to online government information include the following:

- Often the most current issue of a government journal has a URL ending in something like "current issue." When the next issue is loaded, it becomes the current issue, so all of the references to the previous issue at that URL no longer apply.
- When using a database, a URL may be session-specific. Users trying to find that information using the URL will receive the 404 Not Found error message.
- A newer version of a cited resource may exist in the cited location. For numeric data, numbers may be updated or completely refreshed; for text, a new version of a publication may be loaded or a corrected version may overwrite the previous one.
- After the change in presidential administrations, the whitehouse.gov website is moved to the National Archives and has a new domain created (like http://georgewbush-whitehouse.archives.gov). In addition to the presidential websites moving, agency websites may also be overhauled at this point, resulting in new organization and perhaps new policies and other content. Users end up with dead links to even well-referenced publications.

The Indiana University guide (2010) suggests "When citing a full-text electronic source, a good rule of thumb is to follow the format used for print sources, then provide 'access points' for your readers. Access points usually include the name of the full-text service, an indication of the type of service (CD-ROM, online), and the URL for World Wide Web resources." To this list, most style manuals will require an accessed date, so that if something changes, users may be able to find routes to the version that was posted on a specific date.

Citing Laws: P.L., S.A.L. or U.S.C.?

Probably the most challenging citation issue for writers is when to cite to the public law (P.L.), the *Statutes at Large* (S.A.L.) or the *U.S. Code* (see Chapter 5 for a description of each). The P.L.s and S.A.L.s may be considered equivalent citations; however, the S.A.L. has page number as part of the citation, so it is used differently. The *U.S. Code*, however, is very different. While the public laws and *Statutes at Large* may be thought of as more static (once they are passed, it takes a new law to amend them), the *U.S. Code* changes with each new law. In paper form, there is a new version of the *Code* every six years, with annual amendments, so users may be citing the 2001 amendment, for instance, because they are looking at the body of law that has been accumulated to that date.

Here are a few rules to follow:

- Cite the public law (P.L.) when noting the actual piece of legislation passed, such as the GI Bill (P.L. 78-346), the Voting Rights Act of 1965 (P.L. 89-110), or the Whaling Treaty of 1936 (P.L. 74-525).
- Cite the P.L. if the name is the actual name of the law. If the Detainee Treatment Act of 2005 is part of a law with a different name, then let the reader know that: for example, the Detainee Treatment Act of 2005 (Title X of P.L. 109-148).
- Cite the statute (S.A.L.) when writing about a provision of the legislation, for example, the Detainee Treatment Act, Title X of P.L. 109-148 (119 Stat. 2739) contains provisions including.... Use the page number (the part of the citation following Stat.) to take the user to the particular page under consideration.
- Cite the *U.S. Code* (U.S.C.) when discussing the body of law—16 U.S.C. 916 (1997)—at a point in time. For example, the Whaling Convention as law stood in 1997. You would not cite the current *U.S. Code* when talking about the legislation that had passed as of 1936.
- When citing the *U.S. Code*, the year must be included. Then the reader will know that, for example, the writer was citing the 1997 version of 16 U.S.C. 916, as opposed to one from another year.

Version Control

Draft environmental impact statements, an engrossed bill, a proposed rule... all of these things are versions of a work and must be cited as such. A common misunderstanding might be that one version is more important than another, and this might be true in terms of the weight each document is given in decision making; however, the important thing in the world of citations is that the writer is able to accurately identify the version he or she consulted so that others can look at the same material.

When citing congressional bills, the FDsys.gov help (http://www.gpo.gov/help/index.html#about_congressional_bills.htm) lists more than fifty versions of bills—each with its own abbreviation (for some examples, refer to Figure 3.2 in Chapter 3, p. 64). Members of Congress must be specific about which version they are referencing so as to avoid confusion, and writers must to do the same thing. For online versions of bills, the text format and the PDF format will note the version differently. Currently the text versions note the version at the top of the document, for example, CONSIDERED AND PASSED IN THE HOUSE, Job Creation and Unemployment Relief Act of 2008, H.R. 7110, while PDF versions currently note the version at the bottom of the pages as H.R. 7110 CPH. Of course, like all things congressional, this has most likely changed over time, so it is important to understand that versions exist, and to note appropriately.

State legislation may also have multiple versions of bills, as will legislation and rules from intergovernmental organizations.

Citing dates accessed is also vital to referencing the correct version. Then if a newer version of a database or PDF overwrites the version cited, it is easy to note that there may be differences.

Elements of Style (Beyond Citations)

When writing for publication, as discussed above it is necessary to know the citation style used by a journal or a book publisher. In addition to just citations, it is important to pay attention to the other elements of style demanded through these resources.

Many government documents librarians, for example, have looked at government publications for such a long time they are used to seeing *Federal* capitalized, because that is the interpretation government publications and websites give to the *GPO Style Manual* rules on capitalization. Writers in social science journals using *The Chicago Manual of Style*, however, will use the lowercase *federal* unless it is part of a name, as in the Federal Bureau of Investigation or the *Federal Register*. The *GPO Style Manual* has an uppercase bias; *The Chicago Manual of Style* has a lowercase bias.

Style manuals control what gets capitalized, when and if numbers are written out, spelling, punctuation, and more. They don't exist to torment writers (though that may be an added benefit); they exist to ensure consistency across the publication.

Depository Library Programs

Before the Internet there was . . . paper. Lots of paper. Libraries received this paper, along with microfiche and CD/DVDs and a score of other formats, and endeavored to make the material available. These are the government publications that arrive through various depository programs or through gifts, exchange programs, or purchase. Governments at all levels have arrangements to get their publications to people. Depository programs exist for states, the federal government, foreign governments and international organizations. The U.S. version is the Federal Depository Library Program or FDLP (http://www.gpo.gov/libraries/).

The FDLP provides a way to distribute federal government publications to the public through libraries. While the law has been amended many times (see Chapter 1 for an overview), current libraries participating in the program include some 1,200 state, academic, public, law, agency, and a handful of other types of libraries. Since the passage of P.L. 90-620 on October 22, 1968, the program has been divided into selective and regional libraries. Selective libraries can select items they would like from the program, and regional libraries must take, and keep, a copy of everything. Selective depository libraries may also withdraw publications using guidelines set up by their regionals. The FDLP Desktop (http://www.fdlp.gov/) provides information on the program from initial deposit to deselection of materials. This site should be consulted (frequently!) by those with responsibility for depository library operations.

Few other depository library organizations provide the same descriptive information about their programs as does the FDLP about the U.S. depository program. Often headquarters libraries serve as the program managers for state and international organization depository programs. For example, the UN headquarters library, the Dag Hammarskjöld, is the program manager for the United Nations Depository Program, and the California State Library manages the California depository library program. These libraries often provide a high level of assistance for reference inquiries as well as operational questions related to the depository program. A quick Internet search on the phrase *depository libraries* brings up such programs as those mentioned already, and also the World Bank, European Union, the U.S. Patent and Trademark Office, the International Monetary Fund, and programs for Florida, Oklahoma, Texas, and Canada, to name just a few.

Other Help

Guides

In addition to the resources already listed here, there are several other ways to ask for and receive help with either reference or operational questions. One such resource is guides created by librarians. It used to be that the ALA Government Documents Round Table (GODORT) circulated floppy disks to share guides created by others. Now GODORT hosts an online handout exchange (http://wikis.ala.org/godort/index.php/Exchange). While this site might have many guides on local census resources or federal legislation, for example, there may be only a few on subjects such as the British Parliamentary Papers or the Americans with Disabilities Act.

In addition to the GODORT Handout Exchange, many libraries use Springshare's LibGuides to create and organize their guides. As of August 2010, Libguides (libguides.com) hosted upwards of 100,000 guides from more than 1,500 libraries around the world, including some on the same topics as the GODORT Handout Exchange, and they are all publicly available. Guides in either collection may be used to assist in creating your own guide, or for assisting your users to find materials in your collection.

Data Providers

One source of help that is often overlooked is directory or topical listings. Many federal agencies have phone listings/e-mail listings and other methods of contacting individuals within the agency for help on topics specific to that agency. Agencies such as the Departments of Labor and Agriculture and the Census Bureau are data providers, and, as such, have employees who are experts in how the data was created. These employees are often wonderful resources for those with very specific questions about the data. While contacting the agency should not necessarily be your first step, it should always be an option if other methods for finding the answer don't pan out.

The Network: Professional Organizations, Conferences, and Vendors

And finally, don't forget your colleagues out there. Government information specialists, government documents librarians—whatever the name is, there are groups out there where you can meet others who may be able to help you.

Most state library associations have groups that discuss government information issues, and larger metropolitan areas also often have these groups. These are folks who are close geographically and can both share stories and help you answer questions in your area.

At the national level, the American Library Association has the Government Documents Round Table, which started in 1972. This is a group for any librarian interested in government information, but its membership is mostly practicing government documents librarians who work with all levels of government information—local, regional, state, federal, and international. They have useful resources on their wiki (http://wikis.ala.org/godort) such as the handout exchange mentioned previously and toolkits like the Cataloging Committee-Created Toolbox for Processing and Cataloging. GODORT has three task forces and 15 committees and its mission, printed in the Bylaws, is "(a) to provide a forum for the discussion of problems and concerns and for the exchange of ideas by librarians working with government documents; (b) to provide a nexus for initiating and supporting programs to increase the availability, use and bibliographic control of documents; (c) to increase communication between documents librarians and the larger community of information professionals; (d) to contribute to the education and training of documents librarians"

(ALA/GODORT Bylaws, 2010). GODORT often has all day pre-conferences at the ALA Annual Conference.

The American Association of Law Libraries, or AALL, has the Government Relations Committee (http://www.aallnet.org/committee/govr) with a charge of "monitor[ing] all federal and state legislative, regulatory, and judicial developments, with the exception of copyright, that would affect the Association, law librarianship, law libraries, or the dissemination of information" (AALL Government Relations Committee, 2011).

The Special Libraries Association (SLA) has a Government Information Division or DGI (http://units.sla.org/division/dgi/) which provides a forum to discuss the value and use of government information and government libraries. The DGI website features conference reports, a frequently updated blog, and the Government Information Division News Feed. There is also an electronic discussion list and a Facebook group.

For those working in federal government information, be sure to watch the FDLP site (http://www.fdlp.gov/) for news of the spring and fall conferences. The fall conference, held in the Washington, DC, area, is a larger conference (sometimes upwards of 500 attendees); the location of the spring conference varies. Both are great opportunities to meet other librarians and to take advantage of a continuing education opportunity. Unlike most conferences, there is no registration fee and attendees often cut costs by sharing rooms (watch for announcements on GOVDOC-L if you need a roommate).

A regional group worth noting is the Law Librarians' Society of Washington, DC (LLSDC). It was established in 1939 for educational, informational, and scientific purposes. Many LLSDC members work in federal libraries and thus have expert working knowledge of publications and resources within their agencies. The LLSDC website (http://www.llsdc.org/) has a sourcebook that is quite useful to those wanting detailed knowledge of federal legislation, rule-making, and other resources vetted by LLSDC.

This listing should not imply that these are the only library organizations with an interest in government information. Because government publishes on all topics, other organizations within the American Library Association that are interested in government information include the Association of College and Research Libraries (ACRL), the Maps and Geography Round Table (MAGERT), and the Federal and Armed Forces Libraries Round Table (FAFLRT). Other organizations include the Medical Library Association (MLA) and the International Federation of Library Associations and Institutions Government Information and Official Publications Section (IFLA-GIOPS). For almost any group of librarians, there is a tie-in with government information.

Wherever you have your network, this is a group of people who not only will assist you with reference inquiries, but will be colleagues throughout your career. They're the people you'll get together with at conferences and often write letters of recommendations for your next job hunt or your promotion. Treat them with care!

Finally, a group worth knowing is the vendor community. If you are employed in a library, getting to know the folks selling resources in your field is part of your job. While there are those who might think the vendors are just out there trying to sell something (and of course, they are) they also can be useful to funnel information back to make products more usable—and this is also part of your job! Products didn't get to be as useful as they are without constructive feedback from working librarians. It's to your benefit, and the benefit of your institution, to get to know them, and for them to get to know you.

Conclusion

Being a government documents librarian or government information specialist—whatever you want to call it—will bring you in contact with a group of uniquely committed colleagues who are interested not just in the publications themselves, but also in the processes of government. Government documents librarians appreciate, as perhaps no other group of librarians can, the tidbits of arcane knowledge that can assist in helping patrons and colleagues alike— not just by producing the answer, but by teaching how to find it, and being able to explain it all. Learning the basics and staying up-to-date can both start you out and keep you going in a successful career as a government information specialist.

Exercises

1. Read the front page of your daily paper and note when state or federal government is mentioned. Then try to figure out, as specifically as possible, which department, bureau, or committee is being cited.
2. When a catastrophic event takes place, such as a hurricane, oil spill, volcanic eruption, or tsunami, think about which parts of government or international organizations have lead roles or subordinate roles.
3. You read that the federal government prepared a new report on global warming; you have no further information. Discuss the strategies and tools you would use to locate the report.

Sources Mentioned in This Chapter

Sources mentioned in this section do not duplicate the References that follow.

GPO Websites

FDLP Desktop, http://www.fdlp.gov/.
Federal Depository Library Program (FDLP) home, http://www.gpo.gov/libraries/.

FDsys, http://www.fdsys,gov/.
FDsys Help, http://www.gpo.gov/help/index.html#about_congressional_ bills.htm.
SuDocs (Superintendent of Documents) classification system, http://www.access.gpo
.gov/su_docs/fdlp/pubs/explain.html.
U.S. Government Publication Digitization Projects, http://registry.fdlp.gov/.

Electronic Discussion Lists, Journals, and News

DttP: Documents to the People, http://wikis.ala.org/godort/index.php/DttP/.
Free Government Information (FGI), http://www.freegovinfo.info/.
GOVDOC-L, http://wikis.ala.org/godort/index.php/GODORT_Listservs# GOVDOC-L.
Government Computer News (GCN), http://www.gcn.com/.
Government Information Quarterly (GIQ), http://www.elsevier.com/wps/find/journal
description.cws_home/620202/description#description.
INTL-DOC, http://wikis.ala.org/godort/index.php/GODORT_Listservs# INTL-DOC.
New York Times, http://www.nytimes.com/.
Washington Post, http://www.washingtonpost.com/.

Sources for the Monthly Catalog of U.S. Government Publications

*Catalogue of publications issued by the Government of the United States during the month
of . . .* (1976–), http://catalog.gpo.gov/.
Cumulative Subject Index to the Monthly Catalog of U.S. Government Publications, 1895–1899.
1977. Arlington, VA: Carrolton.
Cumulative Subject Index to the Monthly Catalog of U.S. Government Publications, 1900–1971.
1973–1975. Arlington, VA: Carrolton.
Cumulative Title Index to United States Public Documents, 1789–1976. 1979–1982. Arlington,
VA: United States Historical Documents Institute.
OCLC, Government Printing Office Monthly Catalog, http://www.oclc.org/support/
documentation/firstsearch/databases/dbdetails/details/GPO.htm.
Paratext Public Documents Masterfile, http://www.paratext.com/public_document
.html.
ProQuest 1895–1976, http://monthlycatalog.chadwyck.com/marketing about.jsp.

Other Resources

1909 *Checklist*, http://digital.library.unt.edu/ark:/67531/metadc1029.
American FactFinder, http://factfinder.census.gov/.
Bureau of the Census, http://www.census.gov/.
Cheney, Debora, ed. 2002. *The Complete Guide to Citing Government Information Resources:
A Manual for Social Science & Business Research.* 3rd ed. Bethesda, MD: LexisNexis.
The Chicago Manual of Style. 2003. 15th edition. Chicago: University of Chicago Press.
The Chicago Manual of Style. 2010. 16th edition. Chicago: University of Chicago Press.
CIS Index to Executive Branch Documents, 1910–1932.
CIS Index to U.S. Executive Branch Documents, 1789–1909.
FedBizOpps, http://www.fbo.gov/.

Federal Register, http://purl.access.gpo.gov/GPO/LPS1756, SuDoc: AE 2.106 (online), AE 2.7, or GS4.107.

Google Books Library Project, http://books.google.com/.

Google U.S. Government Search, http://www.google.com/unclesam/.

Hathi Trust, http://www.hathitrust.org/.

Indiana University, "Citing U.S. Government Publications," http://www.libraries.iub .edu/index.php?pageId=2558.

International Organizations with Depository Libraries, http://wikis.ala.org/godort/ index.php/Publishing_Policies_and_Practices.

Internet Archive, http://www.archive.org/.

Legislative Source Book, http://www.llsdc.org/fed-reg-cfr/.

Libguides, http://www.libguides.com.

Public Printing and Binding Act (March 1, 1907, P.L. 59-153, 34 Stat. 1012).

Public Printing and Documents Act (October 22, 1968, P.L. 90-620, 82 Stat. 1238).

Non-Depository Government Publications, 1953–2008. Chester, VT: Readex.

State Depository Library Programs listing, http://wikis.ala.org/godort/index.php/ State_Depository_Library_Systems/.

Statistical Abstract of the United States, http://www.census.gov/compendia/statab/.

U.S. *Government Manual*, http://purl.access.gpo.gov/GPO/LPS2410, SuDoc: AE 2.108/2 (online) or GS 4.109.

USA.gov, http://www.usa.gov/.

Wooster College, U. S. Congressional Serial Set Finding List, http://www3.wooster.edu/ library/Gov/serialset/main.htm.

WorldCat, http://www.worldcat.org/.

Professional Associations

American Association of Law Libraries (AALL) Government Relations Committee, http://www.aallnet.org/committee/govr/.

American Library Association, http://www.ala.org/, also provides links to the divisions and round tables.

American Library Association Government Documents Roundtable (GODORT): Wiki, http://wikis.ala.org/godort/; Handout Exchange, http://wikis.ala.org/godort/ index.php/Exchange/.

International Federation of Library Associations and Institutions Government Information and Official Publications Section (IFLA-GIOPS), http://www.ifla.org/en/ giops/.

Law Librarians' Society of Washington, DC (LLSDC), http://www.llsdc.org/.

Medical Library Association, http://www.mlanet.org/.

Special Libraries Association Government Information Division (SLA-DGI), http://units .sla.org/division/dgi/.

Readings

Bernstein, Carl and Bob Woodward. 1973. *All the President's Men*. New York: Simon and Schuster.

Halberstam, David. 1972. *The Best and the Brightest.* New York: Random House.

Noonan, Peggy, 1990. *What I Saw at the Revolution: A Political Life in the Reagan Era.* New York: Random House.

Woodward, Bob, and Scott Armstrong. 1979. *The Brethren: Inside the Supreme Court.* New York: Simon and Schuster.

Texts

Boyd, Anne Morris, and Rae Elizabeth Rips. 1949. *United States Government Publications.* 3rd ed. New York: H. W. Wilson.

Morehead, Joe, and Mary K. Fetzer. 1992. *Introduction to United States Government Information Sources.* 4th ed. Englewood, CO: Libraries Unlimited.

Robinson, Judith Schiek. 1998. *Tapping the Government Grapevine.* 3rd ed. Phoenix: Greenwood.

Schmeckebier, Laurence F. 1925. *The Statistical Work of the National Government.* Baltimore: Johns Hopkins.

Schmeckebier, Laurence F., and Roy B. Eastin. 1969. *Government Publications and Their Use.* 4th ed. Washington, DC: Brookings Institution.

Sears, Jean L., and Marilyn K. Moody. 2001. *Using Government Information Sources: Electronic and Print.* 3rd ed. Phoenix: Greenwood.

References

ALA Government Documents Roundtable. 2010. "Bylaws." American Library Association. Accessed July 5. http://wikis.ala.org/godort/images/5/5b/Bylaws_20090518 .pdf.

The Chicago Manual of Style. 2003. 15th ed. Chicago: University of Chicago Press.

The Chicago Manual of Style. 2010. 16th ed. Chicago: University of Chicago Press.

Elsevier. 2011. "Government Information Quarterly." Accessed January 10. http://www .elsevier.com/wps/find/journaldescription.cws_home/620202/description# description.

Government Printing Office. 2010. FDsys. Accessed July 5. http://www.gpo .gov/projects/ fdsysinfo.htm.

Government Printing Office. 2008. *Style Manual: An Official Guide to the Form and Style of Federal Government Printing.* Washington, DC: Government Printing Office. http:// purl.access.gpo.gov/GPO/FDLP510.

Indiana University. 2010. "Citing U.S. Government Publications." Accessed October 28. http://www.libraries .iub.edu/index.php?pageId=2558.

McKinney, Richard J. 2010. "A Research Guide to the *Federal Register* and the *Code of Federal Regulations.*" In *Legislative Source Book.* Law Librarians' Society of Washington, DC. Revised August 4. http://www.llsdc.org/fed-reg-cfr.

National Archives and Records Administration. 2011. "U.S. Government Manual: Browse." Washington, DC: Government Printing Office. Accessed January 10. http://purl.access.gpo.gov/GPO/LPS2410.

OCLC. 2010. GPO Monthly Catalog (GPO). Description available: http://www.oclc .org/support/documentation/firstsearch/databases/dbdetails/details/ GPO.htm.

Paratext. 2010. Public Documents Masterfile. Accessed August 30. Description available: http://www.paratext.com/public_document.html.

ProQuest. 2010. *Monthly Catalog of U.S. Government Publications, 1895–1976.* Accessed August 30. Description available: http://monthlycatalog.chadwyck.com.

Informational Note

On November 30, 2010, ProQuest announced its acquisition of the Congressional Information Services (CIS) and University Publications of America (UPA) product lines from LexisNexis. The ProQuest announcement indicated that, beginning in 2011, LexisNexis Congressional will be renamed ProQuest Congressional and LexisNexis Statistical Insight will be renamed ProQuest Statistical Insight.

Chapter 3
Congress

Introduction

A health sciences librarian is perfectly comfortable consulting a congressional hearing on government recalls of unsafe food. A public librarian does not miss a beat when asked to trace a congressional bill introduced in April 1999. How did each become proficient with Congress? Both recognize that congressional literature is one of the great hidden collections in our nation's libraries and on the open Internet. It would be a false assumption to think that looking at Congress will only bring the reader into the dry, inexplicable world of lawmaking. On the contrary, congressional publications provide a picture of almost every aspect of American culture and life, including topics as far flung as art, credit card debt, high school debate teams, consumer safety, the readiness of the Navy's fleet, human cloning, and all aspects of medicine and science. Why is this so? Congress looks at problems. Where there is a need that cannot be met at the state government level, via existing federal laws and regulations, or through other institutions, interested parties can bring forth their concerns for Congress to address via legislation, the writing of new laws. The United States Constitution calls for Congress to make "all Laws...necessary and proper" (U.S. Constitution, art. I, sec. 3).

Congress also has oversight authority for the executive branch of government, which means that every agency must be authorized by Congress, and the agency's leadership must go before Congress at regular intervals for funding, known as the appropriations process. Congress must pass 13 appropriations bills by October 1 of each year so that adequate funds may be expended from the U.S. Treasury to give the federal government the money to operate. As each agency defends its spending needs to Congress, the appropriations process becomes a great overview of our national priorities. In this capacity, Congress is the primary decision maker on dollars allotted to federal science and medical initiatives. Vice President Al Gore was once taken to task for making a comment that sounded as though he were taking credit for inventing the Internet while serving as a U.S. senator (Hillman, 2000). While such a claim would be quite an overstatement, it is indeed the case that Congress's actions fund "Big Science." Without the willingness of Congress to commit U.S. research funds to all kinds of scientific, medical, and computing endeavors, progress in these areas would be dramatically slowed or nearly halted. Congress has been called the most influential legislature in the world, with good reason (Oppenheimer, 1983).

Political activists, trade and industry members, and lobbyists have their own interests in Congress; celebrity watchers interested in power and pageantry may have another; historians, journalists, archivists, or political scientists yet another. Librarians are interested in the literature of Congress, the published output, what Congress did and what it produces. We work to collect and preserve that literature and make it more accessible to all. If you spend time with government documents librarians, you will notice that they are enthusiastic about congressional information. They tend to wax rhapsodic about the first time they really "got" the U.S. *Congressional Serial Set* or picked up a hearing that they just could not stop reading. This natural affinity, this chemistry, is simply due to the fact that librarians are interested in all kinds of topics, and so is Congress.

To catch some of that enthusiasm, start by learning about some typical congressional publications:

- Bills, resolutions, and aids for tracking their progress
- Committee hearings
- Research reports and other committee literature
- The U.S. *Congressional Serial Set*
- Main floor transcription (the *Congressional Record*)
- Video proceedings
- Calendars and journals

These official government sources may be consulted directly, but they can be accessed more efficiently, with increased navigation and discovery abilities, by using commercially published summaries, indexes, and digital resources, as well as community-created online resources, which we will cover in the Guides and Indexes section of this chapter.

For Starters: THOMAS

Perhaps even seeing the preceding list has helped make Congress seem more manageable. An online resource known as THOMAS (http://thomas.loc.gov/, named after Thomas Jefferson, of course), the Library of Congress's main site for Congress, is a basic starting place for the novice searcher (see Figure 3.1). THOMAS makes it simple to browse for bills, calendars, hot topics, congressional committees, laws, and congressional history. It is important to note that THOMAS's source for published bills, laws, and other documents is the United States Government Printing Office, the longtime official publisher for Congress. One can also search GPO's holdings directly using the Federal Digital System (http://www.FDsys.gov/). A new congressional researcher would go far simply by setting aside time to learn THOMAS's organization and content.

Getting Specific about Congress and Its Structure

Congress is bicameral, meaning it has two chambers: the House of Representatives, with 435 members apportioned according to each state's population; and the Senate, with two senators from each state for a total of 100 U.S. senators.

Figure 3.1. THOMAS, from the Library of Congress: Access to Bills and Laws

The LIBRARY of CONGRESS THOMAS

The Library of Congress > THOMAS Home

THOMAS

In the spirit of Thomas Jefferson, legislative information from the Library of Congress

Print Subscribe Share/Save

- THOMAS Home
- About THOMAS
- Bills, Resolutions
- Congressional Record
- Presidential Nominations
- Treaties
- Committee Reports
- Government Resources
- For Teachers
- Help

House of Representatives
Senate
U.S. Code

Related Resources at the Library

- Law Library of Congress
- Global Legal Monitor
- Global Legal Information Network
- Century of Lawmaking
- Continental Congress and Constitutional Convention

Find the Law Library on:

In Custodia Legis Blog
 Facebook
 Twitter
 YouTube
iTunes U

Legislation in Current Congress

Search Bill Summary & Status
 Word/Phrase Bill Number

[_____] SEARCH
- Try the Advanced Search
- More Search Options

Browse Bills by Sponsor

Select a Representative GO
Select a Senator GO
- More Browse Options

More Legislative Information

- Search Bill Text for Multiple Congresses
- Appropriations Bills
- Public Laws
- Roll Call Votes
- Contact Members of Congress
- State Legislature Websites

Learn

- THOMAS Orientation
- The Legislative Process
- The Supreme Court
- Declaration of Independence
- U.S. Constitution
- More historical documents

Current Activity
- House Floor Now (video)
- Senate Floor Now
- Passed Congress, Sent to President
- Yesterday in Congress
- Congressional Record Latest Daily Digest
- Schedules, Calendars

Weekly Top Five
- H.R. 5297
- H.R. 6134
- H.R. 4646
- H.R. 3590
- H.R. 4173
- View Top Ten

Tip of the Week

Find links to state legislature websites in THOMAS.
- View Archive of Tips

Feature

In Custodia Legis Blog

A new blog from the Law Library of Congress that will feature information about THOMAS as well as other topics.

Stay Connected with the Library All ways to connect »

Find us on   Subscribe & Comment   Download & Play
                RSS & E-Mail   Blogs   Podcasts Webcasts iTunes U

About | Press | Site Map | Contact | Accessibility | Legal | External Link Disclaimer | USA.gov   Speech Enabled

Combine the two and the result is an ever-fascinating, complex example of representative government.

A congress spans two years, with each session generally lasting one year. Researchers refer to congressional time in terms of congress and session, as in the 111th Congress, second session, or 111-2.

Trivia Time

Many congresses have included a third session, but in the post–World War II era, there has been a consistent pattern of two-session congresses.

The clerk of the House provides background on the history of congressional sessions, and a list of all session dates and years (http://clerk.house.gov/art_history/house_history/Session_Dates/index .html). To learn more, try entering *"session dates" congress* in any Internet search engine, or consult the GPO's easy grid of congress and session years (http://www.gpoaccess.gov/help/congress_table .html).

A vast majority of the work of Congress occurs in committee and subcommittee, not on the floor of the House or Senate. When picturing Congress at work, actively fight the familiar images of impassioned speeches on the "main floor" of the House or Senate, even though both bodies convene in that manner when Congress is in session. Instead, try to imagine smaller gatherings, in much less spectacular office buildings—this is the bread and butter of Congress: committee work. Tracking down a tidbit of congressional information means figuring out the context: did the information come about because of floor action or committee work, and for what purpose? The PBS NewsHour, in its online site @the Capitol, notes that committees

> have been called "scattered nodes of power," fiefdoms and laboratories, and committees are all of these. According to Congress watcher Norman Ornstein, the committee system is the "natural form of division of labor in such a large and complex body as the Congress." Committees are also uniquely American. No other system in the world uses committees. (Public Broadcasting Service, 2009)

There are about 20 committees in each chamber, as well as 5 joint committees, and a handful of select or special committees convened to address specific one-time or recurrent concerns (see sidebar). Recognize committee names from the daily news? Each is further divided into numerous subcommittees. Some subcommittees are so well established that their websites are more developed and useful than those of their parent committees.

Some congressional work is purely ceremonial. This may be shocking to novice searchers, but is familiar to more experienced librarians, who would not even notice a tribute to the founder of Annalee Mobilitee Dolls (Cong. Rec. May 12, 2002) or a heartfelt poem from a constituent ("One Less Angel Will Cry" by contest winner Julie Rich) published in the *Congressional Record* (Cong. Rec., Jan. 23, 2008). The *Congressional Record* and congressional resolutions are the richest sources for these materials, and Professor John D. Wilkerson (e-mail communication, December 10, 2009) found that nearly 3 percent of House bills in a recent session were commemorative in nature: the naming of public buildings, the awarding of medals, and so on. An example is Public Law 111-7, "An Act to designate the facility of the United States Postal Service located at 2105 East Cook Street in Springfield, Illinois, as the 'Colonel John H. Wilson, Jr. Post Office Building.'"

Congress has so many intricacies and offbeat traditions—while it is easy and important to develop a baseline competency and awareness about its literature,

Standing Committees: Senate, House, and Joint

Senate Standing Committees
- Agriculture, Nutrition, and Forestry
- Appropriations
- Armed Services
- Banking, Housing, and Urban Affairs
- Budget
- Commerce, Science, and Transportation
- Energy and Natural Resources
- Environment and Public Works
- Finance
- Foreign Relations
- Health, Education, Labor, and Pensions
- Homeland Security and Governmental Affairs
- Indian Affairs
- Judiciary
- Rules and Administration
- Small Business and Entrepreneurship
- Veterans' Affairs
- Select Committee on Ethics
- Select Committee on Intelligence
- Special Committee on Aging

House Standing Committees
- Agriculture
- Appropriations
- Armed Services
- Budget
- Education and Labor
- Energy and Commerce
- Financial Services
- Foreign Affairs
- Homeland Security
- House Administration
- Judiciary
- Natural Resources
- Oversight and Government Reform
- Rules
- Science and Technology
- Small Business
- Standards of Official Conduct
- Transportation and Infrastructure
- Veterans' Affairs
- Ways and Means
- Permanent Select Committee on Intelligence
- Select Committee on Energy Independence and Global Warming

Joint Committees
- Joint Committee on Printing
- Joint Committee on Taxation
- Joint Committee on the Library
- Joint Economic Committee
- Joint Congressional Committee on Inaugural Ceremonies
- Joint Committee on Taxation

(*Source*: House.gov; Senate.gov.)

it takes a lifetime to become an expert on congressional publishing. Archival information on Congress (office records, members' papers, constituent mail, and so on) is addressed in Chapter 15. A newcomer should be fearless and humble in learning about congressional literature, and look everywhere for answers. What harm could it do to sneak a peek at David Silverberg's *Congress for Dummies* (with a foreword by former Speaker of the House Dennis Hastert and former Senate Majority Leader Tom Daschle) or *The Complete Idiot's Guide to American Government*? If your library does not have these guides, consider adding them as a supplement to more traditional reference works, such as CQ's *Guide to Congress* or the much-loved congressional publication *How Our Laws Are Made*. Whenever using an online system, whether it is THOMAS or something flashier, make sure to use the Help pages, which will undoubtedly help explain congressional terms and traditions. The web has done wonders to "break open" Congress. The fact that the Senate has a candy desk to store caloric confections is no longer a secret: search for it online yourself.

Legislative Process and Publications

About the Legislative Process

Many Americans born in the 1960s or later have enjoyed a series of animated children's videos known as *Schoolhouse Rock!* (Dorough et al., 2002), segments of which may be found on the web via outlets such as YouTube. The *America Rock* grouping includes a variety of lessons in civic engagement, produced in a style reminiscent of early children's television such as *Sesame Street* and *The Electric Company.* The "Just a Bill" segment does a marvelous job of conveying in four minutes the basic path from conception of the idea ("there oughta be a law!") to the struggle to get the introduced bill out of committee. What is portrayed in the video is what is known as the Dance of Legislation, a term made more popular by Seattle-based author and attorney Eric Redman. In his 1973 book with the same title, he describes his job as an intern working for Senator Warren Magnuson, trying to get a particular piece of health care legislation passed.

The dance of legislation is indeed an overwhelming topic to most Americans. Perhaps it is because people rightfully suspect that all kinds of factors—timing, politics, and priorities—go into making legislation succeed. With a very low success rate for each individual bill, it is hard to feel optimistic, much less in command of all the various steps. Bills have to pass both houses and be signed by the chief executive (president) to become law. If the president decides to veto a bill, it returns to Congress, where it must be passed by a two-thirds majority of both chambers. A bill must be passed by the adjournment of the Congress in which it was introduced, or it automatically dies . . . and most bills die.

About Bills and Measures

One could think of an introduced bill or resolution as the first draft of a proposed new law. Resolutions are just like bills, but come in a few different types (joint, concurrent, and simple; see sidebar).

Bills and resolutions, which we will refer to generically as bills or measures, can vary in length from one short page to over 2,000 pages. Who actually writes the text of bills? Bills have to be introduced by a member of Congress, of course, but technically can be written by anyone. The reality is that most bills are written by attorneys or in consultation with attorneys, whether the bill is requested by private industry, a nongovernmental organization, a private citizen, the president, or staff within the executive branch. After a bill is introduced in either the House or Senate, it embarks on its journey toward becoming (or not) an official law. This will involve referral to committee and subcommittee, where it may or may not be considered further, followed by a possible trip back to the main floor and a vote for passage. Once passed by either house, the bill may be referred to as an Act.

Types of Measures

Types of measure	Noted as	Special notes
Bills	H.R. 1	Bills and other measures are numbered sequentially in the order that they are introduced. Bills may be private (affecting only specific individuals or parties) or public; omnibus (on many topics) or target (single topic). Must pass both houses.
	S. 1	
Joint Resolutions	H.J.Res. 1	Tend to have a limited focus or be related to money measures or technical corrections. Constitutional amendments must be introduced as Joint Resolutions and are forwarded to the 50 states for approval (rather than the president). Must pass both houses.
	S.J.Res. 1	
Concurrent Resolutions	H.Con.Res. 1	Internal measures of Congress. Tend to express facts or principles jointly. Used to set time of adjournment, appoint members to joint committees, send congratulatory messages to foreign leaders. Published in *Statutes at Large*.
	S.Con. Res. 1	
Resolutions, sometimes referred to as "Simple Resolutions"	H.Res. 1	Considered only by one chamber, usually refer to procedural matters. Can also express the sentiment of the House or Senate on something over which it has no jurisdiction (ex: 111-1 S. Res. 23, honoring the life of Andrew Wyeth)
	S.Res. 1	
Public Law	P.L. 1	All measures that become law are assigned a Public Law (P.L.) number in the order in which they are passed. P.L.s are published first in a "slip" or paperback edition, and later produced in a bound official edition, *U.S. Statutes at Large*. Can be public or private laws.
United States Statutes at Large	123 Stat. 1776	Official printing of public and private laws (in exact sequence of passage)
United States Code	30 U.S.C. 22	Codified (topically arranged) edition of all public laws *currently in force*; see Chapter 5 (Law)

For further information, see http://www.gpo.gov/fdsys/browse/collection.action?collectionCode=BILLS.

One of the standard questions in government documents libraries over the years has been some variation of "I'm following a bill in Congress and I need to know how far it has gotten in the process," or "I need to know how far a bill went in the last Congress." This is the grand practice of bill tracking or bill status. What users are essentially asking for here is the last official action taken on a particular piece of legislation. When you are viewing a summary of a bill via an online resource such as THOMAS, the bill tracking history can usually be found under a heading like Major Congressional Actions (which provides a list of just the big steps of the process) or All Congressional Actions (much more detail, including the dates of significant meetings related to the bill, comments made on the floor, etc.) or simply Last Action. Frequently, the person asking the question will need to be convinced that a particular bill died in committee, because it is hard to translate lack of action as a kind of action or outcome. No one wants to think that a favorite piece of legislation has died a slow and unceremonious death. For more information about bill tracking, see the Indexes section of this chapter.

Many landmark pieces of legislation (e.g., the Brady Bill) are reintroduced in several congresses before succeeding. They may be known by a popular name that varies from their actual title. Award-winning law librarian Mary Whisner has written a humorous and informative essay on "What's in a Statute Name?" citing everything from the Chain Store Act to the CAN-SPAM Act, explaining that "the Sherman Antitrust Act was not always called that, does not use the word 'antitrust,' and was not even written by Senator Sherman" (Whisner, 2005: 174). Frequently, bills or laws are even known by an acronym.

Many Ways of Referring to Bills and Laws		
Acronym	Popular name or short title	Longer title (stating purpose of bill/law)
ENDA S. 1584	Employment Non-Discrimination Act of 2009	An Act to address the history and widespread pattern of discrimination on the basis of sexual orientation or gender identity by private sector employers and local, State, and Federal government employers, and for other purposes.
HIPAA (P.L. 104-191)	Health Insurance Portability and Accountability Act	An Act to amend the Internal Revenue Code of 1986 to improve portability and continuity of health insurance coverage in the group and individual markets, to combat waste, fraud, and abuse in health insurance and health care delivery, to promote the use of medical savings accounts, to improve access to long-term care services and coverage, to simplify the administration of health insurance, and for other purposes.
The USA-PATRIOT Act (P.L. 107-56)	Uniting and Strengthening America by Providing Appropriate Tools Required to Intercept and Obstruct Terrorism Act of 2001	An Act to deter and punish terrorist acts in the United States and around the world, to enhance law enforcement investigatory tools, and for other purposes.

The Process: It Starts with a Bill,
Leading to Lots of Congressional Literature

Let us walk through the basic legislative process now. Don't worry, this will only hurt a little.

1. Prior to its introduction, each bill must find a champion or advocate within Congress. Bills can originate in either house, except for revenue or appropriations bills, which per the Constitution must start in the House. The bill is introduced by sponsoring and cosponsoring members of Congress and is immediately referred to committee, subcommittee, or multiple committees, sometimes without any comment or debate. All of this is chronicled in the *Congressional Record*, which will be discussed in detail shortly.

> **Bill Introductions from the *Congressional Record***
>
> **Measures Referred**
>
> The following bills were read the first and the second times by unanimous consent, and referred as indicated:
>
> H.R. 1779. An act to amend the Internal Revenue Code of 1986 to allow penalty-free withdrawals from retirement plans during the period that a military reservist or national guardsman is called to active duty for an extended period, and for other purposes; *to the Committee on Finance.*
>
> H.R. 3970. An Act to provide for the implementation of a Green Chemistry Research and Development Program, and for other purposes; *to the Committee on Commerce, Science, and Transportation.*
>
> H.R. 4019. An act to address the participation of Taiwan in the World Health Organization; *to the Committee on Foreign Relations.*
>
> (*Source*: Cong. Rec., April 22, 2004, p. S4299; emphasis added.)

2. If the committee decides to further consider the measure, it may hold *hearings* (see Records of Committee Meetings: Hearings), calling in expert witnesses to testify on the matter at hand, much like a court of law. It may also commission a research report (known as a *Committee Print*) to gain more direct information about the general question. Most measures never get to this point. Committee prints are generally authored by the Congressional Research Service (CRS, an elite research team within the Library of Congress) or committee staff.
3. The committee may vote to change the text of the bill before sending it back to the main floor (bills need to return to the main floor to proceed on their slim chance to passage; this step is critical). This revision process is referred to as *markup*.
4. If the committee members can mostly agree (dissenting views are valued, but a majority must agree), then and only then is the measure reported out of committee. This means that a *committee report* is issued, often providing the revised text and the arguments in support. Reports generally

recommend the bill for passage, and minority dissenting views are sometimes included as well (note that there are other kinds of committee reports published, but this is the primary type). The bill then comes back to the main floor of the House or the Senate for reconsideration, debate, and vote by the entire chamber. Most bills do not make it back to the main floor.

5. Amendments may be offered on the main floor, and voted on. Votes can occur in three ways: by voice (with the presiding officer determining if the ayes or nays have it); by division or standing vote (members literally stand and are counted); or by record vote, also called roll call voting (now done via electronic means, in which both the vote and the voter's identity are recorded).

6. In the House, the bill may also be sent back (recommitted) to committee for further consideration. This can be a stalling mechanism to either encourage or discourage support of the bill.

7. If the bill passes on the floor of one chamber, it is then referred to the other chamber, where it undergoes an identical process. It is also possible to have an identical or nearly identical bill making its way through the other chamber concurrently.

8. If the bill passes the other chamber, but the other chamber changes language or offers amendments, or if the other chamber passes a similar but different bill, a conference committee is appointed with members from each chamber. The conference committee meets to reconcile editorial and substantive differences between the two versions of the bill. Often a conference report is issued with changes noting which chamber's (House or Senate) bill language was used—and in some cases, there is a true mix, borrowing from both texts, or a significant rewriting. This step is not necessary if the two chambers have passed truly identical bills.

9. Once the bill clears the conference committee, this compromise version must be voted on in both chambers (this step is needed only if there were changes from both chambers during the conference).

10. After it has passed both chambers, the bill proceeds to the desk of the chief executive (president) where it is either signed or vetoed within ten days, not counting Sundays. The act of vetoing can be active (the president issues a written veto), or passive (in which the president simply neglects to sign the bill). If Congress is in session, an unsigned bill becomes law; if Congress is not in session, the unsigned bill is effectively vetoed, known as a pocket veto. Vetoes may be overturned by a two-thirds majority of both houses of Congress.

11. The signed bill, now a law, is assigned a public law number (sometimes abbreviated as P.L. or Pub. L.) and is published first in paperback or "slip" form, then more formally in *United States Statutes at Large*.

12. The law becomes codified by the Office of the Law Revision Counsel (http://uscode.house.gov/) and is integrated into the *United States Code*, a topically arranged collection of all federal laws currently in force (see Law, Chapter 5).

All along the dance of legislation, congressional publications are published by the GPO (see Figure 3.2). Most publications are available through FDsys, and print-on-paper and microfiche copies of some types of publications are freely distributed through a system of over 1,000 depository libraries.

More Notes on Bills

New laws usually update existing laws, which can make for excruciatingly dull if not nonsensical reading. The text of many bills begins, "A Bill to Amend..." and involves striking out existing legal text and inserting new phrases. On the other hand, every once in a while a piece of legislation does make inspiring reading, particularly something that breaks new ground and may come to be considered a landmark law. See the Air Quality Act of 1967 for one example, or how about the Servicemen's Readjustment Act of 1944? (Did you guess that this was really the GI Bill?) Bills and laws can be on a single topic (target legislation) or on many different topics (omnibus bills). Unusual phrasing, such as "a bill to do X, and for other purposes," is a telltale sign of an omnibus bill.

The percentage of bills that never find their way out of committee is quite high and has varied over the decades, sometimes reaching as high as 90 percent. In the 1990s, for example, 73 to 89 percent of House bills simply went nowhere. The corresponding range for the Senate in the 1990s was 73 to 78 percent (American Enterprise Institute, 2002).

Congress passes both public and private laws. Public laws apply to the entire population; private laws are for the benefit of specific individuals or organizations. For example, consider the plight of a widow whose home sat within the boundaries of the Rocky Mountain National Park. Upon her husband's death, she might have been forced to move, if not for the Betty Dick Residence Protection Act of 2006 (Private Law 109-1), "to permit the continued occupancy and use of the property...by Betty Dick for the remainder of her natural life." Or what about the plight of Nguyen Quy An, a Vietnamese man who risked his life to save American soldiers during the Vietnam War? Thanks to Private Law 104-4, certain naturalization requirements were waived for An, making it simpler for him to become an American citizen.

Despite their centrality to this process, physical copies of bills have not been widely distributed outside of Congress, probably due to their high volume (sometimes over 8,000 introduced annually) and the number of iterations in each congress. The exception are GPO's microfiche bills on diazo fiche, distributed through the depository program since 1979. Libraries may also purchase historical runs of bills in preservation-quality microform from the Congressional Information Service (CIS), now a division of ProQuest, or Library of Congress Duplication Services. In free online format, bills may be found through the American Memory Project (1799–1875 for the House, 1819–1875 for the Senate; see Figure 3.3 for an example of a bill), then from 1988 on via THOMAS and FDsys. Many commercial publishers offer online access to bills from the late 1980s on as well.

Figure 3.2. A Simplified View of the Legislative Process, Emphasizing GPO's Printing of Bills: How a Bill Becomes Law

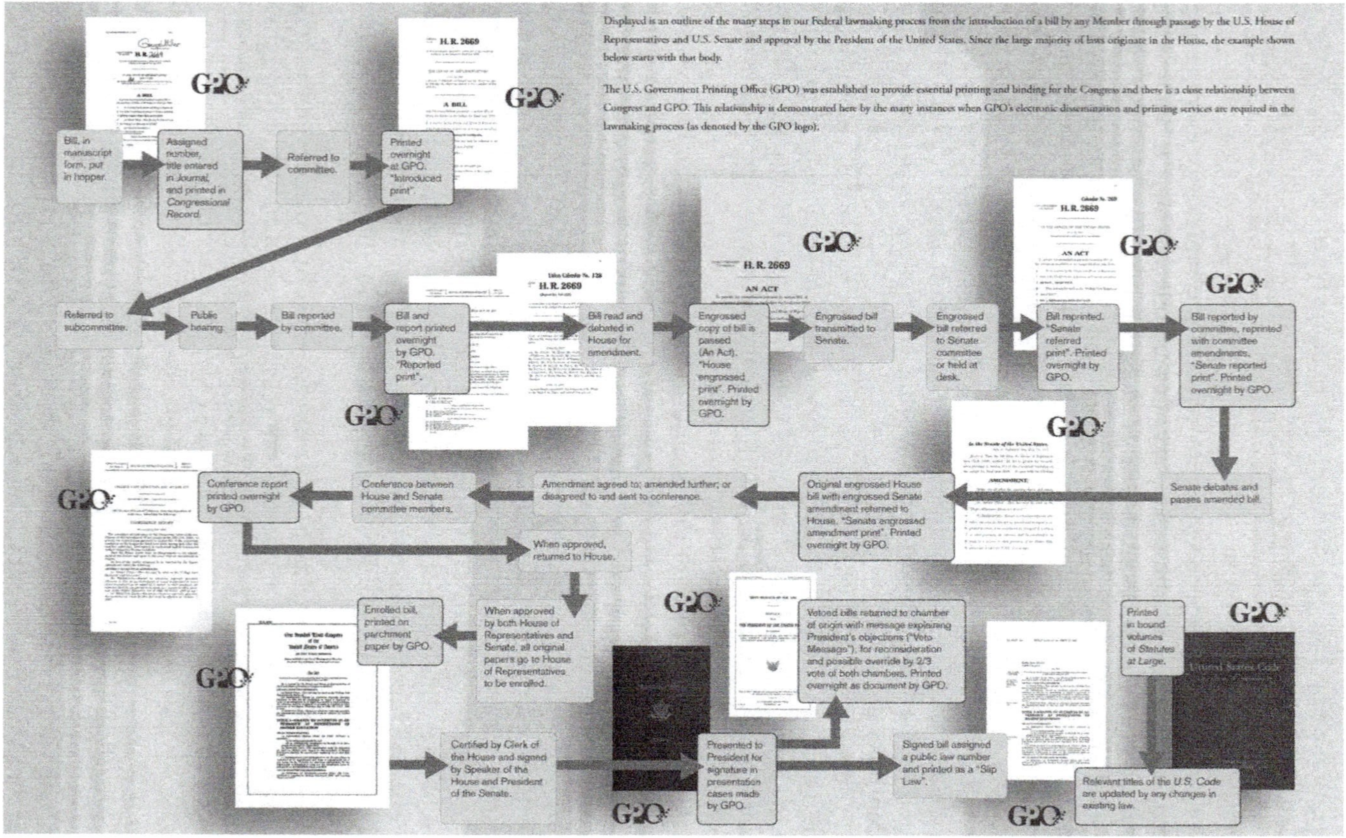
Displayed is an outline of the many steps in our Federal lawmaking process from the introduction of a bill by any Member through passage by the U.S. House of Representatives and U.S. Senate and approval by the President of the United States. Since the large majority of laws originate in the House, the example shown below starts with that body.
The U.S. Government Printing Office (GPO) was established to provide essential printing and binding for the Congress and there is a close relationship between Congress and GPO. This relationship is demonstrated here by the many instances when GPO's electronic dissemination and printing services are required in the lawmaking process (as denoted by the GPO logo).
Bill, in manuscript form, put in hopper.
Assigned number, title entered in Journal, and printed in Congressional Record.
Referred to committee.
Printed overnight at GPO. "Introduced print".
Referred to subcommittee.
Public hearing.
Bill reported by committee.
Bill and report printed overnight by GPO. "Reported print".
Bill read and debated in House for amendment.
Engrossed copy of bill is passed (An Act). "House engrossed print". Printed overnight by GPO.
Engrossed bill transmitted to Senate.
Engrossed bill referred to Senate committee or held at desk.
Bill reprinted. "Senate referred print". Printed overnight by GPO.
Bill reported by committee, reprinted with committee amendments. "Senate reported print". Printed overnight by GPO.
Senate debates and passes amended bill.
Original engrossed House bill with engrossed Senate amendment returned to House. "Senate engrossed amendment print". Printed overnight by GPO.
Amendment agreed to; amended further; or disagreed to and sent to conference.
Conference between House and Senate committee members.
Conference report printed overnight by GPO.
When approved, returned to House.
When approved by both House of Representatives and Senate, all original papers go to House of Representatives to be enrolled.
Enrolled bill, printed on parchment paper by GPO.
Certified by Clerk of the House and signed by Speaker of the House and President of the Senate.
Presented to President for signature in presentation cases made by GPO.
Vetoed bills returned to chamber of origin with message explaining President's objections ("Veto Message"), for reconsideration and possible override by 2/3 vote of both chambers. Printed overnight as document by GPO.
Signed bill assigned a public law number and printed as a "Slip Law".
Printed in bound volumes of Statutes at Large.
Relevant titles of the U.S. Code are updated by any changes in existing law.
H.R. 2669
A BILL
AN ACT
United States Code

Figure 3.3. A Sample Bill from "A Century of Lawmaking for a New Nation," Part of the Larger American Memory Project from the Library of Congress

---

[Printer's No., 403.

41ST CONGRESS,
2D SESSION.

H. R. 1001.

IN THE HOUSE OF REPRESENTATIVES.

JANUARY 28, 1870.

Read twice, referred to the Committee on the Territories, and ordered to be printed.

Mr. CULLOM, on leave, introduced the following bill:

A BILL

To organize the Territory of Lincoln, and consolidate the Indian tribes under a territorial government.

1   *Be it enacted by the Senate and House of Representa-*
2   *tives of the United States of America in Congress assembled,*
3   That there be, and is hereby, created and established within
4   the Indian Territory, bounded as follows, to wit: On the north
5   by the State of Kansas; on the west by the eastern boundary
6   of the Territory of New Mexico and the State of Texas; on
7   the south by the northern boundary of the State of Texas,
8   and on the east by the western boundary of the States of
9   Arkansas and Missouri, a temporary government, by the
10   name of the Territory of Lincoln.

1   SEC. 2. *And be it further enacted,* That the executive
2   power and authority in and over said Territory shall be vested
3   in a governor, who shall be appointed by the President of
4   the United States, by and with the advice and consent of the
5   Senate, and whose salary shall be three thousand dollars per

---

A Bill Is Sent to Committee for Consideration and Markup: Hearings, Committee Reports, Documents, and the Serial Set

RECORDS OF COMMITTEE MEETINGS: HEARINGS

A bill, once introduced and referred to committee or subcommittee, has an uncertain fate. If it rises to the top of the committee's priorities, a hearing may be scheduled and expert witnesses called to testify. Scholars group hearings into four broad types: legislative (considering a bill for passage, creating new law), oversight (reviewing the work of an executive agency), investigative (for example, Watergate or the Iran-Contra affair), and nomination (such as

Supreme Court nominations, the Elena Kagan confirmation hearings being one example).

All hearings are fact-finding investigations and provide an unparalleled glimpse at what Congress—and presumably the nation—deems to be important at the time. Hearings are generally held in Washington, DC, but may be conducted elsewhere as well. These are known as field hearings. The testimony of expert witnesses makes hearings invaluable primary resources for high school level research and beyond. Hearings are a little bit like the *Congressional Record* in their theatrical, read-aloud aspect, but the critical difference is that hearings take place in committee while the *Record* is limited to the floors of the House and Senate (see the section "Back to the Floor: The *Congressional Record*" later in this chapter). Ask librarians to list the top five types of government documents most useful for contemporary and historical research, and hearings will undoubtedly make most people's lists. Recent hearings include titles as diverse as *Hallmark/Westland Meat Recall, Federal Response to the Alzheimer's Epidemic*, and *The Crisis in Tibet: Finding a Path to Peace*.

All aspects of a hearing are vulnerable to political influence: the decision to hold it in the first place, its scheduling and location, to what degree it is widely advertised or promoted, the tenor of questions asked, and the choice of witnesses called. Sevetson (2007) notes that witnesses tend to fall into four overarching groups: political figures (such as Northglenn, Colorado, mayor Kathie Novak); famous personalities (Nick Jonas of the Jonas Brothers); affected individuals (pancreatic cancer patient and author Randy Pausch); and experts (Cornell astronomer Joseph Burns). Witnesses are asked to prepare their remarks ahead of time, but are also subject to questioning, much as in a court of law. Even though the witnesses have prepared statements—which they deposit with the committee clerk, typically two days before testifying—there are also court reporters on hand to make a true transcription.

Getting at the content of hearings or even finding out about hearings has never been easier, but there is still plenty of room for improved access. Every committee and many subcommittees have websites, many of which have RSS feeds or other notification features. With a minimum of effort, the committee can push information to interested individuals. Frequently, there are links to videos of hearings and also to (uncorrected) court reporter transcripts.

Consult published hearings from GPO, even if you have to wait weeks or months for them to be released: fully published hearings include evidence submitted for the record, correspondence, and other relevant material provided to the committee (Sevetson, 2007: 1), all of which can make up over half of the content of a published volume. Published hearings include both versions of the testimony: the version submitted to the clerk, and the transcript of what was actually spoken aloud, along with questions and answers. Frequently, copyrighted material such as newspaper articles is inserted into a hearing; this has been an impediment for hearings digitization projects on the web. A number of limited collections of digitized hearings exist on the web. The University of New Orleans' Earl K. Long Library offers selected digitized U.S. House and Senate committee hearings and publications (http://louisdl.louis

libraries.org/cdm4/index_p120701coll25.php?CISOROOT=/p120701coll25), and the Stanford University Libraries provide digitized hearings from the Joint Committee on Atomic Energy, 1946–1977 (http://collections.stanford.edu/atomicenergy/), as two examples.

Hearings continue to be distributed to many depository libraries in print (as they have been for over 100 years), on microfiche (from the 1970s on), and digitally (from 1994 on). As noted, official, GPO-produced hearings may not be published for months after the hearings are held, and some closed-door hearings, known as unpublished hearings, are withheld from distribution for years due to concerns of confidentiality, national security, trade secrets, and other factors. Broad keyword searching for hearings in a library's online catalog can be as simple as combining a search term with "hearing" (uranium AND hearing). More sophisticated searching (by factors such as witness and bill number) requires special tools (see the Indexes section of this chapter). ProQuest Congressional, a subscription service, offers comprehensive indexing and digital access to current and historic hearings back to 1824 through the Congressional Hearings Digital Collection.

Consider a specific hearing from 2007: the issue at hand was mental health care for veterans, particularly those returning from Iraq and Afghanistan. One particular bill (110 Stat. 2162) had been introduced and referred to the Senate Committee on Veterans Affairs on October 15, 2007. Nine days later (very quickly in congressional terms), a formal hearing was convened on this bill, along with four other bills on veterans' health, with the nondescript title *Hearing on Pending Legislation* (see sidebar). The ultimate fate of this particular bill? It became Public Law 110-387 (that's the number of the Congress, the 110th, followed by the designation for the 387th public law passed), known as the Veterans' Mental Health and Other Care Improvement Act of 2008. Because they needed a tremendous amount of factual information on this topic, including how the Department of Defense works with the Department of Veterans' Affairs, members of Congress asked the Congressional Research Service (CRS) to prepare an informative report. The CRS prepared a May 2007 report, *Veterans Health Care Issues*, updating it in June and November (Panangala, 2007). The report contains a variety of data, including statistics on the major medical diagnoses of VA-treated veterans from the wars in Iraq and Afghanistan:

Example of the Question and Answer Period of a Congressional Hearing

SENATOR MURRAY: OK. Can you give us today what the wait times are?

DR. KUSSMAN: For?

SENATOR MURRAY: For all veterans. Can you tell us what the wait time is?

DR. KUSSMAN: As I reported, we believe on the basis of the data that we have, 95 percent of the 39 million appointments that we see every year are done within the 30-day expectation. These are not urgent or emergency appointments, but routine appointments and things for veterans within 30 days of when they ask for it.

SENATOR MURRAY: Can you give me a reason why the *Charlotte Observer's* information is so different?

DR. KUSSMAN: I will have to get back to you on that.

(*Source: Hearing on Pending Legislation*, 2007: 25–26.)

over 100,000 veterans suffering from mental disorders and 93,093 from "symptoms, signs, and ill-defined conditions" (Panangala, 2007: 17).

RESEARCH REPORTS

The legislative branch documents most likely to be read by a broad audience are research reports. There are at least four different kinds of legislatively relevant government research reports:

1. **Committee Prints**: Committee prints are information briefings or research reports requested by a committee member as part of a deliberative process or simply to investigate an issue. Prints are frequently quite short in length. Most members of Congress are not scientists, but still their job requires them to make decisions about complex technical matters. Bluntly stated, they need to be educated. Sometimes they not only need the help of expert witnesses at hearings, but also need to read a book on the subject at hand. Committee prints are concise, factual reports compiled by committee staff, the Congressional Research Service, or other scholars. As you can imagine, committee prints can also be of great use to generalist researchers. Some prints are more helpful than others; the less exciting ones are simply compilations of readings, much like a course pack, or gathering of facts to support a certain viewpoint. An example of a recent print is *Safeguarding America's Seniors: What We Can Do to Prepare for National Emergencies* (S. Prt. 109-69). Committee prints were not distributed through the depository program until the mid-1970s.

2. **Government Accountability Office Reports**: The Government Accountability Office (GAO), a legislative branch agency, is frequently referred to as a "watchdog" or auditing agency for the entire federal government. GAO has been churning out slim, well-researched reports for decades, initially under its former name, the General Accounting Office. GAO reports tend to be 30 pages or less in length and focus specifically on government efficiency, with a special eye to government waste. Recent titles here include *Disaster Housing: FEMA Needs More Detailed Guidance and Performance Measures to Help Ensure Effective Assistance after Major Disasters* (GAO-09-796, August 2009); *Ryan White CARE Act: Health Resources and Services Administration's Implementation of Certain Provisions Hampered by Lack of Timely and Accurate Information* (GAO-09-1020, September 2009); and *Medicare Physician Services: Utilization Trends Indicate Sustained Beneficiary Access with High and Growing Levels of Service in Some Areas of the Nation* (GAO-09-559, August 2009).

3. **Congressional Budget Office Reports**: Congressional Budget Office (CBO) reports are highly valued as dispassionate cost estimates. As legislation is drafted, particularly at the point when it is reported out of committee, CBO estimates are required so that Congress will know the actual price tag of a proposed new law. This is another office that is held up as a standard for nonpartisan assessments. Terry Gross of National Public Radio's *Fresh Air* interviewed the former director of the CBO, Douglas Holtz-Eakin, who described the challenges of helping Congress

understand the projected economic consequences of its actions (Holtz-Eakin, 2006).

4. **CRS Reports**: CRS reports are the most famous of this genre, with the reports themselves having been a topic of news in recent years. CRS reports (which also tend to be under 30 pages) can be requested by members of Congress for any reason at all: to satisfy constituent needs; to offer background material or a literature review before a bill is drafted; or to perform specialized, frequently investigative, research. This makes them broader in scope than committee prints, also generally authored by CRS, because prints reflect a specific committee's needs. Recent CRS reports include *U.S. Immigration Policy on Haitian Migrants* and *The Future of NASA: Space Policy Issues Facing Congress*. The CRS is a bureau within the Library of Congress employing over 700 staff, including many librarians. Because these reports were historically excluded from the Federal Depository Library Program, several notable efforts have taken place to ensure their wider distribution.

On the commercial side, Penny Hill Press of Damascus, Maryland, sells the reports directly (http://www.pennyhill.com/). ProQuest offers CRS reports, together with committee prints, online as an add-on subscription to its ProQuest Congressional product. On the open web, the Federation of American Scientists (FAS) has been collecting CRS reports and putting them online for years, the University of North Texas has added historic runs of reports to its well-curated digital holdings (http://digital .library.unt.edu/govdocs/crs/), and OpenCRS.com boasts a large collection. The search functionality and completeness of these free resources varies. Although Daniel P. Mulhollan, director of CRS, has argued that Congress's confidential relationship with CRS would be at risk were all reports to be instantly released to the public (Congressional Research Service, 2007), the real value of these well-produced reports makes them perfect candidates for unauthorized release on the web by information activists. Legislation introduced to mandate the reports' wider distribution has not yet succeeded.

COMMITTEE REPORTS

As previously discussed, when a bill makes it through the committee phase and moves on to the House or Senate floor, one says that it is *reported* out of committee. The committee releases a report, almost always recommending passage (the releasing of reports has been the practice for some decades but was not always consistently done in earlier years). Committee reports tend to contain a general statement of the committee's rationale for supporting the bill, a copy of the marked-up bill, a CBO cost estimate, and a brief legislative history. They may also include a tally of how many committee members voted yea and nay on various clauses of the bill, and minority and additional views. Senate executive reports concern treaties or nominations of individuals. Courts and legislative historians use reports, typically many years later, to help determine legislative intent (like what Congress really intended in passing P.L. 108-173, the Medicare Prescription Drug, Improvement, and Modernization Act). Other types of committee reports include findings of congressional investigations, and a wide range of administrative and miscellaneous publications, including reports requested by the House or Senate. Committee reports are included in the U.S. *Congressional Serial Set*.

COMMITTEE DOCUMENTS
Another form of congressional literature is simply referred to as documents. Documents are far more varied than one might expect: Senate executive (or "lettered") documents contain the text of treaties as presented to the Senate for ratification by the president of the United States. In 1981, Congress started using the more descriptive term *Senate treaty documents*, and these materials are now numbered instead of lettered alphabetically. House and Senate documents contain a wide variety of other materials ordered printed by both chambers of Congress. Documents can include reports of executive departments, agencies, and independent organizations; reports of special investigations made for Congress; and annual reports of nongovernmental organizations (Government Printing Office, 2004).

THE U.S. *CONGRESSIONAL SERIAL SET*: REPORTS, DOCUMENTS, AND SO MUCH MORE
Hundreds of libraries across North America consider the U.S. *Congressional Serial Set* to be part of their most valued holdings. An earlier sister publication, the *American State Papers*, consists of the papers and reports of Congress from colonial times to 1838. The *Serial Set*, as it is known, is a specially bound, sequentially numbered set of House and Senate reports and documents from 1817 onward. When performing a legislative history, it is in the *Serial Set* that one will find the reports and documents vital to the quest, and reports frequently include the marked-up version of the bill, as well as an abbreviated legislative history. In the earlier era, the *Serial Set* included all kinds of special reports *to* Congress, such as those of various expeditions and explorations, communications from the president, reports from executive branch agencies, as well as the House and Senate Journals from 1817 to 1952. Its official binding was once sheepskin, so it was known as the Sheep Set, and the paper-bound materials were, for many years, clustered together for binding based on their size (not the most intuitive method for efficient retrieval). This practice stopped somewhere between 1973 and 1980, as printers instituted measures to control the format of the set and bound the reports and documents in numerical order. Users who have a House or Senate report or document number and would like to locate the material in the *Serial Set* will need a conversion table to identify the proper *Serial Set* volume number. See one such example supplied by the Law Librarians' Society of Washington, DC, at http://www.llsdc.org/sch-v/. The set is numbered continuously, with the first volume starting at 1. Volumes are now up well over 15,000.

The *Serial Set* continues on today, though libraries (except regional federal depository libraries) stopped receiving the bound volumes in the 1990s, along with the *Congressional Record*—the printing for both was simply prohibitively expensive. The *Serial Set* is also available, both on deposit and commercially, in microform, for those collections that desire a tangible copy of this historic gem. So valued are the individual printed volumes of the set that the University of North Texas hosts an inventory of *Serial Set* volumes held in American libraries (University of North Texas, 2009).

The early 2000s saw the emergence of two commercial online editions of the *Serial Set*, produced by LexisNexis Congressional (now ProQuest Congressional) and Readex. For researchers, it is worthwhile to seek out an institution subscribing to either. The dawn of these digital editions has ushered in a grand new era of congressional research. These digital editions have made possible advanced text mining, searches for individual or geographic names, the linking of related documents, the viewing of beautiful full-color digitized maps and illustrations, and navigation with immeasurably improved subject access. It is as if the earlier surges forward in access, like the blossoming of advanced government documents indexing and MARC cataloging in the 1970s, have been replicated in the early twenty-first century context with a digital flourish. Figure 3.4 shows a sample record from the Readex edition.

Back to the Floor: The Congressional Record

Next, we consider a transcript of floor activity—an edited, inexact transcript with a checkered past, the *Congressional Record*. When the House or Senate convenes as a whole, there is a need to record what transpired. How often does Congress meet? In the latter half of the twentieth century, Congress has been open for business anywhere from 224 to 375 days per session (a session can last longer than a calendar year if necessary) (American Enterprise Institute, 2002).

What a long and colorful history the *Congressional Record* has! In 1802, *National Intelligencer* publisher Samuel Smith successfully lobbied the Senate to allow stenographers to take notes at its meetings, a practice the House already allowed. Smith eventually sold his thrice-weekly Washington newspaper to a firm that would become a famous capital area publisher, Gales and Seaton. Gales and Seaton published a *Register of Debates* (1824–1837) which was a first- and third-person accounting of congressional activity. After losing their government contract to cover ongoing legislation, they secured congressional funding to essentially compile a prequel: the *Annals of Congress*, in which they used newspaper accounts and other sources to create a "reconstructive" account of the years 1789–1824. Their competitors, Blair and Rives, produced the *Congressional Globe* starting in 1833, and by law (17 Stat. 510), GPO took over the production of the congressional gazette starting on March 4, 1873, for reasons of efficiency and economy (Hernon et al., 2002).

The *Congressional Record*, published daily when Congress is in session, makes for surprisingly interesting reading. As with any transcript, it can become a bit of a theatrical play, and the arena of congressional discourse has been called "great theatre" (Weisberg and Patterson, 1998). On the main floor of either house, each day usually includes a prayer and the Pledge of Allegiance. There will likely be introduction of bills and resolutions with immediate referral to committee, along with the inevitable suspension of the rules in order to accomplish some task. There may be debates of bills currently under consideration,

Figure 3.4. A Sample Page of the Readex U.S. *Congressional Serial Set, Digital Edition*

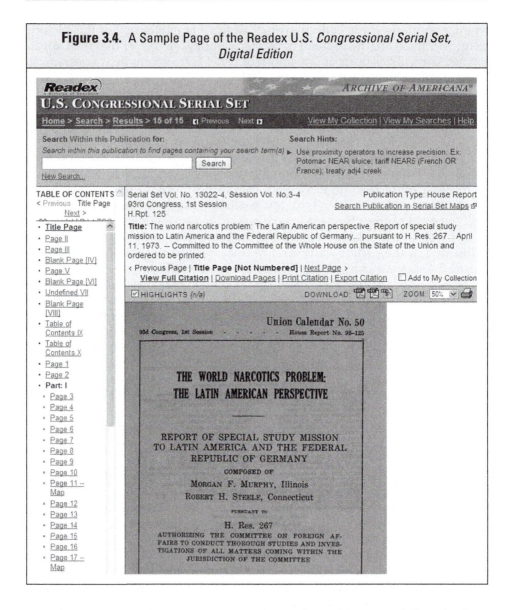

speeches, or voting. In many cases, ceremonial proclamations follow, such as National Polycystic Kidney Disease Awareness Week (154 *Cong. Rec.* S8142).

How usable is the *Congressional Record*? One area of potential confusion: there are two different editions of this serial. The red, hardbound *Congressional Record* is considered the official edition, and its pagination varies from the daily (newsprint, paperback) edition. So when considering a citation to the *Congressional Record*, or *CR*, verify that the reference is to the official edition, *not* the daily. The official edition is considered the default, especially for legal contexts. The daily edition is divided into four distinct sections: House (the H pages),

Senate (the S pages), the Daily Digest (the D pages, a summary of that day's actions), and the Extension of Remarks (the E pages). The official edition uses continuous pagination for each session, so the numbers can get to be quite high (into the tens of thousands), and it does not use the H, S, and E designation that are used in the daily edition, but integrates and repaginates the sections, and offers a separate bound compilation of all Daily Digests. The daily edition is indexed biweekly and the official edition at the end of each session, or annually. Also appearing in the sessional index (from 1873 on) is a list of yea and nay votes, showing which way members of Congress voted on a particular measure. Although it is enjoyable to read in its bound, official edition, the physical books have been hard to come by since 1990 and may be printed and indexed ten or more years after the discourse has occurred. Due to the exorbitant cost of producing the volumes, GPO had to limit the distribution to regional federal depository libraries, or approximately one library per state. Other depository libraries would receive the *CR* in its daily edition, with a microfiche official version arriving at a later time.

There is another interesting wrinkle to the *Congressional Record*: it is not a verbatim record. Practices have varied over the years, but there has been lenience (curtailed in recent decades) in letting members edit their own remarks before the publishing of the official edition. The establishment of an Extension of Remarks section helped clarify those words actually spoken on the floor and those simply added to the record after the fact. In the official version, the Extension of Remarks section is integrated into the main *Record*. Even today, remarks not made on the floor are indicated in a different font or with a bullet, depending on the chamber.

A Century of Lawmaking for a New Nation was an early effort by the Library of Congress to digitize congressional material for the first century of the republic, up to the year 1875 (see Figure 3.5). An online collection within the larger American Memory Project, it includes bills, laws, the *Congressional Record* and all its predecessors, the House and Senate *Journals*, and selected volumes of the U.S. *Congressional Serial Set*. Although the optical character recognition system is not equivalent to today's standards, and the search function has fewer advanced options than most of today's electronic texts, the project was a very important step for the Library of Congress and it is still quite usable and navigable. As its title implies, *A Century of Lawmaking* covers only 100 years, 1774–1875, and it is not comprehensive even for those years.

You can access the full text of the Internet-era (1993–present) CR via THOMAS and FDsys, and commercial editions are available via ProQuest Congressional, Westlaw, CQ.com, and others. ProQuest and William S. Hein are two vendors currently supplying a full-text online *Congressional Record* (official edition) back to its earliest years.

C-SPAN and Video Proceedings

Public perception of Congress changed irrevocably with the dawn of C-SPAN, a television station and website dedicated to video coverage of congressional proceedings, covering both houses since 1986. C-SPAN is a private, nonprofit

---

Figure 3.5. A Century of Lawmaking for a New Nation

The Library of Congress

AMERICAN MEMORY

A Century of Lawmaking
For a New Nation
U.S. Congressional Documents and Debates
Search All Titles 1774-1875

Continental Congress and the
Constitutional Convention
Journals of the
Continental Congress
Letters of Delegates
to Congress
Elliot's Debates
Farrand's Records

Journals of Congress
House Journal
Senate Journal
Senate Executive
Journal
Maclay's Journal

Statutes and Documents
Bills and Resolutions
Statutes at Large
American State Papers
U.S. Serial Set

Debates of Congress
Annals of Congress
Register of Debates
Congressional Globe
Congressional Record

Search: **All Titles** | **Browse Titles by Category: Continental Congress and the Constitutional Convention** | **Journals of Congress** | **Debates of Congress** | **Statutes and Documents**

Beginning with the Continental Congress in 1774, America's national legislative bodies have kept records of their proceedings. The records of the Continental Congress, the Constitutional Convention, and the United States Congress make up a rich documentary history of the construction of the nation and the development of the federal government and its role in the national life. These documents record American history in the words of those who built our government.

Books on the law formed a major part of the holdings of the Library of Congress from its beginning. In 1832, Congress established the Law Library of Congress as a separate department of the Library. It houses one of the most complete collections of U.S. Congressional documents in their original format. In order to make these records more easily accessible to students, scholars, and interested citizens, *A Century of Lawmaking for a New Nation* brings together online the records and acts of Congress from the Continental Congress and Constitutional Convention through the 43rd Congress, including the first three volumes of the *Congressional Record*, 1873-75.

The mission of the Library of Congress is to make its resources available and useful to Congress and the American people and to sustain and preserve a universal collection of knowledge and creativity for future generations. The goal of the Library's National Digital Library Program is to offer broad public access to a wide range of historical and cultural documents as a contribution to education and lifelong learning.

The Library of Congress presents these documents as part of the record of the past. These primary historical documents reflect the attitudes, perspectives, and beliefs of different times. The Library of Congress does not endorse the views expressed in these collections, which may contain materials offensive to some readers.

Special Presentations:

The Making of the U.S. Constitution
Timeline: American History as Seen in Congressional Documents, 1774-1873
The Revolutionary Diplomatic Correspondence of the United States
Indian Land Cessions in the United States, 1784 to 1894 (includes Maps)
The Louisiana Purchase: Legislative Timeline - 1802 to 1807
Journal of the Congress of the Confederate States of America, 1861-1865
The Impeachment Trial of President Andrew Johnson, 1868
Presidential Elections and the Electoral College, 1877

Understanding the Collection	Working with the Collection
About the Collection	Citation Guide
Selected Bibliography	Building the Digital Collection
Using the Collection	How to View: Text & Page Images
Related Resources	Copyright and Other Restrictions
Collection Connections	Acknowledgments

American Memory | Search All Collections | Collection Finder | Learning Page

The Library of Congress   Contact Us   Please Read Our LEGAL NOTICES

May-01-2003   [-] FEEDBACK

---

company financed by the cable television industry as a public service. In its current incarnation, C-SPAN covers the House; C-SPAN II the Senate. Its video archive in West Lafayette, Indiana, includes all aired programs back to 1987. Since 1993, archived programs have been freely available online at http://www.cspan.org/. In March 2010, C-SPAN made its entire backfile free as online streaming video, a tremendous public benefit. An advanced search function allows users to search the backfile by date, tag, format (e.g., debate, forum, interview, moot court, remarks, etc.), program title, program summary, person name or title, geographic location, organization, and program text (taken from the closed captioning). Digital video recording and web archiving of public meetings has nearly become standard practice even in many local governments, and one can now find many video proceedings of congressional activity directly from the House.gov and Senate.gov sites (usually on committee pages).

Calendars and Journals Help Us Stay Organized

The official calendars for Congress are the *Calendars of the U.S. House of Representatives and History of Legislation* (a wordy title, basically the House calendar and a list of measures under consideration) and the *Senate Calendar of Business* (a similar resource, but with more emphasis on committee activity). Both are issued daily when Congress is in session and list the official days of the session and recess, and the expected business for the day. Senate committees also publish their own distinct legislative calendars. The House calendars started in 1935; the Monday issues and the final issue for each Congress provide an excellent way to track legislation in both the House and Senate. The calendars are organized into different chapters around the legislation and are concise and thus fairly simple to look through, consisting of maybe 150 pages for each session. Today, calendar information is available on House and Senate websites, as well as THOMAS, although official calendars and journals are also still produced.

The Constitution (U.S. Constitution, Article I, Section 5) called for a journal of proceedings of Congress. Thus the House *Journal* and the Senate *Journal* were born. These journals fulfill the constitutional requirement, although the *Congressional Record* is another example of the spirit of that early mandate. The journals are summations of actual actions, in outline (not narrative) form. Just as with personal calendars and journals, these are helpful for historic research and determining the sequence in which congressional actions took place as they are organized chronologically. The journals, starting in 1789, provide an excellent way to track legislation back to the origins of the country. Earlier legislative processes did not include hearings or even reports to leave a trail for tracking legislation. The journals (published as part of the *Serial Set* from 1817 to 1952) allow users to see where a bill went and what happened during the process. Today, the journals include bill number, name, title, and subject indexes as part of a "History of Bills and Resolutions" feature.

Guides and Indexes

Guides

A college professor was recently overheard to remark: "There's got to be something between the two-second sound bite you hear on the news and some

900-page congressional report." There is, and it is up to librarians to make these intermediate tools more accessible and widespread. For decades, selected publishers have been invaluable to librarians as we try to make Congress and its daily actions understandable to our patrons and to policy makers themselves. The publications of Congressional Quarterly and its division, CQ Press, some of which are now accumulated and synthesized in CQ.com, are perhaps the best example of translating congressional action into "plain English." What makes CQ publications especially useful? Articles are written at a high school English level, and congressional action is summarized, frequently in the form of "box scores" telling the reader the ultimate outcome on a certain issue. The publisher is trusted in the industry and has earned the confidence of researchers in terms of providing accurate summaries. Librarians may be familiar with resources such as *CQ Researcher*, which provides scholarly summaries on pressing issues of the day, such as immigration rights. The same summaries and encapsulations helpful in *Researcher* are available in CQ's other products.

For decades, reference librarians kept current with Congress by reading the *CQ Weekly Report*, newspapers, and possibly the Daily Digest section of the *Congressional Record* daily edition. One could argue that the *CQ Weekly Report* is still a better approach than the newspaper because CQ cites actual bills, hearings, or reports with full identifying information, whereas newspaper articles continue to be notoriously poor in that regard. This has improved in the digital age, when articles and especially blogs can include hyperlinks to real congressional documents. One can learn an entire year's congressional highlights by consulting the *CQ Almanac*, and several years via *Congress and the Nation*. This approach is still very useful and CQ has greatly increased accessibility and searchability with CQ.com, a subscription service that includes *CQ Today Online News*. Importantly, the *CQ Almanac* is also available for purchase online, both the current and historic volumes, back to its start in 1945, and many of CQ's other monographs are also available as e-books. So valued are *CQ Almanacs* that one could expect to see them at medium-sized public libraries and up, and at most academic and state government libraries.

Congressional Digest is another worthwhile publication. It is a monthly magazine devoted to congressional affairs, known for its pro-con format and guest columns written by legislators and congressional analysts. It began publication in 1921, when publisher Alice Gram Robinson wanted to educate newly franchised voters (i.e., women) on controversial topics of the day. Each issue has a single theme (credit card reform, compulsory national service, biofuels expansion, etc.). It is available online via aggregator services, including EBSCOhost. There are also long-standing newspapers (now online as well) focusing on Congress: *The Hill*, *Roll Call*, and the "Congress" subsection of the "Politics" tab on the online *Washington Post*. Looking for reference books on Congress in your local academic or public library? They tend to be listed under JK in the Library of Congress system, and 328 (the legislative process) in the Dewey Decimal system.

Community-Created Online Guides to Congressional Research

There are many ways to discover congressional guides authored by librarians and other information specialists (see Chapter 2 for professional associations and the GODORT Handout Exchange, which includes resources on Congress). Guides built using SpringShare's LibGuides platform are easy to find by entering **libguides congress** into any search engine. Independent groups as diverse as the Sunlight Foundation (http://www.opencongress.org) and Project Vote Smart (http://www.votesmart.org/) supply congressionally oriented information in line with their advocacy positions, often offering valuable "remixed" content not found elsewhere. The Law Librarians' Society of Washington, DC, founded in 1939, has a particularly useful set of guides grouped together as LLSDC's Legislative Source Book (http://www.llsdc.org/sourcebook/). Other notable collections include the following:

- University of California, Berkeley, http://sunsite3.berkeley.edu/wikis/congresearch/
- Indiana University, http://congress.indiana.edu/
- Policy Agendas Project, http://www.policyagendas.org/

Indexes

The CIS Index *and ProQuest Congressional*

The Congressional Information Service, now a division of ProQuest, was founded by Jim and Esthy Adler in 1969 (see sidebar). The Adlers' vision was to make the riches of congressional publishing more accessible to the general public, and they started a minor revolution. The first printed index, known in the profession simply as the *CIS Index Annual*, provided subject, title, witness, SuDoc number, bill number, and report number access to material that had been difficult to find, or lacking altogether, in the nation's card catalogs. Suddenly, access to all these content-rich congressional committee publications (hearings, reports, documents, and committee prints) that librarians had in their federal depository collections became much easier. To offer the libraries a complete collection, CIS also produced high quality (silver halide) microfiche of all extant congressional committee publications for that year. The index also featured legislative histories, which point users to all the congressional publications associated with a particular piece of legislation. The printed index used abstract-style entries that corresponded to a CIS accession number on the microfiche.

Names and Abbreviations Might Be Confusing

Those new to the world of government documents sometimes confess that they get lost in the abbreviations and names of various publishers. The publishers wisely choose authoritative, governmental-sounding names for their companies. Here are the ones most apt to be confusing. CQ (Congressional Quarterly) publishes a myriad of reference products including almanacs, guides to government, *CQ Researcher*, CQ.com, and much more. CIS (Congressional Information Service) is a division of ProQuest, and its *CIS Index* forms the backbone of ProQuest Congressional. Traditionally CIS produced printed reference guides with accompanying microfiche sets, although most CIS publishing is now digital, incorporated into ProQuest Congressional. CIS is not to be confused with the Congressional Research Service (CRS), a division of the Library of Congress.

The era of CIS began in 1970. The company then went on to replicate its success, tackling committee publications from colonial times to 1969, as well as so-called unpublished hearings, the U.S. *Congressional Serial Set*, and even executive branch documents not included in the *Serial Set*. In each case, the original source material was released on high quality microfiche, with accompanying printed indexes. CIS indexes provide bibliographic organization and generally include brief abstracts and multiple access points. These powerful indexes opened up the world of congressional research materials to a general audience, and evolved from paper indexes to an online resource through LexisNexis, acquired in late 2010 and repackaged as ProQuest Congressional, which includes far more than the original *CIS Index* and its sister indexes. As one academic reviewer noted, "The Congressional Information Service (CIS) [now a division of ProQuest] has long been noted for quality productions, including finding aids and microfiche collections. Their publications are part of a core reference collection that any government documents collection should consider" (Lamont, 1997).

Bill-Tracking Aids and Other Resources

Much general congressional research can be accomplished with tools mentioned thus far. As previously mentioned, bill tracking is a common research task. Bill tracking is available on THOMAS only back to 1973...what if one needed to track a bill from a previous time period? The *Congressional Record's* official edition includes a "History of Bills" section in the bound index volumes for that year. For many years, librarians relied on the *Digest of Public General Bills and Resolutions*, an annual volume printed by the GPO, and a privately produced resource, Commerce Clearing House's *Congressional Index*, which included status tables arranged by bill number. (The *Congressional Index* is a great example of a loose-leaf publication, and veteran library technicians will remember replacing the thin onionskin pages in a three-ring binder when the latest Bill Status Tables arrived.) For further information on bill tracking as a part of legislative history, consult Joe Morehead's detailed discussion of legislative history (Morehead, 1999: 159–164). Beyond bill tracking, the sidebar shows the type of questions government documents librarians field every day, and some of the sources they consult.

Conclusion

This chapter explored the rich, complex literature of Congress. Knowing the context of any particular piece of congressional information—where it falls in the legislative process—is critical. Learning about Congress is manageable if done incrementally, and is easier for those who can tolerate the messiness of the legislative process. Although the sheer volume of congressional output is staggering, there are plain English summaries from specialized news organizations and publishers like CQ, indexing services (both commercial and

Frequently Requested Materials and Recommended Sources	
Type of information needed	**Suggested resource**
Plain English explanation of Congressional activity	**Daily**: CQToday Online News, Daily Digest section of the *Congressional Record (Daily Ed.)*, newspapers, blogs **Weekly**: *Roll Call*, *The Hill*, Congress section of "Post Politics" *(Washington Post)*, *CQ Weekly* **Monthly**: *Congressional Digest* **Annually**: *CQ Almanac* **Span of years**: *Congress and the Nation*, scholarly published books
Bill summary, status	THOMAS, FDsys, CQ.com, ProQuest Congressional, House and Senate Journals
Legislative history	THOMAS, FDsys, CQ.com, ProQuest Congressional, HeinOnline's U.S. Federal Legislative History Library
Information about members of Congress	*Congressional Directory*, members' own websites, THOMAS, CQ.com, ProQuest Congressional, *Biographical Directory of the United States Congress*, *CQ's Politics in America*, OpenCongress.org
Historical sources (selected)	*Congressional Record* and its predecessors, U.S. *Congressional Serial Set*, House & Senate *Journals*, published and unpublished hearings
Voting (tally of members' votes on bills, etc.)	"Yea and Nay Votes" section of the *Congressional Record Index*, *ProQuest Congressional*, *CQ Almanac*, *Congressional Index*

governmental), and boiled-down reports (like those from the Congressional Research Service). If one were limited to using only five free websites for congressional research, the best bets might be THOMAS, House.gov, Senate.gov, FDsys, and the nonprofit, nongovernmental C-SPAN.org. Congress, like every other sector of our government and our lives, is opening up rapidly with the help of new technology; perhaps even the most profound changes are yet to come.

Exercises

1. Watch C-SPAN, C-SPAN2, or any video coverage of congressional activity for 15 minutes, with the aim of sharpening your skills. Pay particular attention to the kind of information exchanged and the technical knowledge of the

speaker or witness. Can you identify the convener of the proceedings? Keep a tally of how many times the following kinds of congressional literature or actions are mentioned:

- Bill
- Amendment
- Vote
- Hearing
- Report

- Calendar
- *Congressional Record*
- Conference
- House or Senate *Journal*

2. Find out the following for your home address:

   Your congressional district:
   Your representative:
   Your senators:
   Sources consulted:

3. Try your skill at tracking legislation. Use THOMAS, FDsys, House.gov, or Senate.gov to select current legislation that interests you. Commit to following this legislation: devise a mechanism that works for you to check its status monthly until the end of the current congress (could be as long as two years). Even if you do not follow through and check on your legislation, what system would you have set in place to do so?

4. Follow a medical issue or concern through Congress. Using secondary sources (CQ publications, newspapers, journal articles, books), identify congressional literature concerning a specific medical topic (diabetes, stem cell research, smoking cessation, and multiple sclerosis are but a few examples). What kind of attention has Congress paid to this topic over the years or decades?

5. One more angle on congressional attention: choose an NGO (nongovernmental organization) or nonprofit focusing on a specific medical condition. Explore this group's website, and determine how well you can learn about relevant legislation via their resources. Possibilities include the following organizations:

   - The National Multiple Sclerosis Society (http://www.nationalmssociety.org/)
   - Susan G. Komen for the Cure (http://www.komen.org/)
   - Children and Adults with Attention Deficit/Hyperactivity Disorder (http://www.chadd.org/)

6. Using the digital archive at the University of North Texas (http://digital.library.unt.edu/govdocs/crs/), use CRS reports to answer the following question: do terns die from eating fish infected with *Pfiesteria*?

7. Can you find the Congressional Budget Office estimate for S. 952, the Harmful Algal Blooms and Hypoxia Research and Control Amendments Act of 2009? According to the estimate, what would be the estimated outlay of spending under S. 952 for the year 2014?

Sources Mentioned in This Chapter

Sources mentioned in this section do not duplicate the References that follow.

American State Papers, http://memory.loc.gov/ammem/amlaw/lwsp.html.
Annals of Congress, http://memory.loc.gov/ammem/amlaw/lwac.html.
Calendars of the U.S. House of Representatives and History of Legislation. 1935–.
　　Washington, DC: Government Printing Office.
Century of Lawmaking for a New Nation, http://memory.loc.gov/ammem/amlaw/.
CIS Index Annual. 1971–. Ann Arbor, MI: ProQuest Congressional.
Congress and Session Years, http://www.gpoaccess.gov/help/congress_table.html/.
Congress and the Nation. 1964–. Washington, DC: Congressional Quarterly, Inc. and CQ Press.
Congressional Globe, http://memory.loc.gov/ammem/amlaw/lwcg.html.
Congressional Index. 1938–. Chicago: Commerce Clearinghouse.
Congressional Record (daily). 1873–. Washington, DC: Government Printing Office. Avail-
　　able online (1994–), http://www.fdsys.gov/.
Congressional Record (bound). 1873–. Washington, DC: Government Printing Office.
　　Available online (1999–), http://www.fdsys.gov/.
CQ Researcher. 1991–. Washington, DC: Congressional Quarterly and EBSCO.
CQ Weekly (title varies). 1956–. Washington, DC: CQ Press.
CQ.com. 2000–. Washington, DC: Congressional Quarterly.
CQ's Politics in America. 1999–. Washington, DC: CQ Press.
C-SPAN, http://www.cspan.org.
Federal Digital System (FDsys), http://www.gpo.gov/fdsys/.
Federation of American Scientists, http://www.fas.org/.
Guide to Congress (6th ed.) 2008. Washington, DC: CQ Press.
HeinOnline. 2000–. Buffalo, NY: William S. Hein.
The Hill, http://www.thehill.com/.
How Our Laws Are Made, http://thomas.loc.gov/home/lawsmade.toc.html.
Journals (House and Senate), http://memory.loc.gov/ammem/amlaw/.
Law Librarians' Society of Washington, DC. http://www.llsdc.org/.
OpenCRS, http://www.opencrs.com/.
ProQuest Congressional, http://library.lexisnexis.com/ws_display.asp?filter= Congressional
　　%20Overview (description only).
Register of Debates, http://memory.loc.gov/ammem/amlaw/lwrd.html.
Roll Call, http://www.rollcall.com/.
Senate Calendar of Business, http://www.gpo.gov/fdsys/browse/collection.action?
　　collectionCode=CCAL/.
Session Dates and Years, http://clerk.house.gov/art_history/house_history/Session_
　　Dates/.
THOMAS, http://thomas.loc.gov/.
United States Code, http://www.gpo.gov/fdsys/.
U.S. *Congressional Serial Set*. 1817–. Washington, DC: Government Printing Office.
United States Statutes at Large. 1789–. Washington, DC: Government Printing Office.
University of North Texas Digital Library, http://digital.library.unt.edu/gov docs/.

References

American Enterprise Institute for Public Policy Research and Brookings Institution. 2002. *Vital Statistics on Congress, 2001–2002*. Washington, DC: American Enterprise Institute. Tables 6-1 & 6-2: 146–147.

Congressional Quarterly, Inc. 2008. *Congress A to Z*. Washington, DC: CQ Press.

Congressional Record (Daily Ed.). 2008. "One Less Angel Will Cry." January 28. http://www.gpo.gov/fdsys/pkg/CREC-2008-01-23/pdf/CREC-2008-01-23-pt1-PgE64-2.pdf.

Congressional Record (Daily Ed.). 2002. "Tribute to Manchester Airport." May 12. http://www.gpo.gov/fdsys/pkg/CREC-2002-05-17/pdf/CREC-2002-05-17-pt1-PgS4535.pdf.

Congressional Research Service. 2009. "CRS Policy Statement: CRS Products Distribution to Non-Congressionals." Washington, DC: Federation of American Scientists. Available: http://www.fas.org/sgp/crs/crs032007.pdf.

Dorough, Bob, Lynn Ahrens, George Newall, Dave Frishberg, Tom Yohe, Rich Mendoza, et al. 2002. *Schoolhouse Rock!* Burbank, CA: Buena Vista Home Entertainment.

Government Printing Office. 2004. "Congressional Documents: About." Updated August 26. http://www.gpoaccess.gov/serialset/cdocuments/about.html.

Hearing on Pending Legislation: Hearing Before the Committee on Veterans' Affairs. 2007. Washington: Government Printing Office. http://frwebgate.access .gpo.gov/cgi-bin/getdoc.cgi?dbname=110_senate_hearings&docid=f: 40547.pdf.

Hillman, G. Robert. 2000. "Exaggerating the Exaggeration?: Gore's Internet Quote, Other Remarks Keep GOP's Spin Machine Humming." *Dallas Morning News*, April 6: 1A.

Holtz-Eakin, Douglas. "The President's (Former) Economy Guru." By Terry Gross. Fresh Air, January 26, 2006, http://www.npr.org/templates/story/story.php?storyId=5173072.

Lamont, Melissa. 1997. "CIS Index to Unpublished US Senate Committee Hearings (review)." *Journal of Government Information* 24, no. 6: 607.

Library of Congress Congressional Research Service. 1978. *Major Studies and Issue Briefs of the Congressional Research Service*. Supplement. Bethesda, MD: LexisNexis.

Morehead, Joe. 1999. *Introduction to United States Government Information Sources*. Englewood, CO: Libraries Unlimited.

Oppenheimer, Bruce I. 1983. "How Legislatures Shape Policy and Budgets." *Legislative Studies Quarterly* 8, no. 4 (Nov.): 551–597.

Panangala, Sidath Viranga. 2007. *Veterans' Health Care Issues*. Washington, DC: Congressional Research Service, Domestic Social Policy Division. Nov. 30, 2007.

Public Broadcasting Service. 2010. *@THE CAPITOL: Overview: The Committee System in the U.S. Congress*. Washington, DC: PBS. Accessed January 27. http://www.pbs.org/newshour/@capitol/committees/committees_overview.html.

Redman, Eric. 2001. *The Dance of Legislation*. Seattle: University of Washington Press.

Roll Call. 2011. Washington, DC: CQ Roll Call, Inc. Accessed January 11. http://www.rollcall.com.

Sevetson, Andrea. 2006. "An Insider's View of the Serial Set." Bethesda, MD: ProQuest. http://wiki.proquest.com/congressional/index.php?title=Congressional_Downloads_and_Articles_Index#White_Papers.

Sevetson, Andrea. 2007. "Hearings and the LexisNexis Congressional Hearings Digital Collection." Bethesda, MD: ProQuest. http://wiki.proquest.com/congressional/index.php?title=Congressional_Downloads_and_Articles_Index#White_Papers.

Whisner, Mary. 2005. "Practicing Reference . . . What's in a Statute Name?" *Law Library Journal* 2005-09: 169–183. http://www.aallnet.org/products/pub_llj_v97n01/2005-09.pdf.

Informational Note

On November 30, 2010, ProQuest announced its acquisition of the Congressional Information Services (CIS) and University Publications of America (UPA) product lines from LexisNexis. The ProQuest announcement indicated that, beginning in 2011, LexisNexis Congressional will be renamed ProQuest Congressional and LexisNexis Statistical Insight will be renamed ProQuest Statistical Insight.

Chapter 4

Regulations

Introduction

When it comes to selecting their favorite foods and beverages, Americans in the know read nutritional labels. The list of food ingredients is rank-ordered, with the most prevalent ingredient listed first—this is a point of common public awareness. It is also widely understood that the nutritional content—often expressed in percent daily values or %DV—is based on recommended dietary guidelines put forth by the United States Department of Agriculture (USDA). Anyone who consumes alcohol may have seen the government warnings on bottles of beer, wine, or liquor, enforced by the U.S. Bureau of Alcohol, Tobacco, Firearms, and Explosives. Those familiar with these simple details from everyday life may not realize that they already have a baseline appreciation of federal regulations. The labeling of food (for nutritional content) and alcohol (with health warnings) are both examples of regulations in action.

All three branches of government (legislative, executive, judicial) produce material that carries the force of law: legislation, regulation, and case law, respectively. The legislative branch *passes* laws, the executive branch *enforces* laws, and the judicial branch *interprets* laws. One might say that in passing laws (also known as statutes or statutory law), Congress authorizes or "empowers" the executive branch agencies to put forth regulations, or that regulations are "the last step in the legislative process" (Arrigo, 2003: 99). Regulations are the agency-based enforcement of laws mandated by Congress. Regulations are also referred to as administrative or bureaucratic law. Rules are synonymous with regulations, and the regulatory process is also referred to as the rulemaking process.

There are plenty of good reasons why people might cringe at the thought of learning more about federal regulations. Most Americans are not coached to think of stewarding the nation's regulations as part of the good citizen role, although one could argue that regulations deserve that kind of attention and regard. Everyday citizens know little about where regulations come from and underestimate their own role in influencing government regulations. Regulations may be avoided as dry and dense reading, which they can be. Americans may also experience a fundamental conflict in thinking about regulations. Federal tax rules may seem overly restrictive, (e.g., one may be granted an extension on one's personal federal income tax return, but the extension "shall not be in excess of six months" (26 C.F.R 1.6161-1)); still, many of us probably appreciate safety regulations, such as rules from the Federal Aviation Administration

(FAA) requiring a uniform set of symbols and terms concerning flight (14 CFR 97.3). Many regulatory scholars actually divide regulations into two large categories, economic and social (the latter would include safety rules, a manifestation of the consumer protection movement of the twentieth century).

A recent government study concluded that

> Federal regulations are among the most important and widely used tools for implementing the laws of the land—affecting the food we eat, the air we breathe, the safety of consumer products, the quality of the work-place, the soundness of our financial institutions, the smooth operation of our businesses, and much more. Despite the central role of rulemaking in executing public policy, both regulated entities (especially small businesses) and the general public find it extremely difficult to follow the regulatory process; actively participating in it is even harder. (Committee on the Status and Future of Federal E-Rulemaking, 2008: 1)

In this chapter, we offer a brief overview of the process and literature of federal regulations.

One of the simplest encapsulations of the regulatory process is as follows:

> After congressional bills become laws, federal agencies are responsible for putting those laws into action through regulations. This process may include the following steps:
>
> 1. An agency initiates a rulemaking activity, and adds an entry to its Regulatory Agenda.
> 2. A rule or other document is published to Regulations.gov.
> 3. The public is given the opportunity to comment on this rule for a specified timeframe.
> 4. Final rules can be accessed on Regulations.gov.
>
> Rules are published every business day [in the *Federal Register*]. (Regulations .gov, 2009)

This chapter will explore the *Code of Federal Regulations*, in which all current regulations are codified, along with its companion sources the *Unified Agenda*, the *Federal Register*, the *List of CFR Sections Affected* (known as the *LSA*), and the *e-CFR*. We will consider the ongoing development of e-rulemaking; two fundamental web resources, Regulations.gov and Reginfo.gov; and one innovative visual diagram that makes regulations much more understandable, the Reg Map.

Unified Regulatory Agenda and Reginfo.gov

The Regulatory Information Service Center (RISC) is a help center within the United States General Services Administration (GSA) (Figure 4.1). RISC is responsible for compiling the *Unified Agenda of Federal Regulatory and Deregulatory*

Actions (known as the *Unified Agenda*) as well as Reginfo.gov, probably the best source for understanding all things regulatory. According to Reginfo.gov,

> (RISC) was created in June 1981. The Center undertakes projects that will facilitate development of and access to information about Federal regulatory and deregulatory activities. It accomplishes this by gathering and publishing information on Federal regulations and their effects on society. The Center provides this information to the President, Congress, agency officials, and the general public to help them better understand and manage the regulatory process. The Center's principal publication is the *Unified Agenda,...* published in the spring and fall of each year. Since 1978, Federal agencies have been required ... to publish agendas of regulatory and deregulatory activities. The *Regulatory Plan,* which is published as part of the fall edition of the Agenda, *identifies regulatory priorities and contains additional detail about the most important significant regulatory actions that agencies expect to take in the coming year* (emphasis added). (Current Unified Agenda of Regulatory and Deregulatory Actions, 2009)

So one can see that the very least agencies must do is to produce a list of the regulatory actions they expect to put forth in the next year. The twice-annual (spring and fall) *Unified Agenda* and the annual (fall) *Regulatory Plan* may be found online, both the current and historical volumes, at Reginfo.gov. The *Agenda* is a listing of specific regulatory actions organized by agency, while the *Plan* is a compilation of narrative essays from each agency stating general priorities or themes in regulation. RISC assigns a Regulation Identifier Number or RIN to each entry in the *Unified Agenda*. The RIN can be used to track a currently proposed regulation. It can also be used years after the fact to identify earlier regulatory efforts, link to related RINs, and trace success/failure rates.

The *Unified Agenda* provides a first-time user of regulations a picture of the enormousness and diversity of the nation's 12-month regulatory plans. What kinds of problems are the agencies trying to fix? In browsing the spring 2009 *Unified Agenda,* one can find the finalizing of "regulations [to] help prevent the artificial spread of boll weevil into noninfested areas of the United States and the reinfestation of areas from which the boll weevil has been eradicated" (Animal and Plant Health Inspection Service, 2009) and also that the government is concerned with safety and efficacy of over-the-counter pediatric cough and cold products (Food and Drug Administration, 2009). No subject, grand or small, escapes the possibility of regulation.

The Regulatory Process

To review the steps of the regulatory process in greater detail, one can use a helpful chart known as the Reg Map (Figure 4.2). The Reg Map was created by ICF, Incorporated in 2000 and revised in 2003 with the cooperation of the U.S.

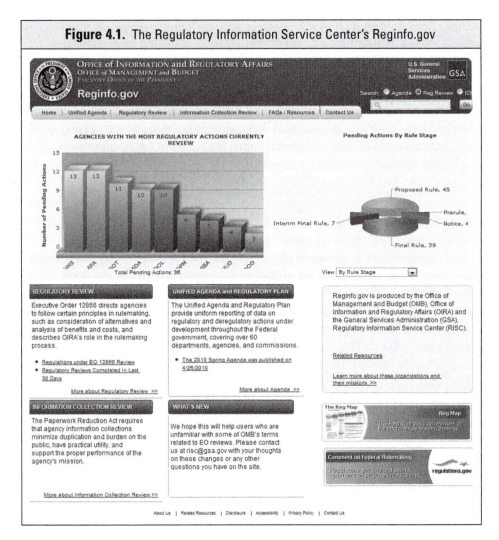

Figure 4.1. The Regulatory Information Service Center's Reginfo.gov

General Services Administration's Regulatory Information Service Center. Although disclaimers state that the map is not endorsed by the GSA as a legal document, it has proven to be a substantially accurate and a helpful, informal guide to the regulatory process. Unlike the legislative process, which schoolchildren learn about in textbooks illustrated with diagrams and stick figures, the regulatory path will be new to many. Using the map in conjunction with more updated tools at Reginfo.gov will serve the professional librarian well.

To start the rulemaking process, there needs to be an "initiating event" or compelling need for new regulations. The push to regulate may come from a legal requirement, a lawsuit or petition, a regularly scheduled review, or sources outside the agency: Congress, the president, other agencies, state governments, advisory committees, the public, the commercial sector, and advocacy groups. Initiating events can also come from within the agency, based on reaction to new scientific information that would impel new rules, or even a current event or an accident or tragedy. Even though there is forward momentum (see Step One in Figure 4.2), concerned parties must first determine that rulemaking is an appropriate response to this particular initiating event (see Step Two in Figure 4.2). To do so, they review relevant sections of the federal Administrative Procedure Act (5 U.S.C. 553).

The Administrative Procedure Act (APA), passed in 1946 as P.L. 79-404, is the law that delineates the rulemaking process. The APA, like the *Federal Register* itself, came in the wake of embarrassing moments in the mid-1930s when it became clear that federal government officials could not determine which federal regulations were in force (Office of the Federal Register, 2006). The APA underwent a major revision on September 6, 1966, with the passage of P.L. 89-554, which further elaborated the kinds of steps one sees reflected in the Reg Map today.

If the action under consideration has met the criteria of the APA as noted in Step Two (see Figure 4.2), agency officials then need to let the public know that they are considering developing a new regulation; they must publish a notice of proposed rulemaking and call for public input (see Step Three in Figure 4.2). This process is referred to by regulators as notice and comment. As one becomes more experienced in moving around the *Federal Register* or Regulations.gov, one learns to look for notices of proposed rulemaking (NPRMs), frequently listed in an Action category or column. An NPRM is the first widely published evidence, subsequent to the agency's published regulatory agenda, that specific rulemaking is underway. At this stage, there is also the possibility of a process called negotiated rulemaking, wherein stakeholders actively negotiate aspects of a proposed rule.

The notice and comment functionality is improving with better technology. In the future, the public may enjoy enhanced (and simpler) tracking of notices published, public hearings held (and summaries/transcripts of hearings), comments received, agency responses to comments, and agency drafting of proposed rules. As it stands now, the Office of Management and Budget (OMB) must review the proposed rule before it is published (see Step Four in Figure 4.2).

Proposed and final rules include a preamble section that provides a plain English background for the action under consideration. Preambles are considered such rich, concise summaries that they are sometimes collected and reprinted as separate publications. A *Federal Register* preamble compilation covering the years 1936–1978 in the field of radiological health is one example (Food and Drug Administration, 1980).

Let us suppose that the agency has published its NPRM and asked for public comment (usually in a period of 30, 60, or 90 days). Officials now take the time to consider the input they have received. All comments, whether received via Regulations.gov, e-mail, fax, or print-on-paper letter, are considered part of the official record, could be published online for public review, and should therefore not contain sensitive, personal, or confidential material. (Although many agencies have their comments published directly on Regulations.gov, over 100 agencies are considered nonparticipatory in auto-publishing their comments

Figure 4.2. The Reg Map™

The Reg Map

Informal Rulemaking

Step One

Initiating Events

Agency Initiatives

Agency initiatives for rulemaking originate from such things as:
- Agency priorities and plans
- New scientific data
- New technologies
- Accidents

Required Reviews

Statutory Mandates

Recommendations from Other Agencies/External Groups/States/Federal Advisory Committees

Lawsuits

Petitions

OMB Prompt Letters

Step Two

Determination Whether a Rule Is Needed

Administrative Procedure Act Provisions

Under the Administrative Procedure Act provisions that are included as part of the Freedom of Information Act at 5 U.S.C. 552, agencies are required to publish in the *Federal Register*:
- Substantive rules of general applicability
- Interpretive rules
- Statements of general policy
- Rules of procedure
- Information about forms
- Information concerning agency organization and methods of operation

Step Three

Preparation of Proposed Rule

Proposed Rule

A notice of proposed rulemaking proposes to add, change, or delete regulatory text and contains a request for public comments.

Administrative Procedure Act Provisions

Under the Administrative Procedure Act provisions at 5 U.S.C. 553, rules may be established only after proposed rulemaking procedures (steps three through six) have been followed, unless an exemption applies. The following are exempted:
- Rules concerning military or foreign affairs functions
- Rules concerning agency management or personnel
- Rules concerning public property, loans, grants, benefits, or contracts
- Interpretive rules
- General statements of policy
- Rules of agency organization, procedure, or practice
- Nonsignificant rules for which the agency determines that public input is not warranted
- Rules published on an emergency basis

Note: Even if an exemption applies under the Administrative Procedure Act provisions, other statutory authority or agency policy may require that proposed rulemaking procedures be followed.

Optional Supplementary Procedures to Help Prepare a Proposed Rule

Advance Notice of Proposed Rulemaking
An advance notice of proposed rulemaking requests information needed for developing a proposed rule.

Using The Reg Map

The Reg Map is based on general requirements. In some cases, more stringent or less stringent requirements are imposed by statutory provisions that are agency specific or subject matter specific. Also, in some cases more stringent requirements are imposed by agency policy.

(Continued)

Figure 4.2. The Reg Map™ *(Continued)*

Step Four
OMB Review of Proposed Rule

OMB Review Under Executive Order 12866

OMB reviews only those rulemaking actions determined to be "significant."

Independent agencies are exempt from OMB review.

Step Five
Publication of Proposed Rule

Administrative Procedure Act Provisions

The Administrative Procedure Act provisions at 5 U.S.C. 553 require proposed rules to be published in the *Federal Register*.

Step Six
Public Comments

Comments

Under the Administrative Procedure Act provisions of 5 U.S.C. 553, an agency must provide the public the opportunity to submit written comments for consideration by the agency.

As required by Public Law No. 107-347, agencies must provide for submission of comments by electronic means and must make available online the comments and other materials included in the rulemaking docket under 5 U.S.C. 553 (c).

Executive Order 12866 established 60 days as the standard for the comment period.

The holding of a public hearing is discretionary unless required by statute or agency policy.

Specific Analyses for Steps Three and Seven

Regulatory Planning and Review (E.O. 12866)

Would the rule have a $100 million annual impact, raise novel issues, and/or have other significant impacts? ➡ **If yes** Prepare economic impact analysis.

Regulatory Flexibility Act (5 U.S.C. 601–612)

Is a notice of proposed rulemaking required by law? ➡ **If yes**

Would the rule "have a significant economic impact on a substantial number of small entities"? ➡ **and yes** Prepare regulatory flexibility analysis.

Note: Under limited circumstances analyses also are required for certain interpretive rules involving internal revenue laws (5 U.S.C. 603, 604).

Paperwork Reduction Act (44 U.S.C. 3501–3520)

Does the rule contain a "collection of information" (reporting, disclosure, or recordkeeping)? ➡ **If yes** Prepare information collection clearance package for OMB review and approval, and prepare request for public comments.

Unfunded Mandates Reform Act (2 U.S.C. Chs. 17A, 25)

Does the rulemaking process include a proposed rule? ➡ **If yes**

Does the rule include any Federal mandate that may result in the expenditure (direct costs minus direct savings) by State, local, and tribal governments, in the aggregate, or by the private sector, of $100 million in any one year (adjusted annually)? ➡ **and yes** Prepare unfunded mandates analysis (unless an exclusion applies).

(Continued)

Figure 4.2. The Reg Map™ *(Continued)*

Step Seven

Preparation of Final Rule, Interim Final Rule, or Direct Final Rule

Final Rule

A final rule adds, changes, deletes, or affirms regulatory text.

Special Types of Final Rules

Interim Final Rule
An interim final rule adds, changes, or deletes regulatory text and contains a request for comments. The subsequent final rule may make changes to the text of the interim final rule.

Direct Final Rule
A direct final rule adds, changes, or deletes regulatory text at a specified future time, with a duty to withdraw the rule if the agency receives adverse comments within the period specified by the agency.

Step Eight

OMB Review of Final Rule, Interim Final Rule, or Direct Final Rule

OMB Review Under Executive Order 12866

OMB reviews only those rulemaking actions determined to be "significant."

Independent agencies are exempt from OMB review.

Step Nine

Publication of Final Rule, Interim Final Rule, or Direct Final Rule

Congressional Review Act (5 U.S.C. 801-808)

An agency must submit most final rules, interim final rules, and direct final rules, along with supporting information, to both houses of Congress and the General Accounting Office before they can take effect.

Major rules are subject to a delayed effective date (with certain exceptions).

Action by Congress and the President could have an impact on the rule.

Administrative Procedure Act Provisions

Under the Administrative Procedure Act provisions that are included as part of the Freedom of Information Act at 5 U.S.C. 552, agencies are required to publish final rules, interim final rules, and direct final rules in the *Federal Register*.

Federal Register Act (44 U.S.C. 1501-1511)

The Federal Register Act at 44 U.S.C. 1510 (implemented at 1 CFR 8.1) requires rules that have general applicability and legal effect to be published in the *Code of Federal Regulations*.

Drafting Requirements for Rulemaking Documents

Agendas for Rules Under Development or Review

Source: Published online at http://www.reginfo.gov/public/reginfo/Regmap/regmap.pdf. Copyright © 2007 by ICF Incorporated. All rights reserved. This document may not be reproduced in any form without permission.

this way. The list of nonparticipators is diverse, including the Central Intelligence Agency, the Federal Communications Commission, the Library of Congress, and many others.) The concerns voiced during the comment period must be addressed in some way by the proposed rule. Like a congressional bill that dies in committee (see Chapter 3), some initiating events do not result in regulations. Instead, many attempts see parties going back to the drawing board—back to the initiating event stage to start over (see sidebar for one example of a failed regulation). For the purposes of this discussion, a positive outcome is assumed at every stage.

Fresh Idea, Failed Attempt

In 2007, the Sierra Club and three other groups petitioned the Environmental Protection Agency, calling for stricter labeling and regulating of air freshener products (which, they claim, tend to contain carcinogens along with lovely scents). This is a perfect Step One: the initiating event is a petition. Although their petition was denied (Environmental Protection Agency, 2007), their efforts are an example of how advocacy groups may bring forward an issue for executive agency consideration. Although the term *lobbying* is usually reserved for the legislative branch, such targeted advocacy (the petition) is certainly a form of lobbying directed at executive branch agencies. In the case of the petition, the issue never made it past Step Two, but instead a notice was published in the *Federal Register*, explaining that a petition had been received and, in the expert opinion of the EPA, failed to meet the criteria of Section 2 of the Toxic Substances Control Act, so no further action would be pursued.

The petition quite likely played a part in raising general public awareness of air fresheners and carcinogens. A simple literature search reveals that, since 2007, there has been increased government activity to regulate the sale of air fresheners at the state level. Because Regulations.gov also makes available the public comments submitted in the course of the rulemaking process, one can read a letter from attorneys at the Reckitt Benckiser company, a firm that "provides high quality air fresheners, marketed under the brand name Air Wick®, meeting the needs of consumers and institutional customers to eliminate odors and improve the quality of the environments in which the products are used." When the petition was made public, many corporations, groups, and individuals went on record to voice support or disapproval. According to the Reckitt Benckiser letter, "Air fresheners are used in 70% of homes in the United States and consumers consider them to be a vital component of their home care regimen to help eliminate offensive odors, provide ambiance, and create an atmosphere that makes them feel good about their homes" (Moyer, 2007).

After review by OMB, the regulation-in-the-making can be published as a proposed rule (PR) in the *Federal Register* and Regulations.gov (see Step Five in Figure 4.2). At this point, stakeholders have something definite to which they can react and on which they can comment. The PR must be accompanied by another call for comments (see Step Six in Figure 4.2).

Assuming that the agency receives comments on the PR, it works (within its mission and statutory authority) to respond to the concerns in its writing of the final rule. The final rule is prepared (see Step Seven in Figure 4.2), and again OMB reviews it (see Step Eight in Figure 4.2), since it may have changed significantly since its proposed stage. In Step Nine (see Figure 4.2), Congress and the General Accounting Office have an opportunity to review the final rule. If it passes through all of these steps without what is known as a negative incident, it becomes a final rule, is published in the *Federal Register* and Regulations.gov, and will be integrated into the next edition of the printed *Code of Federal Regulations*, and its presence will be duly noted in the *List of CFR Sections Affected*. Final rules become effective no sooner than 60 days after they are printed in the *Federal Register*.

The *Federal Register*, FederalRegister.gov, and Regulations.gov

Although the *Code of Federal Regulations* is the final official destination for a regulation, proposed regulations must first be published in the *Federal Register*, a Monday to Friday daily newspaper of the federal government that has been published since 1936, subsequent to the passage of P.L. 74-220, the Federal Register Act, on July 26, 1935. The *Federal Register* is considered the official publishing outlet of the executive branch of government, so in addition to proposed regulations, it also contains presidential executive orders, proclamations, and decision directives; announcements of public agency hearings (these announcements are known as Sunshine Act notices); alerts about federal grant opportunities; notices about future rulemaking; and more. The National Archives and Records Administration produces a readable ten-page history of the *Federal Register* that provides easy background on this publication so pivotal to the daily functioning of the government (Office of the Federal Register, 2006), as well as a practical guide to its use (Office of the Federal Register, 2009). See Figure 4.3 for a typical page from this daily publication. The official online *Federal Register* is available via FDsys at http://www.gpo.gov/fdsys/, back to 1994. Using the advanced search feature, one can perform complex fielded searching in just the *Federal Register*, or browse an entire issue or its table of contents. As with many GPO products, it is delivered in PDF (bearing a digital signature of authenticity), XML, or text.

For years, librarians relied on a guide entitled *The Federal Register: What It Is and How to Use It* (Wickliffe, 1992). Although the guide has not been published since 1992, and the same information is largely available online in the various FAQ sites, a dedicated scholar of regulations would still find this a useful and informative resource. The *Federal Register* in its printed form is not the easiest source to navigate; each issue is organized by agency, and the table of contents (there is no daily index) lists the agencies and their proposed actions. The *Federal Register* is continuously paginated, so page numbers reach into the tens of thousands each year, and it is cited by volume number, page number, and date. The example in Figure 4.3 would be cited as 74 FR 63866 (December 4, 2009). A twice-monthly index, searchable by agency and broad subject, is cumulated in an annual index volume. A commercially published index, the *CIS Federal Register Index*, was published from 1984 to 1999 only. Starting in 1994, with widespread searchable online access to the current *Federal Register* through GPO and numerous private publishers, use of printed indexes declined, although the

Figure 4.3. A Page from the *Federal Register*

63866　　　　Federal Register / Vol. 74, No. 232 / Friday, December 4, 2009 / Proposed Rules

SECURITIES AND EXCHANGE COMMISSION

17 CFR Parts 240 and 249b

[Release No. 34–61051; File No. S7-28-09]

RIN 3235–AK14

Proposed Rules for Nationally Recognized Statistical Rating Organizations

AGENCY: Securities and Exchange Commission ("Commission").

ACTION: Proposed rules.

SUMMARY: The Commission is proposing rule amendments and a new rule that would impose additional requirements on nationally recognized statistical rating organizations ("NRSROs"). The proposed amendments and rule would require an NRSRO to furnish a new annual report describing the steps taken by the firm's designated compliance officer during the fiscal year with respect to compliance reviews, identifications of material compliance matters, remediation measures taken to address those matters, and identification of the persons within the NRSRO advised of the results of the reviews; to disclose additional information about sources of revenues on Form NRSRO; and to make publicly available a consolidated report containing information about revenues of the NRSRO attributable to persons paying the NRSRO for the issuance or maintenance of a credit rating. The Commission is proposing these rules, in conjunction with a separate release being issued today adopting certain rule amendments, to further address concerns about the integrity of the credit rating procedures and methodologies at NRSROs. Finally, at this time, the Commission is announcing that it is deferring consideration of action with respect to a proposed rule that would have required an NRSRO to include, each time it published a credit rating for a structured finance product, a report describing how the credit ratings procedures and methodologies and credit risk characteristics for structured finance products differ from those of other types of rated instruments or, alternatively, to use distinct ratings symbols for structured finance products that differentiated them from the credit ratings for other types of financial instruments. The Commission is also soliciting comments regarding alternative measures that could be taken to differentiate NRSROs' structured finance credit ratings from the credit ratings they issue for other types of financial instruments through, for

example, enhanced disclosures of information. The Commission also is soliciting comment on whether the rule amendments being adopted today in a separate release designed to remove impediments to determining and monitoring non-issuer-paid credit ratings for structured finance products should be extended to create a mechanism for determining non-issuer-paid credit ratings for structured finance products that were issued prior to the rule becoming effective (e.g., to allow for non-issuer-paid credit ratings for structured finance products of the 2004–2007 vintage). The Commission strongly encourages market participants and all others to provide their views.

DATES: Comments should be received on or before February 2, 2010.

ADDRESSES: Comments may be submitted by any of the following methods:

Electronic Comments

• Use the Commission's Internet comment form (*http://www.sec.gov/rules/proposed.shtml*); or
• Send an e-mail to *rule-comments@sec.gov*. Please include File Number S7-28-09 on the subject line; or
• Use the Federal eRulemaking Portal (*http://www.regulations.gov*). Follow the instructions for submitting comments.

Paper Comments

• Send paper comments in triplicate to Elizabeth M. Murphy, Secretary, Securities and Exchange Commission, 100 F Street, NE., Washington, DC 20549–1090.

All submissions should refer to File Number S7-28-09. This file number should be included on the subject line if e-mail is used. To help us process and review your comments more efficiently, please use only one method. The Commission will post all comments on the Commission's Internet Web site (*http://www.sec.gov/rules/proposed.shtml*). Comments are also available for public inspection and copying in the Commission's Public Reference Room, 100 F Street, NE., Washington, DC 20549, on official business days between the hours of 10 a.m. and 3 p.m. All comments received will be posted without change: we do not edit personal identifying information from submissions. You should submit only information that you wish to make publicly available.

FOR FURTHER INFORMATION CONTACT: Michael A. Macchiaroli, Associate Director, at (202) 551–5525; Thomas K. McGowan, Deputy Associate Director, at (202) 551–5521; Randall W. Roy,

Assistant Director, at (202) 551–5522; Joseph I. Levinson, Special Counsel, at (202) 551–5598; Sheila Dombal Swartz, Special Counsel, at (202) 551–5545; Rose Russo Wells, Special Counsel, at (202) 551–5527; Rebekah E. Goshorn, Attorney, at (202) 551–5514; Marlon Q. Paz, Senior Counsel to the Director, at (202) 551–5756; Division of Trading and Markets, Securities and Exchange Commission, 100 F Street, NE., Washington, DC 20549–7010.

SUPPLEMENTARY INFORMATION:

I. Background

On February 2, 2009, the Commission adopted amendments to its existing rules governing the conduct of NRSROs under the Securities Exchange Act of 1934 ("Exchange Act").[1] The Commission proposed these rule amendments in June 2008 to further the purposes of the Credit Rating Agency Reform Act of 2006 ("Rating Agency Act") to improve ratings quality for the protection of investors and in the public interest by fostering accountability, transparency, and competition in the credit rating industry.[2] The amendments also were designed to further address concerns about the integrity of the process by which NRSROs rate structured finance products, particularly mortgage related securities.[3] Concurrent with the

[1] *See Amendments to Rules for Nationally Recognized Statistical Rating Organizations*, Exchange Act Release No. 59342 (February 2, 2009), 74 FR 6485 (February 9, 2009) ("*February 2009 Adopting Release*").

[2] Exchange Act Release No. 57967 (June 16, 2008), 73 FR 36212 (June 25, 2008) ("*June 2008 Proposing Release*"). The Commission adopted the initial set of NRSRO rules in June 2007. *See Oversight of Credit Rating Agencies Registered as Nationally Recognized Statistical Rating Organizations*, Exchange Act Release No. 55857 (June 5, 2007), 72 FR 33564 (June 18, 2007) ("*June 2007 Adopting Release*"). In July 2008, the Commission also proposed a series of amendments to rules under the Exchange Act, Securities Act of 1933 ("Securities Act"), and Investment Company Act of 1940 ("Investment Company Act") that would eliminate references to ratings issued by NRSROs in certain rules and forms. *See References to Ratings of Nationally Recognized Statistical Rating Organizations*, Exchange Act Release No. 58070 (July 1, 2008), 73 FR 40088 (July 11, 2008); *Securities Ratings*, Securities Act Release No. 8940 (July 1, 2008), 73 FR40106 (July 11, 2008); *References to Ratings of Nationally Recognized Statistical Rating Organizations*, Investment Company Act Release No. 28327 (July 1, 2008), 73 FR 40124 (July 11, 2008).

[3] The term "structured finance product" as used throughout this release refers broadly to any security or money market instrument issued by an asset pool or as part of any asset-backed or mortgage-backed securities transaction. This broad category of financial instrument includes, but is not limited to, asset-backed securities such as residential mortgage-backed securities ("RMBS") and to other types of structured debt instruments such as collateralized debt obligations ("CDOs"), including synthetic and hybrid CDOs, or collateralized loan obligations ("CLOs").

Law Library Microform Consortium (LLMC) has digitized the historic run of (GPO-produced) annual printed indexes. HeinOnline's Federal Register Library, a commercial subscription, offers one-stop historic searching of the source and its indexes. Today's users of the free online versions from GPO and the Office of the Federal Register can choose to peruse an online table of contents or a cumulative index for each year as navigation aids, in addition to the general and advanced search capabilities.

Figure 4.4. Regulations.gov Screenshot

Significantly, GPO and the Office of the Federal Register collaborated on a completely new approach to the *Federal Register*, rolled out to the public in July 2010 at http://www.federalregister.gov/. This much more visually appealing, truly interactive (XML-based) edition invites the user to browse, search, follow eye-catching headlines, or view brief videos. The broad categories in the initial release are Money, Environment, World, Science and Technology, Business and Industry, and Health and Public Welfare. A thin banner across the top of the page quantifies that day's content (e.g., 122 Notices, 13 Proposed Rules, 20 Rules, and 2 Significant Regulations, in 264 pages). Its rendering in XML means that it can easily be digested or incorporated into other online spaces. A disclaimer makes it clear that this is a prototype and does not serve as a legal substitute for the FDsys digital edition or the print-on-paper GPO edition.

Another significant online resource, developed earlier than http://www.federalregister.gov/, is http://www.Regulations.gov/, updated daily (Figure 4.4). What makes this web portal particularly useful is that any member of the public can read a proposed regulation and comment on it at the same time. Regulations.gov is administered by an executive committee comprising representatives from 30 federal departments and agencies. Since its launch in 2003, the site has been a truly collaborative project. It could be said that the revolution in easy public access to regulations online started with Regulations.gov, which purports to be "your voice in federal decision-making." Users can search, comment, and read others' comments about proposed rules, final rules, and other agency matters from hundreds of federal government entities. Comments submitted here are considered as official as those submitted via fax, e-mail, or U.S. mail. In recent years, more and more supporting and related regulatory materials have been contributed by agencies. A system of docket folders is used to group related materials. One can limit a search by keyword, agency, date, comment period, docket number, title of document, and document type, and one can sort results by any of these dimensions as well. The interface is simple and intuitive. For those wishing to improve their regulatory research skills, visiting Regulations.gov every now and then and perusing regulations currently up for comment is an educational practice—and sometimes quite interesting, and even entertaining. RSS feeds are available as well, for all postings added to Regulations.gov or just postings from a specific agency.

The *Code of Federal Regulations*

All federal government regulations currently in force are published in the *Code of Federal Regulations* (*CFR*) in a codified, or topical, arrangement. A basic working understanding of the *CFR* and the *Federal Register* (*FR*) is a relevant skill for any public service librarian, educator, or public official. Many veteran librarians will be familiar with the look and feel of the printed *CFR*, as it occupies approximately eight shelves of brightly colored paperbacks in most of the print-on-paper reference collections in the country, and is most apt to be found in health sciences, government, law, and special libraries, as well as medium-to-large public libraries.

The *CFR*'s 50 titles, or topical areas, range from Protection of the Environment (Title 26) to Internal Revenue (Title 40) to Public Health (Title 42); see the full listing in the following box. These numbers have no numeric correlation to the titles of the *United States Code* (*U.S.C.*), a common misperception—and, depending on context, either resource could be referred to as "The Code"—though generally that term is used for the *U.S.C.* The *CFR* is compiled by the Office of the Federal Register and published in online, print, and microfiche formats by the GPO, and made available for sale by many commercial publishers as well. Since the *CFR* is used as a current tool—to determine whether a rule is in force—most libraries retain only the most current edition, relying on law libraries and online vendors to supply older, superseded volumes. Specialized legal research sometimes requires understanding prior regulations, and the William S. Hein Company offers an online searchable version of every edition back to 1938, as well as the complete historical run of the *Federal Register*, via HeinOnline. The printed *CFR* comes with an annual index volume, allowing the user to search the *CFR* by agency or broad topic area. Commercially produced indexes, providing more fine-grained subject access, have been published over the years, notably the *CIS Index to the Code of Federal Regulations* (annually, 1977–2001) and *West's Code of Federal Regulations: General Index* (annually, 2006–present).

CFR Titles: *Code of Federal Regulations*	
1: General Provisions	26: Internal Revenue
2: Grants and Agreements	27: Alcohol, Tobacco Products and Firearms
3: The President, Compilation & Reports	28: Judicial Administration
4: Accounts	29: Labor
5: Administrative Personnel	30: Mineral Resources
6: Homeland Security	31: Money and Finance: Treasury
7: Agriculture	32: National Defense
8: Aliens and Nationality	33: Navigation and Navigable Waters
9: Animals and Animal Products	34: Education
10: Energy	35: Panama Canal
11: Federal Elections	36: Parks, Forests, and Public Property
12: Banks and Banking	37: Patents, Trademarks and Copyrights
13: Business Credit and Assistance	38: Pensions, Bonuses and Veterans' Relief
14: Aeronautics and Space	39: Postal Service
15: Commerce and Foreign Trade	40: Protection of the Environment
16: Commercial Practices	41: Public Contracts and Property Management
17: Commodity & Securities Exchanges	42: Public Health
18: Conservation of Power & Water Resources	43: Public Lands: Interior
19: Customs Duties	44: Emergency Management and Assistance
20: Employee Benefits	45: Public Welfare
21: Food and Drugs	46: Shipping
21: (previous year only) Food and Drugs	47: Telecommunications
22: Foreign Relations	48: Federal Acquisition Regulations System
23: Highways	49: Transportation
24: Housing and Urban Development	50: Wildlife and Fisheries
25: Indians	INDEX

The *CFR* is published annually in rolling updates, with the total set divided into quarters: titles 1–16 are published to be current as of January 1; titles 17–27 to be current as of April 1; titles 28–41 to be current as of July 1; titles 42–50 to be current as of October 1. In the print-on-paper world, if there are no regulatory changes in a particular volume for an entire year, the library or individual subscriber still receives a new cover to place over the previous year's volume. New regulations may strike out, amend, or update older ones, and the entire *CFR* is updated over the course of one year. Watching the (printed) *CFR* covers change color is a marker of a year's passage for many documents and law librarians. One title, Title 3 (*The President, Compilation & Reports*) should not be replaced when the new edition arrives; all of its volumes must be retained for historic purposes. Title 3 contains materials such as executive orders and proclamations, not codified like the rest of the *CFR*, and so must be retained (see Chapter 6 on the presidency). Take note when you visit a library: the *CFR* shelves should include all the old Title 3 volumes back to 1938 (Hartnett, 2006). GPO and the Office of the Federal Register have teamed up to create an e-*CFR*, updated daily instead of quarterly. The result, not considered a legal version of the *CFR* at the time of this writing, is online at http://ecfr.gpoaccess.gov. This differs from the FDsys version (referred to as the *CFR Annual Edition*), which matches the updating pattern of the paper edition. A final note on the *CFR*: reading regulations can be challenging, but some passages are quite straightforward (see sidebar for part of the *CFR* on FAA air procedures).

An Excerpt from the *Code of Federal Regulations*
(Explanations and editorial comments are added in italics.)

Title 14—Aeronautics and space *(This is the "Title" or broad, overarching topic.)*

(The Title is further subdivided into increasingly specific areas.)

CHAPTER I—FEDERAL AVIATION ADMINISTRATION, DEPARTMENT OF TRANSPORTATION

(Within Titles, each Chapter is reserved for a federal agency.)

SUBCHAPTER F—AIR TRAFFIC AND GENERAL OPERATING RULES

PART 97—STANDARD INSTRUMENT PROCEDURES

§ 97.3 Symbols and terms used in procedures

(The part number is the lowest unit of citation. Not all regulations are overly technical, as the following illustrates.)

HAA means height above airport and is expressed in feet.

HAL means height above landing and is the height of the DA/MDA above a designated helicopter landing area elevation used for helicopter instrument approach procedures and is expressed in feet.

HAS means height above the surface and is the height of the DA/MDA above the highest terrain/surface within a 5,200-foot radius of the missed approach point used in helicopter instrument approach procedures and is expressed in feet above ground level (AGL).

HAT means height above touchdown.

(The CFR is cited by Title, Part, and Year of Publication. The above excerpt is properly cited 14 CFR 97.3, 2009.)

The *List of CFR Sections Affected* or *LSA*

If one were a regulatory devotee who lived, breathed, and died by the *CFR*, a recurrent task would be determining which sections of the *CFR* would be affected by all the new rules being published daily in the *Federal Register* and on Regulations.gov. Suppose the FAA updated its regulations mid-year. Aside from reading the daily *Federal Register*, how would one keep up with this, since the print-on-paper *CFR* is only revised annually? The answer lies in a slim paperback monthly volume (and online resource) entitled the *List of CFR Sections Affected (LSA)*. For those in industry, or in healthcare, environmental safety, business, and many other fields, a typical task is monitoring the regulations in your field. Such individuals know which section of the *CFR* title, chapter, and part they need to follow. The *LSA* section shown in the sidebar includes the part number (of Title 14, *CFR*) on the left side, and the page numbers of that year's *Federal Register* (still the preferred legal method of citing) on the right margin. Even "our" FAA section, 14 CFR 97, has been updated with some new developments since its last annual *CFR* compilation. The print-on-paper *LSA* includes only those updates occurring in one month, and the online version includes daily updates of revisions occurring that month. See the sidebar for an example of a daily *LSA* pulled directly from the *Federal Register*, where it is also published daily.

A List of *CFR* Sections Affected, as It Appears in the *Federal Register*

14 CFR – Aeronautics & space

CFR Part....................Federal Register page number

61..........53643
71..........52130, 52131, 52398, 52399, 53160, 53161, 53162, 53163, 53402, 53403,
          53404, 53405, 53406, 53407, 53408, 53648, 54896, 54897, 55449
73..........51076, 53649
91..........53643
93..........52132, 52134
95..........50920
97..........50696, 50698, 54457, 54460, 55451, 55453

E-rulemaking: The Hope for Greater Efficiency and Transparency

Rulemaking was once the epitome of print-on-paper governance. The print or microfiche edition of the *Federal Register* was the primary public forum for the rulemaking activities. Print-on-paper letters, delivered via U.S. mail, or in-person remarks at public hearings were the normal means of comment, although fax and e-mail were adopted as these technologies became available. During the Reagan years, the regulatory process changed with Executive Order 12291, which gave the OMB extensive powers over the regulatory apparatus—perhaps the single most important reform of the rulemaking process since the APA in 1946. The order empowered the OMB to identify duplication, overlap, and conflict in rules, which federal agencies then were required to rectify; and to review existing and new rules for consistency with administrative policies. The order required the use of cost-benefit analysis and established a "net benefit" criterion for rulemaking. (CQ Press, 2008: 7)

In the George W. Bush era, an e-government, or electronic government, initiative emerged, one major focus of which was e-rulemaking, an effort that continues to move forward today. In simple terms, it makes sense that each step taken by agencies (preparing notices, managing a regulatory agenda, handling comments received during the notice-and-comment period, analyzing actions taken in regards to comments, etc.) be done in a uniform, consistent matter, handled by robust technology. There should be agreed-upon elements in the records kept across agencies and in the compatibility of systems used to manage the records. The Federal Docket Management System (http://www.fdms.gov/), a system closed to the public but used by authorized federal employees, helps manage electronic documents related to rulemaking.

E-rulemaking is the use of technology (particularly, computers and the World Wide Web) to: (i) help develop proposed rules; (ii) make rulemaking materials broadly available online, along with tools for searching, analyzing, explaining and managing the information they contain; and (iii) enable more effective and diverse public participation. E-rulemaking has transformative potential to increase the comprehensibility, transparency and accountability of the regulatory process. (Committee on the Status and Future of Federal Rulemaking, 2008: 1)

Regulations.gov, e-CFR, FDsys, and FederalRegister.gov are prime examples of e-government. Although most debuted during the George W. Bush era, all fit in with the Obama-era Open Government Policy (White House, 2009), which calls for agencies to use modern technology, especially the web, to maximize transparency, participation, and collaboration.

Exploring Agency Websites for Regulatory Content

Out of the universe of federal departments, agencies, commissions, and quasi-official establishments, between 60 and 300 have significant regulatory functions, depending on criteria used. The Federal Motor Carrier Safety Administration makes a good case study of a regulatory agency at http://www.fmcsa.dot.gov/ (see Figure 4.5). On its website, a Rules & Regulations section covers drivers, vehicles, and company policies. Clicking on any of the topics allows the user to read the regulations exactly as they are printed in the *CFR*. For most topics, a guidance or interpretation is also available in FAQ style. Other notable regulatory sites include the Food and Drug Administration (http://www.fda.gov/),

Figure 4.5. The Federal Motor Carrier Safety Administration: Rules & Regulations

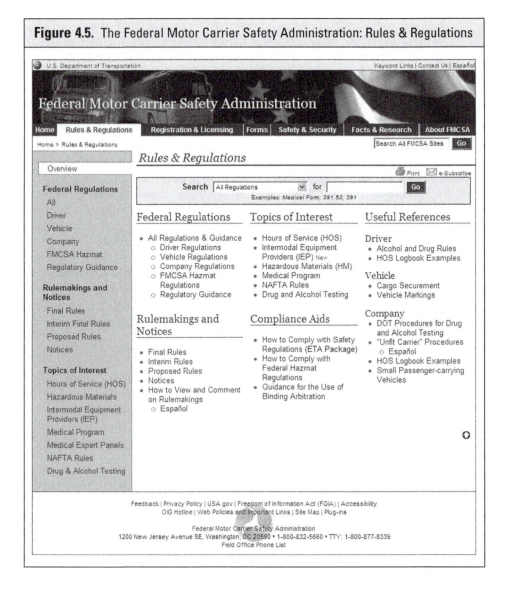

the Nuclear Regulatory Commission (http://www.nrc.gov/), and the EPA (http://www.epa.gov/lawsregs/). One can imagine that much of the regulatory content found by casual users of the web comes through such federal agency sites.

Regulatory agencies also contain adjudicative bodies similar to courts of law; they hear cases regarding regulations and publish decisions, directives, opinions, orders, and reports. These agency actions are subject to judicial review (Hernon, 2002). The University of Virginia Library offers a list (by agency or subject) of "Administrative Decisions and Other Actions" (http://www2.lib.virginia.edu/govtinfo/fed_decisions_agency.html).

State and Local Codes

Just as states have their own constitutions, legislatures, and court systems, all states have executive agencies whose rulemaking parallels that of the federal government. These agencies announce their rulemaking activities in publishing outlets similar to the *Federal Register* (the *Washington State Register*, the *Colorado Register*, and the *Pennsylvania Bulletin*, for example). After a notice and comment period, the agencies publish their final rules in these same publications. Next, the final rules are integrated into the state equivalents of the *CFR*; these compiled, codified regulations are generally called administrative codes (e.g., the *Washington Administrative Code*, the *Colorado Code of Regulations*, the *Pennsylvania Code*)— your state's title may vary. You can find all 50 states' administrative codes linked to from many different online guides, two of the most notable being the National Association of Secretaries of State, which has an Administrative Codes and Registers Section (http://www.administrativerules.org/) and the Public Library of Law (http://www.plol.org/) under the Regulations tab.

The pattern is replicated at the county and municipal levels as well. Your local government has a municipal or county code or both (depending on the governance structure), with sections covering topical areas such as safety, parking violations, and parks and recreation. Most people are aware of their local county health departments, but do not have any idea where to find the county health code or how they might work to change it. It is also common for smaller jurisdictions to adopt wholesale already established codes from industry or safety organizations. The practice of adopting an external set of rules or standards into one's own code is called incorporation by reference, a common practice with building and fire safety regulations, and it can take place at the federal level as well. The major legal publishers (e.g., West, LexisNexis) provide subscription services aggregating state and local codes. The Law Librarians' Society of Washington, DC, maintains a helpful list of state legislatures, state laws, and state regulations (http://www.llsdc.org/state-leg/), as does the Law Library of Congress (http://www.loc.gov/law/help/guide/states.php). In many cases, these state links lead to city and county regulatory sources (codes) within two or three clicks.

Recommended Sources of Additional Information

The Office of Management and Budget's Office of Information and Regulatory Affairs (OIRA), a coordinative and oversight office established in 1980, is a pivotal office within the regulatory realm. The public webpage at http://www.whitehouse.gov/omb/inforeg_default/ describes OIRA's exact role in everything from analyzing the quality of information going into the regulatory process, to monitoring privacy and confidentiality concerns within the federal government sphere, to coordinating certain aspects of federal statistics. For those interested in further readings on regulations, the introductory chapter of CQ Press's *Federal Regulatory Directory* is a readable, in-depth, plain English guide to the regulatory process and the history of regulation.

As with other sectors of the government, the regulatory arena draws many advocacy groups and watchdogs. The Center for Regulatory Effectiveness (http://www.thecre.com/) monitors access to regulations and access to quality data, and shares its independent analyses with Congress. OMB Watch (http://www.ombwatch.org/rulemaking) promotes transparency, sound government processes, and citizen involvement.

Emerging Projects

Two new, completely distinct initiatives aim to increase public awareness of the regulatory process. First is GovPulse (http://www.govpulse.us), an activist-conceived online application that aims to guide the user to regulations currently open for comment, with the ability to search by geographic area as well. The second project, Regulation Room (http://www.regulationroom.org/), with the motto "people talking to people talking to government," is a project of the Cornell e-Rulemaking Initiative (CeRI), hosted by the Legal Information Institute (LII). It differs from Regulations.gov in its livelier interface and respondents' opportunity to discuss regulations with each other, instead of just filing comments. CeRI faculty and students moderate the discussion, and the project has research, teaching, and learning goals as well as a civic purpose. The existence of both projects may indicate a tipping point in public interest about regulations.

Conclusion

One can expect continued reform of the federal regulatory system and increased public awareness due at least in part to online tools like Regulations.gov, as well as the proliferation of online advocacy groups and new online projects. Increased regulation usually follows in the wake of a disaster, and indeed there has been reform in banking rules subsequent to the bank collapse of 2008 and oil drilling rules after the 2010 Deepwater Horizon incident. In the words of the federal committee examining regulatory improvements,

> Continuing to develop a powerful and flexible e-rulemaking system is one of the rare federal projects in which every segment of the public, as well as the government, stands to gain. But before e-rulemaking's potential benefits can become a reality, Congress, the President and OMB must recognize that the current system– while a remarkable accomplishment given where the Initiative started—is only a first step, and that achieving the great potential of technology-supported rulemaking now demands a fundamentally new approach. (Committee on the Status and Future of Federal Rulemaking, 2008: 6)

Exercises

1. Experiment with http://www.govpulse.us/, seeing if there are any regulatory actions affecting your local area, state, or region. What do you find?
2. According to the latest Unified Agenda, which agency has more rulemaking planned for the next six months: the FDA or the EPA?
3. Find a federal regulation currently in force regarding the safe handling of human blood. Can you cite the resource properly?
4. Is the marbled murrelet on the federal Endangered Species List?
5. What is the most recent Final Rule enacted by the federal government?

Sources Mentioned in This Chapter

Sources mentioned in this section do not duplicate the References that follow.

Administrative Decisions and Other Actions, http://www2.lib.virginia.edu/govtinfo/fed_decisions_agency.html.

Administrative Procedure Act, http://www.archives.gov/federal-register/laws/administrative-procedure/.

Center for Regulatory Effectiveness, http://www.thecre.com/.

CIS Federal Register Index, http://www.worldcat.org/oclc/10139759/.

CIS Index to the Code of Federal Regulations, http://www.worldcat.org/oclc/6260698/.

Code of Federal Regulations, http://www.gpo.gov/fdsys/.

CQ Press's *Federal Regulatory Directory*, http://www.worldcat.org/oclc/5250786/.

e-CFR, http://ecfr.gpoaccess.gov/.

Federal Register, http://www.gpo.gov/fdsys/.

Federal Register: What It Is and How to Use It, http://www.worldcat.org/oclc/36755617.

FederalRegister.gov, http://www.federalregister.gov/.

GovPulse, http://www.govpulse.us/.

HeinOnline's Federal Register Library, http://www.worldcat.org/oclc/123028992.

Law Librarians' Society of Washington, DC: State Legislatures, State Laws, and State Regulations, http://www.llsdc.org/state-leg/.

Law Library of Congress, http://www.loc.gov/law/help/guide/states.php.

List of CFR Sections Affected, http://www.gpo.gov/fdsys/.

National Association of Secretaries of State, Administrative Codes and Registers Section, http://www.administrativerules.org/.

Office of Management and Budget's Office of Information and Regulatory Affairs (OIRA), http://www.whitehouse.gov/omb/regulatory_affairs/default/.

OMB Watch, http://www.ombwatch.org/rulemaking/.

Public Library of Law, http://www.plol.org/.

Reg Map, http://www.reginfo.gov/public/reginfo/Regmap/index.jsp.

Reginfo.gov, http://www.reginfo.gov/.

Regulation Room, http://www.regulationroom.org/.

Regulations.gov, http://www.regulations.gov.

Unified Agenda of Federal Regulatory and Deregulatory Actions, http://www.reginfo .gov/public/do/eAgendaMain/, http://www.gpo.gov/fdsys/.

West's Code of Federal Regulations General Index, http://www.worldcat.org/oclc/ 64195650/.

References

Animal and Plant Health Inspection Service. 2009. *Boll Weevil Quarantine and Regulations.* RIN: 0579-AB91. Accessed November 25. http://www.reginfo.gov/public/do/ eAgendaViewRule?pubId=200904&RIN=0579-AB91.

Arrigo, Paul. 2003. "Federal Rules and Regulations: What are They, Where Did They Come From, and How Do I Find Them?" In *Government Publications Unmasked: Teaching Government Information Resources in the 21st Century,* edited by Wendy Mann and Theresa R. McDevitt, 73–84. Pittsburgh, PA: Library Instruction Publications.

Committee on the Status and Future of Federal e-Rulemaking and American Bar Association Section of Administrative Law and Regulatory Practice. 2008. *Achieving the Potential: The Future of Federal e-Rulemaking: A Report to Congress and the President (Executive Summary).* http://ceri.law.cornell.edu/documents/executive-summary .pdf.

CQ Press. 2009. *Federal Regulatory Directory.* Washington, DC: CQ Press.

D'Arista, Jane. "Rebuilding the Framework for Financial Regulation." EPI Briefing Paper #231, Economic Policy Institute, Washington, DC, 2009. http://epi.3cdn.net/ 878d45bddadc3a4305_0vm6iiofp.pdf.

Environmental Protection Agency. 2007. "Air Fresheners; TSCA Section 21 Petition." *Federal Register* 72 (245), December 21. http://www.gpo.gov/fdsys/pkg/FR-2007- 12-21/pdf/07-6176.pdf.

Executive Office of the President. 2003. *E-Government Strategy Implementing the President's Management Agenda for e-Government.* http://permanent.access.gpo.gov/ lps36050/2003egov_strat.pdf.

Federal Motor Carrier Safety Administration. "Rules & Regulations." 2009. Accessed December 6. http://www.fmcsa.dot.gov/rules-regulations/rules-regulations.htm.

Food and Drug Administration. 1980. *Radiological Health: March 1936–March 1978.* Rockville, MD: Dept. of Health, Education, and Welfare, Public Health Service, Food and Drug Administration.

Golan, Elise, Lisa Mancino, and Laurian Unnevehr. 2009. "Food Policy: Check the List of Ingredients." *Amber Waves* 7, no. 2 (June): 16–21.

Hartnett, Cass. 2006. "Government Regulations: Protective, Restrictive, and Influenced by the Public." *DttP: Documents to the People* 32, no. 2 (Spring): 29.

Hernon, Peter, Harold C. Relyea, Joan F. Cheverie, and Robert E. Dugan. 2002. *United States Government Information: Policies and Sources.* Westport, CT: Libraries Unlimited.

Katel, Peter. 2007. "Consumer Safety: Do Government Regulators Need More Power?" *CQ Researcher* 17, no. 36 (October 12): 841–864.

Mackey, Mary Alton, and Marilyn Metz. 2009. "Ease of Reading of Mandatory Information on Canadian Food Product Labels." *International Journal of Consumer Studies* 33, no. 4 (July): 369–381.

Moyer, Eileen J. 2007. "Reference #7: Comments Submitted by Eileen J. Moyer, Director of Regulatory Relations, Reckitt Benckiser, Inc., on the TSCA Section 21 Petition on Air Fresheners." November 6. http://www.regulations.gov/#!documentDetail;D= EPA-HQ-OPPT-2007-1016-0035.14.

Obama, Barack. 2009. "Remarks on Signing the Family Smoking Prevention and Tobacco Control Act of 2009." *Compilation of Presidential Documents* (DCPD200900493). June 22. http://www.gpo.gov/fdsys/pkg/DCPD-200900493/pdf/DCPD-200900493.pdf.

Office of the Federal Register. 2006. *The Office of the Federal Register: A Brief History Commemorating the 70th Anniversary of the Publication of the First Issue of the Federal Register March 14, 1936*. Washington, DC: Office of the Federal Register, National Archives and Records Administration. http://www.archives.gov/federal-register/the-federal-register/history.pdf.

Office of the Federal Register. 2009. "About the Federal Register." Accessed November 25. http://www.archives.gov/federal-register/the-federal-register/about.html.

Regulations.gov. 2009. "Frequently Asked Questions: Rulemaking Process." Accessed November 4. http://www.regulations.gov/search/Regs/home.html#faqs.

Regulatory Information Service Center. 2009. "Current Unified Agenda of Regulatory and Deregulatory Actions." Accessed November 25. http://www.reginfo.gov/public/do/eAgendaMain.

The White House. 2010. "Open Government Policy." Accessed August 8. http://www.whitehouse.gov/open/about/policy.

Wickliffe, Jim, Ernie Sowada, and United States. Office of the Federal Register. 1992. *The Federal Register: What It Is and How to Use It: A Guide for the User of the Federal Register, Code of Federal Regulations System*. Washington, DC: Government Printing Office.

Chapter 5

Law

Introduction

Law research is fascinating but challenging. There's a reason that lawyers go through rigorous schooling and must pass bar exams. There's a reason that states have laws preventing non-lawyers from practicing law and potentially misleading clients. But as a reference or government information librarian who understands the basic sources and strategies for *finding* the law, it can be very empowering—not to mention a lot of fun—to connect patrons with legal resources and the law itself. While most librarians can easily and quickly navigate their way around almost any bibliographic database or discovery tool, it takes special knowledge to understand how to find the law, making the librarian who is comfortable doing so ever valuable. Once one gets past the initial intimidation factor and understands the basic nature of law, finding law is not always hard.

This chapter will introduce primary sources of law (the laws themselves) and strategies for using them. And always remember: you may lead a patron to the law, but after that, step back. Interpreting the law is up to them, or preferably, a lawyer, as often

> patrons in search of legal information are also looking for someone to validate their argument or assure them that they have a "good case." A librarian's responsibility ends after providing assistance in finding information and stops short of providing validation or an opinion; patrons then need to be told to consult with an attorney licensed to practice law in their state. Telling patrons how to interpret the details of a law or how a law applies to them, or dispensing any kind of legal advice, are all acts that can be construed as the unlicensed practice of law, which is illegal. (Knapp, 2009: 1439).

In fact, the term *legal research* often denotes the research that lawyers do for their clients. This chapter focuses on basic aspects of legal research—finding the text of laws and cases—not the deeper work of analyzing and synthesizing legal information to reach a legal conclusion. This chapter will further focus on the free law resources available from governments. A full-fledged law library does not necessarily use the same resources. For instance, the *United States Code* (discussed later in this chapter) is a standard source of statutory law, and the government's version of it is available in depository libraries and free online. A law library engaged in frequent and in-depth research, however, will use not only these free versions, but also the value-added versions available for purchase from various legal information publishers and vendors.

The Kinds of Law

There are four types of federal law. The first and simplest is the U.S. Constitution and its amendments. It is easily found online and in the standard sets of statutory law discussed later in this chapter.

The second type of law is statutory law. The Constitution states that Congress shall make the laws. The laws that Congress makes (through the process described in Chapter 3) are collectively known as statutory law. These laws are referred to as statutes.

The third type of law is case law, or judicial law. Case law originates in the court system (the judicial branch of government). Courts apply law in particular disputes between parties (in contrast to statutes and regulations, which are written for broad categories of people or institutions). Courts apply both statutory law and principles drawn from centuries of precedent, the common law. Courts, via cases, examine the validity of current laws as they relate to the Constitution and existing law, whether statutory or judicial. In our common law system, such decisions of the courts are treated as law unless overturned by a higher court or superseded by subsequent statutory law or a subsequent judicial decision (so common law mainly means that once an issue is decided by a court in one case, that decision is adhered to in similar circumstances elsewhere, known as precedent). Case law is the type of law most difficult to locate using government information sources. Historically, only Supreme Court decisions were easily accessible; lower court decisions were published in private legal sets often outside the scope and access of libraries lacking large legal reference collections. The web has made such case law easier to access, although private publishers remain important in case law publishing.

The final type of law is administrative law, also referred to as regulatory law (covered in Chapter 4). This is the law that is found in rules and regulations from executive departments and agencies. These rules largely detail how the executive branch will perform its constitutional mandate to enforce the laws of Congress. To a lesser extent, administrative law also refers to the works and actions of the president's office, through executive orders and proclamations, legal decisions, and orders from the Office of Management and Budget (covered in Chapter 7).

While this brief summary of the types of law is from a federal perspective, states and local governments produce most of the actual laws that govern society. For instance, read the Constitution; it doesn't say anything about murder. Does that mean that murder was not officially illegal unless an early Congress passed a law preventing it? Not quite. For many, many years after the founding of the nation, the federal government and its lawmaking were generally limited to affairs of the running of the federal government itself. It was states and local governments that did (and still do) most of the lawmaking that governed the lives of the citizenry. So at the time of the U.S. Constitution, it was the state constitutions, statutes, and common law that addressed basics such as preventing murder and theft, and even these early state constitutions often in part simply adopted English common law.

States generally have the same four sources of law. Each state has its own constitution; its own statutory law consisting of the laws passed by its legislative branch; its own administrative law comprising the rules made by state executive agencies; and its own case law, the law derived from opinions of state courts. Further, counties and cities promulgate law via local codes and ordinances that deal with local issues.

This chapter will discuss finding statutory and case law. It begins with the compilation of statutory law; continues with the codification of statutory law; and then discusses finding case law. It concludes with a brief discussion of treaties and international law relevant to the United States. Remember that administrative law is covered in Chapters 4 and 6.

Primary versus Secondary Legal Resources

Government information resources related to the law are all primary sources: they are the laws themselves. Governments are generally not in the habit of producing secondary legal sources. Law libraries, however, rely on many secondary sources to aid access to primary sources: hornbooks, digests, treatises, law review articles, and other reference items that may explain and annotate some aspect or topic of the law and contain citations to the appropriate primary source. Most academic and public libraries do not acquire many secondary legal sources. Likewise, most legal material freely available online is primary. That said, general secondary sources like Wikipedia can and do sometimes provide useful roadmaps to a major legal subject or case, with appropriate citations... although in nothing like the detail of a true secondary legal source as found in a law library. (A rare but notable exception: Congress, with the help of the Congressional Research Service, prepares a weighty secondary source, *The Constitution of the United States of America: Analysis and Interpretation*. This resource, updated with biennial supplements, summarizes significant Supreme Court interpretations of every clause of the U.S. Constitution.)

Because most secondary legal sources are not government information, this chapter focuses mainly on primary government information sources.

Compilation of Statutory Law

Chapter 3 described the process of tracing legislation from a bill to a public law. Yet simply finding public laws is often not sufficient for law research needs. Older laws, especially those enacted before the advent of the web, are often not available in print or online as public laws. One cannot use THOMAS (the congressional finding tool discussed in Chapter 3), for instance, to find the *Civil Rights Act of 1964*; the law predates THOMAS. Likewise, one usually cannot go to the local library to find the slip version (the slim, individual issuance) of older public laws.

To find all public laws—all laws enacted by Congress which govern the nation—requires the *United States Statutes at Large*. The *Statutes at Large* is the chronological compilation of every federal law ever enacted and is the standard source of federal statutory law. The name of the set derives from its history: each session of Congress is considered a statute; each law a chapter.

For the first hundred years of the nation, each law (statute) appears in the *Statutes at Large* in the order that it was passed but there is no numbering system. Public law, or P.L., numbers were first used to number laws in 1901, appearing in the margins of the law as printed in the *Statutes at Large*. In 1957 these public law numbers began to be used in the head (at the beginning of the law) and the current arrangement by public law number became clear. With this current arrangement, chronological numbering by public law numbers is straightforward.

For instance, the first law enacted during the 111th Congress is designated as Public Law 111-1; the second, Public Law 111-2. The *Civil Rights Act of 1964* is Public Law 88-352—the 352nd law passed by the 88th Congress. And since the 1964 volumes of the *Statutes at Large* compile chronologically all public laws passed by the 88th Congress, the *Civil Rights Act of 1964* is followed by the next law passed: 88-353, a measure about federal credit unions. The GI Bill (known as the Servicemen's Readjustment Act of 1944, Public Law 78-346), meanwhile, is in the 1944 volumes of the *Statutes at Large*, from the 78th Congress. The No Child Left Behind Act (Public Law 107-110) is in the 2002 volumes of the *Statutes at Large*, which contain all of the laws passed during the 107th Congress.

After passage, the Office of the Federal Register in the National Archives prepares the public laws for placement into the *Statutes at Large*. Laws passed since 1994 are available online from the GPO (and may also be discovered via THOMAS). Public laws from the current Congress won't be bound as the *Statutes at Large* until several years after the end of the session of Congress; still, these newest laws do appear in FDsys (GPO's Federal Digital System and the successor to GPO Access), shortly after the end of the session, exactly as they will look in the *Statutes at Large* volume, and include the *Statutes at Large* citation.

History of the *United States Statutes at Large*

This process of printing federal laws is itself governed by law. One of the very first laws enacted by Congress (the fourteenth law ever passed, in fact) called for copies of all new laws to be delivered to the secretary of state. The secretary of state was then responsible for delivering copies of each law to all senators and representatives, having each law published in at least three newspapers (a practice that continued until 1875), and delivering copies to each state. In this manner, it was hoped that citizens of the new nation could stay informed of new federal laws. The secretary of state was further charged to "carefully preserve the originals, and shall cause the same to be recorded in books" (1 Stat. 68) (see Figure 5.1). So the secretary of state (which, we might add, only became known as the secretary of state in this very same law; previously, the Department of State was known as the Department of Foreign Affairs) was charged to function as printer, library, and archives of our nation's laws!

Six years later, in what was the fiftieth law ever passed by Congress (Congress is much more active now: in the 110th Congress, 460 laws were passed in a single two-year session), this arrangement was amended, and Congress ordered a compilation of laws (1 Stat. 448), with 4,500 copies of these compilations of statutory law to be printed and distributed around the young nation. Called the *Laws of the United States*, this edition—known as the Folwell edition (for its printer Richard Folwell)—is the first collection of published federal laws and the first precursor to the *Statutes at Large*.

In 1845 another law was passed (5 Stat. 798) calling for an updated compilation of laws, and, more importantly, an *ongoing* compilation of new laws.

Figure 5.1. Text of 1 Stat. 68, the First Law Mandating the Publication of Laws

68 FIRST CONGRESS. SESS. I. CH. 14. 1789.

STATUTE I.

Sept. 15, 1789.

[Obsolete.]

[Act of July 27, 1789, ch. 4.]

Department of foreign affairs changed to the department of state.

Additional duties assigned the secretary of the said department.

CHAP. XIV.—*An Act to provide for the safe-keeping of the Acts, Records and Seal of the United States, and for other purposes.*

SECTION. 1. *Be it enacted by the Senate and House of Representatives of the United States of America in Congress assembled*, That the Executive department, denominated the Department of Foreign Affairs, shall hereafter be denominated the Department of State, and the principal officer therein shall hereafter be called the Secretary of State.

SEC. 2. *And be it further enacted*, That whenever a bill, order, resolution, or vote of the Senate and House of Representatives, having been approved and signed by the President of the United States, or not having been returned by him with his objections, shall become a law, or take effect, it shall forthwith thereafter be received by the said Secretary from the President; and whenever a bill, order, resolution, or vote, shall be returned by the President with his objections, and shall, on being reconsidered, be agreed to be passed, and be approved by two-thirds of both Houses of Congress, and thereby become a law or take effect, it shall, in such case, be received by the said Secretary from the President of the Senate, or the Speaker of the House of Representatives, in whichsoever House it shall last have been so approved; and **the said Secretary shall, as soon as conveniently may be, after he shall receive the same, cause every such law, order, resolution, and vote, to be published in at least three of the public newspapers printed within the United States, and shall also cause one printed copy to be delivered to each Senator and Representative of the United States, and two printed copies duly authenticated to be sent to the Executive authority of each State; and he shall carefully preserve the originals, and shall cause the same to be recorded in books to be provided for the purpose.(*a*)**

Act of March 2, 1799, ch. 30, sec. 1.

Published by Little, Brown, this set—the first to be titled the *United States Statutes at Large*—included the Articles of Confederation, the Constitution, and all laws enacted since the first session of Congress. This edition is held by many larger libraries, and appears online in the Library of Congress's *A Century of Lawmaking*. In 1874 responsibility for publishing the *U.S. Statutes at Large* transferred from this private publisher to GPO, where it remains today.

The volume of laws passed by each Congress has risen consistently over time. For instance, just eight volumes of the *Statutes at Large* are able to cover all the laws from 1789 to 1845. Beginning in 1865, each volume corresponded to a single congress (covering the two years between congressional elections), and in 1939, each volume corresponded to one session of Congress (generally one year). Note that recent volumes of the *Statutes at Large* are usually broken into multiple parts, as even a single session of modern Congress usually produces too much law to bind into one physical volume.

Using the *United States Statutes at Large*

The *Statutes at Large* is available in print at depository libraries. Surprisingly, the complete set is not yet truly online. As noted above, the Library of Congress' *American Memory* project does contain *A Century of Lawmaking*, consisting of scanned versions of the Little, Brown set of the *Statutes at Large*, which covered early congresses all the way up to 1875. And the GPO has .PDF versions of *Statutes at Large* volumes from 2003 forward. But *Statutes* within the large time period between 1875 and 2003 have, as of this writing, been digitized only in fee-based private versions, and some free but incomplete nongovernmental scanning projects. The former include offerings from HeinOnline and Lexis-Nexis; the latter includes a mostly complete version free online via the Constitution Society that lacks the indexes and other supplemental materials (so to use this, one really needs to know exactly what one wants beforehand). Other mass scanning projects, such as the Google Books Library Project, do not yet yield a complete, accessible, or particularly user-friendly presentation. So amazingly, for many years of coverage, print remains the best format for accessing and using the *Statutes at Large* free of charge.

Because the *Statutes at Large* presents only laws as they are passed, and not necessarily the current law, the set is in *some* respects a tool for historical research rather than pure legal research. For instance, when Congress passed the Brady Bill (officially the Brady Handgun Violence Protection Act) in 1994, it wasn't the first gun control law ever passed, nor did it erase all previous federal law related to gun control. What it did was add some new gun control law, edit some existing gun control law, and remove some existing gun control law. Reading the Brady Bill, then, does not present the complete federal gun control law. To piece together the current state of federal gun control law, one would need to examine all public laws ever passed about gun control. A *codification* of federal law addresses this need, and is covered in the next section.

In the meantime, finding laws in the *Statutes at Large* is relatively straightforward. Each volume contains a handy subject and title index. Finding a known law such as the Civil Rights Act of 1964, then, could scarcely be simpler—check the index to the 1964 volumes. Likewise, if one wants to see the text of the large welfare reform law of 1996, the subject index in the 1996 *Statutes at Large* under Welfare leads to the Personal Responsibility and Work Opportunity Reconciliation Act of 1996. Note that the subject and title indexes are repeated within each volume, so one need not be in the correct part to use the index for the entire volume. Knowing that the welfare reform law was passed in 1996 was necessary, but knowing its nonintuitive title was not. If one can get to the right Congress, the index to any physical volume will suffice.

This raises our next issue: the preceding strategy is easy if one is fortunate enough to know the date and name or subject of the desired law (and aided by the web in general, dates and actual names for significant legislation can often be found quite easily). Lacking this information, however, one can use a table of popular names. These tables are designed for use when one knows a name of a law, but not necessarily the official name, or the date. The official table of popular names appears in the *United States Code* (a set discussed in detail later in this chapter), and is also available online at http://uscode .house.gov/popularnames/popularnames.htm. Cornell's Legal Information Institute provides an alternative, very useful popular names table, available at http://www.law.cornell.edu/uscode/topn. For instance, if one did not know the date of the Civil Rights Act, one could use one of these tables to see a correct citation for the major civil rights acts that have been passed (in this case, however, since there are multiple civil rights acts, one still might not know which one is desired).

Yet if one did *not* have the date of the big welfare reform law, or one was looking for the original GI bill, even these popular name tables are insufficient, as neither of those acts is listed under alternative popular names (as noted, the GI bill is officially the Servicemen's Readjustment Act of 1944). To find laws under these circumstances, secondary sources—whether the web, encyclopedias, or secondary legal resources—should be consulted to narrow the search. And frequently, users come to the *Statutes at Large* through citations in the *United States Code*, as you will see.

Once in the *Statutes at Large*, the reader finds useful information. Since 1903, each law contains reference to the original bill number, which is useful when researching the legislative history as described in Chapter 3. Further, beginning in 1963 with the slip law versions, and 1975 in the *Statutes at Large*, brief legislative histories are included with each law (see Figure 5.2). Finally, and of large importance, specific sections of each public law contain notations as to where in the *United States Code* that text will be inserted. The *United States Code* will be discussed shortly.

Compilation of State Statutory Law

All fifty states generally follow a similar publication process with their state statutory law, although the titles vary widely. Do not be confused by the terms *statutes* and *code*. A word associated with one type of publication in a particular

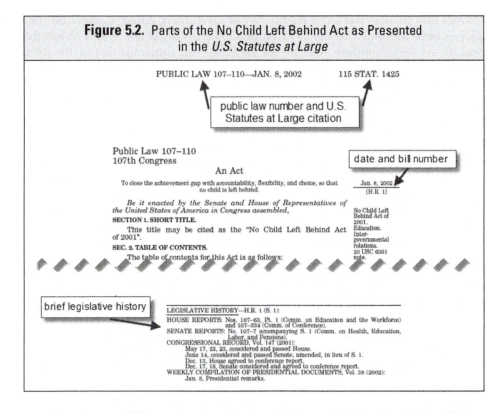

Figure 5.2. Parts of the No Child Left Behind Act as Presented in the *U.S. Statutes at Large*

state may have a different connotation in another state. You should familiarize yourself with your state's compilation of statutory law. In Illinois, for instance, new laws are called public acts and are available free online. The Illinois equivalent to the *U.S. Statutes at Large* is called *Laws of the State of Illinois*. California's new statutory laws are called chaptered bills or chapter laws, with recent laws also free online, and are compiled into the *California Statutes and Amendments to the Codes*. Every state now publishes recent laws online. The Public Library of Law and Justia are two popular free online legal resources that can point you to state statutory law; of course, the fee-based legal reference databases Westlaw and Lexis also contain such law, as do their slimmer brethren LexisNexis Academic and West Campus Research.

Codification of Statutory Law

Most current law on any particular topic is the result of more than one particular public law. The original civil rights law, for instance, has also seen various modifications over the years. To understand civil rights law, then, requires a codification of all the laws that have been passed and are currently in force into a single subject arrangement.

This means that all of the laws about civil rights or gun control, for instance, are integrated in one place to reflect the *current* law on any particular topic. So the text of all of the laws that deal with gun control, no matter when or how they were passed, are brought together—codified—into one narrative gun control law. For federal law, this is done in the *United States Code*. As a result, the *United States Code* is the law of the land, reflecting all current federal statutory law.

History of the *United States Code*

In the decades after the founding of the country, it became increasingly difficult to determine the current state of federal law. Congress might pass any number of new laws that alter, modify, rescind, or add on to very specific portions of previously passed laws. In order to find the current law on a topic, then, one had to comb through all of the public laws on that topic over the years and ascertain what was current and how they fit together.

This was obviously a difficult way to research the law, prone to frustration and error. To address this problem, in 1866 Congress passed a law establishing a commission "to revise, simplify, arrange, and consolidate all statutes of the United States, general and permanent in their nature" (14 Stat. 74). In other words, this commission of lawyers and legal experts was charged with gathering into a single arrangement the currently in-force law of the land. The result was called the *Revised Statutes of the United States*. The *Revised Statutes* contained 70 titles (each title was a broad subject) and was published in an 1875 volume of the *U.S. Statutes at Large*. So these *Revised Statutes* reflected all of the current federal law by topic by omitting whatever had been repealed, and amending whatever had been amended, up to when it was published.

So this worked nicely, sort of, for a while. But it wasn't long before the whole mess started building up again with new laws! So one could start with the *Revised Statutes*, but one still then had to go through every subsequent law to see what had changed since then. Eventually, West Publishing stepped in and published its own subject-arranged code (*U.S. Compiled Statutes Annotated*); several competing codifications were also privately produced.

During the 69th Congress, in 1925, another congressionally mandated codification was put together (with the help of private publishers, who now had experience with such codification), and this codification assumed its eventual name and format: the *United States Code*, with 50 titles. Later in the 1920s, several additions were produced to correct errors in this first *U.S. Code*. More importantly, Congress also passed legislation at this time establishing annual supplements (prepared by the House Committee on Revision of Laws) to update each title of the *U.S. Code*, and, every six years, the content of those supplements was incorporated into an entirely new set of the *U.S. Code*. So finally an official, government-produced, relatively current codification of federal statutory law was ensured.

This process continues to this day, keeping the *U.S. Code* current as the law of the land. Since 1975 the task of keeping the *U.S. Code* up to date has fallen to the U.S. House's Office of the Law Revision Counsel, which monitors public laws and quickly determines their codification status into the *U.S. Code*.

Using the *United States Code*

The *U.S. Code* comprises 50 titles, each of which covers a particular topic. Each is the equivalent to one or sometimes several physical volumes in size. For instance, title 8 covers Aliens and Nationality; title 21 Food and Drugs; title 26 is the Internal Revenue Code; title 43 Public Lands; title 50 War and National Defense. Each title is further divided into chapters, so title 21 on Food and Drugs features chapter 3, Filled Milk; chapter 8, Narcotic Drugs; chapter 12, Meat Inspection; and so on. Within each chapter are more detailed sections.

> **Federal Statutory Law Citations**
>
> - *United States Statutes at Large*: 118 Stat. 1125 (volume-publication-page)
> - *United States Code*: 15 U.S.C. § 7801 (2006) (title-publication-section, usually includes edition year in parentheses).

The *U.S. Code* is cited by title and section (so cites do not specifically include information on the chapter). Sections are numerical throughout a title. For instance, the citation 21 U.S.C. 615 refers to section 615, *Inspection of carcasses, meat of which is intended for export* (Figure 5.3), of the Food and Drug title of the *U.S. Code* (which happens to fall in the chapter on meat inspection).

The *U.S. Code* is free online via GPO's FDsys. It is also available via the excellent Cornell Legal Information Institute site at http://www.law.cornell.edu/uscode/. GPO's version is based on the latest, six-year update version described above. So as of this writing (2010), GPO is using the 2006 version of the *Code*, up to date as of January 2007. Cornell, on the other hand, adds a very useful feature: when looking up the latest portion of any law in the *U.S. Code*, Cornell includes links to Pending Updates, whereby newer public laws are monitored for content that will be added (or deleted) into that particular section of the *U.S. Code* by integrating the *United States Code Classification Tables* (more on these *Tables* later in this section). This keeps the Cornell version current

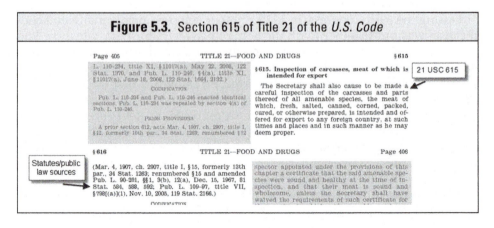

Figure 5.3. Section 615 of Title 21 of the *U.S. Code*

to within days. Privately produced versions of the *U.S. Code*, used by law libraries and law firms, feature even more robust updating.

In any case, a patron who wants to know the current law on any topic, such as educational standards or health records privacy, would need to use the *United States Code*. Finding the right section(s) of the *U.S. Code* can be a difficult process, and at times such a request may be best referred to a law librarian. But there are a few strategies for finding the right section. The simplest is using the index, either in print or by searching online. Because of the sheer volume of federal law, searching the *U.S. Code* online is at times difficult. Keywords can appear in dozens of different titles of the *U.S. Code*, and narrowing the search down to the title or two relevant to current needs can take persistence in looking through various possibilities. It is helpful to pay attention to the titles of the code sections that yield results. If you seek health records privacy law, and search accordingly, results may include sections from topics as far flung as military, natural resources, or transportation. The desired law is more likely in a result appearing in a health volume, or a volume about government records that might include law about privacy. Even within the right volume, finding the desired law can be difficult. If you seek the *U.S. Code* section related to privacy of health information resulting from the oft-cited HIPAA law (Health Insurance Portability and Accountability Act of 1996, 110 Stat. 1936), a search of "health records privacy" leads to dozens of results that are not related to HIPAA. Unlike Google and other search engines, the *U.S. Code* does not rank search results by popularity, and the voluminous content of the code often means that search results are somewhat sprawling and scattered—and not always useful.

Considering these difficulties, the *U.S. Code* is often approached from other directions. One frequent approach is via the public law that was a primary source of the law. As previously discussed, public laws include *U.S. Code* notations throughout, indicating where in the *U.S. Code* that particular public law or even a specific part of a public law will be codified. So if you want the current federal law related to health privacy and HIPAA, you can start by finding HIPAA in the *Statutes at Large* and tracing its notations to *U.S. Code* sections (see Figure 5.4). Every word of text in the *U.S. Code* can thus be traced back to its origins in the *Statutes at Large*.

While a public law like HIPAA is pretty straightforward, with the entire law related to health insurance, some large public laws incorporate multiple completely distinct measures, and have their pieces incorporated into countless different places in the subject arrangement of the *U.S. Code*. For instance, the Consolidated Omnibus Budget Reconciliation Act of 1986 (100 Stat. 82) is a single law that covers a diverse range of topics that might otherwise have been passed as separate laws. There are frequently such sprawling, diverse omnibus laws when Congress tries to pass budgets and get other business finished near the end of a term. Measures within this one particular piece of legislation are integrated into hundreds of different places in the *U.S. Code*, reflecting the hundreds of different subjects all covered by this omnibus law. Browsing the law (and its table of contents) and finding the part about continuation of health insurance enables you to find the needed portion of the law, and then to follow

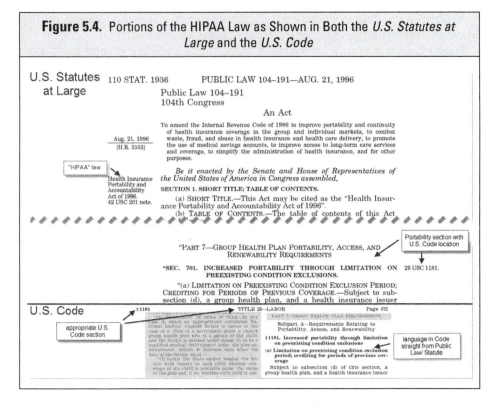

Figure 5.4. Portions of the HIPAA Law as Shown in Both the *U.S. Statutes at Large* and the *U.S. Code*

it to the pertinent *U.S. Code* section (see Figure 5.5). In this case this particular provision was so influential that it is known popularly as COBRA, even though the actual COBRA law deals with dozens of other topics totally unrelated to health as well.

This approach—from the public law to the *U.S. Code*—is sufficiently useful that an entire specialty index volume, the *United States Code Classification Tables*, exists and lists each section of all public laws with notations on where in the *U.S. Code* the new statutory law will be inserted (see Figure 5.6). The *United States Code Classification Tables* are kept very current online at http://uscode .house.gov/classification/tables.shtml (sometimes within days) and also may be found in a volume of the *U.S. Code*.

You can also work backward, from the *U.S. Code* to the statutory law, and see where exactly each piece of the *current* federal law in force originated. This is because each section of the *U.S. Code* cites its source in statutory law. In other words, you can trace each word in the *U.S. Code* to the words in the laws as passed and as they appear in the *U.S. Statutes at Large*. For instance, section 1133 of Title 12 of the *U.S. Code*, which deals with allowable activities in federally protected wilderness, is several pages long. At the end of the section, notes reveal that this section of the *U.S. Code* first originated in Public Law 88-577, the original Wilderness Act. The *U.S. Code* section goes on to note three other laws that amended that section of the *U.S. Code*. By using these notes, you

Figure 5.5. Portions of the COBRA Law, with Notations to Pertinent Locations about Health Insurance in the *U.S. Code*

100 STAT. 82 PUBLIC LAW 99–272—APR. 7, 1986

Public Law 99–272
99th Congress

An Act

Apr. 7, 1986
[H.R. 3128]

To provide for reconciliation pursuant to section 2 of the first concurrent resolution on the budget for fiscal year 1986 (S. Con. Res. 32, Ninety-ninth Congress).

Be it enacted by the Senate and House of Representatives of the United States of America in Congress assembled,

Consolidated
Omnibus Budget
Reconciliation
Act of 1985.

SHORT TITLE

SECTION 1. This Act may be cited as the "Consolidated Omnibus Budget Reconciliation Act of 1985".

large
"COBRA" law

TABLE OF CONTENTS

Title I. Agriculture programs.
Title II. Armed services and defense-related programs.
Title III. Housing and community development programs.
Title IV. Transportation and related programs.

popular section
related to health
insurance

Title V. Corporation for Public Broadcasting and Federal Communications Commission.
Title VI. Maritime, coastal zone, and related programs.
Title VII. Energy and related programs.
Title VIII. Outer Continental Shelf and related programs.
Title IX. Medicare, Medicaid, and Maternal and Child Health programs.
Title X. Private health insurance coverage.

TITLE X—PRIVATE HEALTH INSURANCE COVERAGE

U.S. Code
location

SEC. 10001. EMPLOYERS REQUIRED TO PROVIDE CERTAIN EMPLOYEES AND FAMILY MEMBERS WITH CONTINUED HEALTH INSURANCE COVERAGE AT GROUP RATES (INTERNAL REVENUE CODE AMENDMENTS).

26 USC 162.

(a) DENIAL OF DEDUCTION FOR EMPLOYER CONTRIBUTION TO PLAN.— Subsection (i) of section 162 of the Internal Revenue Code of 1954 (relating to deduction for trade or business expenses with respect to group health plans) is amended by redesignating paragraph (2) as paragraph (3) and by inserting after paragraph (1) the following new paragraph:
"(2) PLANS MUST PROVIDE CONTINUATION COVERAGE TO CERTAIN INDIVIDUALS.—

could examine each of the four cited public laws and see the origin of each word that is currently in force in that section of the *U.S. Code*, as shown in Figure 5.7.

Codification of State Statutory Law

All 50 states follow a similar process for codifying their statutory laws. Frequently, such codifications are produced by private legal publishers. As noted,

Figure 5.6. Excerpt from the *United States Code Classification Tables*

UNITED STATES CODE

TABLE OF CLASSIFICATIONS FOR PUBLIC LAWS

111th Congress, 1st Session

([Final] Public Laws 111-1 to 111-125, 111-128 to 111-135 and 111-137)

Columns 1 and 2

List U. S. Code titles and sections according to the Public Law from which they are derived. The letter "A" in column 4 means Appendix.

Prepared by
Office of the Law Revision Counsel
U.S. House of Representatives
February 1, 2010

Source of U.S. Code sections by Public Law and Statute

U. S. Code Title	Section	Description	Pub. L.	Sec.	123 Stat.
5	5312	nt new	111-1	1	3
42	2000a	nt new	111-2	1	5
42	2000e-5	nt new	111-2	2	5
42	2000e-5		111-2	3	5
29	626		111-2	4	6
42	2000e-5	nt new	111-2	5(a), (b)	6
29	794a		111-2	5(c)(1)	6
42	2000e-16		111-2	5(c)(2)	7
29	633a		111-2	5(c)(3)	7
42	2000e-5	nt new	111-2	6	7
42	1305	nt new	111-3	1(a)	8
42	1396	nt new	111-3	1(c)	8
42	1396	nt new	111-3	2	10
42	1396	nt new	111-3	3	10
42	1397dd		111-3	101-103	11, 15
42	1397ee		111-3	104	17
42	1397dd		111-3	105, 106(a)(1)	23
42	1397dd	nt new	111-3	106(a)(2)	24
42	1397dd		111-3	106(b)	24
42	1397ee		111-3	107(a)	24
42	1397ee	nt repealed	111-3	107(b)	25
42	1308		111-3	109	25
42	139711	new	111-3	111(a)	26
42	1397cc		111-3	111(b)(1)	28
42	1397bb		111-3	111(b)(2)	28

it was private publishers that first began codifying federal statutory law before the federal government stepped in; for states, the private publishers have sometimes retained the primary codification role, although most states do offer some free access online, often in some partnership with the private publisher. For instance, the state of California does not publish an official codification; *West's Annotated California Codes* and *Deering's California Codes, Annotated* are two competing codifications of California statutory law. One advantage of these private compilations is their annotations to court cases, previous law, and

Figure 5.7. *U.S. Code*: 16 U.S.C. 1133, with Listing of the Public Laws That Created This Section

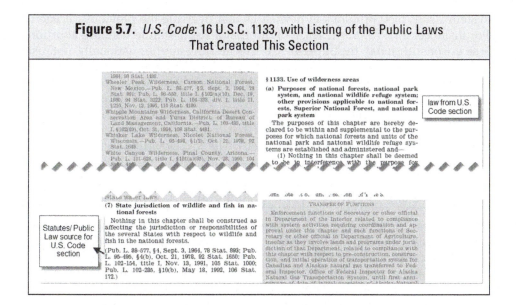

other helpful materials. California does make an unannotated version of its codification available free online as the *California Code.*

As with state statutory law, actual titles vary widely, so don't be confused by the terms *statutes* and *code*. The official codification of Illinois statutory law is called the *Illinois Compiled Statutes* (Illinois also has a privately produced codification, Smith-Hurd's *Illinois Compiled Statutes Annotated*). So while the word *statutes* means *compilation* at the federal level, it refers to Illinois's *codification.*

States also may have an equivalent to the *United States Code Classification Tables* to aid in keeping codified statutory law current with newly passed laws. In California, for instance, the *Table of Sections Affected* indexes sections of the *California Code* affected by newly passed state laws.

As noted, the Public Library of Law and Justia are two popular free online legal resources that can point you to state legal resources including codifications, as do the fee-based services Westlaw, Lexis, LexisNexis Academic, and West Campus Research. You should make yourself familiar with the appropriate publications for your state.

Judicial or Case Law

Congress makes the laws; the executive branch enforces the laws (largely through regulations); and the judicial branch interprets, or examines the validity of laws. The results of these examinations are judicial opinions, which taken together are known as case law. As noted, in our common law system, the decisions of courts have the effect of law, as they set legal precedent. These court decisions, then, remain law unless Congress enacts new laws, or the court system issues new opinions in new cases that overrule the previous decision. For instance, in 1973, *Roe v. Wade* found that a Texas statute banning abortion was unconstitutional; the Supreme Court's holding applies nationally, not just to the Texas statute that was challenged. Abortion will remain legal unless the court system hears a new abortion case (based on a challenge to statutory or constitutional law) and makes a ruling that changes the previous *Roe v. Wade* ruling (a constitutional amendment would also override the original court ruling, and Congress could pass laws that might limit abortions, although Congress can't overturn *Roe v. Wade* itself). The text of judicial opinions is the final published portion of the law.

Background of Court System in the United States

When people think of courts, they might think of cases that they were personally involved in: a criminal or civil case for which they were members of the jury, a disputed traffic violation, or a divorce or bankruptcy proceeding. Results of these cases are not generally of interest to libraries and their patrons. While the decisions and the records of the proceedings are often public records, and may be viewed upon inquiry at the court in question, these decisions are not easy to access and generally have nothing to do with case law. Case law results only from the decisions in the small portion of cases that actually involve an original ruling on a legal question.

Generally, there are two tracks of court cases: state and federal (see Figure 5.8). Most cases begin in a state or local court, which, depending on location, might be called a municipal court, a county court, a district court, or something else. These lowest level courts are trial courts—the courts where the parties present witnesses and a judge or jury decides the case. It's in these courts that people often have personal experience (and theirs are the courtroom dramas seen in

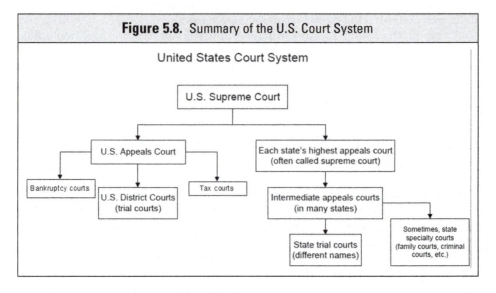

Figure 5.8. Summary of the U.S. Court System

movies). If a decision of such a court is in dispute and a party believes that a legal error has been made, the decision may be appealed to a state appellate court, also known as a state court of appeals. Most states have such a system of state appellate courts to handle appeals of cases decided in the local courts. Beyond the state appellate courts, states have a final state court of appeals, usually—but not always—called the state supreme court. Note that several states do not have intermediate state appellate courts; they have only their local courts and a final court of appeals, which hears all appeals.

The decisions of these state appellate courts are sometimes significant enough to be published and become case law in the state. To be published and become case law, the decision must have some significant or potential impact beyond the case at hand. Once a case escalates to a state's final appellate court or supreme court, it is more likely to be published and become case law in that state. Finally, if a decision of a state supreme court is still in dispute and it involves federal law, parties may appeal the decision to the U.S. Supreme Court.

While most cases begin in local courts and move through the state court system, a much smaller number of cases begin in federal courts, also known as federal district courts. In order for a federal court to hear a case rather than a state court system, there must be a federal question, usually some dispute about a federal law, or a dispute between two states. These federal district courts are also trial courts. There are some 90 federal trial courts in the United States, with at least one in every state. Decisions of federal district courts may be noteworthy enough to be published, but the percentage of noteworthy decisions is still a very small fraction of the total caseload.

When parties appeal decisions of federal district courts because they feel that a legal error has been made, the case goes to a federal court of appeals. There are 12 numbered circuits (e.g., United States Court of Appeals for the First Judicial Circuit), plus the District of Columbia circuit, and one court of appeals for the federal circuit, which hears a special class of cases. Even at this level—just one step below the final appellate court, the U.S. Supreme Court— still only about 20 percent of decisions are considered worthy enough to be published and become case law.

Finally, a party may ask the U.S. Supreme Court to review a federal appeals court decision. So the U.S. Supreme Court reviews cases from federal courts of appeals and from state supreme courts. The document requesting that the Supreme Court review a case is a "writ of certiorari"; when you read or hear that the Court "granted cert," that means that it agreed to hear the case. Although asked to hear some 8,000 cases per year, the Supreme Court ultimately only takes on about one in every 100 of these requests. So someone can claim that they'll fight "all the way to the Supreme Court," but that doesn't mean the Supreme Court will listen. Supreme Court decisions are always published and become case law.

Legal Citations

When judicial decisions are noteworthy enough to be published and become case law, they are published in sets (called reporters) by courts. For instance,

U.S. Supreme Court decisions are published in the set called the *U.S. Reports*. Decisions are published sequentially within the volumes, not unlike how public laws are printed in the *Statutes at Large*.

Citations to cases in these reporters begin with a volume number; then an abbreviation indicating the legal set, and therefore the court; and finally a page number. So, for instance, the 2005 Supreme Court case *Kelo v. City of New London* is cited as 545 U.S. 469, meaning it appears in the 545th volume (one of the volumes from 2005) of the standard set of U.S. Supreme Court decisions, the *U.S. Reports*, and that this decision begins on page 469 of that volume.

This particular case came to the U.S. Supreme Court on appeal from the Connecticut Supreme Court. The *state* court decision (also titled *Kelo v. City of New London*) is cited as 268 Conn. 1, meaning it begins on page 1 of volume 268 of the Connecticut Reports (from 2004). The *Connecticut Reports* is the official reporter of Connecticut Supreme Court decisions. Citations are similar for other sets of decisions from other courts.

Parallel Citations

A single case may have multiple citations, as various private legal publishers compile court decisions in their own sets, adding value along the way (the value added usually by arrangement or annotations). So often a case will include a string of citations. The first citation listed is considered the official citation and refers to the official publication of case law for that court and jurisdiction. The subsequent citations are called parallel citations, and refer to publication of the same case in different sets. For instance, the previously noted U.S. Supreme Court case *Kelo v. City of New London* has the following cites, each one separated by a semicolon: 545 U.S. 469; 125 S. Ct. 2655; 162 L. Ed. 2d 439; 2005 U.S. LEXIS 5011; 60 ERC (BNA) 1769; 10 ALR. Fed. 2d 733; 35 ELR 20134; 18 Fla. L. Weekly Fed. S 437. The first is the official version from *U.S. Reports*. For our purposes, this first cite is all that is necessary; the others are all reprints in various private legal sets, all of which provide some added value to legal professionals but are beyond the scope of this chapter.

Finding Case Law

Finding case law by subject is a task that is often best left to a law library. Many private codifications of law compile not only the statutory law, but also summaries of relevant case law. Legal researchers also use a variety of secondary sources, including encyclopedias (e.g., *American Jurisprudence*), *Restatements* (summaries of common law prepared by the American Law Institute, an influential group of scholars and lawyers), and *American Law Reports* (a series of articles collecting case summaries on particular topics). Further secondary sources may focus on statutory and case law in depth on one subject, such as torts, copyright, or securities laws, while law review articles may provide in-depth analysis of the statutory and case law on a particular subject. Online legal services such as Westlaw and LexisNexis provide access to both cases and numerous secondary finding tools. These specialty tools are for the most part beyond what most government information professionals use, and are found in law libraries and elsewhere in support of law research.

Less robust and more general products that nonetheless contain many legal resources, such as West's Campus Research and LexisNexis Academic, offer secondary sources (notably law reviews and *American Jurisprudence)* as well as access to a substantial number of law reviews, but their legal sources are primarily the cases themselves. If you have access to one of these services, a good research strategy is often to begin with a secondary source to gain an overview of the topic and citations to relevant statutes and cases before moving on to search the cases themselves.

This section will discuss accessing the official sources for judicial decisions, and also freely available access to case law. It will also focus on finding known cases, because this is generally the most frequent legal government information need handled outside of law libraries.

Historically, the only reporter of immediate interest to government documents librarians was the *U.S. Reports,* the decisions of the U.S. Supreme Court. This is because the *U.S. Reports* was—and remains—the only reporter of judicial decisions that is part of the depository program for U.S. government information. Decisions of the lower federal courts—the federal district courts and federal appeals courts—are published by West (and in this chapter, the name *West* refers to the publisher that has gone through many name changes in recent decades, such as West Publishing, West Group, and Thomson West) and access to these sets requires subscriptions to large and expensive legal sets and databases, usually held only by law libraries. Due largely to a long history of publishing such decisions, these private sets are the standard, official reporters, despite the relative difficulty of access to citizens. Of particular importance is the fact that these private publishers didn't just print the decisions; they established the standard numbering and citation system for court decisions at nearly every level outside of the U.S. Supreme Court.

Until relatively recently the numbering and citation system that private publishers used for these sets was considered protected by copyright. Thus, even though the decisions themselves were in the public domain, the fact that private publishers were the official reporters of such cases and that the corresponding citation and pagination for such cases was considered protected by copyright meant that for all intents and purposes, such cases fell outside of free public access. Not surprisingly, this remained a contentious issue, because, as Joe Morehead states in an excellent survey of the subject of legal citations and public access, "a good ol' clash between the public interest and business profits is as American as, well, Microsoft, and usually makes good copy" (Morehead, 1999: 126). A federal court of appeals case (158 F.3d 693) helped free judicial citations from the exclusive hold of West, greatly opening up the world of case law to citizens.

While these reporters remain the official source of case law, and citations to these sets are the standard citations, the court decision above and the web in general have led to much wider access to court decisions. You can increasingly find decisions free online, complete with the official citation. And these online decisions are key, because

> The debate about whether print or electronic resources are better for legal research ended essentially because the consumers of the resources made a decision. Electronic resources are now used so overwhelmingly for legal research that their relative merit seems almost irrelevant. Faculty, attorneys, and law students voted with their feet, and their feet led them to the computer terminal. (Bintliff, 2007: 249)

While many of these faculty, attorneys, and law students may have access to expensive online legal databases, the vast majority of librarians do not have such access, and will forge ahead with what's freely available first. Understanding the court system as outlined here is very important to finding these decisions, as free online access is often available only via a particular court's website.

Federal Case Law

Federal district court opinions that are published appear in the West set called the *Federal Supplement*. For instance, the district court opinion that eventually led to the Supreme Court case *Tasini v. New York Times* may be found at 972 F. Supp. 804. District court opinions also appear selectively online, free, via the court's website. Court websites may be found via http://www.uscourts.gov/courtlinks/. Decisions may also be found via one of the free online legal sources (the Public Library of Law, Justia, and Findlaw, to name three) as well as in the databases from West and LexisNexis discussed previously. Google Scholar also contains federal case law.

When a federal district court case is appealed, it goes to the second level of federal courts, a court of appeals. Federal appeals court opinions are published in a West set called the *Federal Reporter*. The *Tasini* case was appealed from the district court; a federal appeals court heard the appeal and reversed the district court's decision. This reversed ruling, then, is found in the *Federal Reporter* (206 F.3d 161). Like district court opinions, recent decisions of the appeals courts are usually online via the particular court's website, and via the Public Library of Law, Justia, and Google Scholar. Note that even at this level only 20 percent of all decisions are actually considered noteworthy enough to warrant publishing.

Finally, a party to a case at a federal appeals court may petition to have the case heard by the U.S. Supreme Court, all of whose decisions are published in the *U.S. Reports* (as well as in several private sets); these decisions are widely, freely available online, recently at the Supreme Court website, and completely (all historical decisions) via the other online services, both free and fee, noted earlier in this chapter. The *U.S. Supreme Court Case Finder* is a useful way to track down known opinions, and is available at http://www.supremecourt.gov/opinions/casefinder.aspx.

The decisions themselves are relatively straightforward (Figure 5.9). For instance, the decision in the 2005 Supreme Court case *Kelo v. City of New London* (545 U.S. 469) begins with the citation, a brief summary of the case, and a summary of the decision (together, called the syllabus). It also details the decision (who wrote it and who joined in the majority), often includes other concurring opinions (for instance if one justice agrees with the decision but

Figure 5.9. Elements of a U.S. Supreme Court Decision

OCTOBER TERM, 2004   469

Syllabus

KELO ET AL. *v.* CITY OF NEW LONDON ET AL.

CERTIORARI TO THE SUPREME COURT OF CONNECTICUT

No. 04–108. Argued February 22, 2005—Decided June 23, 2005

After approving an integrated development plan designed to revitalize its
ailing economy, respondent city, through its development agent, purchased most of the property earmarked for the project from willing
sellers, but initiated condemnation proceedings when petitioners, the
owners of the rest of the property, refused to sell. Petitioners brought
this state-court action claiming, *inter alia*, that the taking of their properties would violate the "public use" restriction in the Fifth Amendment's Takings Clause. The trial court granted a permanent restrain-
ing order prohibiting the taking of some of the properties, but denying
relief as to others. Relying on cases such as *Hawaii Housing Authority* v. *Midkiff*, 467 U. S. 229, and *Berman* v. *Parker*, 348 U. S. 26, the
Connecticut Supreme Court affirmed in part and reversed in part, upholding all of the proposed takings.

Held: The city's proposed disposition of petitioners' property qualifies as
a "public use" within the meaning of the Takings Clause. Pp. 477–490.

> Summary of case
> and decision

268 Conn. 1, 843 A. 2d 500, affirmed.

STEVENS, J., delivered the opinion of the Court, in which KENNEDY,
SOUTER, GINSBURG, and BREYER, JJ., joined. KENNEDY, J., filed a concurring opinion, *post*, p. 490. O'CONNOR, J., filed a dissenting opinion, in
which REHNQUIST, C. J., and SCALIA and THOMAS, JJ., joined, *post*, p. 494.
THOMAS, J., filed a dissenting opinion, *post*, p. 505.

> End of syllabus
> summarizes
> opinions

472   KELO *v.* NEW LONDON

Opinion of the Court

JUSTICE STEVENS delivered the opinion of the Court.

In 2000, the city of New London approved a development
plan that, in the words of the Supreme Court of Connecticut

> Court opinion

The judgment of the Supreme Court of Connecticut is
affirmed.

It is so ordered.

JUSTICE KENNEDY, concurring.

I join the opinion for the Court and add these further
observations.

This Court has declared that a taking should be upheld as
consistent with the Public Use Clause, 467 U. S., at

> Concurring opinion

494   KELO *v.* NEW LONDON

O'CONNOR, J., dissenting

JUSTICE O'CONNOR, with whom THE CHIEF JUSTICE, JUS-
TICE SCALIA, and JUSTICE THOMAS join, dissenting.

Over two centuries ago, just after the Bill of Rights was
ratified, Justice Chase wrote:

> "An ACT of the Legislature (for I cannot call it a law)
> contrary to the great first principles of the social com-

> Dissenting opinion

expresses a different approach to the decision), and dissenting opinions. It also
lists who argued the case and entities that filed amici curiae briefs with the
court supporting one side or the other. The decisions themselves, including the
concurring and dissenting opinions, are the most important elements of the
case. Other legal materials related to a case, such as pleadings, motions, and

briefs, are sometimes available but are beyond the scope of this chapter. The Supreme Court website does, however, have selected transcripts of oral arguments before the court; The Oyez Project (http://www.oyez.org/) also collects multimedia from the Supreme Court.

More serious users of federal court opinions and documents might also want to register to use PACER (Public Access to Court Electronic Records, http://www.pacer.gov/), providing online access to materials from federal courts, including district, appeals, and bankruptcy courts. Searchable fields include party, judge, and attorney name. PACER includes case status, case histories, and selected documents submitted to the courts by the parties. Regrettably, access to these federal court documents is not free. From 2007 to 2009, GPO and the Administrative Office of the U.S. Courts piloted free PACER access via a select group of depository libraries, but ongoing free access is not available at the time of this writing. In 2009, government transparency activists took a controversial approach: they developed an Internet browser extension, cleverly named RECAP, to harvest PACER materials and automatically deposit the files in the free Internet Archive at http://www.archive.org/details/usfederal courts/.

State Case Law

Most states maintain websites for their court system that include links to recent state appellate court decisions. These include opinions from a state's highest court of appeals, often called its supreme court, and often also include opinions from intermediate state courts of appeal. Lower state courts rarely publish opinions.

For instance, the Illinois courts website (http://www.state.il.us/court/) contains recent decisions of the Illinois Supreme Court and the Illinois appellate courts, including a decision archive going back to 1996. Likewise, the California courts website leads to recent opinions of the California Supreme Court and California appellate courts. Other states generally have similar access to recent years' opinions.

For known opinions, the Public Library of Law and Google Scholar also contain state appellate court decisions (for all 50 states) for recent years; deeper coverage may be found in the fee-based legal databases. For instance, take two U.S. Supreme Court cases, *Romer v. Evans* from 1996 and *Kelo v. City of New London* from 2005. In addition to the U.S. Supreme Court decisions, both the Public Library of Law and Google Scholar contain the prior decisions from the appropriate state supreme courts as well: the Colorado Supreme Court case *Romer v. Evans*, and the Connecticut Supreme Court case *Kelo v. City of New London*. The fee-based legal databases Westlaw and Lexis, however, contain not only the state cases, but also the text for the decisions prior to even those: cases in the Colorado Court of Colorado, Denver County, and in the Superior Court of Connecticut.

The official reporters vary by state and you must discover the appropriate title. Illinois appeals court decisions, for instance, are published in *Illinois Appellate Court Reports*, and Illinois Supreme Court opinions in *Illinois Reports*. In New York, meanwhile, the highest appeals court is called the New York Court of Appeals, and the official reporter for its opinions is called *New York Reports*. New York's intermediate appellate courts report their opinions in *New York Appellate Division Reports*, while a few lower court opinions are published in *New York Miscellaneous Reports*. All of these courts include selected decisions free online as well, via the courts' websites. Librarians will want to familiarize themselves with their own states' court systems and decision publishing mechanisms, and will definitely want to know the closest place to get help from a law librarian.

Federal Case Law Overview

U.S. District Courts
- Federal cases start here. Also called trial courts. More than 90 courts, at least one in each state.
- Recent decisions published on the particular court's website (see http://www.uscourts.gov/courtlinks/), and also in the Public Library of Law, Justia, Google Scholar, and fee-based legal databases.
- Official decisions are published in West's *Federal Supplement*, citations look like: 984 F. Supp. 1288 (decisions from the free websites are cited by party names only).

U.S. Courts of Appeals
- Called appellate courts; 13 circuits (first through eleventh, DC, and federal).
- Recent decisions published on the particular court's website (see http://www.uscourts.gov/courtlinks/), and also in the Public Library of Law, Justia, Google Scholar, and fee-based legal databases.
- Official decisions are published in West's *Federal Reporter*, citations look like: 169 F. 3d 646 (decisions from the free websites are cited by party names only).

U.S. Supreme Court
- Final court of appeals for federal and state cases.
- Decisions 1937–1975 and 1992–2000 online in Supreme Court decisions database via FDsys; 1991– available online at Supreme Court website at http://www.supremecourtus.gov/. All historical Supreme Court Cases back to 1893 available via Public Library of Law, Justia, Google Scholar, and fee-based legal databases.
- Official decisions are published in *United States Reports*; citations look like: 206 U.S. 285.

International Law and Treaties

According to Article VI of the Constitution,

> This Constitution, and the laws of the United States which shall be made in pursuance thereof; and all treaties made, or which shall be made, under the authority of the United States, shall be the supreme law of the land; and the judges in every state shall be bound thereby, anything in the Constitution or laws of any State to the contrary notwithstanding (U.S. Constitution, art. 6).

So treaties are the final major piece of the law. The Constitution further assigns the task of negotiating treaties to the president (or those he designates), who then submits the treaty to the Senate. If the Senate ratifies the treaty, the treaty has the force of law.

There are generally two types of treaties: bilateral treaties, between two nations, which are often on specific topics such as trade or extradition; and multilateral treaties, which are between multiple nations, and usually cover global issues such as human rights, oceans, or the Antarctic. To cite a famous example of the treaty process, the United States signed the Kyoto Protocol on climate change in 1998, but the Senate never ratified it (actually, no president ever even presented it to the Senate to consider for ratification), so the United States' signature on the treaty is largely symbolic, and the treaty is not law in the U.S.

Until 1950, all treaties to which the United States was a party were published in the *U.S. Statutes at Large*. Two early volumes, volumes seven and eight, include all treaties from 1776 to 1845. Beginning in 1950, *United States Treaties and Other International Agreements (UST)* became the official compilation of ratified treaties. *UST* lags far behind currency; recent treaties are published in slip form (individually) in the set *Treaties and Other International Acts Series (TIAS)*. For content prior to 1950, you can also refer to *Treaties and Other International Acts of the United States 1776–1949*. This set is often known by the name of its editor, Bevans, and is available via HeinOnline. The *United Nations Treaty Series* (UNTS) is a standard compilation of treaties, bilateral and multilateral, worldwide.

Treaties in Force lists and indexes treaties to which the United States is a party, and is available online or in print, updated annually. It contains two sections: bilateral treaties (i.e., treaties between the United States and one other country) and multilateral treaties (multiple countries). The bilateral section is arranged first by country, and then by subject; the multilateral section is arranged by subject. Each treaty contains its title, date, and citation in *TIAS*, *UST*, or the *U.S. Statutes at Large*, and the *UNTS*, as appropriate. The free *UNTS* database is searchable by name, participant, or full text.

In-depth treaty research is often best done with the more robust treaty resources available via the fee treaty databases in Lexis, HeinOnline, TIAO, or Westlaw. A useful free resource is EISIL: Electronic Information System for International Law (http://www.eisil.org/), from the American Society for International Law, which includes many multilateral treaties and agreements.

Finally, the International Court of Justice (also known as ICJ or the World Court) arbitrates certain disputes between nations and about treaties. ICJ rulings, unlike treaties ratified by the Senate, are not necessarily law in the United States.

For excellent research guides on a number of international law topics, see the American Society of International Law's ASIL Electronic Resources Guide (http://www.asil.org/erghome.cfm).

Foreign Law

The nature of and access to foreign countries' law is as varied as the governments of the world's nations. Non-law libraries can find some foreign law free online. The big fee-based legal databases Lexis and Westlaw also include some foreign law, but are in no way comprehensive. Some countries' law is extremely difficult to find. But many countries do publish their law free online. The Global and Comparative Law Resources from the Law Library of Congress (http://www.loc.gov/law/find/global.php) is an excellent place to begin this search. New York University's GlobaLex (http://www.nyulawglobal.org/globalex/index.html) also offers excellent guides for many jurisdictions.

Further Legal Research Resources

Legal research is the subject of its own entire books. What do you do if you need to go further with legal research than this chapter's introduction? A great starting place is the Public Library Toolkit (http://www.aallnet.org/sis/lisp/toolkit.htm), prepared by the Legal Information Services to the Public Special Interest Section of the American Association of Law Libraries. It includes a short guide, "How to Research a Legal Problem"; guides for each state list important sources (print and online) and law libraries in the state with their referral policies. A wide variety of guides is available on LLRX.com (http://www.llrx.com/) and Zimmerman's Research Guide (http://law.lexis nexis.com/infopro/zimmermans/).

Good, accessible texts on legal research include the following:

- Cohen, Morris L., and Kent C. Olson, 2010. *Legal Research in a Nutshell.* 10th ed. St. Paul, MN: West.
- Elias, Stephen. 2009. *Legal Research: How to Find and Understand the Law.* 15th ed. Berkeley: Nolo.
- Olsen, Kent C. 2009. *Principles of Legal Research.* St. Paul, MN: West.
- Barkan, Stephen, Roy Mersky, and Donald Dunn. 2009. *Fundamentals of Legal Research.* 9th ed. St. Paul, MN: West.

Conclusion

Many law and legal needs are properly referred to law libraries, law librarians, and lawyers. However, the law is a fundamental aspect of government information; perhaps *the* fundamental piece of government information. It is important and necessary to understand how law is created (Chapter 3), and how it is published and codified, and how all the pieces fit together with compilations, codifications, and cases.

Exercises

1. After the 2009 financial crisis and recession, a patron wants to see the "bailout" law and the "stimulus" law. What are the official titles for each of these? What are the public law numbers? What are the *U.S. Statutes at Large* citations?

2. A patron sees on http://www.healthcare.gov/ that the health care plan of 2010 includes a provision to provide health insurance to citizens denied coverage because of a preexisting condition. First, find the official title and public law number of the health care law. Using the public law, find the referred provision about coverage for those denied because of preexisting conditions. Cite the place in the *U.S. Code* where this particular section will go.

3. A number of states have passed laws legalizing marijuana for some medical uses. What is the name and website of the codification of California laws? In this codification, find and cite the section regarding legal, medical use of marijuana.

4. A patron believes that "Freon" is banned or regulated to protect the ozone layer. Find and cite the *U.S. Code* section that lists substances that are banned or managed so as to reduce damage to the ozone layer. What is the statutory authority for this section of the *U.S. Code* (list the public law(s)/*Statutes at Large* citation)? What is the name of the public law that most recently updated this list?

5. Cite the Supreme Court decision that is credited with striking down sodomy laws. Find the text of the official decision online and include the URL. Cite the decision that the Supreme Court was considering (the case that was appealed to the Supreme Court). Of the nine justices, list who wrote the opinion of the court, who wrote any concurring opinions, and who wrote any dissenting opinions.

Sources Mentioned in This Chapter

Sources mentioned in this section do not duplicate the References that follow.

Administrative Office of the U.S. Courts. PACER, Public Access to Court Electronic Records. http://pacer.psc.uscourts.gov/.

Congress, Office of Law Revision Counsel. *United States Code Classification Tables*. Washington, DC: U.S. Congress, Office of Law Revision Counsel. http://uscode.house.gov/uscct.htm/.

Cornell Law School, Cornell Legal Information Institute, http://www.law.cornell.edu/.

Google Books, http://books.google.com/.

Google Scholar, http://scholar.google.com/.

Government Printing Office. FDsys (Federal Digital System). http://www.gpo.gov/fdsys.

Government Printing Office. 2006. *United States Code*. Washington, DC: Government Printing Office. http://www.gpoaccess.gov/uscode/index.html. Also available at http://www.law.cornell.edu/uscode.

Government Printing Office. 1875–. *United States Statutes at Large*. Washington, DC: Government Printing Office (1789–1874 published by Little, Brown). Recent volumes available at http://www.gpo.gov/fdsys/; unofficial historical volumes at http://www.constitution.org/uslaw/sal/sal.htm.

Justia, http://www.justia.com/.

Lexis Total Research System, http://www.lexis.com/.

LexisNexis Academic, http://www.lexisnexis.com/us/lnacademic/.

Library of Congress. *A Century of Lawmaking for a New Nation: Statutes at Large.* http://memory.loc.gov/ammem/amlaw/lwsl.html.

Oyez Project, http://www.oyez.org/.

PACER (Public Access to Court Electronic Records), http://www.pacer.gov/.

The Public Library of Law, http://www.plol.org/.

RECAP U.S. Federal Court Documents, http://www.archive.org/details/usfederal courts/.

Supreme Court. 1790–. *United States Reports.* Washington, DC: U.S. Supreme Court. http://www.supremecourtus.gov/opinions/boundvolumes.html.

United Nations. 1946–. *United Nations Treaty Series.* New York: United Nations.

United States. 1789. *The Public Statutes at Large of the United States of America from the Organization of the Government in 1789, to March 3, 1845.* Boston: Charles C. Little and James Brown. http://purl.access.gpo.gov/GPO/LPS52578.

United States. 1799. *Laws of the United States.* Washington, DC: Folwell.

United States. 1941–. *Treaties in Force: A List of Treaties and Other International Acts of the United States In Force On. . . .* Washington: Government Printing Office. http://www .state.gov/s/l/treaty/tif/index.htm.

United States. 1946. *Treaties and Other International Acts Series.* Washington, DC: Department. of State. Limited online access: http://www.state.gov/s/l/treaty/tias/index .htm.

United States. 1950. *United States Treaties and Other International Agreements.* Washington, DC: Department of State.

West Campus Research. http://campus.westlaw.com/.

West Publishing. 1880–. *Federal Reporter.* St. Paul, Minn: West Publishing.

West Publishing. 1933–. *Federal Supplement.* St. Paul, Minn: West Publishing.

Westlaw, http://www.westlaw.com/.

William S. Hein & Co, HeinOnline, http://www.heinonline.org/.

References

Bintliff, Barbara. 2007. "Context and Legal Research." *Law Library Journal* 99, no. 2 (Spring): 249–66. http://www.aallnet.org/products/pub_llj_v99n02/2007-15.pdf.

Knapp, Jeffrey. 2009. "Legal Research: An Introduction to Key Online and Print Sources." *Choice* 46, no. 8: 1439–1449.

Morehead, Joe. 1999. "Citation Wars." *The Reference Librarian* 31, no. 65: 125–136.

Chapter 6

The President

We owe it, therefore... to declare that we should consider any attempt on their part to extend their system to any portion of this hemisphere as dangerous to our peace and safety.

Four score and seven years ago our fathers brought forth, upon this continent, a new nation...

Let me assert my firm belief that the only thing we have to fear is fear itself, nameless, unreasoning, unjustified terror...

I believe that this nation should commit itself to achieving the goal, before this decade is out, of landing a man on the moon and returning him safely to the earth.

—Presidential Speeches

Introduction

These are wonderful, famous quotes from speeches given by United States presidents. Are the speeches easy to locate? What about the other speeches and writings from the presidents? Go beyond the very public statements and think about memos to generals, cabinet secretaries, and more. What about orders that may be signed by the president dealing with issues of national security—can we get those? What about letters to family members, loved ones, or even girlfriends? And what about 100 years ago? Can we get all of the documentation from, say, the Wilson administration?

Think about what you know of the daily activities of the president. He gets up; eats breakfast; works out or goes for a run; goes into the Oval Office; writes or signs letters, laws, or other documents; meets with cabinet secretaries; lunches with someone, maybe the vice president or legislative leaders; reviews drafts of policies and upcoming speeches; meets with more people, maybe even the National Security Council; goes out to a dinner and makes a speech; and goes back to the residence and works some more. That is, of course, if the president is home for the day. If the president is outside of Washington, DC, there may be more speeches, meetings, photo opportunities, and dinners with foreign dignitaries or heads of state. Every minute is scheduled and letters, papers, speeches, memoranda, and more come from the White House every day. In fact, the *Compilation of Presidential Documents* lists more than 120 different items coming from the White House in June 2010. This includes the weekly addresses, letters to Congress, remarks at different events, notices, messages, memoranda, and more. A remarkable output for one person—and that is just what is documented on the FDsys website.

Once you've thought about the president's daily life, think about major events—national disasters and catastrophes, the State of the Union address, inaugurations, press conferences, or responses to the death of an important person. For each of these, the president is looked to for a statement or for action. The presidency is a big job, and has gotten bigger and bigger through the years as demands on the president's time have increased. The first administration of President Truman had fewer than 75 public appearances annually, while President Clinton, in 1993–1994, had more than 350 (Ragsdale, 1996). And these are just the documented public events; that figure doesn't include all of the meetings, phone calls, and other items of business that make up a president's day.

Where does it all start—what exactly is the president's job and from what does presidential authority stem? It starts with the powers invested in the president by the Constitution, which are heavily intertwined in checks and balances between the branches of government. For instance, the president can propose laws and veto legislation, but the Congress makes law; the president appoints judges and high-ranking executive branch officials, but the senate confirms the appointments; the president is the commander in chief of the armed forces, while Congress has the power to declare war and to appropriate defense funding; the president can negotiate treaties, but the Senate must ratify any treaties before they take force; the president oversees the executive branch, but Congress passes laws to create and govern the executive branch, as well as—here it is again—to authorize budgets, a power that cannot be underestimated (CQ Press, 2008: vii).

Presidential power has grown over the years, as reflected in books such as *The Growth of Presidential Power: A Documented History* by William Goldsmith (1974), and the *Powers of the Presidency* (2008), both of which discuss presidential power using the same types of divisions: unilateral powers of the presidency, chief of state, chief administrator, legislative leader, chief diplomat, commander in chief, and chief economist. Reviewing those constitutional powers can explain a lot of the way the presidential powers are divided and discussed, and watching the published daily activities of the president can tell you a lot about what is going on.

President's Schedule

July 27, 2010

9:45 a.m.	The President receives the Presidential Daily Briefing.
10:00 a.m.	The President receives the Economic Daily Briefing.
11:00 a.m.	The President meets with bipartisan members of Congress.
12:00 p.m.	The President delivers a statement to the press.
12:20 p.m.	The President has lunch with House Members.
3:05 p.m.	The President congratulates the Warner Robins Softball World Series Champions.
4:00 p.m.	The President meets with Secretary of the Treasury Geithner.
4:30 p.m.	The President meets with Secretary of Defense Gates.
7:00 p.m.	The President attends a DNC Fundraising Dinner.

(*Source*: "President's Schedule, The White House, July 27, 2010." http://www.whitehouse.gov/schedule/president/2010-07-27/.)

So how and where is all of this activity documented? There is now a well-established White House press corps to document the president's activities for the news world—be it via television, newspapers, blogs, or the Internet. Internally, there are other methods of organizing and collecting all of the documentation, which includes personal diaries, letters, memos, and records of all of the activities of office, and White House staff is assisted in organizing this material for posterity by staff from the National Archives—from the material's creation to its deposit at the National Archives at the conclusion of the presidential term of office.

While past presidents may not have thought in terms of saving papers and correspondence for posterity, the passage of the Presidential Records Act (PRA) of 1978 (see p. 144, Ownership of Presidential Documents) changed the ownership of the materials from private, belonging to the president, to public, belonging to the nation. Under 36 C.F.R. 1270.30, the president must first consult the archivist of the United States before disposing of papers.

Presidential Documents

In an article from 1974, librarian Arnold Hirshon wrote that presidential documents could be divided into four categories: public, executively controlled, official, and personal. Looking for papers, speeches, and other documents, it is easy to see that the presidents have done a rather haphazard job of collecting this information for posterity prior to the PRA. Martin Van Buren burned correspondence he deemed of little value, while Millard Fillmore directed his executor to burn all family correspondence (Hirshon, 1974: 380, 382). Teddy Roosevelt was the first president to present his papers to the Library of Congress in 1917. Prior to that, the Library of Congress had simply purchased most of the papers from former presidents or their heirs.

Speeches such as the State of the Union and inaugural addresses have always been easy to find, and there are many privately printed compilations of these as well as those produced by government. Other materials have proven more challenging. Reviewing Hirshon's division of types of documentation makes it easier to ascertain which papers will be easy to find, which may take more digging, and which may be close to impossible (1974). Those divisions are examined in more detail here.

Public Papers and Speeches

These documents relate to the public role of the president—the speeches such as the State of the Union message, news conferences, press releases, executive orders and proclamations, and other materials released by the White House. All of these are considered in the public domain and may be relatively easy to find.

Executive orders and proclamations belong to a broader grouping of documents known as presidential directives—that is, the president directing some action. Executive orders and proclamations are not defined in law, but most executive orders relate to how the government works, while most proclamations announce something.

It would seem from this that most executive orders, as they may be considered inward facing, wouldn't affect the general population; however, that isn't true. They have a larger significance as, for example, E.O. 9066, issued by President Roosevelt on February 19, 1942, directs the "Secretary of War, and the Military Commanders to prescribe military areas in such places and of such extent as he or the appropriate Military Commanders may determine, from which any or all persons may be excluded...." This was the executive order that was used to round up those of Japanese ancestry living on the West Coast for internment (Roosevelt, 1942).

Proclamations tend to be more celebratory in nature and may be used to announce holidays, commemorative months, and other occasions. The sidebar shows examples of some presidential proclamations and executive orders.

Proclamations and Executive Orders from January 2007

- Executive Order 13422—Further Amendment to Executive Order 12866 on Regulatory Planning and Review
- Executive Order 13423—Strengthening Federal Environmental, Energy, and Transportation Management
- Executive Order 13424—Further Amendment to Executive Order 13285, Relating to the President's Council on Service and Civic Participation
- Proclamation 8099—Martin Luther King, Jr., Federal Holiday, 2007
- Proclamation 8100—Religious Freedom Day, 2007
- Proclamation 8101—National Sanctity of Human Life Day, 2007
- Proclamation 8102—Fifth Anniversary of USA Freedom Corps, 2007
- Proclamation 8103—National African American History Month, 2007

(*Source*: FDsys.gov, *Compilation of Presidential Documents*, January 2007.)

Executive orders, compilations, speeches, and other communications are currently funneled into at least one (or more) of four established outlets: the White House website, Whitehouse.gov; the *Public Papers of the Presidents of the United States* (a bound compilation of presidential papers and records); the (formerly weekly, now daily) *Compilation of Presidential Documents*; and the *Federal Register* (for executive orders, proclamations, and directives only). Depending on the import of a speech or appearance, it may also be in newspapers such as the *New York Times* and the *Washington Post*. All public papers are, and remain, in the public domain.

Executively Controlled Documents

Executively controlled documents are those created by other agencies in the executive branch, but over which the president, as chief executive, has authority. Documents in this category include the daily briefings, memos, and other materials from various executive branch agencies.

There is no clear channel by which these executively controlled documents move into the public domain, as they are not strictly controlled by the president and don't fit into the sources used for public papers. Some may be unclassified or released by the agency through normal procedures, and others may be produced when a sitting or former president releases them. Probably the biggest concern for researchers needing this material is that, like the other document categories that follow (Official Papers and Personal Papers), there is no single place to locate these documents, once released— they may show up on an agency website, or a newspaper, but there is no central source.

The daily briefing, the first meeting of the president's day, is a national security update on foreign intelligence and domestic terrorism. It is now noted on the schedule (see sidebar on p. 138), and first came to light "... with the disclosure that President Bush was informed by the August 6 (2001) version that terrorists associated with Osama bin Laden might try to hijack an airplane" (Pincus, 2002: A33). While the presidential daily briefings, or PDB, have apparently been going on for years, very little is known of the briefings and what they contain. There are, however, several websites containing unattributed content providing background on the PDB. Pincus continues "one irony about the public flap over the Aug. 6 PDB item is that it has highlighted a long-standing argument about the CIA's determination to keep all PDBs from being turned over to anyone not on its distribution list."

Another example of executively controlled material is the March 14, 2003, opinion on interrogation from John Yoo while serving in the (G.W.) Bush Administration's Office of Legal Counsel in the Department of Justice. The Yoo memo (Yoo, 2003), "Military Interrogation of Alien Unlawful Combatants Held Outside the United States," is referenced in many congressional hearings, but actually finding a copy on government websites is difficult, if not impossible. After the 2008 declassification of the memo, it is much easier to find on nongovernmental websites; however, a version from an official government source is still difficult to come by. There are many reasons why this 81-page memo is considered controversial, many of which were brought up in the press, on blogs, and by Congress. Principal among these was the claim in the memo that the president was above the law (*Los Angeles Times*, 2008). With claims like these, it's no wonder the president wanted to keep this memo classified and that Congress (and the press) wanted to examine it.

A president may claim executive privilege to withhold information if it is requested. In the George W. Bush administration, there were more instances of this than prior administrations. For background on this trend, as well as its overall effect on government, check the Secrecy News site, a service of the Federation of American Scientists (http://www.fas.org/blog/secrecy/). In 2007, Pulitzer Prize–winning newspaper reporter Charlie Savage released a book-length consideration of this topic, and presidential power in general, in *Takeover: The Return of the Imperial Presidency and the Subversion of American Democracy* (Savage, 2007). It is a lively and well-documented read on both executive privilege and how the White House works behind the scenes.

Unlike the executive orders and proclamations discussed earlier, some presidential directives fall into the category of executively controlled documents, as they are "cloaked in official secrecy" (Relyea, 2008: 2). Over the years, depending on the president and the purpose, these directives from the president have been referred to by different titles such as National Security Directives, National Security Action Memoranda, Presidential Review Directives, and Presidential Decision Directives. Some of these may not see the light of day for 25 years or longer. A Congressional Research Service report describes such activities for each administration, starting with Eisenhower, and gives some details about the nature and number of directives and what they are called, making it easier for the reader to infer whether or not the directives are public or classified (Relyea, 2008: 9–12). One example from the Nixon administration may demonstrate the kinds of material gathered and usage of that material by the president:

> When Richard Nixon became President, he appointed Henry Kissinger as his national security advisor. Kissinger recruited a substantial and influential NSC staff, and they produced national security position papers which were designated National Security Study Memoranda (NSSM). They were developed through the use of various interdepartmental working groups composed of high level representatives from pertinent agencies. Beginning with a study answering 26 questions on Vietnam, multiple NSSMs were immediately assigned.... The NSSMs were among the resources used by the President when determining national security policy, which he would express in National Security Decision Memoranda (NSDM). (Relyea, 2008: 10)

Another group of presidential directives stem from the president's National Security Council (NSC). The NSC was created by the National Security Act of 1947 and has been revised many times. The NSC advises the president "with respect to the integration of domestic, foreign, and military policies relating to the national security so as to enable the military services and the other departments and agencies of the Government to cooperate more effectively in matters involving the national security" (50 U.S.C. 402).

One of the things the NSC does is to direct intelligence, and these directives are particularly hard to come by in a timely fashion. For example, a top-secret memo dated December 9, 1947 (declassified March 30, 1983), "instructs the CIA director to initiate and conduct covert psychological operations designed to counteract Soviet and Soviet-inspired activities that threaten world peace" (*Index*, 1994: 7).

In trying to review the NSC directives, a report from the General Accounting Office states:

> Because NSC did not give us access to the directives we could not analyze NSDs [national security directives] issued by the [George H.W.] Bush administration. We do not know how many NSDs have been issued by the Bush administration, but we do know that 51 were issued

through the fall of 1990. We examined unclassified NSC summaries of five NSDs issued by the administration and concluded that four of the five NSDs make U.S. policy. (General Accounting Office, 1992: 1)

The report goes on to say:

> Most of the directives issued during the Truman and Eisenhower administrations (1947–69) have been declassified and are maintained in the National Archives and Records Administration. In contrast, most of the presidential directives written since 1961 remain classified, and details about them are largely unavailable for congressional or public scrutiny.
>
> In 1988 we issued a report on the use of presidential directives to make and implement U.S. policy. The report includes an analysis of the directives that were publicly released between 1961 and 1988. We found that at least 1,042 presidential directives had been issued, and 247 had been publicly released. We also found that 116, or about half of the 247 examined served three functions; they established policy, directed the implementation of policy, and/or authorized the commitment of government resources. (General Accounting Office, 1992: 2)

Some unclassified national security directives may be found at the Federation of American Scientists' website (http://www.fas.org/). The Homeland Security Directives of the George W. Bush administration are found in the *Weekly Compilation of Presidential Documents* and on the (now archived) White House website from his administration (Relyea, 2008: 15–16). Finally, University Press of America has a microfilm collection entitled *Documents of the National Security Council* that contains many of the documents created for the NSC.

Official Papers

Papers in this category are also referred to as private papers or White House files. Papers may contain draft proposals, personal notes, memoranda, personal correspondence, and other documents that circulate behind the scenes and are directly related to the particular president's work. Hirshon further divides these into two categories: working papers, and records of office. Working papers are stuff that surrounds office life—drafts of speeches, interoffice communications, and memoranda. The records of office are the historical files that Hirshon claims "do not bear directly upon the actions of the president, but which provide a chronicle of those actions" (Hirshon, 1974: 368). Examples include audio recordings, diaries, and notes of meetings.

Official papers are of great interest to those trying to see just where a particular thought or phrase entered a policy, or who actually said what in a meeting, as recollections months or years later often prove fuzzy. In fact, it was the release of the tapes from the Nixon White House that seemed to hasten the resignation of President Nixon. Perhaps the realization that everyone would be privy to exactly what had been said regarding the Watergate break-in and the attendant cover-up provided the impetus.

Personal Papers

Finally, we have personal papers. Hirshon quotes Chief Justice Marshall: "Letters to the president in his private character, are often written to him in consequence of his public character, and may relate to public concerns" (1974: 371). Certainly there are types of documents that are personal in nature—notes between spouses, love letters, and now e-mails. Hirshon notes in his appendix that "in 1964 there was a dispute over 'love letters' which President Harding had sent to Carrie Phillips. These letters cannot be disclosed until 2014 due to a court order" (1974: 387).

Often controversy surrounds these documents because they give a view of the president and his character unseen by the public. In the twenty-first century we have new concepts of privacy because of what may be shared on social networking sites and via texts and tweets from cell phones, but these discussions are not new to the White House, where it seems that everything the president says and does may be considered of interest.

Controversies

Ownership of Presidential Documents

Often presidents' heirs have controlled papers, resulting in instances like the case of an heir to George Washington's cutting up fragments of documents to give to requestors for anything "that bears the impress of his venerated hand" (Hirshon, 1974: 372) and Martha Washington's burning almost all of her correspondence with her husband.

While Theodore Roosevelt was the first president to give his papers to the Library of Congress, his was not the first set of papers collected there. In fact, with a few exceptions, the Library of Congress has been relatively successful in collecting papers of the presidents. (For background on the disposal of presidential papers, see Hirshon, 1974: 377–389). Online guides to holdings of presidential papers include the following:

- The Miller Center of Public Affairs at the University of Virginia, http://www.millercenter.org/scripps/onlinereference/presidentialpapers/
- The Library of Congress (see the LC Archival Finding Aids by name of president), http://www.loc.gov/rr/mss/f-aids/mssfa.html

Prior to 1974, the materials from a term of office were considered the president's property. With the criminal proceedings against Nixon, Congress passed the Presidential Records and Materials Preservation Act (P.L. 93-526) on December 19, 1974, some four months after Nixon's resignation. Papers that had been impounded as evidence in the Watergate hearings were transferred to the General Services Administration. The law also abrogated an agreement giving Nixon ownership of his papers, and established the National Study

Commission on Records and Documents of Federal Officials. The commission explored issues of ownership, control, disposition, and preservation of historical materials (Schick, 1989: 16). President Nixon challenged this law, but lost in 433 U.S. 425 (1977), *Nixon v. Administrator of General Services.*

The Presidential Records Act (PRA) of 1978, P.L. 95-591, based on the work of the commission, was amended by P.L. 98-497 (44 U.S.C. 2201-2207) and governs the official records of presidents and vice presidents created or received after January 20, 1981—everything from Ronald Reagan forward. In essence, the PRA changed the legal ownership of the official records of the president from private to public, and established a new statutory structure under which presidents must manage their records.

Specifically, the Presidential Records Act:

- Defines and states public ownership of the records.
- Places the responsibility for the custody and management of incumbent Presidential records with the President.
- Allows the incumbent President to dispose of records that no longer have administrative, historical, informational, or evidentiary value, once he has obtained the views of the Archivist of the United States on the proposed disposal.
- Requires that the President and his staff take all practical steps to file personal records separately from Presidential records.
- Establishes a process for restriction and public access to these records. Specifically, the PRA allows for public access to Presidential records through the Freedom Of Information Act (FOIA) beginning five years after the end of the Administration, but allows the President to invoke as many as six specific restrictions to public access for up to twelve years. The PRA also establishes procedures for Congress, courts, and subsequent Administrations to obtain special access to records that remain closed to the public, following a thirty-day notice period to the former and current Presidents.
- Requires that Vice-Presidential records are to be treated in the same way as Presidential records. (National Archives and Records Administration, 2010a)

To date, the PRA has been amended by three different executive orders, each revoking the previous one: E.O. 12667 (54 Fed. Reg. 3403, January 1989); E.O. 13233 (66 Fed. Reg. 56025); and E.O. 13489 (74 Fed. Reg. 4669). Reading these executive orders, and all of the detail contained, can make one's eyes roll when trying to figure out the nuances and the differences. E.O. 12667 and E.O. 13489, issued by President Reagan and President Obama, respectively, appear relatively straightforward. The second executive order, E.O. 13233, issued by President George W. Bush, differs from the executive orders before and after in, among other things, citing *Nixon v. Administrator of General Services* in establishing precedent for a "demonstrated, specific need" for access to particular records, as well as a lot more detail in all areas of implementation. Bush also added the final bullet to the list, bringing vice presidential records in line with those of incumbent or former presidents (Bush, 2001).

Versions aside, where these issues get really interesting is with the disclosure of records relating to individuals who have served in multiple administrations. Two examples from nominees to the Supreme Court serve to illustrate the issues. Supreme Court Justice Elena Kagan worked first for President Clinton as associate counsel to the president (1995–1996) and then as deputy assistant to the president for domestic policy and deputy director of the Domestic Policy Council (1997–1999). An earlier nominee to the Supreme Court, Harriet Miers, served as White House counsel for George W. Bush before he nominated her to the court.

Why does it get interesting? Members of the Senate get to confirm presidential appointments, and, as part of the confirmation process, the Senate can ask to review documentation that was generated under the current or previous administrations and has been attributed to the nominee. Presidents can be generous, or stingy, in allowing the memos and other material to be a part of that confirmation process. For the nomination of Elena Kagan, President Obama and former President Clinton allowed the release of the thousands of documents from the Clinton administration. With Harriet Miers, however, when the Senate called for release of documents related to her service, incumbent President George W. Bush declined, "deeming it an infringement of executive privilege" (Baker and Murray, 2005: A01) to a great hue and cry in the press. However, the documents were never released. Who is to say if this had an impact on the process that resulted in the withdrawal of her nomination?

It is safe to say that the declassification of classified materials from the White House is an ongoing saga, and will likely continue. A note on the Bush Library website reminds users of current restrictions: "The George W. Bush Presidential records are governed by the Presidential Records Act (PRA). Under the provisions of the PRA, George W. Bush Presidential records are not available to public access requests for the first five years after the end of the Administration. George W. Bush Presidential records will become subject to Freedom of Information Act requests on January 20, 2014" (National Archives and Records Administration, 2010b).

The (Weekly) Compilation of Presidential Documents

With the Obama administration, the *Weekly Compilation of Presidential Documents* became more simply known as the *Compilation of Presidential Documents* or CPD (and is now updated continuously rather than weekly). The compilation (1965–present) was originally issued every Monday and contains statements, messages, and other presidential material released by the White House press secretary during the preceding week (see Figure 6.1).

The lack of official editorial standards has come into play at least once in determining what is printed in the *Weekly Compilation*. Donald Smith detailed a controversy in the Reagan administration when Deputy Press Secretary Larry Speakes admitted to fabricating presidential comments that were then included in the series. Smith writes, "not all off–the–cuff remarks are included—or are they? Moreover, readers do not know who officially makes, and thereby has

---

Figure 6.1. President Obama's Remarks on Signing the Lilly Ledbetter Fair Pay Act of 2009, from January 29, 2009, *Compilation of Presidential Documents*

Administration of Barack H. Obama, 2009

Remarks on Signing the Lilly Ledbetter Fair Pay Act of 2009
January 29, 2009

All right, everybody please have a seat. Well, this is a wonderful day. First of all, it is fitting that the very first bill that I sign—the Lilly Ledbetter fair pay restoration act—that it is upholding one of this Nation's founding principles: That we are all created equal and each deserve a chance to pursue our own version of happiness.

It's also fitting that we're joined today by the woman after whom this bill is named; someone who Michelle and I have had the privilege to get to know ourselves. And it is fitting that we are joined this morning by the first woman Speaker of the House of Representatives, Nancy Pelosi. It's appropriate that this is the first bill we do together. We could not have done it without her. Madam Speaker, thank you for your extraordinary work—and to all the sponsors and Members of Congress and leadership who helped to make this day possible.

Lilly Ledbetter did not set out to be a trailblazer or a household name. She was just a good, hard worker who did her job, and she did it well, for nearly two decades before discovering that for years she was paid less than her male colleagues for doing the very same work. Over the course of her career, she lost more than $200,000 in salary and even more in pension and Social Security benefits; losses that she still feels today.

Now, Lilly could have accepted her lot and moved on. She could have decided that it wasn't worth the hassle and the harassment that would inevitably come with speaking up for what she deserved. But instead, she decided that there was a principle at stake, something worth fighting for. So she set out on a journey that would take more than 10 years, take her all the way to the Supreme Court of the United States, and lead to this day and this bill which will help others get the justice that she was denied.

Because, while this bill bears her name, Lilly knows that this story isn't just about her. It's the story of women across this country still earning just 78 cents for every dollar men earn—women of color even less—which means that today, in the year 2009, countless women are still losing thousands of dollars in salary, income, and retirement savings over the course of a lifetime.

Equal pay is by no means just a women's issue; it's a family issue. It's about parents who find themselves with less money for tuition and child care; couples who wind up with less to

---

responsibility for, decisions concerning what is released" (Smith, 1989: 215). Those who were around in the 1980s will remember that President Reagan, during a microphone test, said, "My fellow Americans, I'm pleased to tell you I just signed legislation which outlaws Russia forever. The bombing begins in five minutes." This gaffe was covered heavily in the press, and yet doesn't appear in any compilations of his papers—perhaps because, as noted by Doder in the *Washington Post*, "White House spokesman Larry Speakes continued to insist that the remark was off the record and as such would not be acknowledged by the White House. 'I have not commented on it and I don't intend to,' he said, according to United Press International" (1984: A26). Another quote, President Clinton's response to the question of "boxers or briefs," was, in fact,

included in the *Weekly Compilation*, as it was a question asked during an appearance on MTV (Clinton, 1994: 848).

Today's scholars can take some comfort in resources such as C-SPAN to replay important speeches and DVRs to record them. These may be checked against the official transcriptions of each public interaction. Whether or not more such documented instances occur, the ability to rewrite history is certainly worth keeping in mind as users and librarians alike look for what was actually reported in the *Weekly Compilation of Presidential Documents*.

Signing Statements

A more recent controversy, though not a recent issue, concerns presidential signing statements. While to the casual reader, the concept of a signing statement might be any speech that a president makes while signing a piece of legislation, the term *signing statement* has come to have a very specific meaning. Halstead (2007: summary) explains that presidential signing statements:

> are official pronouncements issued by the president contemporaneously to the signing of a bill into law that, in addition to commenting on the law generally, have been used to forward the President's interpretation of the statutory language to assert constitutional objections to the provisions contained therein and, concordantly, to announce that provisions of the law will be administered in a manner that comports with the Administration's conception of the President's constitutional prerogatives.

According to Halstead, the first signing statement belonged to Andrew Jackson in 1830 when he claimed

> but as the phraseology of the section which appropriates the sum of $8,000 for the road from Detroit to Chicago may be construed to authorize the application of the appropriation for the continuance of the road beyond the limits of the Territory of Michigan, I desire to be understood as having approved this bill with the understanding that the road authorized by this section is not to be extended beyond the limits of the said Territory" (2007: 2). (Jackson, 1830)

However, Woolley (2010) claims that Monroe issued the first signing statement in 1822! Signing statements remained rare through the Roosevelt administration, but President Truman issued nearly 16 signing statements per year, and the number has gone up with each succeeding administration (Halstead, 2007).

It was during the Reagan administration that the presidents began to use signing statements to assert the "constitutional prerogatives of the presidency" (Halstead, 2007: 3), both to question the constitutionality of certain laws and to direct executive branch agencies in their actions. The controversy gained most ground during the George W. Bush presidency as he used signing statements "to insulate executive power from congressional and judicial oversight, especially in matters pertaining to national and homeland security" (Nelson, 2008: 181).

On April 30, 2006, Charlie Savage of the *Boston Globe* published ten examples of the president's signing statements. One of the most discussed signing statements was in response to Congress passing H.R. 2863 (which, after being signed by the president, became P.L. 109-148), Article X of which is known as the Detainee Treatment Act of 2005. This section of the law says that prisoners of war (i.e., detainees) "shall not be subject to any treatment or technique of interrogation not authorized by and listed in the United States Army Field Manual on Intelligence Interrogation" (119 Stat. 2739). The signing statement, under the title "President's Statement on Signing of H.R. 2863, the Department of Defense, Emergency Supplemental Appropriations to Address Hurricanes in the Gulf of Mexico, and Pandemic Influenza Act, 2006," states:

> The executive branch shall construe Title X in Division A of the Act, relating to detainees, in a manner consistent with the constitutional authority of the President to supervise the unitary executive branch and as Commander in Chief and consistent with the constitutional limitations on the judicial power, which will assist in achieving the shared objective of the Congress and the President, evidenced in Title X, of protecting the American people from further terrorist attacks.

In Savage's words, "The president, as commander in chief, can waive the torture ban if he decides that harsh interrogation techniques will assist in preventing terrorist attacks" (Savage, 2006). Talking about the number and import of the Bush signing statements Halstead notes:

> The qualitative difference in the Bush II approach becomes apparent when considering the number of individual challenges or objections to statutory provisions that are contained in these statements. Of President Bush's 152 signing statements, 117 (78%) contain some type of constitutional challenge or objections, as compared to 70 (18%) during the Clinton Administration. Even more significant, however, is the fact that these 188 signing statements are typified by multiple constitutional and statutory objections, containing challenges to more the 1,000 distinct provisions of law. (Halstead, 2007: 9)

While the long-term effect of the signing statements is not yet decided, signing statements work, in effect, as a line-item veto; the statements are telling the executive branch what will and won't be done as regards enforcing the law, even though the Constitution doesn't give the president the right to veto specific provisions in the laws he is signing (Rudalevige, 2008). Halstead notes that the Take Care clause in the Constitution (Article II, section 3, clause 3: the president "shall take Care that the Laws be faithfully executed"), judicial precedent, and the participation of the president in the initial drafting of legislation imply that signing statements lack persuasive authority; he states, "there is little evident support for the notion that signing statements are instruments with legal force and effect in and of themselves" (Halstead, 2007: 15). This doesn't mean, of course that there hasn't been an outcry in the press and in Congress, as there have been several hearings on the matter. As with the other issues discussed in this section, there are more chapters to be written before the issue is decided.

Signing statements are considered public documents and, as such, are available through the *Compilation of Presidential Documents*, the *Public Papers of the Presidents of the United States*, or the *Compilation of Messages and Papers of Presidents, 1789–1897*, and online through the online equivalents of these publications and the American Presidency Project. For those interested in following this issue, Green (2010) has a list of presidential signing statements from 2001 with citations to the [*Weekly*] *Compilation of Presidential Documents*.

Presidential Libraries

While many politicians have donated or sold their papers to archives, since the 1950s there has been a system of presidential libraries. As noted earlier, the maintenance of presidential papers of all kinds had been haphazardly handled. Franklin Roosevelt thought that the presidential papers were an important part of the national heritage and should be accessible to the public (National Archives, 2010c). Roosevelt used the Rutherford B. Hayes library as a model for his idea, and developed the concept of presidential libraries constructed and equipped with private funds and administered by the National Archives (Schick, 1989: 6). President Truman asked archivist Wayne Grover to "insert a clause into the draft of the proposed Federal Records Act that would make it possible for presidents and high government officials to deposit their papers in the National Archives" (Schick, 1989: 10–11).

The passage of the Presidential Libraries Act in 1955 (P.L. 84-373, 69 Stat. 695) allowed living and future presidents to create libraries for their papers, and set up the libraries as field branches of the National Archives. These field branches were built with private funds, but are federally maintained. Prior to 1955 there were seven presidents with papers in historical libraries or other special libraries, and since that date, 13 presidential libraries have been established, as President Hoover also established a library after passage of the act (this was in addition to the Hoover Institution at Stanford University).

It wasn't until the Presidential Records Act (PRA) of 1978 that the government took legal ownership of the papers; the Presidential Libraries Act allowed for deposit of the papers, not ownership. A subsequent law, the Presidential Libraries Act of 1986 (P.L. 99-323, 100 Stat. 495), required endowments for each library created, and made some attempt at limiting the size of the libraries so as to control costs. The 1986 legislation created the interesting situation of placing the president in the role of fund raiser. It also allows the archivist of the United States to solicit funds for these libraries.

The libraries (and they also serve as museums) often reflect the interests of the president, with the Roosevelt library having interests in naval history, and the Carter library showing evidence of his strong interest in human rights. Each of the libraries now has a website hosted by the National Archives; see http://www.archives.gov/presidential-libraries/ for a complete listing. The Hoover Library website currently has posted an orientation film hosted by his great-granddaughter, shows information about current exhibits, shows lesson plans emphasizing primary resources for students, and has some games (including a trivia game about the states, allowing the unwary to while away hours crossing the country with First Lady Lou Hoover), while the recently created George W. Bush Library website is still in its initial stages.

Sources for Speeches and Publications from the Executive Office

Listing every possible source for presidential speeches and publications, from *Vital Speeches of the Day* to one's local hometown newspaper, would be an over-whelming prospect. With a few exceptions, this list will focus on official sources for these publications, as they are widely available at depository libraries (with notes indicating online availability). Where available, Super-intendent of Documents (SuDocs) classifications are listed; however, individual libraries may classify these with their non-documents collections.

Compilations

The *Code of Federal Regulations*, or *CFR* (Title 3, The President) contains pres-idential proclamations and executive orders from 1936 forward. The first exec-utive order included in Title 3 is #7316 (March 13, 1936). The first proclamation included in Title 3 is #2161 (March 19, 1936). Title 3 of the *CFR* is the only title of the set that does not get replaced annually—proclamations and executive orders are published chronologically, and so are not codified like the rest of the *CFR*. As with all of the other materials in the *CFR*, these materials are posted initially in the *Federal Register*, or *FR*, and then printed in the *CFR*.

Availability: The *CFR* and the *FR* are widely available in print and online through public and commercial sites. Most depository libraries have good col-lections of Title 3 of the *CFR*, print may be classified as SuDoc: GS 4.108/2, and *CFR* (1997–) is online at http://www.gpo.gov/fdsys/browse/collectionCfr .action?collectionCode=CFR. The *FR* is online (1994–present) at http://www .gpo.gov/fdsys/browse/collection.action?collectionCode=FR, and the print may be classified as SuDoc: AE 2.7, or GS 4.107.

There is also a codification of presidential proclamation and executive orders at the National Archives website (http://www.archives.gov/federal-register/ codification/index.html) spanning 1945–1989; it was distributed to depository libraries under the SuDocs number AE 2.13:. Note: when searching by date in the *Federal Register*, be sure to search for dates beyond the date of issuance as it may take some time for things to appear. For example, Executive Order 13491 (Ensuring Lawful Interrogation) was signed by President Obama on January 22, 2009, but wasn't printed until another five days later, on January 27.

Compilation of Messages and Papers of Presidents, 1789–1897 is also known as the Richardson Set. In April 1895, James Richardson, a representative from

Tennessee, was charged with compiling all of the official papers of the presidents; to this end, ten volumes were produced from 1896 to 1899.

This compilation contains most of the presidential papers through Cleveland's second administration ending March 4, 1897. The index volume (volume 10) also contains many of the papers of the earlier presidents which were omitted in their proper place and the papers of President McKinley relating to the Spanish-American War. Sadly for those hoping for comprehensive coverage, there are interesting omissions, such as Lincoln's Gettysburg Address. Users researching presidential materials from this first century will probably need materials in addition to this compilation. This compilation was updated in an edition published by the Bureau of National Literature to include presidents Benjamin Harrison through Woodrow Wilson. Because there was both a public version and a repaginated privately published version, citations may prove confusing. A more comprehensive review of this title is available in Schmeckebier (1939: 311).

Availability: As with other materials from this time period, it was included in both the *Congressional Serial Set* (volumes 3265-1 through 3265-10, as H. misdoc 210) and printed separately and given the SuDocs classification Y4.P93/1:3/(volume number). Hathi Trust has posted the edition from the Bureau of National Literature, available at http://catalog.hathitrust.org/Record/001137867, and other editions may be available online.

Executive orders are a special challenge to researchers. The first executive order was issued in 1789, but none was numbered or issued uniformly until 1907. At that time, the State Department began a numbering system and designated an 1862 order as executive order #1. Orders issued between 1789 and 1862 are referred to as unnumbered executive orders. There was no governmental compilation of executive orders prior to the 1930s (when they were included in the *CFR*), so in the 1980s the Congressional Information Service created the *CIS Index to Presidential Executive Orders* (with an accompanying microfiche set). The compilation provides access to some 75,000 orders from 1789 to 1983. (Note: CIS was acquired by LexisNexis in 1988, and those product lines were acquired by ProQuest in 2010.)

The **Public Papers of the Presidents of the United States** (1929–1933, 1945–present) is published by the Office of the Federal Register (OFR) and is the official publication of United States presidents' public writings, addresses, and remarks (see Figure 6.2). Each volume contains that year's papers and speeches of the president of the United States issued by the Office of the Press Secretary. This title does, in fact, overlap in coverage with the *Compilation of Presidential Documents*. Prior to the 1977 volume, the *Public Papers of the Presidents* was an edited version of the *Compilation of Presidential Documents*. Beginning with the Carter administration, the *Public Papers* were expanded to include virtually all materials published in the *Compilation*, plus a color photographic section.

Availability: Beginning in 1991 (George H.W. Bush), the series is available at http://www.gpo.gov/fdsys/browse/collection.action?collectionCode=PPP. The University of Michigan Digital Library has a complete series at http://quod.lib.umich.edu/p/ppotpus. Print versions may be classified as SuDoc: GS 4.113.

Figure 6.2. President Eisenhower's Remarks upon Signing the Proclamation Admitting Alaska to the Union

Dwight D. Eisenhower, 1959 ¶ 4

3 ¶ Remarks Upon Signing the Proclamation Admitting Alaska to the Union and the Executive Order Changing the Flag of the United States. *January* 3, 1959

GENTLEMEN, I think that all of us recognize this as an historic occasion. Certainly for myself I feel very highly privileged and honored to welcome the forty-ninth State into the Union.

Such a ceremony has not taken place in almost half a century, so at least I have the feeling of self-gratification that I am not just one of a group in this kind of ceremony.

To the State itself, to its people, I extend on behalf of all their sister States, best wishes and hope for prosperity and success. And to each of you gentlemen elected to high office to represent your new State, in both State and Federal offices, my congratulations, my felicitations, and my hope that we will all work together to the benefit of all forty-nine States.

Certainly, I pledge to you my cooperation in that effort.

And now, as far as these pens are concerned, I hope there's one for each of you people who has worked so hard to bring this about.

NOTE: The ceremony was held in the Cabinet Room at noon. Among those present were Senators-elect E. L. Bartlett and Ernest Gruening, Representative-elect Ralph J. Rivers, Acting Governor Waino Hendrickson, Michael A. Stepovich, former Governor of Alaska, and Robert Atwood, Publisher of the Anchorage Daily Times.

The new 49-star flag, to become official on July 4, was unfurled immediately after the President signed the documents.

Proclamation 3269 "Admission of the State of Alaska into the Union" and Executive Order 10798 "Flag of the United States" are published in the Federal Register (24 F.R. 79 and 81, respectively).

Source: From *Public Papers of the Presidents*, 1959.

The *Compilation of Presidential Documents* (1965–present) was originally issued every Monday and contains statements, messages, and other presidential material released by the White House during the preceding week. It includes such material as proclamations, executive orders, speeches, press conferences, communications to Congress and federal agencies, statements regarding bill signings and vetoes, appointments, nominations, reorganization plans, resignations, retirements, acts approved by the president, nominations submitted to the Senate, White House announcements, and press releases. Prior to the Carter administration, materials in the *Weekly Compilation* were not necessarily included in the *Public Papers of the Presidents*, so libraries needed to keep both titles to ensure a complete record. Starting with the Obama administration, on January 29, 2009, the *Weekly Compilation* has been replaced by the *Daily Compilation of Presidential Documents*.

Availability: From 1993 to present at http://www.gpo.gov/fdsys/browse/collection.action?collectionCode=CPD, SuDoc: GS 4.114.

And don't forget the *Congressional Record* (and predecessors) and the *Serial Set* (both covered in Chapter 3). While we typically think of the *Record* as a place to find congressional debates, votes, sometimes the texts of bills, and more, the *Record* includes many important speeches, documents, and correspondence from the president and executive departments. The Gettysburg Address, for example, is found there on January 16, 1895 (although its inclusion was 32 years after the actual address!). State of the Union addresses are also included in the *Record* (because they are delivered to Congress) and the *Serial Set*, as are many more pieces of correspondence and speeches. These congressional sources are widely held by libraries, with commercial digital editions available, and so are important sources when researching the presidency.

The State of the Union, Inaugural Addresses, Vetoes, and More

Article II, section 3 of the Constitution says the president "shall from time to time give to the Congress information of the state of the union, and recommend to their consideration such measures as he shall judge necessary and expedient...." This **state of the union** is one of the few constitutional requirements of the president; as a result, copies of these speeches are thick on the ground by comparison with other materials from the president. It is interesting to note that until the twentieth century, these speeches may not have been actually delivered in front of Congress (though some were), but may have been sent to Congress in written form. Because this is information delivered to Congress, these also appear in the *Congressional Record* (and its predecessors, the *Congressional Globe*, the *Register of Debates in Congress*, and the *Annals of Congress*); in the *Congressional Serial Set* and predecessor *American State Papers*; and, of course, in the *Public Papers of the Presidents* and the Richardson compilation. Online, they are available from 1790 forward at the American Presidency Project (http://www.presidency.ucsb.edu/).

Inaugural addresses are also quite easy to come by. They are in the Richardson compilation, in the *Public Papers of the Presidents*, and at the American Presidency Project, and some are reproduced in the *Serial Set* individually. There are also occasional volumes produced by (congressional) inaugural committees that compile all of the addresses, such as *Inaugural Addresses of the Presidents of the United States from George Washington 1789 to George Bush 1989* (the latest was printed as Senate document 101-10).

There are many individual **veto messages** printed as part of the *Serial Set* and the *Compilation of Presidential Documents*. Two committee prints, *Presidential Vetoes, 1789–1988* (SuDoc: Y1.3:S.Pub.102-12) and *Presidential Vetoes, 1989–2000* (SuDoc: Y1.3:S.Pub.107-10) provide a comprehensive list of all vetoes to 2000, indicate if there was a message along with the veto (and provide a document number), and note whether the veto was sustained or overridden.

Internet Sites

The **American Presidency Project** (http://www.presidency.ucsb.edu/), located at the University of California, Santa Barbara, was established in 1999 and currently contains more than 88,000 documents related to the presidency. While this is the best gathering of materials available online, it focuses on the public papers (speeches, executive orders, and so on) gathered from the various compilations, so will generally not have the type of material outlined in the other categories: the executively controlled, official, or personal papers.

WhiteHouse.gov, the official website of the president, is something of a mixed blessing. It is a great resource for materials on the sitting president, including speeches, press releases, featured legislation, photos, and the schedule. Unfortunately, once a president leaves office, no resources, other than biographical material of previous presidents and first ladies and similar material, stays on that site—it is essentially wiped clean with each new administration. Older material is captured by the National Archives and migrated to the presidential libraries section of the National Archives website (http://www.archives.gov/presidential-libraries/).

Declassified Documents Reference System (DDRS), a commercial product from the Gale Group, is a growing collection of more than 100,000 declassified documents from presidential libraries. Many of the documents in this file fall into the executively controlled category and contain White House confidential files as well as material from the CIA, FBI, the National Security Council, and more. Material in the database dates back to the years immediately following World War II, when declassified documents were first made widely available, and now reaches into the 1980s. Nearly every major foreign and domestic event of these years is covered: the Cold War, the Vietnam War, foreign policy shifts, the civil rights movement, and more. The documents range in size and scope from telegrams, correspondence, and unevaluated field reports to lengthy background studies and detailed minutes of cabinet level meetings.

Conclusion

What does the president do in a day? More than just sign laws or give speeches—though that is part of the job. Foreign affairs, executive orders, proclamations, policies—all of these are the result of public and private meetings and "strategery." Presidential documents are an interesting mix of public and executively controlled documents—and with every word and action being documented for posterity, they keep researchers busy.

Exercises

1. When listening to the news or reading the paper, listen for mentions of the president and think about which of the four categories of presidential documentation may apply to that particular news story.
2. If a researcher wants a letter from Teddy Roosevelt to his wife, where would you look? What about correspondence with John Muir?

3. The day after an inaugural address, where would you look for the speech text? What are your options six years later?
4. If the president sends a BlackBerry message to a cabinet secretary, which of Hirshon's categories of documents does this fall into?
5. Of the ten George W. Bush signing statements detailed in Charlie Savage's article, which do you think is most important? Has Barack Obama issued any signing statements indicating disagreement with the legislation he is signing?

Sources Mentioned in This Chapter

Sources mentioned in this section do not duplicate the References that follow.

Executive Orders and Legislation (Chronological Order)

Presidential Libraries Act of 1955, P.L. 84-373, 69 Stat. 695 (1955).
Presidential Records and Materials Preservation Act, P.L. 93-526, 88 Stat. 1695 (1974).
Presidential Records Act of 1978, P.L. 95-591, 92 Stat. 2523 (1978).
National Archives and Records Administration Act of 1984, P.L. 98-497, 98 Stat. 2280, 44 U.S.C. § 2201-2207 (1984).
Presidential Libraries Act of 1986, P.L. 99-323, 100 Stat. 495 (1986).
Exec. Order No. 12,667, 54 Fed. Reg. 3403 (January 16, 1989).
Exec. Order No. 13,233, 66 Fed. Reg. 56025 (November 1, 2001).
Department of Defense, Emergency Supplemental Appropriations to Address Hurricanes in the Gulf of Mexico, and Pandemic Influenza Act, 2006–, P.L. 109-148, 119 Stat. 2680 (2005); Title X is known as the Detainee Treatment Act of 2005.
Exec. Order No. 13,489, 74 Fed. Reg. 4669 (January 21, 2009).

Other Sources

American Presidency Project, http://www.presidency.ucsb.edu/.
CFR, Title 3, The President. http://purl.access.gpo.gov/GPO/LPS494; SuDoc: AE 2.106/3:3 (online) or GS 4.108/2.
CIS Index to Presidential Executive Orders & Proclamations 1789–1983. Washington, DC: Congressional Information Service, c1986–c1987.
Codification of Presidential Proclamation and Executive Orders (1945–1989), http://www.archives.gov/federal-register/codification/index.html.
Compilation of Messages and Papers of Presidents, 1789–1897, available as *Serial Set* volumes 3265-1 through 3265-10 (H. misdoc 210); printed separately as SuDoc: Y4.P93/1:3/; online as http://catalog.hathitrust.org/Record/001137867.
Compilation of Presidential Documents (1965–present), http://purl.access.gpo.gov/GPO/LPS1769; SuDoc: AE 2.109: (online) or GS 4.114.
Congressional Record, http://purl.access.gpo.gov/GPO/LPS1671; SuDoc: X 1.1/A:.
Declassified Documents Reference System (DDRS), http://www.gale.cengage.com/.

FDsys, http://www.fdsys.gov/.

Federal Register, http://www.gpo.gov/fdsys/browse/collection.action?collectionCode= FR; SuDoc: AE 2.106 (online), AE 2.7, or GS4.107.

Inaugural Addresses of the Presidents of the United States from George Washington 1789 to George Bush 1989 (S.doc. 101-10), SuDoc: Y 1.1/3:101-10.

Library of Congress Archival Finding Aids by Name, http://www.loc.gov/rr/mss/f-aids/ mssfa.html.

Miller Center of Public Affairs at the University of Virginia, http://www.millercenter .org/scripps/onlinereference/presidentialpapers/.

New York Times, http://www.nytimes.com/.

Nixon v. Administrator of General Services, 433 U.S. 425 (1977).

Presidential Libraries (National Archives), http://www.archives.gov/presidential- libraries/.

Presidential Vetoes, 1789–1988, SuDoc: Y1.3:S.Pub.102-12.

Presidential Vetoes, 1989–2000, SuDoc: Y1.3:S.Pub.107-10.

Public Papers of the Presidents of the United States (1929–1933, 1945–present) available at http://www.gpo.gov/fdsys/browse/collection.action?collectionCode=PPP (1991–), complete series at University of Michigan Digital Library, http://quod.lib.umich .edu/p/ppotpus; SuDoc: AE 2.114: (online) or GS 4.113.

Savage, Charlie. 2006. "Examples of the President's Signing Statements." *Boston Globe*, April 30. http://www.boston.com/news/nation/articles/2006/04/30/examples_ of_the_presidents_signing_statements/.

Savage, Charlie. 2007. *Takeover: The Return of the Imperial Presidency and the Subversion of American Democracy*. New York: Little, Brown.

Secrecy News, Federation of American Scientists, http://www.fas.org/blog/secrecy/.

University Press of America. 1980–2004. *Documents of the National Security Council*, mul- tiple supplements.

U.S. *Congressional Serial Set*, http://purl.access.gpo.gov/GPO/LPS839, Final bound ver- sion SuDoc: Y 1.1/2:.

Washington Post, http://www.washingtonpost.com/.

WhiteHouse.gov, including the President's Schedule, http://www.whitehouse.gov/ schedule/president/2010-07-27.

References

Baker, Peter, and Shailagh Murray. 2005. "Bush Defends Supreme Court Pick; President Reassures Conservatives on a Range of Issues." *Washington Post*, October 5: A01.

Bush, George W. Exec. Order No. 13,233, 66 Fed. Reg. 214 (November 5, 2001).

Clinton, William J. 1994. "Interview on MTV's 'Enough is Enough' Forum" *Weekly Com- pilation of Presidential Documents*. April 19: 836-49. http://www.gpo.gov/fdsys/ pkg/WCPD-1994-04-25/pdf/WCPD-1994-04-25-Pg836.pdf.

CQ Press. 2008. *The Powers of the Presidency*, 3rd ed. Washington, DC: CQ Press.

Doder, Dusko. 1984. "President Said to Voice 'His Secret Dream'; Moscow Calls Reagan's Quip 'Self-Revealing.'" *Washington Post*, August 15: A26.

Executive Power and Its Constitutional Limitations: Hearing Before the Committee on the Judiciary. 110th Cong. 2 (2008).

Gale Group. 2008. "Declassified Documents Reference System Fact Sheet." http://www
.gale.cengage.com/pdf/facts/ddrs.pdf.

Goldsmith, William M. 1974. *The Growth of Presidential Power: A Documented History.*
New York: Chelsea House.

Green, Joyce A. 2010. "List of Laws Subjected to Presidential Signing Statements."
Coherentbabble.com. Accessed August 31. http://www.coherentbabble.com/list
LAWSall.htm.

Halstead, T.J. 2007. *Presidential Signing Statements: Constitutional and Institutional Implications.* Washington, DC: Congressional Research Service. http://www.fas.org/
sgp/crs/natsec/RL33667.pdf.

Hirshon, Arnold. 1974. "The Scope, Accessibility, and History of Presidential Papers."
Government Publications Review 1: 363–390.

*Impact of the Presidential Signing Statement on the Department of Defense's Implementation of
the Fiscal Year 2008 National Defense Authorization Act: Hearing Before the Oversight and
Investigations Subcommittee of the Committee on Armed Services.* 110th Cong. 2 (2008).

Index to Documents of the National Security Council. 1994. Bethesda, MD: University Publications of America.

Jackson, Andrew. 2010. "Special Message, May 30, 1830." The American Presidency Project. Accessed August 25. http://www.presidency.ucsb.edu/ws/?pid=66775.

Los Angeles Times. "Torture Memos: How Did We Get Here? Justice Department Writings
Reveal the Origins of 'Enhanced' Interrogation." April 4, 2008. http://articles
.latimes.com/2008/apr/04/opinion/ed-yoo4.

National Archives and Records Administration. 2010a. "Presidential Records Act (PRA)
of 1978." Accessed July 23. http://www.archives.gov/presidential-libraries/laws/
1978-act.html.

National Archives and Records Administration. 2010b. "George W. Bush Presidential
Library." Accessed July 23. http:// www.georgewbushlibrary.gov/.

National Archives and Records Administration. 2010c. "Presidential Libraries, A Brief
History." Accessed August 23. http://www.archives.gov/presidential-libraries/
about/history.html.

National Security: The Use of Presidential Directives to Make and Implement U.S. Policy
(GAO/NSIAD-92-71). Washington, DC: U.S. General Accounting Office, 1992.

Nelson, Michael, ed. 2008. *CQ Guide to the Presidency,* 4th ed. Washington DC: CQ Press.

Pincus, Walter. 2002. "Under Bush, the Briefing Gets Briefer: Key Intelligence Report by
CIA and FBI Is Shorter, 'More Targeted,' Limited to Smaller Circle of Top Officials
and Advisers." *Washington Post,* May 24: A33.

Presidential Speeches:
  Lincoln, Abraham. "National Military Park, Gettysburg, PA." 27 Cong Rec, 1039 (1895).
  Monroe, James. *Message of the President of the United States, at the commencement of the
    First Session of the Eighteenth Congress.* American State Papers (ASP05 For.rel.360),
    December 2, 1823.
  Roosevelt, Franklin. "First Inaugural Address, Saturday, March 4, 1933." In *Inaugural
    Addresses of the Presidents.* Washington, DC: Government Printing Office, 1989.
  Special Message to the Congress on Urgent National Needs, 107 Cong. Rec. 8887 (1961).

Ragsdale, Lyn. 1996. *Vital Statistics on the Presidency: Washington to Clinton*. Washington, DC: Congressional Quarterly.

Relyea, Harold C. 2008. *Presidential Directives: Background and Overview*. Washington, DC: Congressional Research Service, Government and Finance Division. November 26, 2008. ProQuest Congressional Research Digital Collection.

Roosevelt, Franklin. Exec. Order No. 9,066, 42 Fed. Reg. 1563 (February 19, 1942). http://www.presidency.ucsb.edu/ws/?pid=61698.

Rosenberg, Morton. 2008. *Presidential Claims of Executive Privilege: History, Law, Practice and Recent Developments*. Washington, DC: Congressional Research Service, American Law Division. August 21. ProQuest Congressional Research Digital Collection.

Rudalevige, Andrew. 2008. "Unilateral Powers of the Presidency." In *CQ Guide to the Presidency*, 4th ed, edited by Michael Nelson, 511–540. Washington, DC: CQ Press.

Savage, Charlie. 2006. "Examples of the President's Signing Statements." *Boston Globe*, April 30.

Schick, Frank L., Renee Schick, and Mark Carroll. 1989. *Records of the Presidency: Presidential Papers and Libraries from Washington to Reagan*. Phoenix: Oryx Press.

Schmeckebier, Laurence F. 1939. *Government Publications and Their Use*. Washington DC: Brookings Institution.

Smith, Donald C. 1989. "The Rhetoric of the *Weekly Compilation of Presidential Documents*: 'We Make that Decision on a Daily Basis.'" Government Publications Review 16: 213–217.

Woolley, John T. 2010. "Presidential Signing Statements, Hoover—Obama, Frequently Asked Questions." The American Presidency Project. Accessed August 25. http://www.presidency.ucsb.edu/signingstatements.php.

Yoo, John, 2003. "Memorandum for William J. Haynes II, General Counsel of the Department of Defense, Re: Military Interrogation of Alien Unlawful Combatants Held Outside the United States." United States Department of Justice, Office of the Deputy Assistant Attorney General, Washington, DC. March 14. http://www.aclu.org/files/pdfs safefree/yoo_army_torture_memo.pdf.

Informational Note

On November 30, 2010, ProQuest announced its acquisition of the Congressional Information Services (CIS) and University Publications of America (UPA) product lines from LexisNexis. The ProQuest announcement indicated that, beginning in 2011, LexisNexis Congressional will be renamed ProQuest Congressional and LexisNexis Statistical Insight will be renamed ProQuest Statistical Insight.

Part II
Government Information in Focus

Chapter 7

The Executive Branch

Introduction

Few librarians have the time to sit and think intentionally about the executive branch of government. Many may have a mental diagram of the three branches of government, perhaps with the executive branch represented by an image of the White House. Although the Executive Office of the President resides in the executive branch, so do hundreds of other agencies. The executive branch is a coordinated group of agencies authorized by Congress to carry out the laws of the land (see Chapter 4 for a discussion of the executive branch's regulatory function). Notably, it contains no elected officials, with the exception of the president and vice president. We refer to this executive sector of government as administrative, or with a word that may have negative connotations: bureaucratic. Bureaucracy is governance "in which most of the important decisions are taken by state officials rather than by elected representatives" (*Oxford Dictionary of English*, 2005). One hallmark of democratic governments is this exact mix of government branches: elected, administrative, and judicial/appointed. The organization of U.S. federal departments and agencies has changed dramatically over the decades. Some relatively recent changes include the establishment of the Department of Veterans Affairs (upgraded to a department from Veterans Administration); the Department of Homeland Security (established in January 2003 by the Homeland Security Act of 2002, P.L. 107-296); the Bureau of Ocean Energy Management, Regulation, and Enforcement (formerly Minerals Management Service); and the coordination of intelligence agencies into an Intelligence Community, with the Office of the Director of National Intelligence (DNI) beginning its operations in April 2005 (Office of the Director of National Intelligence, 2010).

Executive branch literature offers readers an unparalleled view of government functioning over the years, and a glimpse of American society of the time. Think of the stories government agency publications might tell during just the twentieth century:

- The development of federal guidelines for modern aviation by a Hoover Administration bureau, the Aeronautics Branch
- World War II–era War Relocation Authority manuals providing instruction on the relocation and internment of those of Japanese ancestry
- Atomic Energy Commission and later Nuclear Regulatory Commission reports revealing the brave new world of nuclear energy and warfare
- The surgeon general's report in January 1964 demonstrating with clinical evidence the negative health effects of smoking

- The declassified Department of Energy reports showing the government radiation experiments conducted on human subjects without proper consent
- The public remarks of Federal Reserve Chair Alan Greenspan, to which stockbrokers and homeowners alike listened with bated breath in the booming 1990s
- USDA pamphlets promoting household cleaning methods now seen as unsafe (see Figure 7.1)

Learning about executive branch structure can strengthen the overall information skills of any librarian or information specialist.

To better understand the executive branch, the adventuresome librarian could start by becoming more familiar with the names and functions of government agencies. It makes sense to start with the agencies most relevant to one's everyday work, and be willing to learn about agencies that are complete mysteries. Perhaps you have already heard of the Office of Head Start or the National Eye Institute, but what about the National Portrait Gallery, the Federal Grain Inspection Service, or the Migratory Bird Conservation Commission? This is not to neglect the U.S. Military Academy at West Point, the Prints and Photographs Division of the Library of Congress, the Office for Victims of Crime, the Secret Service, the Selective Service, the St. Lawrence Seaway Development Corporation, or the Institute of Peace. All of the aforementioned federal entities have a publishing history, are represented in the SuDocs numbering scheme, have had their publications distributed to depository libraries, and, in addition, are actively publishing online.

It's in the Details

The simple details of American daily life reveal the pervasive presence of the bureaucratic state—the dollars in our wallets, printed by the Treasury Department; the peanut butter we eat, subsidized and regulated by the U.S. Department of Agriculture (USDA); the pain medications we take, approved and governed by the Food and Drug Administration (FDA); the cars we drive, produced in factories regulated by the Occupational Safety and Health Administration (OSHA) and themselves regulated by the Environmental Protection Agency (EPA) and the National Highway Traffic Safety Administration; the national parks and forests, in which we ski, fish, hike, hunt, climb, and camp, governed by the Forest Service and the Department of Interior; and the $425.3 billion in checks that our elderly and disabled receive annually from the Social Security Administration.

—Professor Daniel Carpenter of Harvard University (Carpenter, 2005: 41)

The work of many specific executive agencies is scattered throughout this book, such as the Bureau of Labor Statistics in Chapter 8, Statistical Information; the Department of Health and Human Services in Chapter 9, Health Information; the Department of Education in Chapter 10, Education Information; the Environmental Protection Agency in Chapter 12; the National Archives and Records Administration in Chapter 16, Historical and Archival Information; and so forth.

Figure 7.1. Excerpt from a 1949 USDA Consumer Pamphlet That Encouraged Americans to Spray the Insecticide DDT, Banned since 1972 as a Harmful Substance, Directly onto Mattresses and Baseboards in the Home

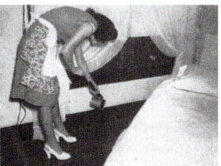

Treating Mattress for Bedbugs   Spraying Baseboard for Bedbug Control

A pair of guides should be in every librarian's arsenal for understanding federal executive branch structure, both already mentioned in this book. First is the A–Z list of agencies at http://www.usa .gov/Agencies/Federal/All_Agencies/index .shtml, and second is the *U.S. Government Manual.* For decades, the opening chapters of the *Manual* have included the Declaration of Independence, the Constitution, and an organizational chart of the federal government (see Figure 7.2). It does not get much simpler than this, in terms of starting places. A third guide, a print-only publication, *Guide to U.S. Government Publications*, is for those truly desiring a comprehensive look at federal publishing patterns as reflected in the depository library program. The book, long referred to as Andriot after its original editors, is organized by agency and SuDoc class stem (the part of the classification number before the colon). It provides a list of series titles and types of materials published under each SuDoc stem, inclusive dates, and importantly, agency genealogy—which agencies have ceased, which have changed names, and which new ones have been established, with the exact chronology. With a quick glance at Andriot, one can discover that the Office of Federal Employees' Compensation existed only from 1972 to 1974; produced three different types of publications (annual reports, general publications, and pamphlets); and was replaced by the Office of Workers' Compensation Programs (Batten, 2010).

Cabinet-Level Departments

Under the large central box in Figure 7.2, the executive office of the president, small boxes show the 15 departments frequently referred to as cabinet-level agencies. Although the cabinet is a top-level advisory body, Bledsoe and Rigby point out that "membership in the president's cabinet is not limited to the secretaries of the executive departments . . . presidents are free to promote any

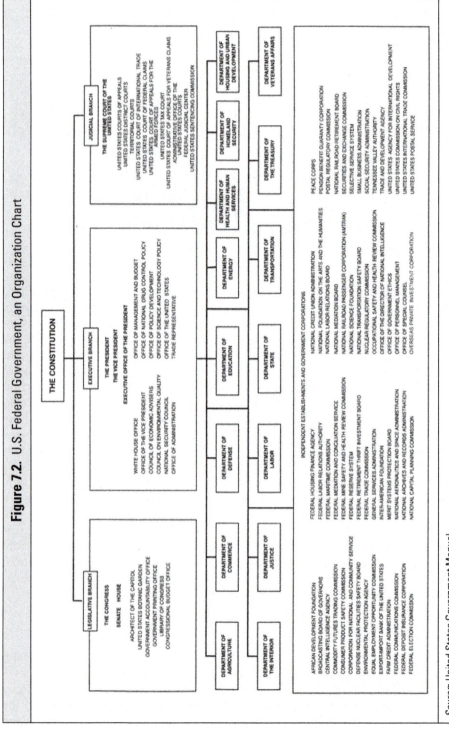

Figure 7.2. U.S. Federal Government, an Organization Chart

Source: United States Government Manual.

[other] government official they please to cabinet-rank status" (1997a: 77). Since the earliest days of our government, four of the departments have been those pertaining to foreign affairs (Department of State), military affairs (Department of Defense), the legal system (Department of Justice), and fiscal affairs (Department of Treasury). Today, each executive department is headed by a secretary (except for Justice, headed by the attorney general). Secretary positions are filled via nomination by the president, with confirmation following in the Senate. According to Article II, Section 2 of the U.S. Constitution, the president "shall nominate, and with the advice and consent of the Senate, shall appoint...Officers of the United States" but may allow agency heads to appoint their own "inferior officers" as needed (Bledsoe and Rigby, 1997b: 145). (Today, *The U.S. Government Policy and Supporting Positions*, also known as the Plum Book, available via http://www.fdsys.gov/, lists over 7,000 presidentially appointed federal employees, excluding the judges of the judicial branch—it is released after every change in presidential administrations.) Each department contains a number of agencies and subordinate offices; these are described in the *Government Manual*, in numerous other general guides to government, and on the agencies' own websites. Although it is conceivable that a government agency might exist that would be wholly uninteresting to the public or to librarians, the authors have not found one yet. There is simply too close a tie between government functioning and our everyday lives.

Independent Agencies and Government Corporations

Beneath the cabinet-level departments is a box listing the independent agencies and government corporations (see Figure 7.2), those that do not fall under a larger department. The chief administrators and governing boards of these agencies are accountable to Congress and the president, and are required to post updates in the *Federal Register*. Some of the best known of these include the Environmental Protection Agency, the Nuclear Regulatory Commission, the Peace Corps, and the U.S. Postal Service. Bledsoe and Rigby (1997b) group these bottom-listed agencies into three categories: regulatory agencies (example: the Federal Trade Commission or FTC, which regulates broadcast media), independent executive agencies (example: National Aeronautics and Space Administration or NASA), and government corporations (example: the

> **The U.S. Postal Service**
>
> The creation of post offices was originally called for by Article I, Section 8 of the Constitution, and for decades the Post Office was part of the president's cabinet. With the passage of the Postal Reorganization Act of 1970 (P.L. 91-375), the U.S. Postal Service became an independent federal agency, with an appointed board of governors, and the postmaster is no longer an automatic member of the cabinet. Although the agency needs to be self-sustaining over time, supporting itself by charging for postage and other products and services, it cannot close down rural post offices simply because they don't make money: it is a government agency mandated to connect the nation by relaying correspondence.

National Railway Passenger Corporation or AMTRAK). "A government corporation has a board and directors and managers, but it does not have any stockholders ... [one] cannot buy shares of stock. If the government corporation makes a profit, it does not distribute the profit as dividends [nor does it pay taxes on the profits, the profits remain with the corporation]" (Schmidt, 2009: 503). Although an administrator of these freestanding executive branch units may or may not serve in the president's cabinet, some such administrators have been quite well known: George W. Bush appointed former New Jersey governor Christine Todd Whitman as EPA administrator, for example.

The Quasi-Government

There's actually a misleading aspect to the organizational chart (Figure 7.2). Not all federally affiliated entities are included. One can find dozens more listed in the *Budget of the United States* and in the back of the *U.S. Government Manual* under "Boards, Commissions, and Committees," "Quasi-Official Agencies," "Selected Multi-Lateral Organizations," and "Selected Bilateral Organizations," with a further note that the *Manual* completely omits yet another category: federal advisory commissions. None of these are found on the organizational chart, perhaps for visual simplicity, but also because some are more nongovernmental than governmental. Their creation was mandated and/or partly funded by Congress, but their operations and infrastructure resemble a private, for-profit organization, except that their initial charters may include extra benefits or privileges not usually accorded the private sector, and their activities are proscribed by their government charters. Scholars have dubbed this sector "the quasi-government."

One could categorize the array of quasi-governmental agencies on a numbered scale, with 1 being a purely governmental agency (both its funding and mission generated by government); 2 being a "quago" (mostly a government organization with some private sector attributes, for example the Legal Services Corporation); 3 being a "quango" (a private organization with some governmental sector attributes, such as the Red Cross); and 4 being a purely private organization (funding and mission established privately) (Moe, 2005). Quasi-governmental agencies would fall in a range of fine gradations within 2 and 3, due to the many different types of organizations. The Boy Scouts of America, for example, cannot be considered purely private. The Boy Scouts were granted a federal charter in 1916 (P.L. 64-94); they must forever remain nonprofit and file a report to Congress on April 1 each year detailing their activities (this can be found in the *Serial Set*). Thanks to the law, they retain sole and exclusive rights to their name and their emblem. As the Congressional Research Service notes, "There is nothing modest about the size, scope, and impact of the quasi government. Time will tell whether the emergence of the quasi government is to be viewed as a symptom of decline in our democratic government, or a harbinger of a new, creative management era where the purported artificial barriers between the governmental and private sectors are breached as a matter of principle" (Moe, 2005: 2).

CRS analysts trace the era of the quasi-government era back to the establishment of the Communications Satellite Corporation (ComSat) in 1962 (Moe, 2005: 5). Other examples of the quasi-government are government-sponsored enterprises (GSEs), hybrid financial structures such as the Federal Home Loan Bank System and the Farm Credit System. These exhibit legal characteristics of both public and private fiscal organizations. Quasi-government entities are not agencies as defined by Title 5 of the *United States Code*. For an extremely detailed discussion of this topic, consult *The Quasi Government: Hybrid Organizations with Both Government and Private Sector Legal Characteristics* (Moe, 2005).

Publications of Executive Branch Agencies

Agency Mission Is Paramount

Want to learn more about an agency's information output? First consider its purpose. Agencies are established by law and funded by Congress to carry out specific missions. For example, taxpayers expect the Internal Revenue Service to help us "understand and meet...tax responsibilities and enforce the law with integrity and fairness to all" (Internal Revenue Service, 2010), but not to establish new taxes or a higher rate of taxation (Congress does that) or to produce a fresh supply of pennies, nickels, and other coins (the job of the U.S. Mint). The National Institute of Occupational Safety and Health (NIOSH, an institute within the Centers for Disease Control and Prevention) conducts research to help prevent work-related injury and illness, so it is not surprising that it has produced both a four-page consumer fact sheet on worker illnesses at indoor water parks (NIOSH, 2010) and a detailed 64-page *Investigation of Employee Symptoms at an Indoor Waterpark* (NIOSH, 2008). However, one would look to the Occupational Safety and Health Administration (OSHA), primarily a regulatory rather than a research agency, for an online database of federal safety interventions at workplaces (http://www.osha.gov/pls/imis/establishment.html). One can search this OSHA database for interventions at Great Wolf Lodges, other indoor waterparks, or any place of employment by name, geography, or industrial code (Occupational Safety and Health Administration, 2010).

Leaders whose agencies drift too far off course may be accused by Congress or even the courts of "mission creep." One can easily discover agency mission statements in the *U.S. Government Manual* and on agency websites. Gormley and Balla (2010) note that an agency with a single, straightforward mission, such as the National Weather Service, is likely to perform its functions well and receive high ratings, especially when that mission enjoys wide support. And even the National Weather Service (NWS) can have its mission challenged, as it did during the mid-2000s controversies regarding privately owned weather services competing with the NWS (Newmyer, 2007). For tips on how best to navigate agency websites, refer to Chapter 2.

Types of Agency Publications

As discussed in Chapters 1 and 2, the Superintendent of Documents (SuDocs) classification scheme is based on issuing agency rather than subject. The system also provides a useful framework for understanding the different documents issued by federal agencies. In the SuDocs scheme, the numeral that comes directly after the first letter/number combination (i.e., after the department designation) indicates the subagency and publication category: annual reports; general publications (unnumbered publications of a miscellaneous nature); bulletins; circulars; laws (administered by the agency and published by it); regulations, rules, and instructions; releases; handbooks, manuals, guides; bibliographies and lists of publications; directories; maps and charts; posters; forms; addresses and lectures; and so on. For example, HE 20 is the Department of Health and Human Services; anything classed in the HE 20.300s is from the Indian Health Service, and HE 20.312: is reserved for posters from the Indian Health Service, such as HE 20.312: D 54, *Shoes and Socks, Take 'Em Off!: If You Have Diabetes, Have Your Doctor Check Your Feet* (Indian Health Service, 1999). When mining the riches of agency publications, expect most agencies to publish in at least these simple categories. Spending some time perusing the *List of Classes* (see Chapter 1) or the *Guide to U.S. Government Publications* (Andriot) will provide you with at least a broad mental map for output from executive agencies. This technique is helpful even now when the vast majority of government content is online, never published in a tangible form and never captured by the Depository Library Program. Today, it is necessary to expand one's mental map to include ever-changing documents: interactive forms, user-generated tables, and endlessly customizable, continuously updated resources, which are becoming the new normal in publishing.

GPO and the EPA Web-Harvesting Experiment

One of the more interesting chapters in federal depository library history was GPO's 2007 experiment to mechanically harvest content from the Environmental Protection Agency website and analyze the results, seeing what kind of publications might turn up that would be useful for cataloging and preservation in the now electronic depository library program. GPO hired two different companies, referred to here as X and Y, to download everything from the http://www.epa.gov/ domain. Both companies performed electronic site crawls over a period of six months, identifying within their results distinct documents that would be appropriate as online FDLP materials. Company X identified roughly 83,000 documents in scope for the program, while Company Y uncovered 239,000 (Government Printing Office, 2007).

The startling difference between the two numbers brings old questions to mind: what constitutes an individual document or publication; and what deserves permanent preservation as a worthwhile public document? The project was also valuable in its jarring quantification of online government publishing. If one agency produced even conservatively half of the lower number—41,500 relevant government documents—imagine multiplying that by the number of federal agencies, which ranges from 70 to 1,400, depending on what one counts as a distinct agency (*Securing Cyberspace*, 2005: 14), and projecting this figure, clearly numbering in the millions, decades or centuries into the future. The experiment provided a valuable perspective as FDsys, GPO's new system for storing, preserving, and retrieving government publications, was in active development.

How to Find Executive Branch Documents

Consider the *Serial Set*

In learning about executive branch publishing, keep in mind two watershed dates—or, more accurately, transitions—in publishing patterns. A significant year for many documents librarians is 1976, when GPO instituted full online MARC cataloging according to Library of Congress standards. From 1976 forward, depository documents are simply easier to find in library catalogs, as full cataloging records were available for purchase commercially; in this sense, no special finding tips are needed for this period, as you can simply search WorldCat, your library's online catalog, or GPO's Catalog of Government Publications.

Another watershed occurred during the early 1900s. As we learned in Chapters 1 and 2, the federal government funneled most of its reports through Congress in the 1800s, printed as part of the U.S. *Congressional Serial Set*. We learned that the Public Printing and Binding Act (March 1, 1907, P.L. 59-153) changed the distribution so that only a very few libraries (sometimes referred to as posterity libraries) continued to receive the more complete *Serial Set* which included large runs of executive branch materials. The two commercially digitized versions of the *Serial Set* (by ProQuest and Readex) have scanned from the fuller, posterity library editions. One can see vestiges of the earlier funneling-through-Congress well into the mid-twentieth century: in 1969, for example, one can still find the *Army Register* (SuDoc D 2.109) printed as part of the depository edition *Serial Set* (the *Army Register*, a directory of U.S. military personnel, is a good report to know about too). For more examples of ongoing executive branch serials included in the *Serial Set*, consult a guide produced by the College of Wooster library (McMullen, U.S. Congressional Serial Set Finding Guide, http://www3.wooster.edu/library/Gov/serialset/main.htm/).

From the late 1970s through the mid-1990s, microfiche was the dominant dissemination medium from GPO, with some recurrent reports fluctuating in format between paper, microfiche, then back to paper, and so on—making their use and bibliographic control quite a challenge. Also in this era, librarians were concerned with the privatization of government information (see Chapter 9 for one current example) and the trend of "Less Access to Less Information By and

About the U.S. Government" (American Library Association, 2010) in the wake of the Paperwork Reduction Act (P.L. 96-511).

Starting in the 1990s and continuing into today, the next challenge for information seekers was that of creating coherence (especially for time series data or a run of a government serial) in pre- and post-Internet publishing. Certain long-running publications disappeared in the Internet world, replaced by many separate web files. Librarians could once direct users to a section of their library's collection (using print, microfiche, or CD-ROM) to find, for example, the latest economic census, including special reports arranged by industrial classification and state. Today's economic census will have neither tangible reports nor online PDF releases; it will be available solely as interactive data via American FactFinder (http://factfinder.census.gov/). The Census Bureau is not the only agency to radically change publication patterns as a result of the Internet, but it is one that easily springs to mind for many documents librarians.

CIS Index to U.S. Executive Branch Documents

Starting in 1990, a commercially produced index made historical administrative documents more findable: the *CIS Index to U.S. Executive Branch Documents, 1789–1909: Guide to Documents Listed in Checklist of U.S. Public Documents, 1789–1909, Not Included in the U.S. Serial Set*. CIS followed its publishing pattern of the day, issuing a multivolume index set with the actual documents available on silver halide microfiche. The *Executive Branch Documents* set, as it is known, was released in two waves: the 1990 release indexed documents published 1789–1909, while the 1996 release covered documents from 1910 to 1932. The beauty of this resource is that it provides users with subject/name, title, author, agency report number, and SuDocs number access to tens of thousands of agency publications, and the microfiche established preservation-quality copies of documents for those libraries able to purchase the set. Today the indexing is available as bibliographic records, easily loaded into libraries' online catalogs. This stands as a powerful way to access historical executive branch documents, along with the indexing provided for federal statistical publications by ProQuest Statistical Insight (the online successor to the printed *American Statistics Index*, from 1970 forward). The *Readex Non-Depository Government Publications* collection (on microform) is yet another source of federal executive material and more, covering the years 1953–2008.

Additional Tools and Everyday Searching

Today federal documents librarians have another ace up their sleeves: commercially produced digital editions of the historic *Monthly Catalog of U.S. Government Publications*, like the version available from Chadwyck-Healey, a division of ProQuest, covering the years 1895–1976. Using a mix of these resources, and benefitting from increased library cataloging of pre-1976 federal depository documents (records available via http://www.worldcat.org/), and seemingly limitless possibilities on the open web, today's users are probably better positioned to find federal agency publications than they have been at any point in history. GPO even hosts a "government book talk" site (http:// govbooktalk.gpo.gov/) for those who just want to find a good document to read. GovBookTalk highlights interesting or popular government releases and gives the public the chance to review and discuss works in an open forum.

A librarian colleague recently confessed, "I now use WorldCat more than the *Monthly Catalog*, and Google is my new *Monthly Catalog*." There is no shame in pointing out that most of us, even trained documents librarians, start our government searches with WorldCat or the open web; there is no one database that captures all federal executive publications. Neither one of these resources would be as effective as it is today without the contributions of thousands of information specialists producing cataloging (WorldCat) and metadata (the open web) or designing automated means of producing descriptive data. Advanced searchers know when to search a mass digitization repository (Google Books, the Hathi Trust, the Internet Archive), a specialized tool (FDsys), or the deep science web via http://www.ScienceAccelerator.gov/.

Spotlight on Selected Federal Agencies and Departments

Many of the most important information-producing agencies are discussed elsewhere in this book; some are the subject of entire chapters. The following description of a small subset of agencies and their publications is meant as only a modest introduction, providing the reader with a launching point for learning more about the administrative branch of government. And in a broad sense, these four agencies provide a blueprint for the variety of publications and information available at all executive agencies. We have chosen to focus on the Departments of Commerce, Defense, State, and Treasury. We also briefly address the Office of Management and Budget because of its role in information policy. All of the cabinet-level departments and independent agencies have significant output and are worthy of ongoing study and attention.

Executive Office of the President, OMB, and the Budget

The Executive Office of the President (EOP) was established in 1939, a cluster of federal agencies directly serving the president. Some of the agencies, established by Congress or the president, have come and gone; others (like the White House Office and the Office of Management and Budget, originally called the Bureau of the Budget) have endured. In recent presidencies, the office has contained nine to fifteen distinct subagencies. The EOP has been characterized variously as a "managerial or coordinative auxiliary, a national symbol, or a haven of political patronage." (Relyea, 2008: 1). The Congressional Research Service provides a thorough and readable 32-page history of the EOP in its *Executive Office of the President: An Historical Overview* (Relyea,

2008). So even the presidential office, which one might think of as relatively straightforward, is a conglomeration of agencies, only one of which is the White House.

Established in 1939 as the Bureau of the Budget, and moved to within the EOP (and renamed) in 1970, the Office of Management and Budget (OMB) exists primarily to assist the president with the preparation of the federal budget and to establish government-wide management practices. Government documents librarians note OMB's roles with federal information. OMB promulgated Circular A-130 (Management of Federal Information Resources), a government rule defining *government information*, *government document*, *information life cycle*, and other terminology, bringing these concepts into the electronic age. In Chapter 4 (Regulations), we discuss the fact that OMB review is a required step in the regulatory process, providing some uniformity across the incredible universe of regulatory information. Observant users may have at least noticed that federal forms bear an OMB control number, denoting among other things that the form meets Paperwork Reduction Act requirements, minimizing respondents' time in replying.

Over the decades, OMB's role has evolved to include the issuing of standards, regulatory guidance, and directives followed by all federal agencies. In collecting survey data, federal agencies must conform to OMB's five-race classification system, with two ethnicity possibilities (see sidebar). OMB developed these standards in coordination with 30 federal agencies to promote standardized record-keeping and reporting (Office of Management and Budget, 2000).

OMB's website, a branch of the WhiteHouse.gov tree, looks deceptively lean at first, but links to: About OMB, President's Budget, Management, Information & Regulatory Affairs, Legislative Information, Intellectual Property, and Agency Information. The latter category is impressive, providing an archive of OMB's Bulletins, Circulars (back to 1952), Memoranda, Policy Guidance, and Reports. Government transparency advocates, including some librarians, are concerned with OMB's extensive reach and the public's lack of knowledge about this blandly named federal agency (see Chapter 6 for its regulatory role). Such concerns are summarized on

> ### What Are the Requirements for Collecting Individual Data on Race and Ethnicity?
>
> ...The OMB standards for data on race and ethnicity provide a minimum set of two categories for data on ethnicity:
>
> - Hispanic or Latino and
> - Not Hispanic or Latino,
>
> and five categories for data on race collected from individuals:
>
> - American Indian or Alaska Native,
> - Asian,
> - Black or African American,
> - Native Hawaiian or Other Pacific Islander, and
> - White.
>
> Note: "other race" is not a response category.
>
> Respondents are to be offered the option of selecting one or more racial designations. Based on research findings, the recommended forms for the instruction are *Mark one or more*, *Select one or more*, or *Choose one or more* (not check all that apply).
>
> (*Source*: U.S. Office of Management and Budget, 2006: 49–50.)

nonprofit foundation sites such as http://www.ombwatch.org/ (a group monitoring OMB since 1983), in mainstream news articles, and in public policy literature.

Certainly OMB's function most evident to the public is the preparation of the federal budget. When one imagines the physical publishing of the federal budget—and its release is an annual media event—one needs to picture a multi-volume set that does not have the same content or volume structure from year to year (it tends to vary by presidential administration). In recent decades, there was an effort to produce a citizen-friendly guide to the budget, so mere mortals could read a single-volume *Budget in Brief* annually from 1972 to 1990. (This content has been incorporated into the larger budget from 1991 forward, but many librarians miss the *Budget in Brief*. A similar title, the *Citizen's Guide to the Federal Budget*, was published from 1996 to 2002.) Most users will start by consulting the main volume, the *Budget of the United States*. If one wishes to understand the budget by broad theme, the *Analytical Perspectives* volumes are useful; if seeking a time series back to 1940, try the *Historical Tables*. To get the most detail by agency, in a line-by-line format, consult the very weighty *Appendix*. The exact format of the budget has varied widely over the years. Remember that this is the president's proposed budget and not all sections will be passed by Congress. The president must submit the budget to Congress in February each year, and it is based on the coming federal fiscal year, or FY, that runs October 1 through September 30. Amounts budgeted may not equal amounts appropriated or expended, so one finds columns listed for FY (est), FY (actual), and so on (see Figure 7.3). The previous one or two years are listed in the current budget. Today, the budget may be found via FDsys at http://www.gpo.gov/fdsys/browse/collectionGPO.action?collectionCode=BUDGET, where the "About the Budget" pages offer a useful overview of the process and its history.

Commerce Department

The U.S. Department of Commerce (http://www.commerce.gov/), which debuted as Commerce and Labor in 1903, and its subagencies and bureaus are key producers of government literature. First there are the sciences within Commerce: the National Institute of Standards and Technology (NIST); the National Oceanic and Atmospheric Administration (NOAA, addressed in Chapter 12, Environment and Energy Information); the National Technical Information Service (NTIS); the National Telecommunications and Information Administration (NTIA); and the Patent and Trademark Office (USPTO) (we cover scientific literature in Chapter 11). Next are major economic, social science, and demographic publishers: the Bureau of the Census and the Bureau of Economic Analysis (BEA), both part of the Economics and Statistics Administration; see Chapters 8 (Statistical Information), 13 (Business, Economic, and Consumer Information) and 14 (Census). We will discuss some of the remaining agencies, the Bureau of Industry and Security (BIS), the International Trade Administration (ITA), and various online projects of the agency.

Figure 7.3. Table 11.3, Outlays for Payments to Individuals, from the *Budget of the United States*

(in millions of dollars)

Program	2010 estimate			2011 estimate			2012 estimate		
	Total	Direct	Grants	Total	Direct	Grants	Total	Direct	Grants
Social security and railroad retirement:									
Social security: old age and survivors insurance	590,374	590,374	....	598,809	598,809	....	624,026	624,026	....
Social security: disability insurance	124,191	124,165	26	130,311	130,286	25	136,697	136,671	26
Railroad retirement (excl. social security)	6,582	6,582	....	6,504	6,504	....	6,665	6,665	....
Total, social security and railroad retirement	721,147	721,121	26	735,624	735,599	25	767,388	767,362	26
Federal employees retirement and insurance:									
Military retirement	50,814	50,814	....	51,746	51,746	....	52,746	52,746	....
Civil service retirement	70,024	70,024	....	72,216	72,216	....	74,829	74,829	....
Veterans service-connected compensation	57,233	57,233	....	51,997	51,997	....	47,000	47,000	....
Other	3,170	3,170	....	3,374	3,374	....	3,341	3,341	....
Total, federal employees retirement and insurance	181,241	181,241	....	179,333	179,333	....	177,916	177,916	....
Unemployment assistance	190,710	190,710	....	104,002	104,002	....	79,031	79,031	....
Medical care:									
Medicare: hospital insurance	249,325	249,325	....	266,072	266,072	....	274,485	274,485	....
Medicare: supplementary medical insurance	279,381	279,381	....	311,542	311,542	....	321,312	321,312	....
Children's health insurance	9,103	....	9,103	10,485	....	10,485	11,805	....	11,805
Medicaid	275,383	....	275,383	296,726	....	296,726	273,715	....	273,715
Indian health	4,505	4,505	....	4,612	4,612	....	4,895	4,895	....
Hospital and medical care for veterans	38,536	37,633	903	41,195	40,133	1,062	43,883	42,851	1,032
Health resources and services	7,558	4,571	2,987	7,515	4,528	2,987	6,539	3,884	2,655
Substance abuse and mental health services	3,349	479	2,870	3,457	494	2,963	3,460	495	2,965
Health care tax credit	200	200	....	141	141	....	122	122	....
Uniformed Services retiree health care fund	8,634	8,634	....	9,356	9,356	....	10,153	10,153	....
Health Reform Allowance	5,500	5,500	....	-7,000	-7,000	....	-17,000	-17,000	....
Other	1,836	1,836	....	1,188	1,188	....	263	263	....
Total, medical care	883,310	592,064	291,246	945,289	631,066	314,223	933,632	641,460	292,172
Assistance to students:									
Veterans education benefits	9,651	9,651	....	10,992	10,992	....	11,168	11,168	....
Student assistance—Department of Education and other	45,299	45,197	102	36,455	36,369	86	40,199	40,151	48

The Bureau of Industry and Security (BIS), known as the Bureau of Export Administration until April 2002, monitors U.S. exports, focusing on high technology and defense-related commodities that could increase a trading partner's military might. Its sister agency, the International Trade Administration (ITA), formerly the Industry and Trade Administration, seeks to "create prosperity by strengthening the competitiveness of U.S. industry, promoting trade and investment, and ensuring fair trade and compliance with trade laws and agreements" (International Trade Administration, 2010). Its Internet domain name reveals ITA's boiled-down purpose: http://www.trade.gov/. The ITA is a much more prolific publisher than the BIS, but examining both agencies' reports and documents shows the incredible complexity of trade with other nations: the observance of treaties, the regulation of the flow of controlled commodities (dangerous substances), and the enforcement of embargoes. By reading the BIS annual report, one learns that Quality Penn Products Inc. had to pay a civil penalty of $6,000 for ordering "the export of pallets of wood to Cuba without the required authorization and with knowledge that a violation would occur" (Department of Commerce, 2009: 37). By reading a recent ITA publication, one learns that "in 2006, approximately 80 percent of [Foreign Direct Investment] inflows . . . came from Europe and Japan. The United Kingdom held the largest FDI position in the United States at $303 billion" (International Trade Administration, 2008). See Figure 7.4 for a sampling of ITA publications.

The year 2010 saw the end of an interesting era within the Department of Commerce: two decades of STAT-USA. STAT-USA was an information resource produced within Commerce yet designed to be cost-recovery. It ceased on September 30, 2010, its fee-for-service model outdated in the new world of free data sharing. STAT-USA provided top economic indicators and aids for exporters, while USA Trade Online (http://www.usatradeonline.gov/) focuses on import/export statistics. As of this writing, USA Trade Online is still in operation, to be managed by the Census Bureau's Foreign Trade Division. Additionally, the Department of Commerce is a core contributor to the free resources http://www.export.gov/ and http://www.tradestatsexpress.gov/, which are addressed in Chapter 13.

Defense Department

Perhaps no other department website showcases our digital era better than http://www.defense.gov/. Photographs and videos flash across the center panel; links to the military's Facebook, Flickr, Twitter, and YouTube sites are just as prominent as links to the Joint Chiefs, Army, Marine Corps, Navy, Air Force, National Guard, and Coast Guard. Thumbnail panels underneath the central panel invite users to watch the Pentagon Channel live (http://www.pentagonchannel.mil/), learn about the national space policy, and read Twitter updates from a recent briefing. The impression is that of a government institution usually characterized as the ultimate closed structure transformed by the interactive web. The promise of e-government is evident in many corners of the .mil domain.

Figure 7.4. A Title Browse of International Trade Administration Documents from a Federal Depository Library's Online Catalog

53 ☐ A basic guide to exporting : the official government resource for small and medium-sized businesses. ;
Washington, D.C. : U.S. Dept. of Commerce, International Trade Administration : [For sale by the Supt. of Docs., U.S. G.P.O.], 2008.

54 ☐ Belgium / prepared by American Embassy Brussels ;
Washington, D.C. : U.S. Dept. of Commerce, International Trade Administration : Available by subscription from the Supt. of Docs., GPO

55 ☐ Belize / prepared by American Embassy Belize City ;
Washington, D.C. : U.S. Dept. of Commerce

56 ☐ Benin / prepared by American Embassy Cotonou ;
Washington, D.C. : U.S. Dept. of Commerce, International Trade Administration : Available by subscription from the Supt. of Docs., GPO

57 ☐ Bermuda / prepared by American Consulate General Hamilton ;
Washington, D.C. : U.S. Dept. of Commerce, International Trade Administration : Available by subscription from the Supt. of Docs., GPO

58 ☐ Big emerging markets, ASEAN ;
[Washington, D.C.?] : U.S. Dept. of Commerce, International Trade Administration, [1996?]

59 ☐ The big emerging markets : ... outlook and sourcebook / U.S. International Trade Administration ;
Lanham, MD : Bernan Press in conjunction with the National Technical Information Service, 1995-

60 ☐ Biotechnology ; United States. International Trade Administration
Washington, D.C. : U.S. Dept. of Commerce, International Trade Administration : For sale by the Supt. of Docs., U.S. G.P.O., 1984

61 ☐ Biotechnology in Western Europe / Robert T. Yuan ; Yuan, Robert T
Washington, D.C. : International Trade Administration, U.S. Dept. of Commerce, [1987]

The history of the United States military is the subject of innumerable books, studies, and documentary films, bearing Library of Congress subject headings such as "United States—Armed forces" and "United States—History, military." United States ground troops (Army) and naval and marine forces all date back to the country's founding (including the Continental Army of 1775), and Congress established the Department of War in 1789 to coordinate all elements of wars. After World War II, the National Security Act of 1947 (P.L. 80-253) established the Department of Defense (DoD), originally (and briefly) called the National Military Establishment. The National Security Act Amendments of 1949 (P.L. 81-216) further delineated the new agency's structure, creating secretaries for the Army, Navy (including the Marine Corps), and newly established Air Force. The general leadership structure today remains that of a civilian secretary of defense, who may not have served in the military during the prior ten years; three undersecretaries; and a nonvoting chair of the Joint Chiefs of Staff. The defense secretary also serves on the National Security Council, the highest-level forum on national security and foreign policy matters.

Today's Defense Department consists of over 1.4 million active duty military and 845,000 reserves.

Since the DoD receives a notoriously large federal budget allocation ($616 billion in 2008), it is not surprising that its published output (found in libraries, at bookstores, and online) is substantial as well. Much DoD material concerns national security, may be highly technical, and falls outside the guidelines for wide distribution and cataloging via the depository library system or through sale to the general public, requiring security clearance to access. As with many other topic areas within government, it is still fascinating to see what *is* publicly released: material as far-ranging as poster-style prints of commemorative battle paintings; technical manuals (like the *Technical Manual for Batteries, Navy Lithium Safety Program Responsibilities and Procedures*); field manuals (like the classic *FM-76: Survival*); popular press items like *Soldiers* magazine; policy papers; innumerable pamphlets (see Figures 7.5 and 7.6); recurrent reports on the nation's defense posture and world terrorism; and even music CDs from the United States Marine Band.

The Defense Department has its own publishing outlet for technical reports: the Defense Technical Information Center (DTIC), also addressed in Chapter

Figure 7.5. Army ROTC Recruiting Brochure

1951

Source: U.S. Department of the Army, 1951.

Figure 7.6. Cold War–Era Department of Defense Alert about the Perils of Communism, Featuring Soviet Premier Nikita Khrushchev

Source: U.S. Department of Defense, 1963.

11. DTIC offers an online index to its materials at http://www.dtic.mil/dtic/. To quote directly from the site,

> DTIC serves the DoD community as the largest central resource for DoD and government-funded scientific, technical, engineering, and business related information available today. For more than 60 years DTIC has provided the warfighter and researchers, scientists, engineers, laboratories, and universities timely access to over 2 million publications covering over 250 subject areas. All visitors can search DTIC's publicly accessible collections and read or download scientific and technical information, using DTIC Online service. DTIC also makes available sensitive and classified information to eligible users who register for DTIC services (DTIC, 2010).

Other agencies specifically geared toward information gathering or dissemination are the Defense Information Systems Agency (http://www.disa.mil/), the Defense Intelligence Agency (http://www.dia.mil/), and the National Geospatial-Intelligence Agency (http://www1.nga.mil/). DISA is a combat support agency developing the systems serving the president and highest members of the cabinet; the DIA provides foreign military intelligence for U.S. military personnel and policy makers, and the NGA develops imagery and cartographic intelligence resources for U. S. navigational and defense purposes.

At least three military universities have played a major role in making military publications more accessible to the general public, even if their primary objective is to assist the forces. First, in 1988, Air University began producing its online Index to Military Periodicals (http://www.dtic.mil/dtic/aulimp/); while it may not always link directly to the article's full text, it functions as a core index to 70 journals. The second is the Staff College Automated Military Periodical Index (http://www.dtic.mil/dtic/scampi/), produced by the Joint Forces Staff College Ike Skelton Library. Third, the Naval Postgraduate School's "Where to Find Military Information" stands as one of the most useful library pages on this subject; see its subject guides at http://www.nps.edu/library/. The Naval Postgraduate School collaborates with the Department of Homeland Security in building and maintaining the Homeland Security Digital Library, a virtual library of tens of thousands of specially selected documents culled from the open web. The materials are abstracted and brought together in a singularly useful collection, built to aid first responders, academic researchers, and homeland security personnel in learning and coordinating best practices.

Whether a user seeks academic content from a defense-related university, statistics on military personnel, or annual reports of military subagencies, these are all apt to be found in a depository library. Military history texts are some of the most appealing books distributed through the federal depository program, with the publication quality of coffee table books. Generally absent from the depository program are military newspapers, including the on-base publication, *Stars and Stripes*. Libraries making special attempts to collect military newspapers have a particularly rich source of primary U.S. historical material.

Military resources are expansive enough to warrant their own chapter or indeed book. Professional organizations such as the Federal and Armed Forces Libraries Round Table (FAFLRT) of the American Library Association and the Military Libraries Division of the Special Libraries Association (founded in 1953) aim to foster continuing education and believe that military libraries are essential to a strong defense.

State Department

The Department of State (http://www.state.gov/) dates back to 1789. When one thinks of the State Department, what comes to mind? United States embassies all over the world, and foreign embassies here in the United States? Diplomacy and the U.S. Foreign Service? The issuing of passports and visas? The crafting of foreign policy, spanning decades of change? The admission of refugees? All of these associations would be valid. Ask a government documents librarian, and the State Department might instantly call to mind these key resources: the *Background Notes* series, *Foreign Relations of the United States*, *Country Commercial Guides*, *Country Reports on Human Rights Practices*, a 1990s era e-archive called DOSFAN, and a departmental website rich with current information about countries of the world and U.S. foreign policy.

Background Notes (http://www.state.gov/r/pa/ei/bgn/) are extremely brief (less than ten pages) overviews of individual nations, compiled annually, comprising what many would call foreign country cheat sheets. Read the *Background Note* on Ghana for an instant summary of the land: its people, government, economy, political conditions, defense, transportation, and relations with the U.S. and other countries. One will discover that although English is the official language, 49 percent of the population speaks Akan (which includes Asante Twi, Akwapim Twi, Akyem, and Fanti), and the population (69 percent Christian) has a 57 percent adult literacy rate, with only nine years of compulsory school (Department of State, 2009). The location of the U.S. embassy is listed (24 Fourth Circular Road, Cantonments, in Accra) as well as that of Ghana's embassy in Washington, DC (3512 International Drive, NW).

Suppose one wanted to find out more about the history of Ghana, specifically about our history of diplomacy with that country. Look no further than another long-standing classic of government literature (back to 1861!), the *Foreign Relations of the United States (FRUS)*, the world's first glimpse of diplomatic history as it unfolds. *FRUS* (http://history.state.gov/historicaldocuments/) is valuable enough that the release of new volumes is usually covered by the news media, including the controversy surrounding the volumes released in 2001 regarding mid-1960s massacres in Indonesia. In *FRUS*, still issued in hardcover as well as online (and also included in the *Serial Set*), one finds now-declassified correspondence between top U.S. officials and foreign officials, domestically and abroad. In recent years, content has included transcriptions from Oval Office audiotapes and material culled from a broader range of agencies, including the Intelligence Community (Department of State, Office of the Historian, 2010). Typically, the material is declassified after a period of 30 years or more. In this particular case, there is not an overwhelming cache of correspondence to and from Ghana, but the materials may be found in the Near East and Africa sub-series. *FRUS* has enjoyed an Internet life as one of the series picked up early for digitization. The University of Wisconsin Digital Collections offers a substantial portion of the series at http://digital.library.wisc.edu/1711.dl/FRUS. Because the series is noncumulative, it is important to retain every volume.

Country Commercial Guides. Preparing to open a new business venture in India, Peru, or Portugal? It would be wise to first consider if your product, service, or manufacturing plant is a good match for the local economy, as well as the basic information vital to operating a business in those locales. To help foster well-informed American business ventures abroad, the State Department (in partnership with the ITA's U.S. Commercial Service and other agencies) maintains up-to-date guides on the business climate of every nation. The Botswana *Country Commercial Guide*, for instance, reveals that the agriculture-related commodities that are currently most in demand are "grains, dairy farming, pet foods, health foods, food service, ostrich farming and processing, leather, fish farming, and veldt products" (Commercial Service, 2009: 31).

Country Reports on Human Rights Practices. Accurate reporting from the field is a critical component in the growing international attention to human rights. Since 1975, the State Department has compiled and submitted to Congress an annual report on the progress made in human liberty and dignity in various countries (not every country is included). The department collaborates with nongovernmental groups such as Amnesty International in bringing together verifiable accounts of each country's general treatment of women, children, and those arrested or imprisoned, as well as inhumane incidents known to have occurred since the previous edition. Although this is some of the most sobering reading within the government documents canon, it is important to know where to find even the grim truth. For Australia, the 2009 report noted verifiable cases of women who "traveled to the country voluntarily to work in both legal and illegal brothels but under conditions that amounted to debt bondage or sexual servitude." The report's authors further acknowledge that Australian law "prohibits all forms of trafficking in persons, but the country continued to be a destination for some trafficked women in the sex industry and trafficked laborers." In Djibouti, the disturbing reality of female genital mutilation, as well as the efforts to end it, is noted.

The State Department offers an organized and useful website. From State's homepage, a user can go just about anywhere, as resources are broken down by country, foreign policy issue, and broad topic. Along with a substantial Media Center, Secretary of State's page, and offerings for youth or those interested in a diplomatic career, the site is naturally useful for anyone traveling abroad, containing travel advisories and explicit directions on visas and passports. The page is a portal to all the aforementioned State publications.

Early on in its Internet history, the State Department entered into an official partnership with the University of Illinois at Chicago (UIC) to electronically archive its web content, known as the Foreign Affairs Network (FAN). The DOSFAN project was an early prototype of a public university helping preserve the vital informational content of democracy, a forerunner of projects like the University of North Texas's involvement in federal web harvests of 2008 (during the transition between presidential administrations). In addition to archiving many of State's pages from 1990 to 1997, librarians at UIC helped answer informational questions about the Department of State, in the days before websites included extensive FAQ and Ask Us pages.

Treasury Department

Even a person professing little interest in money or financial matters can become fascinated by the Treasury Department (http://www.treasury.gov/). A trip to the Treasury website yields everything from a children's game in how to design your own pretend money (http://www.newmoney.gov/newmoney/dyob/index.html) to the Internal Revenue Service page (http://www.irs.gov/), to critical information about the crimes of counterfeiting and money laundering. The Treasury Department is divided into offices that perform the policy-level work and bureaus, in which 98 percent of the Treasury workforce is employed (see sidebar). Together, these bureaus cover a remarkable range of functions.

Bureaus of the Department of the Treasury

- The **Alcohol and Tobacco Tax and Trade Bureau** is responsible for enforcing and administering laws covering the production, use, and distribution of alcohol and tobacco products. TTB also collects excise taxes for firearms and ammunition.
- The **Bureau of Engraving and Printing** designs and manufactures U.S. currency, securities, and other official certificates and awards.
- The **Bureau of the Public Debt** borrows the money needed to operate the federal government. It administers the public debt by issuing and servicing U.S. Treasury marketable, savings, and special securities.
- The **Community Development Financial Institution Fund** was created to expand the availability of credit, investment capital, and financial services in distressed urban and rural communities.
- The **Financial Crimes Enforcement Network** supports law enforcement investigative efforts and fosters interagency and global cooperation against domestic and international financial crimes. It also provides U.S. policy makers with strategic analyses of domestic and worldwide trends and patterns.
- The **Financial Management Service** receives and disburses all public monies, maintains government accounts, and prepares daily and monthly reports on the status of government finances.
- The **Inspector General** conducts independent audits, investigations, and reviews to help the Treasury Department accomplish its mission; improve its programs and operations; promote economy, efficiency, and effectiveness; and prevent and detect fraud and abuse.
- The **Treasury Inspector General for Tax Administration** provides leadership and coordination and recommends policy for activities designed to promote economy, efficiency, and effectiveness in the administration of the internal revenue laws. TIGTA also recommends policies to prevent and detect fraud and abuse in the programs and operations of the IRS and related entities.

(Continued)

Bureaus of the Department of the Treasury *(Continued)*

- The **Internal Revenue Service** is the largest of Treasury's bureaus. It is responsible for determining, assessing, and collecting internal revenue in the United States.
- The **Office of the Comptroller of the Currency** charters, regulates, and supervises national banks to ensure a safe, sound, and competitive banking system that supports the citizens, communities, and economy of the United States.
- The **Office of Thrift Supervision** is the primary regulator of all federal and many state-chartered thrift institutions, which include savings banks and savings and loan associations.
- The **U.S. Mint** designs and manufactures domestic, bullion and foreign coins as well as commemorative medals and other numismatic items. The Mint also distributes U.S. coins to the Federal Reserve banks as well as maintains physical custody and protection of our nation's silver and gold assets.

(*Source*: http://www.ustreas.gov/bureaus/.)

The *Daily Treasury Statement* lists the balance sheet of the U.S. coffers in millions of dollars, similar to a daily printed statement of a personal bank account: money in, money out. This is a daily edition of statistics that are annualized in the *Combined Statement of Receipts, Outlays and Balances*, also known as the *United States Government Annual Report*, online at http://www.fms.treas.gov/ annualreport/index.html. Another frequently consulted Treasury publication is *Statistics of Income*, an aggregated look at individual tax return data for the previous year.

Blast from the Unhappy Past

IRS publications are probably the most known to librarians—numbered publications (many book-length) on various aspects of taxation. These were delivered annually to libraries in paper, along with hundreds of numbered tax forms and instructions known as "reproducibles" held together in binders (the idea being that users could remove and photocopy the forms), later to be complemented by a paperbound depository version referred to as *Package X: Informational Copies of Federal Tax Forms*. Since the IRS was one of the early agencies to migrate its content first to CD-ROM and then entirely online, the era of reproducibles is gone. Gone too is the era of massive direct distribution of IRS 1040 tax forms to post offices and libraries. Librarians were particularly unhappy when shipments were late, not to mention the daily challenge of keeping the forms stocked. Happily, the IRS website contains close to all extant forms and publications back to 1990, with selected forms back to 1980. Taxpayers can print and fill out the online forms and are encouraged (or in the case of many corporate and nonprofit firms, *required*) to use the e-file option.

Conclusion

This chapter explored executive branch structure, noting cabinet-level departments, independent agencies, and a vast array of administratively linked entities and aids to find out about their mission and publications. We reviewed typical categories of publications (annual reports, handbooks, circulars, and more) and how to find historical documents (asking first "Was it published before 1976?" and "Could it have been published as part of the *Serial Set*?" and "Was it published outside the depository library program?"). We discussed the complexity of the current online environment, looking to the EPA web-harvesting experiment as a conceptual framing device to think about the high numbers of public interest documents residing on federal government servers. Many federal publications are no longer documents per se, but are constantly updated, customizable, or interactive online resources, databases, or repositories.

We looked to four federal departments (Commerce, Defense, State, and Treasury) for a more focused introduction to government literature and the importance of an agency's mission to its publishing output. We discussed the role of the Office of Management and Budget and learned about the several different volumes of the *Budget of the United States*.

Output from the executive branch of government will be forever linked to the lives of the American citizens, as agencies—established, authorized, and funded by the people's legislature—aim to meet the challenges of our current age.

Exercises

1. Search a library's online catalog for official government information concerning the response to Hurricane Katrina. List the names of the various agencies whose publications you found. How does this list differ from a search you might perform on the open web, if you were to limit your search to the .gov and .mil domains?

2. Become a pest at your next social gathering. Bring organizational charts of the federal government and your state government. The same friends who can name all of the major league baseball teams in the National and American Leagues should be able to name the cabinet-level agencies in the federal and state government. If they are proficient, ask if they can name any of their local county or city government agencies.

3. Using DTIC and other government resources, what information can you find about the use of dogs in military service, historically and currently?

4. Using the agency list at http://www.USA.gov/, pick an agency with which you are unfamiliar. For the agency chosen, can you locate the following on its official website? (Check all that apply.)
   ___ Agency statutory authority
   ___ Agency budget information, current and historical
   ___ Statement of mission
   ___ News feeds (go ahead, subscribe!)
   ___ Publications

5. Using a list of either federal or state cabinet-level departments, select a department and imagine the possible consequences of eliminating that

agency from government structure entirely (example: Department of Energy). Keeping your response nonpolitical, brainstorm probable changes to everyday life based on the absence of this particular agency. Consider impacts on the following dimensions: human health and safety, everyday conveniences, financial security, science and technology, information-seeking in this subject area, general provision of service in this area (i.e., where people might turn for needed services, if not the federal/state government).

Sources Mentioned in This Chapter

Sources mentioned in this section do not duplicate the References that follow.

Analytical Perspectives, http://www.gpo.gov/fdsys/browse/collectionGPO.action?collectionCode=BUDGET/.

Andriot, see *Guide to U.S. Government Publications*.

Background Notes, http://www.state.gov/r/pa/ei/bgn/.

Budget in Brief, 1972–1990, http://fraser.stlouisfed.org/publications/usbib/.

Budget of the United States, http://www.gpo.gov/fdsys/browse/collectionGPO.action?collectionCode=BUDGET/.

Bureau of Industry and Security, http://www.bis.doc.gov/.

Catalog of Government Publications, http://catalog.gpo.gov/.

CIS Index to U.S. Executive Branch Documents, 1789–1909: Guide to Documents Listed in Checklist of U.S. Public Documents, 1789–1909, Not Included in the U.S. Serial Set. 1990. Bethesda, MD: Congressional Information Service.

CIS Index to U.S. Executive Branch Documents, 1910–1932: Guide to Documents Not Printed in the U.S. Serial Set. 1996. Bethesda, MD: Congressional Information Service.

Citizen's Guide to the Federal Budget, 1996–2002, http://www.gpoaccess.gov/usbudget/citizensguide.html.

Combined Statement of Receipts, Outlays and Balances, http://www.fms.treas.gov/annualreport/.

Country Commercial Guides, http://www.buyusainfo.net/.

Country Reports on Human Rights Practices, http://www.state.gov/g/drl/rls/hrrpt/.

Daily Treasury Statement, http://www.fms.treas.gov/dts/.

Defense Information Systems Agency, http://www.disa.mil/.

Defense Intelligence Agency, http://www.dia.mil/.

Defense Technical Information Center, http://www.dtic.mil/dtic/.

Department of Commerce, http://www.commerce.gov/.

Department of Defense, http://www.defense.gov/.

Department of State, http://www.state.gov/.

Department of the Army. 1869–1976. *Army Register*. Washington, DC: Government Printing Office. Also issued as a House document in the *Serial Set*, 1896–1969.

DOSFAN (Electronic Research Collections), http://dosfan.lib.uic.edu/ERC/.

Executive Office of the President, http://www.whitehouse.gov/administration/eop/.

Federal and Armed Forces Libraries Round Table of the American Library Association, http://www.ala.org/faflrt/.

Foreign Relations of the United States, http://digital.library.wisc.edu/1711.dl/FRUS and http://history.state.gov/historicaldocuments/.

Guide to U.S. Government Publications. 1973–. Detroit: Gale Cengage Learning.

Historical Tables (Budget of the United States), http://www.gpo.gov/fdsys/browse/ collectionGPO.action?collectionCode=BUDGET.

Internal Revenue Service, http://www.irs.gov/.

International Trade Administration, http://www.trade.gov/.

Less Access to Less Information by and about the U.S. Government, http://www.ala.org/ ala/issuesadvocacy/advocacy/federallegislation/govinfo/lessaccess/index.cfm.

Military Libraries Division of the Special Libraries Association, http://units.sla.org/ division/dmil/.

Monthly Catalog of U.S. Government Publications, 1895–1976, http://monthlycatalog .chadwyck.com/home.do/.

National Geospatial-Intelligence Agency, http://www1.nga.mil/.

Non-Depository Government Publications, 1953–2008. Chester, VT: Readex.

Office of Management and Budget, http://www.whitehouse.gov/omb/.

Office of Management and Budget: Agency Information, http://www.whitehouse.gov/ omb/agency/default/.

OMB Watch, http://www.ombwatch.org/.

Package X: Informational Copies of Federal Tax Forms, http://www.worldcat.org/oclc/.

Pentagon Channel, http://www.pentagonchannel.mil/.

ProQuest Statistical Insight, American Statistics Index, http://web.lexis-nexis.com/ statuniv/.

Stars and Stripes, http://estripes.osd.mil/.

Statistics of Income, http://www.irs.gov/taxstats/.

Treasury Department, http://www.treasury.gov/.

U.S. *Congressional Serial Set,* http://www.gpoaccess.gov/serialset/.

U.S. Congressional Serial Set Finding Guide, http://www3.wooster.edu/library/Gov/ serialset/main.htm/.

U.S. Government Annual Report, http://www.fms.treas.gov/annualreport/index.html/.

U.S. Government Manual, http://www.gpo.gov/fdsys/browse/collection.action? collectionCode=GOVMAN.

U.S. Government Policy and Supporting Positions, also known as the Plum Book, http://www.gpo.gov/fdsys/.

USA Trade Online, http://www.usatradeonline.gov/.

USA.gov's A–Z list of agencies, http://www.usa.gov/Agencies/Federal/All_Agencies/ index.shtml.

WorldCat, http://www.worldcat.org/.

References

American Library Association. 2010. "Less Access to Less Information by and about the U.S. Government, 1981–1996." Accessed September 1. http://www.ala.org/ala/ issuesadvocacy/advocacy/federallegislation/govinfo/lessaccess/index.cfm.

Batten, Donna, ed. 2010. *Guide to U.S. Government Publications*. 2011 ed. Detroit: Gale Cengage Learning.

Bledsoe, W. Craig, and Leslie Rigby. 1997a. "The Cabinet and Executive Departments." In *Cabinets and Counselors: The President and the Executive Branch*, 2nd ed., 73–140. Washington, DC: CQ Press.

Bledsoe, W. Craig, and Leslie Rigby. 1997b. "Government Agencies and Corporations." In *Cabinets and Counselors: The President and the Executive Branch*, 2nd ed., 141–179. Washington, DC: CQ Press.

Bureau of Industry and Security. 2010. *Annual Report to the Congress for Fiscal Year 2008*. Accessed March 17. http://www.bis.doc.gov/news/2009/bis_annual_report_2008.pdf.

Carpenter, Daniel. 2005. "The Evolution of National Bureaucracy in the United States." In *The Executive Branch*, edited by Joel D. Aberbach and Mark A Peterson, 41–71. Oxford; New York: Oxford University Press.

Centers for Disease Control. 2010. "Smoking and Tobacco Use: History of the Surgeon General's Reports on Smoking and Health." Accessed June 4. http://www.cdc .gov/tobacco/data_statistics/sgr/history/index.htm.

Columbia University Libraries. 2010. "U.S. Government Documents: Executive Branch Resources." Accessed July 20. http://www.columbia.edu/cu/lweb/indiv/usgd/executive.html.

Commercial Service. 2009. *Doing Business in Botswana: A Country Commercial Guide for U.S. Companies*. http://botswana.usembassy.gov/root/pdfs/botswanaccguide 2009.pdf.

Deeben, John. 2004. "Genealogy Notes: The Official Register of the United States, 1816–1959." *Prologue* 36, no. 4. http://www.archives.gov/publications/prologue/ 2004/winter/genealogy-official-register.html.

Department of Defense. 1963. "We Will Bury You." *Alert Facts for the Armed Forces*, no. 8. Washington, DC: Government Printing Office.

Department of Health and Human Services. 1999. *Shoes and Socks, Take 'Em Off! If You Have Diabetes, Have your Doctor Check Your Feet*. Bethesda, MD: U.S. Department of Health and Human Services.

Department of State. 2010. "Background Note: Ghana (3/10)." Accessed September 3. http://www.state.gov/r/pa/ei/bgn/2860.htm.

Department of the Army. *Your Future in the Army ROTC*. Washington, DC: Government Printing Office, 1951.

Federal Staff Directory. 2009. Mt. Vernon, VA: Staff Directories.

Federal Yellow Book. 2010. New York and Washington, DC: Leadership Directories.

Gale Research Company. 2010. *Encyclopedia of Governmental Advisory Organizations*. 25th ed. Detroit: Gale Research.

Gormley, William, and Steven Balla. 2008. *Bureaucracy and Democracy: Accountability and Performance*. Washington, DC: CQ Press.

Government Printing Office. 2007. *Web Harvesting White Paper, Ver. 1.0*. Washington, DC: Government Printing Office. February 14. http://www.fdlp.gov/home/reposi-tory/doc_download/543-web-harvesting-white-paper.

Internal Revenue Service. 2010. "The Agency, Its Mission and Statutory Authority." Last revised June 23. http://www.irs.gov/irs/article/0,,id=98141,00.html.

International Trade Administration. 2008. *Assessing Trends and Policies of Foreign Direct Investment in the United States*. July. http://www.ita.doc.gov/media/Publications/pdf/fdi2008.pdf.

International Trade Administration. 2010. "About the International Trade Administration." Accessed September 4. http://www.trade.gov/about.asp.

McMullen, Jennifer, ed. 2004. *U. S. Congressional Serial Set Finding List*. College of Wooster Libraries. Last revised April. http://www3.wooster.edu/library/Gov/serialset/main.htm.

Moe, Ronald C., and Kevin R. Kosar. 2005. *The Quasi-Government: Hybrid Organizations with Both Government and Private Sector Legal Characteristics*. Washington DC: Library of Congress, Congressional Research Service. http://digital.library.unt.edu/ark:/67531/metacrs6224.

National Institute for Occupational Safety and Health. 2008. *Investigation of Employee Symptoms at an Indoor Waterpark* (HETA 2007-0163-3062). Washington, DC: National Institute for Occupational Safety and Health. June. http://www.cdc.gov/niosh/hhe/reports/pdfs/2007-0163-3062.pdf.

National Institute for Occupational Safety and Health. 2010. *Reducing Illnesses at Indoor Waterparks* (DHHS (NIOSH) Publication No. 2010–138). Washington, DC: National Institute for Occupational Safety and Health. March 2010. http://www.cdc.gov/niosh/docs/wp-solutions/2010-138/pdfs/2010-138.pdf.

Naval Sea Systems Command. 2004. *Technical Manual for Batteries, Navy Lithium Safety Program Responsibilities and Procedures*. S9310-AQ-SAF-010. August 19. http://www.marcorsyscom.usmc.mil/sites/pmeps/DOCUMENTS/BatteryPolicy/Battery%20Policy%20-%20S9310%20manual%20-%2019%20Aug%2004.pdf.

Newmyer, Tory, and Kate Ackley. 2007. "K Street Files." *Roll Call*, February 7.

Occupational Safety and Health Administration. 2010. "Integrated Management Information System." Accessed September 4. http://www.osha.gov/pls/imis/industry.html.

Office of the Historian. 2010. "About the Foreign Relations of the United States Series." Accessed July 10. http://history.state.gov/historicaldocuments/about-frus.

Office of Management and Budget. 2000. "OMB Bulletin No. 00-02: Guidance on Aggregation and Allocation of Data on Race for Use in Civil Rights Monitoring and Enforcement." March 9. http://www.whitehouse.gov/omb/bulletins_b00-02/.

Office of Management and Budget. 2006. "Memorandum for the President's Management Council: Guidance on Agency Survey and Statistical Information Collections." January 20. http://www.whitehouse.gov/omb/assets/omb/inforeg/pmc_survey_guidance_2006.pdf.

Office of Management and Budget. 2010. "Circular No. A-130, Revised." Accessed July 10. http://www.whitehouse.gov/omb/circulars_a130_a130trans4/.

Office of the Director of National Intelligence. 2010. "History of the Office of the Director of National Intelligence." Accessed September 4. http://www.odni.gov/history.htm.

ProQuest. 2010. *Monthly Catalog of U.S. Government Publications*. Product description: http://www.proquest.com/en-US/catalogs/databases/detail/monthly_catalog.shtml.

Relyea, Harold C. 2008. *The Executive Office of the President: An Historical Overview* (Order Code 98-606 GOV). Washington, DC: U.S. Congressional Research Service. http://www.fas.org/sgp/crs/misc/98-606.pdf.

Schmidt, Steffen, Mack Shelley, and Barbara Bardes. 2009. *American Government and Politics Today, 2009–2010 edition*. Australia and Boston: Wadsworth Cengage Learning.

Securing Cyberspace: Efforts to Protect National Information Infrastructures Continue to Face Challenges: Hearing Before the Federal Financial Management, Government Information, and International Security Subcommittee of the Committee on Homeland Security and Governmental Affairs. 109th Cong. 1 (2005). http://www.access.gpo.gov/congress/senate/pdf/109hrg/23163.pdf.

Soanes, Catherine, and Angus Stevenson, eds. 2005. *Oxford Dictionary of English*. Revised ed. Cambridge: Oxford University Press.

Sobel, Robert, and David B. Sicilia. 2003. *The United States Executive Branch: A Biographical Directory of Heads of State and Cabinet Officials*. Westport, CT: Greenwood.

Informational Note

On November 30, 2010, ProQuest announced its acquisition of the Congressional Information Services (CIS) and University Publications of America (UPA) product lines from LexisNexis. The ProQuest announcement indicated that, beginning in 2011, LexisNexis Congressional will be renamed ProQuest Congressional and LexisNexis Statistical Insight will be renamed ProQuest Statistical Insight.

Chapter 8

Statistical Information

Introduction

Statistics may be the most frequently used type of government information. Among the most widely held titles in OCLC's WorldCat database, United States census volumes are second behind the Bible (and one spot ahead of Mother Goose). And the most popular single government document, the federal government's *Statistical Abstract of the United States* (the Bible of statistics), is the single most held library serial, not counting popular magazines.

So when it comes to counting, governments are remarkably prolific. Gathering statistics might not resonate like other government functions such as fixing potholes and funding schools, law enforcement, parks, firefighters, roads, and the military. But statistics, and counting, is central to the birth of the country itself, as a representative democracy. The fifth paragraph of the Constitution (Article I, Section 2) contains the first government mandate for gathering statistics:

> Representatives and direct taxes shall be apportioned among the several states which may be included within this union, according to their respective numbers, which shall be determined by adding to the whole number of free persons, including those bound to service for a term of years, and excluding Indians not taxed, three fifths of all other Persons. The actual Enumeration shall be made within three years after the first meeting of the Congress of the United States, and within every subsequent term of ten years, in such manner as they shall by law direct. (U.S. Constitution)

So the founding fathers mandated the first government statistical effort, a count of the nation's population within three years of the Constitution and every ten years afterward, in order to apportion representatives. That enumeration became the decennial census. Every ten years the Census Bureau still counts the nation's people and publishes the results, with the reapportionment of congressional representation being only one of countless uses. The decennial census is so large and important that it is covered separately in Chapter 14.

But statistics gathering in the nation has moved well beyond the decennial census. The ensuing centuries have seen numerous laws by Congress establishing further statistical projects in order to understand many things of interest to the country and its citizens, such as measures of business and the economy, health and medicine, education, crime, and other socio-demographic data.

Also, the government participates in activities that, although not specifically designed to count, generate statistics as a byproduct. For instance, while we're swearing in new citizens, we keep track of how many we swear in; when a baby is born, hospitals put another tick on their ledger of births and share those ledgers with government agencies. All in all, the U.S. government is the biggest producer of statistics in the world (see Figure 8.1).

Figure 8.1. Samples of Government Statistical Data

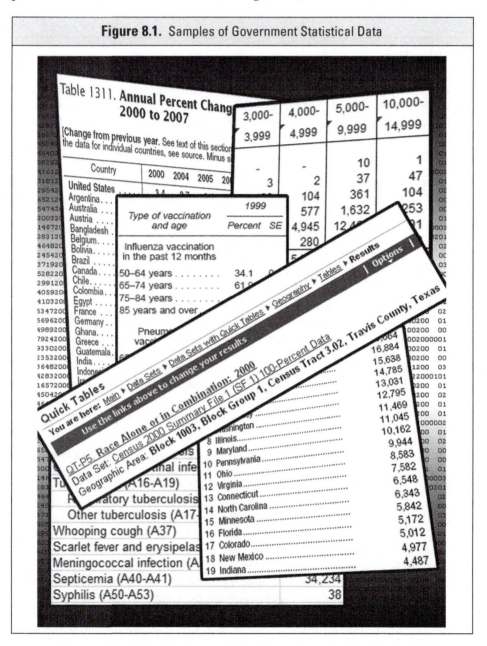

So how does one find and access all of this data? This chapter presents a brief overview of who does the counting; how things are counted; key statistics-producing agencies, initiatives, and resources; and strategies for finding statistical data. Just about all current government statistics are available via agency websites, making their discovery in some ways easier than ever before. This is true despite the fact that Google and other general search engines are not very successful at discovering specific data within statistical tables or datasets. But despite this increased ease of retrieval, identifying proper surveys, datasets, and resources of government statistics remains an area of special expertise. Additionally, with data taking on an ever-increasing role in decision making across society, government information users more frequently want the power to build their own statistical tables based on raw data... if only they could find that raw data. Therefore, this chapter also provides a basic explanation of data sets and how to find them. Finally, although the U.S. federal government is the biggest compiler of statistics in the world, state and local governments, foreign nations, and international organizations also compile statistics. We'll briefly introduce those sources as well.

Who Counts What?

As discussed in previous chapters, one of the most important skills in understanding the mass of government information is a foundation in civics. Knowledge of government functions is conducive to competency in using appropriate search engines, indexes, bibliographies, and sources. Simply knowing the key agencies can be the most important step to finding a desired statistic.

The authority for every government counting effort should have its origin somewhere in the Constitution or in subsequent laws passed by Congress. Take the Census Bureau, for example. Its statistical duties go well beyond the decennial census. A law from 1954 is still on the books (amending earlier laws from the 1920s) requiring the Census Bureau to "collect and publish statistics concerning the amount of cotton ginned" (13 U.S.C. §41). This type of specificity from Congress is not necessarily the rule. It's more common for Congress to establish some broader goals, such as those that lead to the plethora of surveys and reports that the Census Bureau produces about social and economic characteristics. Consider this law (most recently amended in 1976) with its potentially vague mandate to gather population characteristics:

> During the intervals between each census of population required under section 141 of this title, the Secretary, to the extent feasible, shall annually produce and publish for each State, county, and local unit of general purpose government which has a population of fifty thousand or more, current data on total population and population characteristics. . . . Such data may be produced by means of sampling or other methods, which the Secretary determines will produce current, comprehensive, and reliable data. (13 U.S.C. §181)

The law leaves a fair amount of discretion to the secretary (in this case, the Secretary of Commerce, the head of the U.S. Census Bureau's parent agency). The important thing to learn is simply the fact that the Census Bureau is a good place to find statistics about population characteristics. It is often useful to understand the authorizing law for specific statistical efforts to better understand the reasons behind them.

So most useful in finding government statistics is knowing the key statistics-producing agencies and understanding their key statistics programs, resources, and publications. The interagency project FedStats (http://www.fedstats.gov/) lists what it calls the "principal statistical agencies" of the United States federal government:

1. Bureau of Economic Analysis
2. Bureau of Justice Statistics
3. Bureau of Labor Statistics
4. Bureau of Transportation Statistics
5. Census Bureau
6. Economic Research Service, Department of Agriculture
7. Energy Information Administration
8. Environmental Protection Agency
9. Internal Revenue Service, Statistics of Income
10. National Agricultural Statistics Service
11. National Center for Education Statistics
12. National Center for Health Statistics
13. National Science Foundation, Science Resources Statistics
14. Office of Management and Budget
15. Social Security Administration, Office of Policy

Familiarity with these 15 agencies goes a long way toward responding to needs for statistics. Browsing their available data online and knowing their missions provide an overview to these key agencies. The *U.S. Government Manual* (discussed in Chapter 2) also includes the missions of the agencies and sums up the key statistical mandates that these agencies have received from Congress. For instance, the Census Bureau's mission includes the following data collection areas:

- the decennial censuses of population and housing
- the quinquennial censuses of State and local governments, manufacturers, mineral industries, distributive trades, construction industries, and transportation
- current surveys that provide information on many of the subjects covered in the censuses at monthly, quarterly, annual, or other intervals
- compilation of current statistics on U.S. foreign trade, including data on imports, exports, and shipping
- special censuses at the request and expense of State and local government units
- publication of estimates and projections of the population

- publication of current data on population and housing characteristics; and current reports on manufacturing, retail and wholesale trade, services, construction, imports and exports, State and local government finances and employment, and other subjects. (General Services Administration, 2010: 134–135)

So one quickly understands that the Census Bureau is a good place to look for specific statistics such as foreign trade. Similarly, suppose one seeks statistics on inflation? One might intuitively browse the Census Bureau or the Bureau of Economic Analysis; however, the mission of the Bureau of Labor Statistics mandates statistics "relating to employment, unemployment, and other characteristics of the labor force; consumer and producer prices, consumer expenditures, and import and export prices; wages and employee benefits" (General Services Administration, 2010: 289). Familiarity with these key agencies, then, is extremely useful.

A must-read for the serious user of government statistics is the annual *Statistical Programs of the U.S. Government*, prepared by the Office of Management and Budget, which reports directly to the president (and which is discussed in Chapter 6). *Statistical Programs of the U.S. Government* details spending on statistical programs (12.4 billion dollars in fiscal year 2010, which includes 6.9 billion for the decennial census budget), discusses changes and priorities in government statistics collection, and presents long-range plans for federal statistics programs, among other details. The sidebar shows the agencies receiving the most funding for statistics-related work in fiscal year 2010. Census funding is much higher in a decennial census year such as fiscal year 2010 (and also somewhat higher in the years before the decennial census, during preparation). Also note that statistical funding for an agency such as the National Institutes of Health is largely to support research studies that include a statistical component. Those results will most likely be found in the regular scholarly medical literature rather than a government report.

Direct Funding for Major Statistical Programs, Fiscal Year 2010 (in Millions of Dollars): Top Five Agencies	
Agency	**Funding**
Bureau of the Census	
General	7,405
For decennial census	6,901
National Institutes of Health	963
Bureau of Labor Statistics	612
Centers for Disease Control	475
National Center for Education Statistics	330

How Statistics Are Gathered

Before discussing what these agencies produce and how to find it, it is extremely useful to understand how the data is compiled, and where specifically it comes from. Such understanding not only informs efforts to find and use statistics, it helps determine if the data is even likely to exist. Governments use three general counting methods: collecting statistical samples via surveys; conducting a census (which may be a survey but is asked of every instance of a population, and is a complete enumeration); and aggregating administrative records.

A statistical sample is a subset of the potential population about which data is to be gathered, where participants are chosen by some random method, and which is large enough to yield survey results considered statistically accurate for the desired larger population. Although there are dozens of different, ongoing government statistical samples, many citizens may go a lifetime without ever being asked to participate in a government survey outside of the decennial census. Still, such surveys yield highly accurate statistical portraits. Consider the largest effort to measure health indicators of Americans, the annual National Health Interview Survey (NHIS, the source of many basic statistics about the health of Americans). The NHIS surveys approximately 35,000 households annually, covering some 87,000 people. Participants answer a series of questions regarding their health and their demographic characteristics. While this sample of 87,000 people equates to just three out of every 100,000 people, the sample size is nonetheless large enough to provide statistically sound health data for the whole nation by some basic demographic characteristics, such as race, sex, age group, and income range.

Note that while the random sample is conducted to ensure that no geographic area or region is overly represented (we wouldn't, for instance want 80,000 of the 87,000 people surveyed to be from the West Coast, and then claim that represents the entire nation), the sample is *not* large enough to provide data for specific states, cities, or smaller geographic entities. If you want data on the health of the people of Topeka, Kansas (a city of a bit more than 100,000 people), those three interviews are not enough to learn anything about the health of the city's entire population. This is a key point: the smaller the geographic area, the less likely it is that you can find statistics about it. Like the National Health Interview Survey, most statistics based on samples are big enough to provide data only for the United States as a whole, or sometimes for a United States region (such as Northeast, West, South, or Midwest). The same sample is likely too small to yield sound data for states, and in that case, it would definitely be too small to yield data for cities.

A census, on the other hand, is a complete enumeration, which means every single instance is counted. Among statistics about the entire U.S. population, the decennial census is the only complete enumeration of the U.S. population (it being no small feat to ask over 300 million people questions). It is therefore unique in that data about every single person, rather than just a sample, is counted. The difference is significant: from the large sample of three in every

100,000, to all 100,000. The census asks questions of over 100 million households, covering over 300 million people. That's a lot of tick marks.

The upside to all those tick marks is the ability to get detailed information about smaller geographic entities, something a sample of 87,000 cannot do. Not only can one get census statistics about the people in states, counties, cities, and small towns, but one can even go down to ZIP codes and smaller census units called census tracts (neighborhood sized), block groups (yes, like a group of some city blocks) and census blocks (more or less equivalent to a single city block). See Figure 8.2 for a summary of frequently used geographic entities for geography from the 2000 census. So to apply the geographic lesson that we just learned: if you need data for these small geographic entities and you can see that the data was covered in the decennial census, you might be in luck. The decennial census and the American Community Survey are the two most important statistical efforts for which geography is especially important. These will be covered in much greater detail in Chapter 14.

The third category, administrative records, usually acts more as a complete enumeration, albeit one with some specific audience or subject. Much data is collected in the course of conducting government business, a great deal of which is often compiled and published. As mentioned earlier, new citizens are

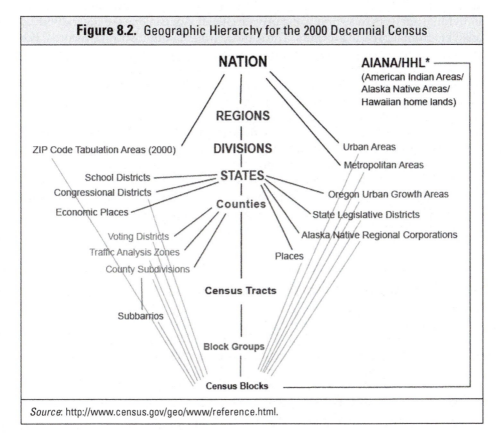

Figure 8.2. Geographic Hierarchy for the 2000 Decennial Census

Source: http://www.census.gov/geo/www/reference.html.

counted this way. Governments also coordinate collection of birth and death statistics in cooperation with hospitals and county health departments, leading to, among other data, statistics on the cause of death. Nearly everyone files taxes, so data on tax revenue from IRS statistics is based on everyone's taxes (not just a sample). Grant makers keep track of awards, so one can find data on recipients of research funding from the National Institutes of Health. The Social Security Administration keeps data on all the checks it sends out—whether for social security, welfare programs, or disability programs—data which is compiled into aggregate statistical data. Governments also collect much scientific data, such as hourly weather conditions; daily pollution samples; nearly real-time stream flow data; and endless sets of cartographic, seismological, meteorological, and other scientific data. Like the decennial census, a few government surveys are mandatory. Some business statistics are collected this way, as are many educational statistics—schools are sent surveys every year and the data collected and published. All told, governments have numerous administrative functions that yield useful data.

An important point to note is that in almost every government statistical undertaking, confidentiality of respondents is required by law. For instance, one cannot find out the identity of a particular living respondent to a government survey. This goes for individuals and businesses; just as one cannot see the individual answers to a survey of a private citizen, nor can one see the individual answers from a private business. The same is true of administrative records. For instance, even when political candidates show the public their tax returns, they do it by choice; citizens cannot ask for or view such personal information. Not every government data collection is confidential, however. Most contributions to political candidates are required by law to be public. And the most notable, partial exception is the decennial census: those records become public 72 years after each census. For instance, if a patron's grandmother is 95 years old, it's possible to go back and access the 1930 census schedules (the actual forms used to gather data) and see what her family filled out. This and the ability to access a few other types of government records (such as old immigration forms, with which one could research the same grandmother's immigration paperwork) are essentially genealogical questions rather than statistical questions. For more about genealogical/historical research, see Chapter 15.

How Statistical Data Is Compiled: Microdata

Understanding the key statistical agencies, and also the methods used to gather data, is useful, but the actual details of data collection are illuminating and increasingly important when finding government statistical information. In early years, before technological improvements, statistical compilation was actually done by making tick marks and adding them up. And while the concept of counting is unchanged, technology now allows those tick marks to be tabulated by computer. A basic understanding of the difference between these tick marks (the raw data, also called microdata) and the tables that are eventually published is of increasing importance, for "when quantitative analysis lies behind a reference question, anxiety and confusion can color even the most competent reference librarian's response" (Gerhan, 1999: 166).

At a glance, it's not too complicated. Generally, data from a survey is entered and coded into microdata files. For instance, examine a tiny piece of the microdata for 2007's National Health Interview Survey (Figure 8.3). Each row of numbers corresponds to one respondent; each column corresponds to one question; and a separate "codebook" or some other documentation explains what each column represents. In this case, the first two columns for all ten respondents in the example below is "30," which the NHIS codebook identifies as meaning they are in the "Adult Sample." The next four digits identify the year of the survey, all "2007," and so on.

Our abbreviated, sample microdata file includes, among others, the following data:

- Column 39 specifies sex (labeled u; 1 for male, 2 for female);.
- Columns 48–49 specify age (labeled vv, in years).
- Column 50 specifies marital status (labeled w, many values; for what is included below, "1" specifies married and living with spouse, "5" divorced", "6" never married, "7" separated).
- Columns 709–710 specify, for smokers, the number of cigarettes smoked per day (labeled xx).
- Columns 722–723 specify number of times of vigorous exercise per week (labeled yy; "95" means never).
- Columns 781–782 specify the number of hours of sleep per night (labeled zz).

Further columns specify geographic location, age, race, sex, and hundreds of other health indicators about each person. Remember, this abbreviated raw data is just a tiny bit of the file, equivalent to a postage stamp on a basketball court. The example includes only some 50 columns; the actual file includes

Figure 8.3. A Small Extract of Microdata from *National Health Interview Survey Sample Adult File*

```
                            u        vvw      xx        yy        zz
30200700000211  \   64031770121201010172 1  \ 00  /   95   \   11
30200700000910  /   157312802112020202601    / 00  \   03   /   08
30200700001110  \   352320902112030303421    \ 30  /   95   \   06
30200700001210  /   792427102212010101621    / 00  \   95   /   08
30200700001310  \   730318001112010101625    \ 00  /   95   \   07
30200700001611  /   003317002112010101321    / 00  \   03   /   08
30200700001810  \   935104702112010101416    \ 09  /   95   \   06
30200700002011  /   218208102112010101311    / 00  \   00   /   07
30200700003311  \   738313101212010101491    \ 00  /   95   \   06
30200700003411  /   365104102112010101587    / 40  \   95   /   06
30200700003810  /   735194102112010101297    \ 20  /   95   \   08
30200700004011  /   965344102212010101197    / 10  \   07   /   03
```

over 1,000 uninterrupted columns representing the answers to the many questions. Vertically, meanwhile, this abbreviated sample includes only 12 respondents, a far cry from the 87,000 in the actual sample.

A statistician or data expert using statistical software could take the raw file shown here and, using the documentation, pull out data by a nearly infinite range of criteria and turn it into something we could read. Figure 8.4 shows a snapshot of selected data including those defined in Figure 8.3 (while our sample of 12 is not necessarily a representative sample of the sample, is it really possible that 8 out of 12 people never exercise?):

Most users, however, are not experts with statistical software packages, and are unable to easily go from the raw data to usable data as done in Figure 8.4. Instead, we seek and rely on published output from the agency. The data culled from the National Health Interview Survey is the basis for many published reports and statistical tables. Figure 8.5 is just one table from the report *Health, United States*, which is the National Center for Health Statistics' flagship annual statistical publication. *Health, United States* features key results from the NHIS and numerous other surveys and data collection efforts (and interestingly, the published table below reveals that the number of inactive people, those who never exercise, isn't quite as bad as our earlier quick look hinted at. And *that's* why they we survey tens of thousands of people and not just a dozen).

Key Statistical Resources

The key agencies mentioned previously all produce numerous, widely used statistical data and reports. Additionally, there are several cross-agency, cross-

Figure 8.4. Small Microdata Extract Transformed into a Readable Chart

Sample?	Year?	Sex	Age	Marital Status	If smoker, cigarettes/ day	vigorous exercise: times/wk.	Sleep: hours/ night
30	2007	2	72	1		95	11
30	2007	1	60	1		3	8
30	2007	1	42	1	30	95	6
30	2007	2	62	1		95	8
30	2007	1	62	5		95	7
30	2007	1	32	1		3	8
30	2007	1	41	6	9	95	6
30	2007	1	31	1		0	7
30	2007	2	49	1		95	6
30	2007	1	58	7	40	95	6
30	2007	1	29	7	20	95	8
30	2007	2	19	7	10	7	3

Figure 8.5. Table 73 from *Health, United States*, 2007

Table 73 (page 1 of 2). Leisure-time physical activity among adults 18 years of age and over, by selected characteristics: United States, 1998, 2005, and 2006

This table has been updated since the printed book

Click here for spreadsheet version

[Data are based on household interviews of a sample of the civilian noninstitutionalized population]

Characteristic	Inactive[1]			Some leisure-time activity[1]			Regular leisure-time activity[1]		
	1998	2005	2006	1998	2005	2006	1998	2005	2006
	Percent of adults								
18 years and over, age-adjusted[2,3]	40.5	40.5	39.5	30.0	29.3	29.5	29.5	30.2	31.0
18 years and over, crude[3]	40.2	40.5	39.5	30.0	29.3	29.6	29.8	30.1	30.9
Age									
18–44 years	35.2	35.9	34.9	31.4	30.5	30.4	33.5	33.7	34.6
18–24 years	32.8	33.5	34.8	30.1	29.1	27.1	37.1	37.4	38.1
25–44 years	35.9	36.7	35.0	31.8	31.0	31.6	32.4	32.4	33.4
45–64 years	41.2	41.2	39.7	30.6	29.7	30.8	28.2	29.1	29.5
45–54 years	38.9	39.5	38.2	31.4	30.1	30.7	29.8	30.4	31.1
55–64 years	44.9	43.6	41.9	29.3	29.2	30.9	25.8	27.2	27.2
65 years and over	55.4	53.9	53.4	24.7	24.9	24.5	19.9	21.3	22.0
65–74 years	49.1	47.8	48.0	26.5	27.0	25.8	24.4	25.3	26.2
75 years and over	63.3	60.6	59.6	22.4	22.6	23.1	14.3	16.8	17.3
Sex[2]									
Male	37.8	39.1	38.5	28.7	29.2	28.4	33.5	31.8	33.1
Female	42.9	41.7	40.3	31.1	29.5	30.7	26.0	28.8	29.0
Sex and age									
Male:									
18–44 years	32.0	34.4	34.2	30.7	30.5	28.8	37.2	35.1	36.9
45–54 years	37.7	40.2	39.0	29.6	29.4	28.4	32.6	30.4	32.7
55–64 years	44.5	43.4	41.1	26.9	28.0	30.6	28.6	28.7	28.2

Source: http://www.cdc.gov/nchs/hus.htm.

jurisdiction sources that compile much data into one place. We'll start by highlighting three cross-agency statistical sources.

Statistical Abstract of the United States

This chapter began by mentioning the popularity of the premier statistical publication, the *Statistical Abstract of the United States*. Published annually since 1878, the *Statistical Abstract* is a Bureau of the Census–produced compendium of key and popular statistics. Because it aims to cover statistical topics comprehensively, it includes data from all agencies, all levels of government (state, county, federal, etc.), and other, nongovernment sources such as associations and organizations (for example, the United Nations), interest groups, and private market research companies. The *Statistical Abstract* is available in print and as an online PDF, and also in a unique web version (see Figure 8.6). There are some 20 main subject chapters, each containing several subchapters with anywhere from one or two to several dozen statistical tables each. The breadth is revealed by looking at just some of the main chapters: Health and Nutrition; Social Insurance and Human Services; Education; Construction and Housing; Science and Technology; Business Enterprise; Births, Deaths, Marriages, and Divorces; Prices; International Statistics; and many, many more. Reflecting the scope and multiple jurisdictions involved, tables in the *Statistical Abstract* may cover data for the United States, states, metropolitan areas, or comparative data for foreign countries.

The *Statistical Abstract* is far and away the single most important statistical resource. Unless one knows otherwise, it is nearly always the place to begin a

Figure 8.6. Web Version of the *Statistical Abstract of the United States*

U.S. Census Bureau   People | Business | Geography

The 2010 Statistical Abstract
The National Data Book

| Abstract Main | Overview | PDF Version | Earlier Editions | Order |

BROWSE SECTIONS:

Accommodation, Food, & Other Services
Agriculture ▸
Arts, Recreation, & Travel ▸
Banking, Finance, & Insurance ▸
Births, Deaths, Marriages, & Divorces▸
Business Enterprise ▸
Construction & Housing ▸
Education ▸
Elections ▸
Energy & Utilities ▸
Federal Gov't Finances & Employment ▸
Foreign Commerce & Aid ▸
Forestry, Fishing, and Mining ▸
Geography & Environment ▸
Health & Nutrition ▸
Income, Expenditures, Poverty, & Wealth ▸
Information & Communications ▸
International Statistics ▸
Labor Force, Employment, & Earnings▸
Law Enforcement, Courts, & Prisons ▸
Manufactures ▸
National Security & Veterans Affairs ▸
Population ▸
Prices ▸

What is the Statistical Abstract?

The *Statistical Abstract of the United States*, published since 1878, is the authoritative and comprehensive summary of statistics on the social, political, and economic organization of the United States.

Use the Abstract as a convenient volume for statistical reference, and as a guide to sources of more information both in print and on the Web.

Sources of data include the Census Bureau, Bureau of Labor Statistics, Bureau of Economic Analysis, and many other Federal agencies and private organizations.

Tables of Interest

345 - Fires and Property Loss for Incendiary and Suspicious Fires and Civilian Fire Deaths and Injuries, by Selected Property Type [Excel 34k] | [PDF 460k]

1057 - State Motor Fuel Tax Receipts, and Gasoline Tax Rates [Excel 36k] | [PDF 461k]

1209 - Adult Attendance at Sports Events by Frequency: 2008 [Excel 29k] | [PDF 461k]

308 - Stalking and Harassment Victimization in the United States: 2006 [Excel 40k] | [PDF 450k]

309 - Fraud and Identity Theft--Consumer Complaints by State: 2008 [Excel 38k] | [PDF 450k]

statistical search. The key reason for this is not just its many statistical tables, but also the source notes associated with each table. Each table cherry-picks the best or most interesting data about a topic, culled from the original source. But since the original sources are so well cited, the *Statistical Abstract* often leads to an even better, more complete source. For instance, the *Statistical Abstract* has statistics on murder; many of the tables about murder are pulled from the FBI publication *Crime in the United States*; using *Crime in the United States* finds more detailed statistics about murder (see Figure 8.7). This same pattern—the *Statistical Abstract* as both source and index—is repeated for each of the 1,000-plus statistical tables, making the *Statistical Abstract* brilliantly useful!

Figure 8.7. Table from the *Statistical Abstract of the United States*

Table 296. **Crimes and Crime Rates by Type and Area: 2007**

[In thousands (1,408 represents 1,408,000), **except rate. Rate per 100,000 population;** based on Census Bureau estimated resident population as of **July 1**. See headnote, Table 295. For definitions of types of crimes, go to <http://www.fbi.gov/ucr/cius2007/about/offense_definitions.html/>

Type of crime	United States		Metropolitan statistical areas [1]		Cities outside metropolitan areas		Nonmetropolitan counties	
	Total	Rate	Total	Rate	Total	Rate	Total	Rate
Violent crime	1,408	467	1,265	504	79	395	64	209
Murder and nonnegligent								
manslaughter	17	6	15	6	1	4	1	3
Forcible rape	90	30	75	30	8	38	8	25
Robbery	445	148	428	170	12	62	5	16
Aggravated assault	856	284	747	298	58	291	50	165
Property crime	9,843	3,264	8,577	3,417	758	3,774	509	1,668
Burglary.	2,179	723	1,859	740	157	783	163	536
Larceny-theft	6,569	2,178	5,698	2,270	565	2,815	305	1,000
Motor vehicle theft.	1,096	363	1,020	406	35	176	40	132

[1] For definition, see Appendix II.

Source: U.S. Department of Justice, Federal Bureau of Investigation, "Crime in the United States"; <http://www.fbi.gov/ucr/cius2007/index.html/>.

Using the *Statistical Abstract* is pretty straightforward, but understanding the indexing is very helpful. The print and PDF versions feature an excellent, comprehensive subject index. The web version requires browsing through the topical sections and subsections, or using the keyword search, neither of which will often find all of the relevant tables in the *Statistical Abstract*. Looking through the print or PDF version of the index remains a better strategy in many instances. Consider a search for statistics about Americans and health insurance. One may easily browse the web version to the Health and Nutrition section, and then the subchapter on Health Insurance, and easily find a half dozen tables about HMOs, types of health insurance by demographic and economic factors, health insurance by state, people without health insurance, and characteristics of employer-sponsored health insurance programs. Using the online keyword search for "health insurance," however, turns up over 1,300 results, partly because it searches beyond simply the *Statistical Abstract* (also, these 1,300 results do not appear in an order resembling an effective relevance search). Using the print or PDF index, meanwhile, turns up some two dozen tables, going beyond the Health Insurance subchapter to many useful tables appearing in other sections, such as Health Expenditures and Income, Expenditures, Poverty, and Wealth (see Figure 8.8).

The *Statistical Abstract*'s usefulness as a statistical reference tool is also underlined by several extremely useful appendices: Guide to Sources of Statistics; Guide to State Statistical Abstracts; and Guide to Foreign Statistical Abstracts. These appendices list major statistical publications of the federal agencies, states, and foreign countries. They stand on their own as excellent reference guides, and are yet more evidence of the *Statistical Abstract*'s usefulness.

With annual volumes since 1878, one can find older statistics and can often piece together lengthy time-series of data over the years by using older

---

Figure 8.8. Part of the Print and PDF Index to the *Statistical Abstract of the United States*

	Table

Gross domestic product (GDP):—Con.
   Relation to national and personal income 657
   Sectoral contributions 1315
   State 655, 656
Gross national product 663
   Foreign countries 1312
Gross private domestic investment ... 651, 652, 724
Gross value added 1315
Ground water used 358
Group health insurance plans 147
Group quarters population 74
Guadeloupe. (See Foreign countries.)
Guam. (See Island areas of the U.S.)
Guamanian population 1277
Guatemala. (See Foreign countries.)
Guernsey. (See Foreign countries.)
Guinea. (See Foreign countries.)
Guinea-Bissau. (See Foreign countries.)
Guns. (See Firearms.)
Guyana. (See Foreign countries.)
Gymnastics 1207
Gypsum and gypsum products .. 721, 870, 871, 874, 927

H

Haddock 866
Haemophilus influenza 178
Haiti. (See Foreign countries.)
Hake, Pacific whiting, imports 863
Halibut 863
Hallucinogenic drugs 202
Ham prices 717
Handguns 299, 320
Handicapped. (See Disability.)
Harrasment victimization 308
Hawaii. (See State data.)
Hawaiian population. (See Native Hawaiian and Other Pacific Islander population.)
Hay 815, 830
Hazardous waste/materials:
   Generation 360
   State data 360, 371

Health care and social assistance industry:—Con.
   Receipts 730, 733, 738, 739, 740, 741
Health insurance (see also Health services, Insurance carriers, Medicaid, Medicare, and SCHIP):
   Contributions 152
   Coverage . 138, 141, 147, 149, 150, 151, 152
   Enrollment and payments ... 138, 140, 144, 145, 146, 148
   Expenditures . 127, 128, 129, 130, 131, 132, 133, 134, 136, 138, 152, 526, 668, 669, 670, 671, 672, 723
   Premiums and policy reserves, life insurance companies 1184
   State Children's Health Insurance program .. 138
Health insurance industry, employment 156
Health maintenance organizations 147, 148
Health sciences, degrees conferred ... 290, 291, 292, 293
Health services:
   Buildings and floor space 971
   Charitable contributions 568, 571
   Construction, value 929, 930
   Coverage 139, 140, 141, 145, 149, 512
   Expenditures:
      Private expenditures . 127, 128, 129, 130, 132, 133, 134, 136, 670
      Public expenditures . 127, 128, 129, 130, 131, 132, 133, 134
      State and local government ... 134, 423, 424, 431
         City government 446
         County government 448
         State government 439, 442
      Foreign countries 1310
      Government employment and payrolls . 450
      Government expenditures:
         Federal government . 134, 420, 422, 462
      Hospitals . 166, 167, 168, 169, 170, 172, 173
      Industry:
         Capital expenditures 757

---

volumes of the *Statistical Abstract*. Note, however, that the farther back one goes, the less data that was collected and the less available statistical data.

Historical Statistics of the United States

Another key, cross-agency and multi-topic statistical resource specifically collects historical data: *Historical Statistics of the United States, Colonial Times to 1970*. Like the *Statistical Abstract*, it includes a comprehensive subject index, detailed source notes (in the form of wonderful bibliographic essays) and a PDF version online. Also like the *Statistical Abstract*, there is a separate web version, although in this case the web version isn't free. Cambridge University Press published an updated and expanded version called *Historical Statistics of the United States: Millennial Edition* (also available in a five-volume print edition) which updates and expands the original *Historical Statistics of the United States*. Note that relevant tables in the *Statistical Abstract* reference previous data available in *Historical Statistics of the United States*.

Indexes to Statistics: FedStats and ProQuest Statistical Insight

A third comprehensive statistical source is the interagency project FedStats (http://www.fedstats.gov/). FedStats attempts to gather together all key online statistical data across agencies. FedStats includes extremely useful links to statistics by subject, offers a search across statistical agencies, and has several other useful tools, such as pointing to data available by geographic level and agency. This last feature, searching by geography, is especially useful, as many statistical needs are dependent on geographic coverage. For instance, if one seeks to know how much money a dietician makes, data for the United States may be less useful than specific data for particular cities (wages by occupation and place are available from the Bureau of Labor Statistics, covered in the next section).

Nearly all of the sources and tools covered in this chapter are freely available online, part of the depository library program, or both. Using free tools such as the *Statistical Abstract* and FedStats is frequently sufficient. However, a commercial product, ProQuest Statistical Insight (from the Congressional Information Service, owned by ProQuest, Inc.), is a powerful database aiming to index statistical data broadly from government and many private and organizational sources. By striving to comprehensively index statistical publications, and by allowing many special search limiters, such as searching for data by geographic, demographic, and other criteria, it provides potentially broader access and discovery to statistical publications and tables. Modules allow searching for publication information (including the ability to search broadly by subject terms, abstracts, and titles of tables within a volume) and by information within tables themselves, such as a particular instance or variable. ProQuest Statistical Insight is based on three classic products from the Congressional Information Service (see Chapter 3): the *American Statistics Index (ASI)*, which indexes and abstracts federal government statistical sources from 1973; the *Statistical Reference Index (SRI)*, which indexes and abstracts state, industry, and about 1,000 other non-federal statistical publications since 1980; and the *Index to International Statistics (IIS)*, which indexes and abstracts about 2,000 international organizations' statistical sources since 1983. These latter two products (and their corresponding modules in ProQuest Statistical Insight) are especially useful for their indexing of nongovernmental sources not covered in the free tools.

Major Statistical Agencies

Beyond these major sources, which cover topics comprehensively, are the works of specific agencies, which are all topic based. This is where a knowledge of civics is useful. Knowing about the National Center for Education Statistics, for instance, makes finding statistics about education *sometimes* as easy as visiting its website and browsing around some pretty clear topic-based links. This pattern is repeated for agencies dealing with health, crime and justice, economics, labor, and transportation, among other topics. And of course the *Statistical Abstract* leads right to numerous agencies, too, even if you don't know your civics. The 15 major agencies noted on p. 194 are all worth knowing about. This section will discuss the most important agencies and their key resources.

The Bureau of Labor Statistics (BLS) is the source of many key economic statistics. These include data on unemployment, prices, and inflation (via the Consumer Price Index, or CPI, and the Producer Price Index, or PPI), wages, and many more specific measures, such as employment by occupation, wages by occupation and city/state, and inflation by city/state. Beyond pure statistics is its work in discussing the characteristics, requirements, and outlook for specific occupations via the annual *Occupational Outlook Handbook*, a classic reference source for career-seekers. The BLS website lays out its wealth of data by specific topic quite clearly, and there is a lot of it.

The National Center for Health Statistics (NCHS) is another excellent example. Also discussed in Chapter 9 on health information, the NCHS conducts many surveys about medicine, health conditions, hospital visitors, and the health care system, and publishes key statistical publications highlighted by the annual *Health, United States* compendium. It also compiles various data from administrative records such as those about vital statistics (births, deaths and deaths by cause, marriages, etc.). Yet the NCHS website lays out topics so simply via its FastStats A–Z section that basic inquiries are easily answered. Finding further statistics requires beginning with FastStats A–Z, checking the source notes of the resulting table(s), and then finding this original source, or perhaps going even further to locate and download the microdata on which the statistics are based. Advanced queries require more robust knowledge of the relevant statistical programs and access tools.

The National Center for Education Statistics (NCES), meanwhile, follows a similar pattern for education-related statistics. Two historical annual statistical publications are still going strong—the *Digest of Education Statistics* and the *Condition of Education*, both available in print or online—yet the NCES website features a statistical portal which gathers the data featured in those two and the numerous other statistical publications arranged by topic: there are Fast Facts and Tables and Figures sections, which both link to statistical tables from various NCES publications. Another option, Surveys and Programs, collects published statistics by the source survey, and also includes information about the survey effort and sometimes information about microdata. These surveys compile data on all levels and aspects of education, from preschools to universities, with data on funding, budgets, personnel, performance indicators, demographics of students at all levels, library statistics, and more. One can even find and compare data about any particular school, both public and private, at all levels. Like with the other agencies, more advanced queries require more advanced understanding of the statistical programs of the agency. Education resources are covered in more detail in Chapter 10 on education resources.

The Bureau of Justice Statistics (BJS) is responsible for producing crime and criminal justice statistics. The long-running flagship publication is from the FBI, *Uniform Crime Reports* (*UCR*, also known as *Crime in the United States*), which, via administrative records from law enforcement at all levels, reports annually the number of crimes committed, crime rates, types of crimes committed, and other characteristics of crime, often for the state, city, and specific jurisdiction. The second major criminal justice publication is the *Sourcebook of Criminal Justice Statistics*, which supplements the *UCR* with data about the justice system, prisons, court cases and loads, sentencing, etc. And like the other statistical agencies, the entire BJS website is set up to lead users to this data by topic.

The pattern for using statistical agency websites should be clear by now. Just about all of them have prepared topic-by-topic portals to their statistical information and reports.

There remains the Census Bureau. As mentioned previously, the Census Bureau compiles many statistics about population and demographics, economics, and foreign trade, among other topics. The Census Bureau's major project, the decennial census, is covered separately in Chapter 14, along with the related American Community Survey, which together provide the most detailed and comprehensive statistical portrait of the nation's inhabitants. Census Bureau economic programs are also prominent. An economic census is conducted every five years, which counts businesses by type of business and location, and also gathers some further information such as number of employees, and a measure of the size of the business, such as value of shipments for a manufacturer. Using the economic census, one can find the number and size of business by type of business and by location. The economic census and other Census Bureau economic and business projects are also covered in Chapter 13 on business and economic information.

The Census Bureau is in charge of numerous other statistical efforts, which may largely be discovered by browsing its website. In addition to the very large American Community Survey covered alongside the decennial census in Chapter 14, two further ongoing surveys provide the basis for much useful census data: the Current Population Survey (CPS) and the Survey of Income and Program Participation (SIPP). The CPS is a monthly survey of 55,000 households that has been ongoing for more than 50 years. While many of the questions on the CPS are the same each month, other questions are asked only annually or even only once, allowing both ongoing reports about specific topics and one-off reports on a special topic. The CPS, conducted in partnership with BLS, is especially prominent for producing data on employment and occupational status, education, marital status, and more. Annual questions as part of the CPS are the basis of many reports about income and poverty. Similarly, SIPP gathers more data on factors and sources of income for people. For CPS, SIPP, and several other Census Bureau surveys, data is available in various reports and tables, relatively easily discoverable via the agency's website.

Census Bureau statisticians also prepare official population estimates and projections, as well as numerous data about international trade, including U.S. imports and exports by product. This will also be covered more in Chapter 13 on business information.

The other agencies listed among the 15 principals are generally not as prolific, but all are very important in gathering statistics in their topic areas. Their websites and mission statements may be explored in a similar fashion to those highlighted to begin to build a knowledge base of their key statistical resources and publications. The sidebar summarizes the basic steps for locating statistical data.

Three Approaches to Finding Statistical Data

1. Start with the *Statistical Abstract of the United States*, and let it either answer the question or, via its excellent source notes, lead you to the statistical publications, programs, and agencies that address the topic in depth.
2. Familiarize yourself with the major statistical agencies and browse to the needed information on that agency's website.
3. Use a search engine. As mentioned earlier, Google can be a bit frustrating in the statistical search. With its popularity-heavy algorithm, searches for statistics can be unfruitful. Better is FedStats (http://www.fedstats.gov/), which searches only statistical tables. Finally, there are private sources that help to identify statistical tables, such as ProQuest Statistical Insight.

Finding Microdata

With the new ease with which statistical tables are discovered, an increasing emphasis is placed on finding and using the raw data behind the tables. While this book does not teach one how to use robust statistical software, one should be prepared to help users find and access data sets for further exploration.

Finding microdata requires shifting through any notes or documentation about a statistical publication and identifying the original microdata data set. Once this source is known, one can browse the appropriate website or inquire of the producers of the statistics about the availability of microdata. In the National Health Interview Survey example from earlier in this chapter, we can check statistical table 73 from *Health, United States*, and check the source notes leading to the National Center for Health Statistics, National Health Interview Survey, family core and sample adult questionnaires. The National Health Interview Survey website then links to the documentation and raw data.

Many Census Bureau statistics are based on the large monthly Current Population Survey discussed previously. When one checks the technical documentation of some popular Census Bureau statistical tables, one is referred back to this ultimate source, the CPS. It doesn't take much digging thereafter to find the microdata files for the CPS, which can be used for further, more customized analysis.

The largest repository of microdata on all topics is the Interuniversity Consortium for Political and Social Research (ICPSR), based at the University of Michigan. It provides a central repository for thousands of raw data sets. While many of these sets are freely available, especially many from governments, others require a membership to ICPSR. If your institution is a member of ICPSR, your users will have free access to this archive of data sets. Most data is now delivered to the end user online.

A recent initiative, Data.gov (Figure 8.9), aims to be a gateway to federally produced data sets. Data.gov is an excellent (and growing) place to identify and access data sets. ProQuest Statistical Insight, meanwhile, includes an optional add-on called Statistical DataSets, which also strives to collect raw data from many different sources into one place. An advantage of Statistical DataSets is the publisher's effort to provide an easier interface to the data sets, making raw data easier to find and extract without knowledge of the robust statistical software usually needed to find raw data. One can extract, export, or even map raw data by using only the web interface.

A final, similar product often used by larger government documents libraries is SimplyMap from Geographic Research, Inc. SimplyMap also takes

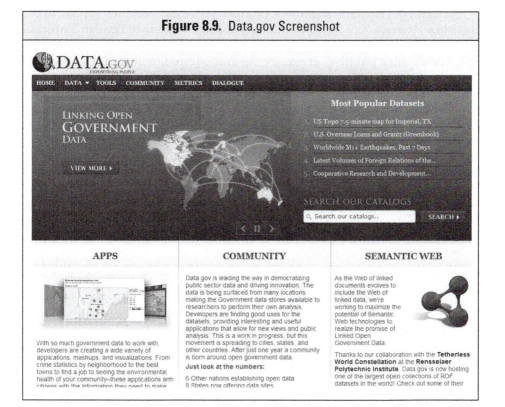

Figure 8.9. Data.gov Screenshot

large data sets and through an easy-to-use interface allows data to be extracted, formatted, and mapped.

State, Local, Foreign, and International Statistics

Up to this point, this chapter focused primarily on statistics from the U.S. federal government. State governments and local governments (city, county, etc.) also compile statistics for their own geographies, albeit on a much smaller scale than the U.S. federal government. Many states have their own equivalents of the *Statistical Abstract*, although frequently the data is simply culled from federal sources. The *Statistical Abstract* appendix Guide to State Statistical Abstracts (to find this online go to the link for the PDF version of the *Statistical Abstract*) lists the closest equivalent in each state.

Further, like the federal government, most states have agencies for education, health, justice, and other functions, and those agencies may produce some further statistics on their subjects within their states. One should be familiar with the statistics that may be available for relevant states. To explore, start with the state's *Statistical Abstract* equivalent and follow source notes to discover further statistical data available from the state.

Foreign governments also often produce statistical volumes similar to the *Statistical Abstract*. The *Statistical Abstract* appendix Guide to Foreign Statistical Abstracts lists those volumes and, when available, a website for each foreign country's primary statistical agency. Several international organizations also produce foreign or comparative international statistics. This international statistics framework bears similarities to that of the U.S. federal government: a few key central, multiple-subject compendiums of statistics, and many other sources of specific, topic-based statistics. For instance, the United Nations acts as a central source, working with foreign governments and other international organizations to gather a variety of statistics about the countries of the world. The United Nations Statistical Division maintains its flagship online statistics compendium, UNdata (free), and also produces an annual *Statistical Yearbook* (economics) and *Demographic Yearbook* (demographics). The World Bank—which one might assume would deal only with banking, finance, and economics—actually publishes comprehensive online statistics (it does so because its mission deals with developing countries in all aspects, not just economically). Much of this is available via the organization's data webpage, highlighted by World Development Indicators, a subscription-based database, with a subset available for free (http://data.worldbank.org). Beyond these comprehensive products are specific organizations and their statistical products. For instance, the International Monetary Fund produces detailed data about international finance; the World Health Organization produces international health statistics; and the International Labour Organization produces detailed international labor-related statistics. Other specific international organizations also produce statistics on their topics. These key organizations' statistical publications and programs, as well as those of major private and nongovernmental sources, are listed in detail in another appendix to the *Statistical Abstract*, Guide to Sources of Statistics. These appendices are yet another reason that the *Statistical Abstract of the United States* is such an important resource.

The Statistical Reference Interview

All of the above, especially the material on how and by whom statistics are gathered, is presented to stress the value of assessing the potential sources and data gathering methods that might lead to needed statistics. Say someone is looking for statistics on the number of broadband Internet users in Aspen, Colorado. One useful exercise is to ask oneself, "If I lived in Aspen, who might be tracking whether or not I use broadband Internet? Does the Federal Communications Commission (FCC) know? Does my Internet provider provide that data to anyone who might publish it? Has anyone ever asked me what kind of Internet access I have (have I been surveyed), and if so, might I find the results in publicly available sources, or has a private entity gathered it somehow and will it only be sold as market research?" Similarly, what if you want to track lung cancer for the nation, and also for a particular area near a polluting factory? By whom, how, and where might that data be collected? Would it be health data from the National Center for Health Statistics, or might an environmental agency gather data about that? Would it be published in the same place? How can I find data about abortions throughout history? By whom and how would those have been counted? And although "every statistics reference question is not a disguised exercise in quantitative analysis" (Gerhan, 1999: 168), you must still consider whether there is microdata behind the source that could be necessary or useful for further exploration.

Because of the potential for statistical queries to be complex, these are the types of questions one should ask oneself when assessing where and how to find needed data. The ability to analyze and access this information should be that which sets apart the librarian or informational professional from the person asking for the information.

Conclusion

Statistics and data are increasingly used for decision making in all aspects of society. The need to understand the nature of statistical data, its sources, and its uses continues to increase. Governments have a long history of gathering and publishing statistical data, and recent efforts such as Data.gov are indicative of the growth of the importance of data. Future years are likely to see further developments in governments' statistical access tools.

Exercises

1. Find statistics on how many people lack health insurance in the United States. Also, how many of these are children? And how many are on Medicare?
2. A student needs statistics about crime on his campus, and how it compares to his city and his state. Where does this data come from ultimately? Is the source of the state data different from the campus data?
3. Find a breakdown of religious affiliation for the United States population. What is the source?
4. A researcher wants statistics on police expenditures for a given year for all cities in the United States. Where should the researcher go, and what approach might she take to get all of this data?
5. A student desires data on the number of engineers working worldwide, by country and by gender. What is the source?

Sources Mentioned in This Chapter

Sources mentioned in this section do not duplicate the References that follow.

Bureau of Justice Statistics, http://bjs.ojp.usdoj.gov.

Bureau of Justice Statistics. *Sourcebook of Criminal Justice Statistics*. Washington, DC: Published annually. http://www.albany.edu/sourcebook/.

Bureau of Labor Statistics, http://www.bls.gov/.

Bureau of Labor Statistics, Consumer Price Index, http://www.bls.gov/epi/.

Bureau of Labor Statistics. *Occupational Outlook Handbook*. Washington, DC: U.S. Bureau of Labor Statistics. Published biennially. Also http://www.bls.gov/OCO/.

Current Population Survey, http://www.census.gov/.

Economic Census, http://www.census.gov/econ/census07/.

Federal Bureau of Investigation. *Crime in the United States*. Washington, DC: Federal Bureau of Investigation. Published annually. http://www.fbi.gov/ucr/ucr.htm.

FedStats, http://www.fedstats.gov/.

Historical Statistics of the United States: Colonial Times to 1970. Washington, DC: U.S. Bureau of the Census, 1975. http://www.census.gov/prod/www/abs/statab.html.

Historical Statistics of the United States Millennial Edition. New York, NY: Cambridge University Press, 2006.

National Center for Education Statistics. *Condition of Education*. Washington, DC: National Center for Education Statistics. Published annually. http://nces.ed.gov/programs/coe/.

National Center for Education Statistics. *Digest of Education Statistics*. Washington, DC: National Center for Education Statistics. Published annually. http://nces.ed.gov/programs/digest/.

National Center for Education Statistics, http://www.nces.ed.gov/.

National Center for Health Statistics. *Health, United States.* Washington, DC: U.S. National Center for Health Statistics. Published annually. http://www.cdc.gov/nchs/hus.htm.

National Center for Health Statistics, http://www.cdc.gov/nchs.

National Center for Health Statistics, National Health Interview Survey, http://www.cdc.gov/nchs/nhis.htm.

Office of Management and Budget. *Statistical Programs of the U.S. Government.* Washington, DC: Office of Management and Budget. Published annually. http://www.whitehouse.gov/omb/inforeg_statpolicy/.

ProQuest Statistical Insight, http://www.lexisnexis.com/academic/1univ/stat/default.asp.

Statistical Abstract of the United States, http://www.census.gov/compendia/statab/.

UNdata, http://data.un.org/.

United Nations Statistics Division. *Demographic Yearbook.* New York: United Nations. Published annually. http://unstats.un.org/unsd/databases.htm.

United Nations Statistics Division. *Statistical Yearbook.* New York: United Nations. Published annually. http://unstats.un.org/unsd/syb/.

United States Census of Population and Housing. Washington, DC: Government Printing Office. Published decennially. http://factfinder.census.gov/.

World Bank. *World Development Indicators.* Washington, DC: IBRD, World Bank. Published annually. Limited data available free: http://www.worldbank.org/data/dataquery.html.

References

13 U.S.C. § 41 (1954).

13 U.S.C. § 181 (1976).

General Services Administration. 2010. *United States Government Manual.* Washington, DC: Government Printing Office.

Gerhan, David. 1999. "When Quantitative Analysis Lies behind a Reference Question." *Reference & User Services Quarterly* 39, no. 2: 166–175.

U.S. Const. art. I, § 2.

Informational Note

On November 30, 2010, ProQuest announced its acquisition of the Congressional Information Services (CIS) and University Publications of America (UPA) product lines from LexisNexis. The ProQuest announcement indicated that, beginning in 2011, LexisNexis Congressional will be renamed ProQuest Congressional and LexisNexis Statistical Insight will be renamed ProQuest Statistical Insight.

Chapter 9
Health Information

ANN GLUSKER

Introduction

Few concerns are as central to our lives as health. With the complexity of health information and the variety of sources available, searching for health information can be a bewildering process for researchers, consumers, and others. Compounding these difficulties is the specialized vocabulary of the medical profession, which can be impenetrable to an untrained information seeker. An additional challenge is the recent proliferation of health information, especially on the Internet, which is often unreliable and can, at its worst, be dangerously inaccurate. Government-created or -sponsored sources can often cut through some of the chaos and offer clear and trustworthy resources.

This chapter will focus mainly on materials that come from the executive branch, since it contains most of the variety of independent government agencies that actively engage in health-related activities (see Chapter 7, The Executive Branch, for more information).

The United States Department of Health and Human Services, the National Institutes of Health, and the National Library of Medicine: Centuries of Progress

The United States Department of Health and Human Services and its sub-agencies produce much of the federal government's output related to health information. The National Library of Medicine is the central organization responsible for its collection, organization, and dissemination. To understand where these agencies stand today, and to be able to do research that spans back over decades, it is helpful to get a sense of their history.

The United States Department of Health and Human Services

The United States Department of Health and Human Services (HHS) is the agency under which most federal activity related to health and health care takes place, and therefore is a prolific creator of government documents on these topics. The secretary of HHS is a member of the president's cabinet. The agency began in 1798 as a division of the Department of the Treasury, part of an act for the relief of sick and disabled seamen (the Treasury Department was selected to oversee it since it was the one equipped to garner seamen's pay to fund the act). In 1870, these services were formalized as the Marine Hospital Service (MHS), which was also given additional responsibilities such as quarantining immigrants. The first supervising surgeon for the Marine Hospital Service, the predecessor of today's surgeon general, was appointed in 1871.

In 1902 the MHS became the Public Health and Marine Hospital Service, its title further condensed to the Public Health Service (PHS) in 1912. In 1939 the PHS was taken over by the Federal Security Agency after the passage of the 1935 Social Security Act, and in 1953 it was subsumed by the cabinet-level Department of Health, Education, and Welfare (HEW). The HEW department was split in 1980 into the Department of Education and the current Department of Health and Human Services, of which the still-existing PHS is a part.

Other important historical milestones include the establishment in 1887 of a disease research lab on Staten Island which became the National Institutes of Health (NIH); the establishment in 1946 of a Communicable Disease Center which became the Centers for Disease Control and Prevention (CDC); and the development of the Department of Agriculture's Bureau of Chemistry, founded in 1862, into today's Food and Drug Administration (FDA). The Medicaid and Medicare programs were created in 1965, and the Health Care Financing Administration was created in 1977 (Kurian, 1998).

The National Institutes of Health

A subagency of HHS, the National Institutes of Health is "the nation's medical research agency . . . [and] the largest source of funding for medical research in the world." Medical advances made by funded researchers have been central to the history of medicine. Not surprisingly, NIH is a productive source of health information, as it is made up of 27 separate institutes and centers, each with its own research focus (National Institutes of Health, 2010b).

In the late 1800s, American physicians were becoming increasingly aware of the work being done by European researchers related to infectious organisms. Newly trained in bacteriological methods, Dr. Joseph Kinyoun established the nation's Hygienic Laboratory under the Marine Health Service, to expand upon the work being done overseas. Over the next decades, the laboratory moved to Washington, D.C., and extended its purview to include noncontagious diseases and other health conditions, as well as the production of vaccines and antitoxins. Hygienic Laboratory personnel were central in exploring and suggesting ways to improve health conditions among the military during both world wars. In 1930, the laboratory was formally named The National Institute of Health, and study fellowships were established.

The years following World War II saw tremendous growth for NIH. Many new institutes were founded. The first was the National Cancer Institute (which was designated a component of the NIH only several years after its creation). Subsequently, the development of new condition-specific institutions

List of HHS and NIH Agencies, Offices, Institutes, and Centers

U.S. Department of Health and Human Services—Agencies and Selected Offices

ACF	Administration for Children & Families
AoA	Administration on Aging
AHRQ	Agency for Healthcare Research & Quality
ATSDR	Agency for Toxic Substances & Disease Registry
CDC	Centers for Disease Control & Prevention
CMS	Centers for Medicare & Medicaid Services
FDA	Food & Drug Administration
HRSA	Health Resources & Services Administration
IHS	Indian Health Service
NIH	National Institutes of Health
OIG	Office of Inspector General
SAMHSA	Substance Abuse & Mental Health Services Administration
OPHS	Office of Public Health and Science
ASPR	Assistant Secretary for Preparedness and Response
OGHA	Office of Global Health Affairs
ONC	Office of the National Coordinator for Health Information Technology

National Institutes of Health—Institutes and Selected Centers

CC	NIH Clinical Center
NCI	National Cancer Institute
NEI	National Eye Institute
NHLBI	National Heart, Lung, and Blood Institute
NHGRI	National Human Genome Research Institute
NIA	National Institute on Aging
NIAAA	National Institute on Alcohol Abuse and Alcoholism
NIAID	National Institute of Allergy and Infectious Diseases
NIAMS	National Institute of Arthritis and Musculoskeletal and Skin Diseases
NIBIB	National Institute of Biomedical Imaging and Bioengineering
NICHD	Eunice Kennedy Shriver National Institute of Child Health and Human Development
NIDCD	National Institute on Deafness and Other Communication Disorders
NIDCR	National Institute of Dental and Craniofacial Research
NIDDK	National Institute of Diabetes and Digestive and Kidney Diseases
NIDA	National Institute on Drug Abuse
NIEHS	National Institute of Environmental Health Sciences
NIGMS	National Institute of General Medical Sciences
NIMH	National Institute of Mental Health
NINDS	National Institute of Neurological Disorders and Stroke
NINR	National Institute of Nursing Research
NLM	National Library of Medicine
NCCAM	National Center for Complementary and Alternative Medicine
NCMHD	National Center on Minority Health and Health Disparities

(*Source*: Department of Health and Human Services, 2010; National Institutes of Health, 2010a.)

created the current NIH structure of categorical disease-based constituent agencies and centers. Funding was also expanding rapidly in this period; the total NIH budget went from $8 million to $1 billion between 1947 and 1966. However, by the early 1980s, the state of the economy and competition for federal funding slowed this growth. NIH turned its attention to maintaining its preeminence as a broadly based research organization, and to developing collaborations and connections with similar institutions in other countries. The National Library of Medicine has been a central resource in this effort.

The National Library of Medicine

The National Library of Medicine (NLM) "is the world's largest medical library. The Library collects materials and provides information and research services in all areas of biomedicine and health care" (National Library of Medicine, 2010a). Today, NLM is a subagency of the NIH, which is itself a subagency of HHS.

This was not always the case; NLM, like the HHS, has military origins, but unlike the HHS, its existence is heavily indebted to two men in particular. The first is Dr. Joseph Lovell, who was appointed the first surgeon general of the United States Army in 1818. It is his reference collection that is the foundation of what is now NLM. His collection was so extensive in its day that in 1836 it was officially named The Library of the Office of the Surgeon General, United States Army (National Library of Medicine, 2010f).

The second central figure in the history of NLM is Dr. John Shaw Billings. He assumed direction of the Army Surgeon General's library after the Civil War, at a time when there was a substantial influx to the library of discarded books from army and other military hospitals. Billings was a dynamo, and during his tenure, from about 1867 to 1895, he turned his library into the largest medical library in the Americas, and one of the largest in the world. He was a tireless collector and visionary. Not only did he expand the collection many times over (from 2,300 to 124,000 volumes), but he created an index-catalog of its holdings, and launched the *Index Medicus*, which will be discussed in more detail below. He even came up with the idea of the punch card, which he suggested to Census Bureau head Herman Hollerith for use in tabulating data from the 1890 census, and which eventually revolutionized information processing (for more on Hollerith, see Chapter 14, The Census) (National Library of Medicine, 2010c).

After Billings' tenure, the Library was renamed the Army Medical Library (1920) and later the Armed Forces Medical Library (1952), before becoming part of the PHS and being named the National Library of Medicine in 1956. In the next decades NLM created a system of Regional Medical Libraries (today's National Network of Libraries of Medicine) and developed information systems which were the basis of its current central resource, PubMed, which will be discussed further in the next section. It also produced the consumer health resource MedlinePlus, released in 1998, which provides reliable, librarian-vetted consumer health information.

The National Library of Medicine and the Organization of Health Information

Figure 9.1 shows the manner in which the library that Billings inherited from his predecessor was first cataloged; its contents were listed (not indexed) primarily by author and secondarily by subject (for example, "Hamilton on Female Complaints"). The innovative Billings cataloged his library with not only author, but also—unusually for the time—subject indexes. Given the extent of the library's holdings, this catalog was considered an exhaustive resource of the medical literature of the time.

However, this was an era in which periodicals were becoming a major source of medical information, meaning that the volume of publications increased dramatically. Billings's main cataloguing project couldn't keep pace

Figure 9.1. Facsimile of Page from "The First Catalogue of the Library of the Surgeon General's Office, 1840"

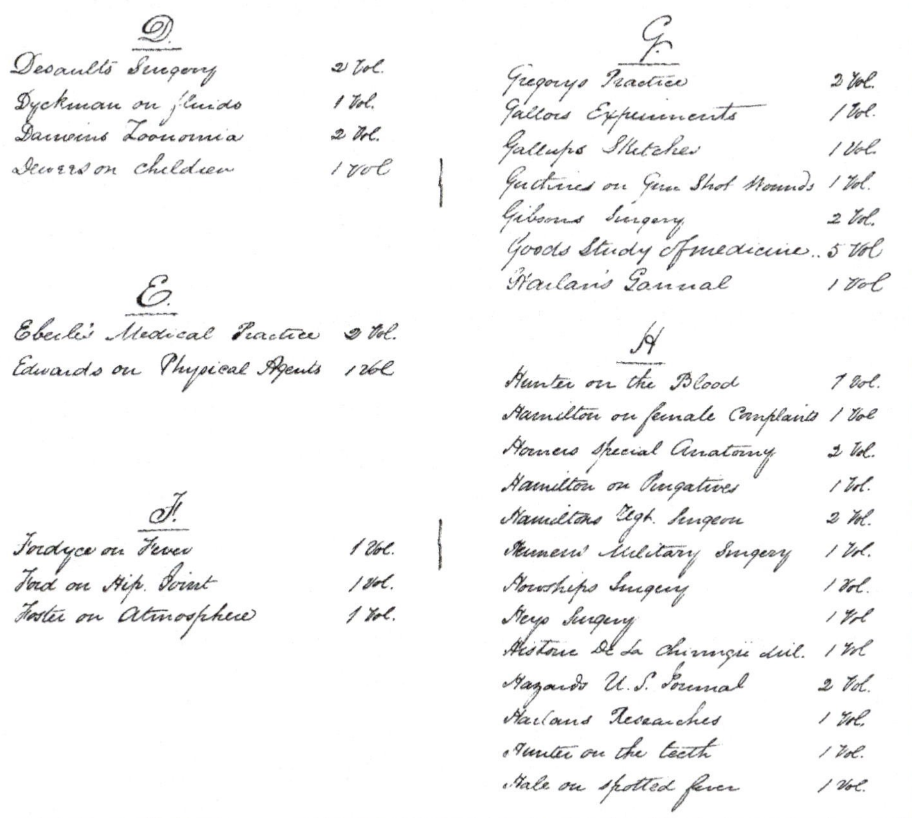

D.

Desaults Surgery	2 Vol.
Dyckman on fluids	1 Vol.
Darwins Zoonomia	2 Vol.
Dewees on Children	1 Vol

E.

Eberle's Medical Practice	2 Vol.
Edwards on Physical Agents	1 Vol

F.

Fordyce on Fever	1 Vol.
Ford on Hip Joint	1 Vol.
Foster on Atmosphere	1 Vol.

G.

Gregorys Practice	2 Vol.
Gallons Experiments	1 Vol.
Gallups Sketches	1 Vol.
Guthries on Gun Shot Wounds	1 Vol.
Gibsons Surgery	2 Vol.
Goods Study of Medicine	5 Vol
Harlan's Journal	1 Vol

H

Hunter on the Blood	1 Vol.
Hamilton on female Complaints	1 Vol
Horners Special Anatomy	2 Vol.
Hamilton on Purgatives	1 Vol.
Hamiltons Regt. Surgeon	2 Vol.
Hennens Military Surgery	1 Vol.
Howships Surgery	1 Vol.
Heys Surgery	1 Vol
Histoire de la chirurgie mil.	1 Vol
Hazards U.S. Journal	2 Vol.
Harlans Researches	1 Vol.
Hunter on the teeth	1 Vol.
Hale on spotted fever	1 Vol.

Source: National Library of Medicine, 1961.

with these new publications, and so he created a separate indexing system for medical periodicals. This became known as *Index Medicus*, which was published monthly by the library starting in 1879. Today's MEDLINE is the modern outgrowth of the printed *Index Medicus* (maintained by NLM until 2004), a chronology of which appears in Figure 9.2.

By the mid-1960s, NLM was able to take the enormous step of computerizing *Index Medicus*, which was still being published in paper form. After some experimentation, the Medical Literature Analysis and Retrieval System (MEDLARS) was launched, using *Index Medicus* as its input. By 1971, MEDLARS was able to be accessed online, and was called MEDLINE (MEDlars onLINE), which still exists today and is the major component of PubMed. Central to the efficient indexing and retrieval of articles within these tools was the introduction, in 1960, of a new list of Medical Subject Headings, known as MeSH (Katcher, 1999). Its structure, which has had an enormous impact on access to health

---

Figure 9.2. Finding Older Medical Journal Articles

Question: How do I find older medical journal articles?

Answer:

To identify articles published from:

1948–present, search PubMed®. Your retrieval will include both MEDLINE® and OLDMEDLINE records, as well as some other citations not indexed with Medical Subject Headings (MeSH®).

prior to 1948, there are a small number of citations included in PubMed Central, searchable via PubMed. Otherwise, there are no online sources from NLM except for IndexCat. You need to use *Index Medicus®* and the other print sources that are described below. These sources can be found at many medical and large university libraries. Note: *Index Medicus®* ceased hard copy publication with the Dec 2004 edition (Volume 45).

Index Title	Years	NLM Call Number	Number of Volumes	Publisher	Description
Index Medicus® (IM)	1879–1926	ZW1 I383	45 volumes in 3 series; 1879–1899, 1903–1920 including war supplement 1914–1917, 1921–1926	Edited by John Shaw Billings, Robert Fletcher, et al.; Published by F. Leypoldt, Carnegie Institution, etc.	Journals, books, pamphlets indexed; Subject arrangement with author indexes; intended to supplement the Index-Catalog, contains some material not in the Index-Catalog.
Bibliographia medica	1900–1902	ZW1 B5836	3 volumes	Edited by Marcel Baudouin; Published by Institut de Bibliographie, Paris	Publication of *Index Medicus®* was suspended from 1899–1902. In the interval, a similar index was issued in Paris by the Institut de bibliographie. In French.

(Continued)

Figure 9.2. Finding Older Medical Journal Articles *(Continued)*

Index Title	Years	NLM Call Number	Number of Volumes	Publisher	Description
Index-Catalog of the Library of the Surgeon-General's Office (ICLSGO)	1880–1961	Z 675 .M4 I38	61 volumes in 5 series; 1880–1895, 1896–1916, 1913–1932, 1936–1955, 1959–1961	Library of Surgeon-General's Office, Army Medical Library, Armed Forces Medical Library, and GPO (Government Printing Office)	Journals, books, pamphlets, theses indexed; Journal articles listed only under subject; Subject-author arrangement each series A-Z, except Series 5 which is A-M only.
Quarterly Cumulative *Index to Current Literature* (QCICL)	1916–1926	ZW1 Q4	12 volumes	American Medical Association	Journal articles indexed; lists of new books, publishers, new gov't pubs; aimed at English-speaking, clinical, American doctors; alphabetical dictionary arrangement.
Quarterly Cumulative *Index Medicus* (QCIM)	1927–1956	ZW1 Q3	60 volumes	American Medical Association; Carnegie Institute helped finance 1927–1931	Journal articles indexed; list of books and publishers; dictionary arrangement.
Current List of Medical Literature (CLML)	1941–1959	ZW1 C969	36 volumes	Army Medical Library; Armed Forces Medical Library	Journal articles indexed; table of contents arrangement with author, subject indexes; *use jointly with QCIM since indexed journals not the same*; 1957-1959 the ONLY index.
Index Medicus® / Cumulated *Index Medicus* (IM/CIM)	1960–2004	ZW1 I384	1960-2004, 45 volumes	*Index Medicus*: NLM ; Cumulated *Index Medicus*: American Medical Association (1960–1964), NLM (1965–2004) [GPO]	Searchable on PubMed. Monthly issues with annual cumulations; subject, author indexes with complete entry under each. Publication ceased with December 2004 edition (Volume 45).

Source: National Library of Medicine, 2010b.

information, has been recognized as a model for controlled vocabulary creation in other arenas and forms the basis of MEDLINE and PubMed searching (Lipscomb, 2000).

PubMed is "the freely accessible online database of biomedical journal citations and abstracts created by the U.S. National Library of Medicine" (National Library of Medicine, 2010d), and is the recommended starting point for any health literature search, whether for government documents or other sources such as citations of articles published in peer-reviewed journals. It is one of the most comprehensive and valuable tools in existence for finding such literature (including the broader Internet). Its building blocks are MEDLINE, with its indexing for 5,400 journals from around the world (although note that PubMed does include content in addition to that from MEDLINE), and MeSH (NLM's controlled indexing vocabulary). Understanding these building blocks makes using PubMed searching far more effective.

MEDLINE citations are useful not only because of the consistency of the record structures retrieved by PubMed, but also because each citation is indexed using these medical subject headings, or MeSH terms. The MeSH terms constitute a controlled vocabulary applied to each MEDLINE entry by NLM indexers. Using these terms is an invaluable tool for creating searches with consistent search strategies, and addressing possible differences in terminology between lay and professional language. For example, any article dealing with the substance vitamin C will be indexed with the MeSH term *ascorbic acid* (this is an example of vocabulary control). However, not every article about that substance will contain the wording *vitamin C*. Using the MeSH term for the search ensures that the search will find all related articles. In this case, either *vitamin C* or *ascorbic acid* would work, since MeSH contains entry terms which cross-reference related terminology; these let PubMed know that if the user types in vitamin C, the MeSH term *ascorbic acid* should be applied.

Using MeSH terms also connects a search in the most efficient way possible to the underlying structure of MEDLINE indexing. MeSH terms themselves are structured in a hierarchy, and searching can be more productive if the search terms are refined according to a particular term's place in that hierarchy. PubMed users can see the MeSH terms related to their initial search terms as part of the search results and can revise them interactively. A searchable graphic of the MeSH hierarchy is also available through PubMed. Not every phrase a user types in has a corresponding MeSH term, so one should always explore the hierarchy and possible related terms that might yield a tighter search. For example, Figure 9.3 shows that the term *health care costs* appears in two different tree structures, with varying related terms and concepts, which in turn may suggest previously unconsidered search strategies.

Another innovation from NLM regarding the organization of health information was the development of its own classification system, in use in many health sciences and other libraries (although not all libraries use the NLM classification, preferring to place corresponding materials in the Library of Congress's "R" class).

Figure 9.3. Example of MeSH Tree Structure

Health Care Economics and Organizations [N03]

  Economics [N03.219]

    Costs and Cost Analysis [N03.219.151]

           Cost Allocation [N03.219.151.080]

           Cost-Benefit Analysis [N03.219.151.125]

           Cost Control [N03.219.151.160] +

           Cost of Illness [N03.219.151.165]

           Cost Sharing [N03.219.151.170] +

          ▶ **Health Care Costs [N03.219.151.400]**

                 Direct Service Costs [N03.219.151.400.325]

                 Drug Costs [N03.219.151.400.350]

                 Employer Health Costs [N03.219.151.400.375]

                 Hospital Costs [N03.219.151.400.687]

                 Health Expenditures [N03.219.151.450] +

Health Care Quality, Access, and Evaluation [N05]

  Delivery of Health Care [N05.300]

           After-Hours Care [N05.300.049] +

           Attitude of Health Personnel [N05.300.100] +

           Attitude to Death [N05.300.125]

           Attitude to Health [N05.300.150] +

           Delivery of Health Care, Integrated [N05.300.262] +

           Dentist's Practice Patterns [N05.300.300]

          ▶ **Health Care Costs [N05.300.375]**

                 Direct Service Costs [N05.300.375.250]

                 Drug Costs [N05.300.375.300]

                 Employer Health Costs [N05.300.375.350]

                 Hospital Costs [N05.300.375.500]

           Health Care Reform [N05.300.380]

           Health Expenditures [N05.300.385]

           Health Priorities [N05.300.400]

           Health Resources [N05.300.420] +

           Health Services Accessibility [N05.300.430] +

           Health Services Needs and Demand [N05.300.450] +

           Healthcare Disparities [N05.300.493]

           Medical Tourism [N05.300.515]

           Needs Assessment [N05.300.537]

           Nurse's Practice Patterns [N05.300.581]

           Physician's Practice Patterns [N05.300.625]

           Professional-Patient Relations [N05.300.660] +

           Uncompensated Care [N05.300.830]

Source: Results of search on "health care costs" at http://www.nlm.nih.gov/mesh/MBrowser.html.

NLM *Classification* covers the field of medicine and related sciences. The scheme is a system of classification intended to be used for the shelf arrangement of all library materials, regardless of format ... [It] is a system of mixed notation patterned after the Library of Congress (LC) Classification where alphabetical letters which denote broad subject categories are further subdivided by numbers. NLM *Classification* utilizes schedules QS–QZ and W–WZ, permanently excluded from the LC Classification Schedules and is intended to be used with the LC schedules which supplement NLM *Classification* for subjects bordering on medicine and for general reference materials. (National Library of Medicine, 2010e)

Where Does Health Information Come From?

In order to assess and understand health information, it's helpful to understand how that information was created, and the cautions that may apply to using it. For example, obesity researchers know that people underreport their weight when asked about it in surveys. So, if obesity researchers look at a table that reports obesity percentages and notes a survey as its data source, they can assume that the percentage reported is on the low side of the true percentage, unlike data that come from a source in which patient height and weight were actually measured. Government documents and sources focus heavily on reporting information about health conditions, using current figures to reflect the health status of the population. In many (but not all) government documents reporting statistics, health information comes from one of three sources: vital statistics, surveys, and research/clinical trials.

Vital Statistics

Most of us are familiar with vital statistics data; anyone who has ever had to show a birth certificate to apply for a driver's license or passport has held a vital statistics reporting instrument in their hands. In general, vital statistics data refer to central events in the life cycle—births, marriages, divorces, and deaths—which are vital milestones in citizens' lives. Information about these transitions is considered essential to government operations. Communicable disease information and hospitalizations are also often considered vital statistics data. Generally this information is collected and collated by state health departments from individual reports of events by health care providers, agencies, hospitals, etc. Designated forms are used, with reporting requirements governed by state codes. The relevant government website or government publication, rather than a secondary source, should be the starting place for checking any of these figures.

Vital statistics data are uniquely valuable, because they cover the entire population which experiences an event. Not only is there complete population coverage, but the data are collected using forms that contain many items of detail about the persons involved. If, for example, researchers are interested in levels of mothers' education, they might be better off researching this question in a state that includes this item on the birth certificate, since by using birth certificate data, they are getting information about every birth that occurred in the state, as opposed to using survey data, which would give them information about only the sample of the population that was asked that question. Vital statistics also offer fairly consistent collection of information through the use of standard certificates. As long as one is fairly sure that the information is filled out completely and accurately for this item on the certificates, there is a high degree of certainty that the levels reported are close to the truth (of course, there are often systemic and other issues with completeness and accuracy of filling out certificates, but that is another discussion). In addition, these data sources can sometimes be linked and considered in conjunction with one another. One such source is infant deaths, which reflect deaths to infants in the first year of life, per 1,000 live births; this information is obtained from linked birth and death records (information from the death certificates of all babies who die under the age of one year are linked, using specific data fields, to the corresponding infant's birth certificate).

Vital statistics data can only go so far, however. They are collected at a particular point in time and with relation to a specific event, and they don't ask questions related to health behaviors and various health conditions. They can't give information such as whether new mothers continue to breastfeed six months after giving birth, whether younger people are more likely to use seat belts than older people, or whether medical expenditures are higher for men or women. For information about health behaviors such as these, and a host of other questions, one must turn to survey data.

Survey Data

Survey data most often come from information gathered from a sample of the population, usually collected following scientific methods that ensure that the sample is representative of the population at large. In general, the kind of survey data reported in government documents come from surveys sponsored and/or administered by government entities. Here are some of the health surveys conducted nationally and/or at the state level that are commonly used in health research and government reporting: the Behavioral Risk Factor Surveillance System; the National Health Interview Survey; the National Health and Nutrition Examination Survey; the National Health Care Surveys; the Medical Expenditure Panel Survey; the Youth Risk Behavior Surveillance System; and some questions on the American Community Survey and the Current Population Survey, both from the Census Bureau.

Survey data can be exciting because they can report on health questions directly. For example, if researchers want to know what percentage of the population gets an annual flu shot, they can ask survey respondents rather than trying to gather that information from health care providers. Survey data are therefore more flexible and responsive to current conditions than vital statistics data. However, this flexibility comes at a price; surveys are very expensive to administer, and therefore often don't completely cover an entire population of interest (for example, people who speak only limited English are commonly underrepresented in surveys). Also, since only a sample of the population is being questioned, the data being reported is an approximation, with associated error. A sample percentage, even if statistically manipulated, may not represent the true rate in the population.

Another issue with survey data is that they can't go into a great deal of depth. For example, phone surveys are kept to a maximum of about 45 minutes of questioning, in order to ensure participation. Surveys also may not focus on a particular issue of interest; for example, a researcher who wants to study attitudes toward binge drinking may find that available surveys ask only two or three questions about alcohol consumption, and nothing about attitudes.

Research/Clinical Trials

For a more in-depth look at a question, a research study may be called for. This is particularly the case if the information being sought is clinical in nature. The range of medical research is vast and beyond the scope of this discussion, including studies funded by private foundations, issue-oriented organizations, pharmaceutical companies, and other entities with health-related interests. For government-sponsored medical research, funding is generally supplied by the NIH in a competitive process. Loosely defined, the funded research may be basic medical research, focusing on laboratory findings, or a clinical trial, which measures the effects of an intervention on human subjects. It may take place in federal, state, or local government agencies, in universities, in health care settings, in free-standing laboratories and research institutions, or a variety of other settings. In addition, researchers who get NIH funding must share the data generated by their research with other researchers.

A final note: remember that in almost all cases, it takes some time for health data to become available to the public. Typically, vital statistics data for a calendar year will become available 12 to 18 months after the end of the year of interest (sometimes longer). Survey data are usually available within about a year of the completion of the survey data collection, depending on the sample size. These delays are due to the time required to gather the information from all sources, and additional time to process it; clean it (for example, remove values where there have been data entry errors, such as a person's age entered as 199 years); test it; analyze it; and prepare data sets, tables, and figures for release to the public.

Federal Resources and Organizations

The array of types and creators of health information is vast, and it can improve search processes to have some familiarity with the main resources and

Figure 9.4. Al Gore Introducing a Surgeon General's Report on Physical Activity (with Tipper Gore, U.S. Department of Health and Human Services Secretary Donna Shalala, and Surgeon General Joycelyn Elders)

organizations involved with the production and dissemination of publications, websites, and other material. This section covers the following topics: federal-level agencies and organizations, print resources, and websites. Remember that these will focus heavily on materials from the executive branch of the federal government. Figure 9.4 shows the executive branch in action; Vice President Al Gore is shown here introducing a surgeon general's report on physical activity and health.

Agencies

At the federal level, remember that government publications correspond to all three branches of government, and publications distributed via the Government Printing Office can be found in the *Catalog of Government Publications* and its predecessor, the *Monthly Catalog of United States Government Publications* (Robinson, 1998). Depending on the subject matter and purpose of a search, health information is contained in the publications of each governmental branch (Boorkman et al., 2004).

The specific question being researched will to some extent determine which agencies' publications to consult (refer to p. 217 for a list of agencies which may publish in various areas of interest). As discussed, HHS is a central organization for health-related information and oversees many federal agencies with associated agendas:

- National Institutes of Health
  http://www.nih.gov/
  Oversees medical research funding and operations, and contains NLM.
- Centers for Disease Control and Prevention
  http://www.cdc.gov/
  Deals with a range of health and safety topics, and oversees the National Center for Health Statistics.
- Agency for Healthcare Research and Quality
  http://www.ahrq.gov/
  Works to improve the nation's health care system.
- Health Resources and Services Administration
  http://www.hrsa.gov/
  Works to improve access to the nation's health care system.
- Food and Drug Administration
  http://www.fda.gov/
  Ensures the safety and efficacy of many of the substances and machines that come into contact with our bodies.
- Centers for Medicare and Medicaid Services
  http://www.cms.gov/
  Works to improve life conditions for older adults and people in financial or medical need.

Each agency's website has a research/data section with lists of publications. One agency that does not fall under HHS but is a central resource for health-related information is the independent Environmental Protection Agency (EPA), which has a mission of protecting not only the environment but also human health. The EPA is discussed in more detail in Chapter 12.

Print Resources

Whatever the research topic, consider starting with classic publications that are still issued in print format. Seeing a report in print can give a better sense of its big picture than exploring it piecemeal online. Tables can be easier to find and use in a printed hard copy than in its online counterpart. Looking at printed reports can be especially valuable for researching health-related trends and other historical questions; regular periodic reports may only have older print versions from the pre-Internet days, and thus the print copies may be the only way to look at a series over time.

The *magnum opus* of print publications related to health is *Health, United States*, published each year by HHS. *Health, United States, 2009* was the thirty-third such report issued. It has nearly 600 pages, including 150 detailed tables and a chartbook, as well as a special section on medical technology (each year's report has a focused section on a current health topic). Each year "*Health, United States* presents trends and current information on measures and determinants of the Nation's health. It also identifies variation in health status, modifiable risk behaviors, and health care utilization among people by race and ethnicity, gender, education and income level, and geographic location" (National Center for Health Statistics, 2010a). In addition to outlining health disparities, the report discusses access to health care and available resources, and health care insurance costs and expenditures, drawing from vital statistics and survey data. *Health, United States* is available both online and in hard copy. However, the information presented in a given year's report will be from the previous year or before, and the report is not likely to have information on a topic at any geographical area smaller than the state level.

Another important print publication (also available online at http://www.cdc.gov/mmwr/) is the *Morbidity and Mortality Weekly Report*, or *MMWR*, from the Centers for Disease Control and Prevention. "Often called 'the voice of CDC,' the MMWR series is the agency's primary vehicle for scientific publication of timely, reliable, authoritative, accurate, objective, and useful public health information and recommendations" (Centers for Disease Control and Prevention, 2010). The exciting aspect of this publication is that it is willing to present preliminary data in the interests of timeliness, which allows swifter tracking of current trends and information than can be found in some of its larger counterparts (such as *JAMA* or the *New England Journal of Medicine*, whose articles often are considered breaking news in the media). While centrally managed, it also reflects information submitted by health departments from all over the United States, many of them local jurisdictions, and it covers a wide range of topics, often crucially important to health care practitioners. The CDC also has more of a stake in surveillance (tracking health and disease patterns in populations) than do some more research-oriented agencies. This makes the *MMWR* (which is searchable via PubMed) the go-to source for questions related to trends in certain health conditions or practices.

The National Center for Health Statistics (a division of the CDC) reports on various areas of its work in its *Vital and Health Statistics Series*, also known as the Rainbow Series (because the original print volumes were printed on different colors of paper). "Series 1 to 6 include information about the NCHS program, reports about the methods its analysts use, international reports and documents that report on the activities of its committees...Series 10 to 16 report on the surveys conducted by the NCHS. These series are the principal vehicle for releasing survey specific results. Series 20 to 24 report on vital statistics including reports based on birth, death, marriage and divorce records and the results of the National Survey on Family Growth" (National Center for Health Statistics, 2010b). While these reports are no longer being issued in print format, the older volumes are invaluable resources for historical health-related research, and are still held in many depository libraries. Most are also available online, along with newer and current releases of this ongoing series.

Other prominent print publications are the *Healthy People* series, currently at *Healthy People 2010*, which sets out desired health status standards and targets for communities, and *Public Health Reports*, the journal of the United States Public Health Service (first published in 1878). Also consider looking at publications from agencies which are not normally considered health-related. For example, the Census Bureau's *Statistical Abstract* has a Health/Nutrition section that can be very useful, as it gathers information from a variety of sources into one unified set of tables.

Websites

Websites with health-related government information abound. These may be gateways to download the publications issued by an agency; they may be databases or interactive query systems to allow access to information; or they may be cross-agency information compendia. The NLM website (http://www.nlm .nih.gov) is a good place to explore, with its thoughtful, organized presentation of trusted sources. Not only can it be used in order to discover a range of websites, agency and otherwise, but it also includes an extensive listing of databases and other electronic resources. While it's not usually a problem to find a report if you know its name or the name of the issuing agency, the NLM site will facilitate finding reports and resources otherwise.

Another fruitful source of website resources can be found in the intersection of medical and government librarianship. Broadly conceived, these two types of librarians approach health-related questions in different ways; the medical librarian tends to start a search process with a focus on the subject matter, and the government documents librarian starts with a focus on relevant agencies, jurisdictions, and statistical sources. However, they will eventually meet in the middle, and their websites are each full of rich guides to best tools. Consider looking at the sites of health sciences libraries for pages listing government documents sites, and vice versa, at the sites of government documents libraries for pages on medical and health-related sites (Columbia University Libraries, 2010; Purdue University Libraries, 2010; The University of Delaware Library, 2010; University of Washington Health Sciences Libraries, 2010). Also be sure to look at the corresponding professional organizations' sites. An example is the "Information Issues and Policy" page of the Medical Library Association (http://www.mlanet.org/government/).

The following are some of the best federal-level government sites, which all health information seekers should have in their toolkits:

Articles and Databases

- PubMed (http://www.pubmed.gov/)
  "Comprises more than 19 million citations from MEDLINE and life science journals" (National Center for Biotechnology Information, 2010). Its content tends towards the academic, and therefore sophisticated search techniques (for example, incorporating MeSH headings into the search strategy, and/or using the advanced search option) can yield better results.

- National Technical Information Service (http://www.ntis.gov/)
  "The largest central resource for government-funded scientific, technical, engineering, and business related information available today," it offers

on the order of three million publications, many of them health-related (National Technical Information Service, 2010).

Consumer Health Information

- MedlinePlus (http://www.medlineplus.gov/)
  One of the best and most reliable websites currently available. Its content is user-friendly, and while it links to outside sites that are not government-produced, all of its links are vetted by librarians from NLM, and are trustworthy.
- Healthfinder (http://www.healthfinder.gov/)
  This HHS site overlaps MedlinePlus in some aspects (for example, both offer health encyclopedias), but is broader in scope and focuses more on connecting with services, and taking action toward healthy living.
- ClinicalTrials (http://www.clinicaltrials.gov/)
  A "registry of federally and privately supported clinical trials conducted in the United States and around the world... [giving] information about a trial's purpose, who may participate, locations, and phone numbers for more details" (National Institutes of Health, 2011).

Statistics

- FastStats (http://www.cdc.gov/nchs/fastats/)
  This service of the National Center for Health Statistics (a section of the CDC) is good for quick statistics, such as the current death rate from heart disease. From allergies to whooping cough, a full spectrum of topics is covered. Each has a page that lists the most current national statistics, links to the source reports (this can be useful itself), and gives additional resources of interest.
- CDC Wonder (http://wonder.cdc.gov/)
  This is a related site from the CDC, with a wider scope of data available, where users can run their own analyses.
- National Institutes of Health "Quick Links" (http://health.nih.gov/)
  This feature offers convenience in finding a range of health facts by topic.

Public Health/Environmental Health

- Public Health Partners (http://www.phpartners.org/)
  This is a "collaboration of U.S. government agencies, public health organizations, and health sciences libraries." It's aimed at the public health workforce, which comprises a number of professional roles and needs, and is one of the more comprehensive health-related sites. Features include "Public Health Topics" and links to "Current Public Health News."
- Environmental Protection Agency (http://www.epa.gov/)
  The EPA site contains a wide range of information on environmental concerns.

- TOXNET (Toxicology Data Network) (http://toxnet.nlm.nih.gov/)
  This NLM site allows searching on a range of databases on toxicology,
  hazardous chemicals, environmental health, and toxic releases.

State, Local, Tribal, and International Resources

Exploring resources produced by local, state, tribal, and international government agencies and organizations can yield valuable information in addition to
that published by the federal government. For example, if you are interested in
health questions at the county level, often federal publications do not contain
data at that level of detail, while state health departments may publish that
information in print and on the Internet. Likewise, many larger local health
jurisdictions will publish health information for areas smaller than counties. It
is harder to find sub-county information for rural areas than it is for urban
areas, as the small population sizes in rural areas usually don't allow for data
analysis and presentation. In fact, much of the health information available at
any level is driven by population or survey sample size.

State and local health departments often develop resources which are
updated regularly, so it is worth checking back with agencies of interest on a
consistent basis. Examples of this kind of resource at the state level are the *Vital
Statistics Annual Reports* from the Texas Department of State Health Services
(2010), and the *Annual Water Quality Report* from the New York State Department of Health (2010). A similar example of a locally produced resource is the
Annual Morbidity/Communicable Disease Reports series, from the County of Los
Angeles Department of Public Health (2010).

When looking for state and local health information resources on the relevant agency's website, consider searching within the site using the following
terms: statistics, vital statistics, data, publications, reports, and annual reports.
Often an agency will have a link to its materials using one of these headings.

For resources related to the health of American Indians, Alaska Natives, and
Native Hawaiians, be sure to look for information published by the tribe or
organization (regardless of whether the group is recognized by the federal government), as well as that released by federal, state, and local governments.
Nationally, the Urban Indian Health Institute (http://www.uihi.org/) and the
HHS Indian Health Service sites (http://www.ihs.gov/) can be excellent
sources of information on the health of these groups.

In addition, even if a question is not specifically international in focus,
looking at information from international government sources, as well as
intergovernmental organizations such as the World Health Organization, can
suggest avenues of inquiry and questions that might not occur to someone in
the United States context. For example, tables that include statistics on maternal
mortality are common in the context of the developing world, and can cast
light on the question of maternal mortality causes and prevention here in the
United States.

Indicator Websites and Additional Sources

A new genre of website is gaining popularity in the health information world: the health indicator website. Health indicators are generally data points which suggest the relative health of populations and groups. For example, life expectancy at birth and infant mortality are considered two basic indicators of a community's health. These websites are compilations of wide varieties of information from many sources, collected in one place for ease of use, which can be very helpful when researching across topics. They may be produced by governmental or nongovernmental organizations, but they almost always use a substantial amount of government-created content.

Some well-known sites of this type are the Community Health Status Indicators site, from the HHS; the Annie E. Casey Foundation's KIDS COUNT Data Center; and the United Health Foundation's America's Health Rankings. There are also a variety of state- and local-level indicator websites, such as the Community Health Indicators site from Public Health—Seattle & King County. Entering the words *health indicator site* in a search engine will yield a number of hits. You can also do a search on the health indicator title itself (for example, life expectancy) if you know it. Two cautionary notes: always double-check that the data included are recent, and be careful when using data from a website that reports a health index (a combined measure created from various separate pieces of health information) unless there is a clear understanding of the components of the index and the method used to combine them.

Last but not least, be persistent in searching for sources, especially grey literature: material that has not been formally published and is often difficult to find through regular channels. The New York Academy of Medicine Library publishes a Grey Literature Report (http://www.nyam.org/library/pages/grey_literature_report) that outlines the latest such health-related publications, some of them government-produced (Association of College and Research Libraries, 2004; Mathews, 2004). Consider exploring materials from legislative and judicial sources. And most importantly, just as one might use Google Scholar as a double check against a PubMed search, remember that any given search engine does not yield a reliable search of the entire Internet—always get a second opinion by repeating searches using a different search engine.

A Word on Consumer Health and Health Literacy

Many of us may never need to research any health topic beyond those related to our own personal situations. These kinds of searches fall under the term *consumer health*. Many resources will differentiate these kinds of questions from those focused on research or academic topics, in order to better serve information seekers' needs. A recent study by the Pew Internet and American Life Project and the California HealthCare Foundation found that 61 percent of Americans (corresponding to 80 percent of Internet users) go online for their health information, spawning the term *e-patient*. In addition, "60% say the information found online affected a decision about how to treat an illness or condition" (Pew Internet and American Life Project, 2009). And this doesn't even include increasing use of the Internet through wireless technologies such as handheld devices.

Clearly, this trend toward using the Internet as a source of personal health information is a phenomenon to be reckoned with, especially with the growing population of digital natives who are most comfortable with Web 2.0 applications. It raises questions such as: where are information seekers finding their information—are the websites they consult accurate and reliable? Current? Free from bias? Do searchers know how to assess the quality of a website—a crucial concern if they are acting on the medical information found online? Are they health-literate? (That is, according to *Healthy People 2010*, "the degree to which individuals have the capacity to obtain, process, and understand basic health information and services needed to make appropriate health decisions"). Among other things, health information seekers urgently need user-friendly tools and techniques for assessing websites' quality. A useful checklist is contained in the University of Washington Health Sciences Libraries' "Finding Health Information Online" (http://healthlinks.washington.edu/howto/finding_healthinfo.html).

The role of government-produced publications in this scenario is central, since their function is to deliver the most trustworthy information available. Government agencies by their very nature have a vested interest in making reliable information available in user-friendly formats and well-publicized sites. As mentioned earlier, MedlinePlus.gov and healthfinder.gov are major resources in this effort. Additionally, these two websites are interesting examples of the ways in which governmental resources can seem to be duplicative, but taken together add up to more than the sum of their parts. As Patricia Anderson, a University of Michigan health sciences librarian, put it in her blog,

> Why [are there] two major consumer health information sites supported by the government? You might as well ask why does the government support websites for both the CDC and the DHHS, or for Cancer.gov and CDC.gov/cancer, or many other examples. Basically, they aren't doing the same thing, they aren't targeting the same audience, they aren't used in the same way, they aren't providing duplicated content, AND having multiple sites maximizes the likelihood of general public searchers discovering quality information. (Anderson, 2009)

More remains to be accomplished, both in educating users about available resources, and in teaching users how to use those resources most effectively. Consumer health librarians are working hard to partner with organizations that can get the message out, and to lobby for ever-improved materials.

In addition to education about availability and use of consumer health resources, health information seekers need a heightened awareness of quality issues related to current health news stories on the Internet and in other news outlets. Media portrayal of health news items should be taken with a grain of salt, no matter what the perceived quality of the information source. Every statistic or finding mentioned is worthy of healthy skepticism.

An example is an article from the *New York Times* published March 23, 2010. In it, Denise Grady (2010) wrote, "Caesarean section has become the most common operation in American hospitals." This is a strong and seemingly clear statement. Grady's source was a recently released report on cesarean deliveries by Menacker and Hamilton of the National Center for Health Statistics. They wrote, "In 2006, cesarean delivery was the most frequently performed surgical procedure in U.S. hospitals" (Menacker and Hamilton, 2010). This statement is very different than the one reported in the *Times*. First, the underlying data was four years old at the time of the *Times'* reporting, but the *Times'* wording implied the information was current; secondly, the terms *operation* and *surgical procedure*, while they may mean the same thing to a layperson, do not have the same meaning in the health care arena (the latter is a more specific term). Digging deeper, it seems that Menacker and Hamilton's statement was referencing yet another source. That source, by C. Allison Russo, Lauren Wier, and Claudia Steiner of the Agency for Healthcare Research and Quality (2009), stated "C-sections were, overall, the most commonly performed operating room procedures in U.S. hospitals in 2006." Considering that not all surgical procedures in hospitals are done in operating rooms, it seems that Menacker and Hamilton and Grady would each have done better to stick with this original study's language. Their slight changes in wording made for differences in meaning that could have a substantial effect on the usefulness of the information for certain seekers. The moral is, if you see a statistic, question it, dig for the original source, and assess its usefulness for the information need at hand.

The Future of Government Health Information

When surveying the changes in information technologies over the last 50 years, it's clear that no one should dare to prognosticate what will happen in the next 50. However, a number of trends bear watching and may revolutionize how health information is delivered by governments. Both the phenomenon of the increasing use of the Internet and wireless technologies for consumers seeking health information, and the impacts these trends will have on the need for reliable and available government publications (in whatever format) online, have already been discussed here. Web 2.0 and its reach is a central aspect of these changes.

Another trend is the open access movement. This movement attempts to have the results of scholarly inquiry published such that they are available to any user, as opposed to being reported solely in scholarly journals from which users are restricted by cost, access to libraries, and other factors. While government information is almost always completely released in open access formats for users (in fact, that is a central tenet relating to any materials held by a depository library), the open availability of additional scholarly publications could have a positive effect on research and the dissemination of health information, government and otherwise. See Chapter 1 for a more complete discussion of this issue.

A further trend of note is the increasing use of the personal electronic health record. The federal government has mandated adoption of electronic health records by 2014 for all patients and providers, meaning that they are set to become a central aspect of the health information scene in the United States (Bradbury, 2009). As individuals' health information is increasingly held in electronic format, and in varied databases which can all be related to each other, health research may be revolutionized; interconnected electronic databases will allow analyses of previously unanswerable and complex health-related research questions. This, of course, may have impacts on government. Both from the researchers' position and from the standpoint of protections needed by research subjects in this scenario, regulatory interventions beyond those already in place are sure to be required.

There are two issues regarding government documents specifically that are perhaps the most immediate, and even most important of these trends. The first is the issue of materials that are no longer being printed, but appear only online. This phenomenon is increasing as printing budgets decline, and as people are more and more likely to turn to the Internet for information. Having reports issued only in online format is seen as efficient and cost-effective. However, there is no assurance that historical material will be kept online indefinitely, creating a problem for health researchers and others who are interested in historical statistics. Many of those in the health information professions are familiar with the scenario in which a health report that has been happily used for years is taken off a website, resulting in a frantic scramble to locate a colleague who can e-mail a PDF of the report. As print versions of government health information cease to be produced (even the venerable *Index Medicus* ceased publication in December 2004, supplanted by online databases), the online versions become ever more important—and our history of publications ever more vulnerable, even more so since government leadership and priorities change so often. Archiving online materials is an important aspect of preserving this history, and such archiving is made even more challenging by the rapid obsolescence of each new information storage technology. In fact, archived materials should be re-archived regularly, using the latest available storage practices, standards, and media.

The second issue is that of government publications which are no longer being printed by the government but by outside organizations, rendering them less freely available, and creating less control by the government over its own information. Many of the arrangements in which a private publisher prints government-produced information are long-standing (see Chapter 5, Law), but there is a trend toward new partnerships of this type.

A case in point is that of the publication *Public Health Reports*. This publication, the journal of the United States Public Health Service, was printed by the Government Printing Office from 1878 until the beginning of 1999. A press release at the time from the Robert Wood Johnson Foundation (a funder of the new project) states:

> The Association of Schools of Public Health developed a plan for *Public Health Reports* to convert from a federally financed (Department of Health and Human Services-Public Health Service) publication to a public-nonprofit partnership with the association. The project's goal was to increase the 117-year-old journal's quality, circulation, and impact on the field of public health by informing the public health community about the latest developments in science, research, policy, and practice. (Robert Wood Johnson Foundation, 1998)

Publication shifted in 1999 from the Government Printing Office to Oxford University Press, and then again in January of 2004 from Oxford University Press to Elsevier. In January 2010, print publication ceased altogether and only an online version was available by subscription or through a depository library. While archives are available online at PubMed Central (http://www.ncbi.nlm.nih.gov/pmc), they do not include the two most recent years' issues (and with health information, two years can be an eternity). Suddenly, the public could gain no-cost access to this journal, a government-sponsored publication, only by going to a depository library and asking for access via a password that a library staff person would have to provide; this is arguably much poorer access than in the past. In this example, we see that funding issues that lead a government to publish in partnership may make the government's connection to its own information vulnerable.

The future of government health information, then, appears to be one of balancing a vast proliferation of information and means of dissemination with the realities of funding and competing interests. It will be fascinating to see how it all plays out.

Exercises

1. A patron tells you he is about to have surgery on his knee. He is anxious, and wants to find a video of the procedure to watch ahead of time. What do you ask him to be sure you find the right source, and where do you look first?
2. Search PubMed for articles related to changes in vision as we age. Develop a list of five topic areas which you might want to research further (for example, glaucoma might be one of the topics).
3. As you do the searches above, jot down the MeSH headings that correspond to the terms you are entering (you can find them in the "search details" box after conducting the search). How much did they vary from the terms you entered?
4. Use your favorite search engine to look for indicator sites which give information on county rankings on health status. Were there certain sites that

stood out in your search? What do you think might be some of the factors that would affect a county's health status ranking? Where might you find component statistics for the rankings?

5. Read your favorite newspaper in either print or online form. Looking at the health-related stories, do you see any that cite statistics that were originally released in government documents? Can you find the document that the statistic came from, and is it accurately reported in the newspaper article?

6. Revisit the exercise you did in Chapter 3, where you followed a medical issue through Congress. Is there anything you might add now to the research resources you used for that question?

Selected Agencies and Sources Mentioned in This Chapter

Sources mentioned in this section do not duplicate the References that follow.

Agencies

Agency for Healthcare Research and Quality, http://www.ahrq.gov/.
Centers for Disease Control and Prevention, http://www.cdc.gov/.
Centers for Medicare and Medicaid Services, http://www.cms.gov/.
Department of Health and Human Services, http://www.hhs.gov/.
Environmental Protection Agency, http://www.epa.gov/.
Food and Drug Administration, http://www.fda.gov/.
Health Resources and Services Administration, http://www.hrsa.gov/.
Indian Health Service, http://www.ihs.gov/.
National Center for Health Statistics, http://www.nchs.gov/.
National Institutes of Health, http://www.nih.gov/.
National Library of Medicine, http://www.nlm.nih.gov/.
National Technical Information Service, http://www.ntis.gov/.
Urban Indian Health Institute, http://www.uihi.org/.
World Health Organization, http://www.who.int/.

Resources

About NLM Classification, http://www.nlm.nih.gov/class//nlmclassintro.html.
Annie E. Casey Foundation, KIDS COUNT Data Center, http://datacenter.kidscount
    .org/.
CDC Wonder, http://wonder.cdc.gov/.
Federal Depository Library Program, Passworded Databases, http://www.fdlp.gov/
    collections/building-collections/137-passworded-databases.
Final NIH Statement on Sharing Research Data, http://grants.nih.gov/grants/guide/
    notice-files/NOT-OD-03-032.html.
Health Information, http://health.nih.gov/.
Healthfinder, http://www.healthfinder.gov/.

Healthy People 2010, http://www.healthypeople.gov/.

Medical Library Association, Information Issues and Policy, http://www.mlanet.org/government/.

MedlinePlus, http://www.medlineplus.gov/.

MeSH Browser, http://www.nlm.nih.gov/mesh/MBrowser.html.

New York Academy of Medicine, Grey Literature Report, http://www.nyam.org/library/pages/grey_literature_report.

Partners in Information Access for the Public Health Workplace, http://www.phpartners.org/.

Public Health Reports, http://www.ncbi.nlm.nih.gov/pmc/journals/333/.

Public Health—Seattle & King County Community Health Indicators, http://www.kingcounty.gov/health/indicators.

PubMed, http://www.pubmed.gov/.

A Short History of the National Institutes of Health, http://history.nih.gov/exhibits/history/index.html.

United Health Foundation, America's Health Rankings, http://www.americashealthrankings.org/.

University of Washington Health Sciences Libraries, Finding Health Information Online, http://healthlinks.washington.edu/howto/finding_healthinfo.html.

References

Anderson, Patricia F. 2009. "MedlinePlus vs. Healthfinder: Must We Choose?" Emerging Technologies Librarian. April 29. http://etechlib.wordpress.com/2009/04/29/MEDLINEplus-vs-healthfinder-must-we-choose/.

Association of College and Research Libraries. 2004. "Gray Literature: Resources for Locating Unpublished Research." Available: http://www.ala.org/ala/mgrps/divs/acrl/publications/crlnews/2004/mar/graylit.cfm.

Boorkman, Jo Anne, Jeffrey T. Huber, and Fred W. Roper, eds. 2004. *Introduction to Reference Sources in the Health Sciences.* 4th ed. New York: Neal-Schuman.

Bradbury, Danny. 2009. "Obama and e-Health Records—Can He Really?" *The Guardian* (London), March 18. http://www.guardian.co.uk/society/2009/mar/18 electronic-medical-records.

Centers for Disease Control and Prevention. 2010. "MMWR Publications." Accessed March 27. http://www.cdc.gov/mmwr/publications/index.html.

Columbia University Libraries. 2010. "U.S. Government Documents, Ready Reference Collection: Health and Social Services." Accessed March 27. http://www.columbia.edu/cu/lweb/indiv/usgd/rref/health.html.

County of Los Angeles, Department of Public Health. 2010. "Acute Communicable Disease Control." Accessed March 27. http://publichealth.lacounty.gov acd/Report.htm.

Department of Health and Human Services. 2010a. "About HHS." Accessed March 27. http://www.hhs.gov/about/.

Department of Health and Human Services. 2010b. "Historical Highlights." Accessed March 27. http://www.hhs.gov/about/hhshist.html.

Department of Health and Human Services. 2010c. "Indian Health Service." Accessed March 27. http://www.ihs.gov/.

Grady, Denise. 2010. "Caesarean Births Are At a High in U.S." *The New York Times*, March 24. http://www.nytimes.com/2010/03/24/health/24birth.html.

Katcher, Brian S. 1999. *MEDLINE: A Guide to Effective Searching*. San Francisco, CA: The Ashbury Press.

Kurian, George T., ed. 1998. *A Historical Guide to the U.S. Government*. New York: Oxford University Press.

Lipscomb, Carolyn. 2000. "Medical Subject Headings (MeSH)." *Bulletin of the Medical Library Association* 88, no. 3 (July): 265–266.

Mathews, Brian S. 2004. "Gray Literature: Resources for Locating Unpublished Research." *C&RL News* 65, no. 3 (March). http://www.ala.org/ala/mgrps/divs/acrl/publications/crlnews/2004/mar/graylit.cfm.

Menacker, Fay, and Brady E. Hamilton. 2010. "Recent Trends in Cesarean Delivery in the United States." NCHS Data Brief no, 35, National Center for Health Statistics, Hyattsville, MD. March 2010. http://www.cdc.gov/nchs/data/databriefs/db35.pdf.

National Center for Biotechnology Information. 2010. "PubMed Overview." Accessed March 27. http://www.ncbi.nlm.nih.gov/entrez/query/static/overview.html.

National Center for Health Statistics. 2010a. *Health, United States, 2009: With Special Report on Medical Technology*. Hyattsville, MD. http://www.cdc.gov/nchs/data/hus/hus09.pdf.

National Center for Health Statistics. 2010b. "Vital and Health Statistics Series." Accessed March 27. http://www.cdc.gov/nchs/products/series.htm.

National Information Center on Health Services Research and Health Care Technology. 2010. "NCHS Published Reports Series." Accessed March 27. http://www.nlm.nih.gov/nichsr/usestats/Example16_NCHS_published_report.html.

National Institutes of Health. 2010a. "Institutes, Centers, and Offices." Accessed March 27. http://www.nih.gov/icd/.

National Institutes of Health. 2010b. "About the National Institutes of Health." Accessed March 27. http://www.nih.gov/about.

National Institutes of Health. 2011. "ClinicalTrials.gov." Accessed January 11. http://www.clinicaltrials.gov/.

National Library of Medicine. 1961. "The First Catalogue of the Library of the Surgeon General's Office, Washington, 1840." Accessed March 27. http://www.nlm.nih.gov/hmd/pdf/library.pdf.

National Library of Medicine. 2010a. "About the National Library of Medicine." Accessed March 27. http://www.nlm.nih.gov/about/index.html.

National Library of Medicine. 2010b. "FAQ: Index Medicus Chronology." Accessed March 27. http://www.nlm.nih.gov/services/indexmedicus.html.

National Library of Medicine. 2010c. "National Library of Medicine: John Shaw Billings Centennial." Accessed March 27. http://www.nlm.nih.gov/hmd/pdf/john.pdf.

National Library of Medicine. 2010d. "What's the Difference Between MEDLINE and PubMed?" Accessed March 27. http://www.nlm.nih.gov/pubs/factsheets/dif_med_pub.html.

National Library of Medicine. 2010e. "NLM Classification." Accessed March 27. http://www.nlm.nih.gov/pubs/factsheets/nlmclassif.html.

National Library of Medicine. 2010f. "The Story of NLM Historical Collections." Accessed March 27. http://www.nlm.nih.gov/hmd/about/collectionhistory.html.

National Technical Information Service. 2010. *Health, United States, 2008 with Special Feature on the Health of Young Adults.* Accessed March 27. http://www.ntis.gov/products/health.aspx.

New York State Department of Health. 2010. "Annual Water Quality Report." Accessed March 27. http://www.health.state.ny.us/environmental/water/drinking/annual_water_quality_report.

Pew Internet and American Life Project. 2009. "The Social Life of Health Information." June. http://www.pewInternet.org/~/media//Files/Reports/2009/PIP_Health_2009.pdf.

Purdue University Libraries. 2010. "Government Documents on Health." Accessed March 27. http://www.lib.purdue.edu/govdocs/health.html.

Robert Wood Johnson Foundation. 1998. "Federally Financed Health Journal Says 'Write On' to Public/Private Venture." November 1. http://www.rwjf.org/publichealth/product.jsp?id=17694.

Robinson, Judith Schiek. 1998. *Tapping the Government Grapevine: The User-Friendly Guide to U.S. Government Information Sources.* 3rd ed. Phoenix: Greenwood.

Russo, C. Allison, Lauren Wier, and Claudia Steiner. 2009. "Hospitalizations Related to Childbirth, 2006." Statistical Brief #71. Rockville, MD: Agency for Healthcare Research and Quality, Healthcare Cost and Utilization Project (HCUP). April. http://www.hcup-us.ahrq.gov/reports/statbriefs/sb71.jsp.

Texas Department of State Health Services. 2010. "Vital Statistics Annual Reports." Accessed March 27. http://www.dshs.state.tx.us/chs/vstat/annrpts.shtm.

The University of Delaware Library. 2010. "Selected U.S. Government Publications: A Research Guide." Accessed March 27. http://www2.lib.udel.edu/subj/godc/resguide/govinfo2.htm.

University of Washington Health Sciences Libraries. 2010. "Health Links." Accessed March 27. http://healthlinks.washington.edu/.

Chapter 10

Education Information

SUSAN EDWARDS

Today, education is perhaps the most important function of state and local governments. Compulsory school attendance laws and the great expenditures for education both demonstrate our recognition of the importance of education to our democratic society. It is required in the performance of our most basic public responsibilities, even service in the armed forces. It is the very foundation of good citizenship.

—*Brown v. Board of Education*, 347 U.S. 483 (1954)

Introduction

We are all deeply affected by education—as children, as parents, as citizens. Education has a profound impact on the quality of life and economic well being of individuals and communities, and is one of the largest expenditures of towns, cities, and states. Conducting education research can be challenging and complex, partly because education is at once both highly decentralized and subject to extensive federal oversight. Funding for education provides one example of the decentralization. The Census Bureau's June 2010 report on public education finances shows that in 2008, the federal government provided about 8 percent of the total funding for public elementary and secondary schools, while the states contributed about 48 percent and local governments provided 44 percent. The federal percentage is estimated to go up to about 10 percent in 2009–2010, with the state percentage going slightly down (Bureau of the Census, 2010).

Unlike many other countries, the United States has no national core curriculum—though there is a growing movement to create one with the Common Core State Standards Initiative (http://www.corestandards.org/). There is no national agreement on what is required to graduate from high school; or the age at which a student begins, or is allowed to leave, school. Decisions about what and how to teach have historically been controlled at or below the state level and can be highly contentious within and even between states, as demonstrated by ongoing battles over whether or how to teach evolution. Another recent controversy emerged when the Texas Board of Education decided, over the objection of historians, educators, and even librarians (Alire, 2010) to introduce a more conservative bias into the state's history and economics textbooks (McKinley Jr., 2010).

Yet within this historical backdrop of decentralization, there is an important and growing federal role in educational assessment, policy, funding, and research. This is in addition to the historic role of promoting equal access to educational opportunities, and preventing discrimination based on sex, race, ethnicity, national origin, or disability. For librarians and researchers, it's particularly important to know that the U.S. Department of Education plays a crucial role, both currently and historically, in collecting and disseminating information from the states about education at the local level.

Education reference questions are challenging, and have real-life implications. They frequently combine the personal and the political, the local and the federal, as in this question: "My child is eight years old and has cerebral palsy. What does the research show is the best practice for children like her? What does the law say she's entitled to, and how can I work with my daughter's teacher and school to make sure she is getting the best education possible?" In this chapter we will explore using government information from a variety of local, state, and federal sources to answer these and many other questions.

Government Involvement in Education

The Tenth Amendment of the U.S. Constitution (the final item in the Bill of Rights), enacted in 1789, provides that "the powers not delegated to the United States by the Constitution, nor prohibited by it to the States, are reserved to the States respectively, or to the people." Since education was not explicitly mentioned in the Constitution, it was deemed a state, not federal, function. However, since education touches on other fundamental rights established by the Constitution and civil rights legislation, and because it is so integrally related with the nation's economic and political well being, the federal government has been involved in education since at least the mid-nineteenth century. This role has expanded greatly through legislation, federal court decisions, and executive action.

State Sources

We think of the United States as having a core commitment to free public education, but this has evolved over time and historically was determined by the state, or even the city or town. The first statewide law requiring free public schools was enacted in 1826 by Massachusetts, which was also the first to make attendance compulsory, in 1852. (We'll see later, however, that in at least one town in Massachusetts, education was compulsory only for three months of the year!) School attendance didn't become mandatory in all states until 1918—though reflecting the decentralized nature of education, many cities passed free school legislation prior to their states' enactment of public school laws (Goldin, 2006).

Some states and local governments published (and continue to publish) annual reports that complement, and may precede, the federal education sources. The titles vary, and it can take a bit of sleuthing in the library catalog or in a secondary source to determine the exact title. In New York, for example, the *Report of the Superintendent of Common Schools* from 1823 provides information on school funding and on the number of students attending school.

As was discussed in Chapter 5, states each have their own statutes, case law precedent, and administrative law which will include education law. Education librarians should be familiar with the main sources for their state. The state department of education also may have a website that provides a helpful entry point for state and federal legislation related to education in your state.

> **Anti-Education Laws**
>
> At the same time that education was becoming more available for some, it was becoming illegal for others. In 1830, Louisiana passed the first law that prohibited teaching slaves to read; Georgia, Virginia, Alabama, and North and South Carolina passed similar laws between 1831 and 1835 (Goldin, 2006).

Federal Collection and Dissemination of Information

In 1867, the U.S. Bureau of Education was established to collect and disseminate information on schools and teaching, a role it continues to fill today through its successor, the U.S. Department of Education. The Bureau published an annual *Report of the Commissioner of Education* from 1869 through 1917 (Goldin, 2006) and it is a treasure trove of information on a wide variety of topics related to education. It contains reports from all the states, including many from towns and cities. These reports, like other primary sources, give a vivid sense of the attitudes, prejudices, and concerns of the time. For example, the *Report* of 1873 offers the following quote from a bishop in Dakota:

> Our missions are placed among a wild people, who, from the oldest down to the youngest, have never known any control, but have lived independent, idle lives, with no higher law than the whim of the moment. It is not easy to induce the children of such people to come to a day-school, and their parents would not think for a moment of compelling them. But they will come to a boarding-school, for there they find what they do not know in their own homes, regular meals, good clothing, and comfortable beds. These wild children become quite docile in the schools and their improvement is decided. (Bureau of Education, 1874: 479)

The *Report* includes articles on special topics, such as *On the Instruction of Deaf Mutes* by E. M. Gallaudet (first superintendent of what was to become Gallaudet University). In addition to his report on the pedagogy of the Clarke Institution for Deaf Mutes in Northampton, Massachusetts, he takes the time to report on an off-topic, but intriguing, overlap between the signs used by American Indians and the sign language of the deaf, including "identical or strikingly similar" signs for love, hate, fear, death, anger, river, and other words (Bureau of Education, 1874: 503).

But the bulk of the *Report* consists of detailed informational essays and statistics about the schools, libraries, museums, orphanages, and institutions for the deaf and blind. It's hard to imagine where else we could we learn that in Pittsfield, Massachusetts, in 1873, school attendance was compulsory for three months of each year for children between the ages of 8 and 14, of which only six weeks need be consecutive; or that in Mississippi eight years after the end of the Civil War, black parents were "forcing the question of mixed schools in cases where there are but two or three colored children in a subdistrict" (Bureau of Education, 1874: 222).

Congress and Higher Education

In 1862 Congress passed the Morrill Land Grant Act, which gave federal land to states which they could use (or sell, and use the proceeds) to found colleges of mechanical arts, military science, and agriculture. This was of great value to the states, but not everyone benefited equally. African Americans were not allowed to attend some of the original land-grant institutions, and in 1890 Congress passed the Second Morrill Land Grant Act. This act gave the Office of Education responsibility for administering support for the original land-grant colleges and universities and also mandated that the facilities be open to all students, or the state must establish separate institutions. In response, the Southern states then established 16 African American land-grant colleges, part of the historically black colleges and universities (HBCUs).

In 1944 Congress passed the GI Bill (you can find the official name in Chapter 5!) which included funding for vocational training and higher education for veterans returning from World War II. The GI Bill had a profound economic and social impact, making a college education attainable for many students who were the first in their families to attend. In 1947, the peak year, veterans made up 49 percent of college admissions. By 1956, when the original bill expired, almost half of all veterans (7.8 million out of 16 million) had participated in an education or vocational training program.

The Higher Education Act of 1965 included provisions for federally funded financial aid for needy college students. It was extended in 1973 with the federal Pell Grant program, and further extended when Congress passed the Taxpayer Relief Act of 1997, establishing the Hope Tax Credits, tax credits for lifelong learning, education IRAs, and the ability to deduct interest on student loans. Today, the federal government is the major source of financial aid for students in higher education.

The Supreme Court and Education

The Supreme Court has decided several key cases involving constitutional rights and education. For example, *Plessy v. Ferguson*, 163 U.S. 537 (1896), upheld racial segregation (including the resistance to integration that resulted in the land-grant funded historically black colleges and universities) with the "separate but equal" doctrine. This validation of racial segregation remained in effect until 1954, when it was overturned by the Supreme Court in *Brown v. Board of Education*. Other education-related Supreme Court decisions include *West Virginia Board of Education v. Barnette*, 319 U.S. 624 (1943), in which the Court held that students could not be compelled to salute the flag; *Engel v. Vitale*, 370 U.S. 421 (1962), which established that states could not require public prayer in schools, even if students were permitted to remain silent or leave the room while the prayer was recited; *University of California Regents v. Bakke,* 438 U.S. 265 (1978), where the Court ruled that while race could be a factor in admissions, racial quotas even in support of affirmative action violated the equal protection clause and could not be used to determine admission to a state-supported school; and *Plyler v. Doe,* 457 U.S. 202 (1982), which held that Texas could not deny access to a free public education to undocumented school-age children.

Federal Education Legislation

The first comprehensive federal education legislation was passed in 1958 in response to the Soviet launch of Sputnik during the Cold War. The goal of the National Defense Education Act (NDEA) was to help Americans remain academically competitive with the Soviets. The NDEA included loans for college students, as well as provisions to improve science, mathematics, and foreign language instruction in elementary and secondary schools (Department of Education, 2010).

In 1965 Congress passed the Elementary and Secondary Education Act (ESEA), the main federal law affecting education from kindergarten through high school. In order to promote equal access to education, ESEA included (and still includes) Title 1 funding. Title 1 directs funding to local school districts to improve teaching and learning for students in high-poverty schools. Sex discrimination in education was prohibited by Title IX of the Education Amendments of 1972, and Section 504 of the Rehabilitation Act of 1973 prohibited discrimination based on disability. In 1975, Congress passed the Individuals with Disabilities Education Act (IDEA) to ensure services to children with disabilities, and to govern how states and public agencies provide early intervention and special education (http://idea.ed.gov/).

In 2001, Congress reauthorized ESEA as the No Child Left Behind Act (NCLB). NCLB expanded the role of the federal government in education by mandating increased accountability from the states, school districts, and schools with the goal of ensuring that no child (or group of children) would be "left behind" in underperforming, high-poverty schools. NCLB required states to implement statewide accountability systems covering all public schools and students based on rigorous state standards. It also required states to measure statewide progress toward meeting the objectives set by the state with assessment results broken out by poverty, race, ethnicity, disability, and limited English proficiency (http://www2.ed.gov/nclb/overview/intro/execsumm.html).

Education Resources: Getting Started

The U.S. government provides numerous resources for education research, including information about education at the state and local level. The first two, the *Condition of Education* and ED.gov, are easy to use and can provide quick answers to some education reference questions. The third, Education Resources Information Clearinghouse (ERIC), is a much larger, more complex and powerful resource, so it is covered here in more depth.

The *Condition of Education*

The *Condition of Education* (http://nces.ed.gov/programs/coe/) is a congressionally mandated report of education in the United States. Published annually since 1975, it provides a national (not state or local) portrait of trends in early childhood through postsecondary education. It includes statistics and a narrative summary of student achievement, educational outcomes, and school environments and resources. Each year also provides in-depth coverage of a specific topic which varies from year to year. For example, the 2010 report provides a detailed analysis of high-poverty schools and a descriptive profile of the students and the people who work there, comparing them to low-poverty public schools in terms of resources and student outcomes.

ED.gov (U.S. Department of Education)

ED.gov ("ED") is a rich electronic portal from the United States Department of Education providing access to education information spanning preschool through graduate school. Educational policy is a particular strength of the site, and ED provides access to an extensive network of legislation, regulation, and policy guidelines on elementary and secondary education, higher education, adult education, special education and rehabilitative services, and vocational education. ED links to research publications and reports, and has a frequently updated news section and blog. ED is also delivering content with Web 2.0 technology, including Facebook, Twitter, and YouTube.

ED provides information in all areas related to the U.S. Department of Education's mission:

- Focus national attention on key educational issues.
- Prohibit discrimination and ensure equal access to education.
- Collect data on America's schools and disseminate research.
- Establish policies on federal financial aid for education, and distribute as well as monitor those funds.

ERIC

The Education Resources Information Clearinghouse (http://www.eric.ed.gov/), from the U.S. Department of Education, is the world's largest digital library of education resources. ERIC indexes published and nonpublished scholarly and professional literature in education. One of ERIC's historic and current strengths is to provide access to material that has not been formally published (also called grey literature or fugitive literature). This includes conference papers, dissertations, and material from research centers, policy and professional organizations, and federal, state, and local agencies. In addition, ERIC currently indexes 950 education and education-related journals.

ERIC began in 1966, and in the early years provided subscribing libraries with unpublished material on microfiche. In 1993 ERIC began migrating to the web (Weiner, 2009), and has actively worked to convert the microfiche to digital form. Some libraries still have ERIC microfiche collections, but much of this material (1966–1992) is now available online. Digital conversion is an ongoing effort, as ERIC continues to seek permission from copyright holders to make the remaining documents available online.

ERIC is not the only tool used to find education research, though it is the only one that is freely available as a government resource. In 2007 Jean-Jacques Strayer analyzed the indexing coverage of ERIC and compared it with some of the commercial databases. He determined that the commercial databases Academic Search Premier, Web of Science, and PsycINFO also uncovered useful education research depending on the topic and the depth of the researcher's information need, but stated that "[a] strong case can be made for starting with the ERIC database" (Strayer 2008: 91). Other commercial databases include Education Research Complete (EBSCO), Education Full Text (Wilson), and Educational Research Abstracts Online (Routledge).

ERIC continues to be a particularly valuable research tool because it has an extremely powerful search interface based on the Thesaurus of ERIC Descriptors (Thesaurus). Like the MeSH subject headings covered in Chapter 9, the Thesaurus provides controlled vocabulary to increase search precision. A word in the Thesaurus (called a descriptor) is not the same as a keyword. A descriptor is applied to the article by an editor to describe what the article is about, as opposed to a keyword, which is any word that appears in the bibliographic record—but which may or may not be the focus of the content. Controlled vocabulary also ensures that related words with the same meaning are brought together into one term. And as terminology changes over time, the descriptors provide links from earlier terms to current terms.

The Thesaurus also organizes the content of the database into a hierarchical list of approximately 40 broad subject categories, and then further refines those categories into numerous more narrowly focused subcategories. Browsing the top level categories gives an overview of the research being done in an area and the language being used to describe it. Like all disciplines, education has its own terminology (or jargon, depending on one's perspective) and using the Thesaurus is particularly helpful for the searcher new to the discipline. For example, the Thesaurus category of Reading further subdivides into areas such as Reading Aloud to Others, Reading Difficulties, Reading Fluency, Speed Reading, and more. The Thesaurus gives a scope note to describe the way the term is used in the database and provides links to additional terms on related topics. Once you find a helpful term it can be added easily to the advanced search query and combined with other descriptors or limits.

Let's look at how to use ERIC's thesaurus to help our parent trying to find research on the best educational practice for children with Cerebral Palsy.

Looking at Search & Browse the Thesaurus, she selects Disabilities. By browsing Disabilities, she can see the array of subtopics available. She selects the subtopic of Cerebral Palsy but notices some other related and relevant terms, such as Speech Impairment and Multiple Disabilities, which can be added to the search if Cerebral Palsy doesn't find enough material. After she adds Cerebral Palsy to the Advanced Search, ERIC displays the results and a panel on the left side of the screen lets her restrict the results in a variety of ways—by date, audience (whether the article is oriented towards teachers, researchers, parents, or another group), source (name of journal), education level, or publication type. Our parent cares most about the grade level, so she chooses to limit by Elementary Education and finds quite a few articles that are worth exploring.

ERIC also has recently implemented Web 2.0 features—so the search results can be shared via social networking sites, or added to an RSS feed reader so the searcher will be notified when new material meets her search criteria.

> **ERIC Research Tip**
>
> Today's searchers are used to typing in a few words and relying on the search engine to retrieve the most relevant results. Sometimes this approach fails—which is when they come to a reference librarian. Power searching a structured database with editor-added content like the Thesaurus and field restrictions can help them locate the precise information they need.

Statistics

Statistics questions are common in education reference, and most frequently involve the demographics of students and staff, school funding and expenditures, and educational attainment or achievement. Our patrons want us to help them find the one number that provides the hard data to support their argument. But statistics are squishy, as this recent newspaper article shows:

> State officials are claiming the state dropout rate declined by almost 11 percent over the last year, but critics say the data being used is flawed and doesn't accurately reflect what's going on in Texas schools. (Associated Press, 2010)

The article elaborates that a state report claims the dropout rate in Texas is 9.4 percent, while other studies estimate a much higher number of dropouts—up to 31 percent according to an independent education advocacy group. How can there be such a difference of opinion on what seems like such a basic question?

The graduation rate, which seems so simple, is actually quite complex—partly because there are different definitions of a dropout and different ways to count them. Different states use different methodologies, as do the Census Bureau and the National Center for Education Statistics. Some of the differences include whether the dropout rate includes students who left school but received a GED, whether students are counted who leave that school and move to another state or country, if students (including students with disabilities or with limited English proficiency) must graduate within four years in order to be counted with their cohort, and whether to count students who are expelled or who are removed to child protective services (Wolfe, 2009).

Different measures have different goals—determining the dropout rate of a given high school for school accountability purposes is a very different goal from measuring the total number of 16- to 24-year-olds who aren't in school and don't have a high school diploma or GED. And different data sources use different methodologies. All of the census data, for example, relies on a sample. It is self-reported data, and people may overreport their educational levels. State data come from administrative records and is more comprehensive—but it is not consistently handled from state to state, and has the built-in problem of not tracking students who leave school. For difficult to find (or understand!) statistics, search ERIC with a limit by the publication type of Numerical/Quantitative. The resulting articles can help explain the numbers, as well as the strengths and weaknesses of the different methodologies. And the sources cited may lead to the exact statistic needed.

An important part of the statistics reference interview is to determine the geographic level of the question. Is the patron interested in national level data? Or does he need the information broken out for a state, school district, or one particular school? Another important question is whether the information needs to be cross-tabulated. For example, does the patron want just the dropout rate by high school, or does she also want it broken down by (cross-tabulated with) race or gender?

The number of statistics reported from over 14,000 local school districts up to the state and the national level is growing, partly in response to No Child Left Behind and other standards-based reforms that require measurable progress towards educational goals. However, to answer some questions, you still need to consult district or individual school sources. One example of a question that requires using the local data is per pupil spending for each school within a district (currently called comparability).

Comparability is an important measure which shows whether fewer dollars are being spent in schools with more low-income students than those with more high-income students within a district. This gap is obscured if you are looking at the aggregate district or state data; it appears only at the individual school level. A recent study of comparability in California by the Center For American Progress (which implemented its own school-by-school finance data collection prior to the federal requirement) showed that "the aggregated salary gap between two otherwise identical schools with the average number of teachers, one with a student poverty rate of 50 percentage points higher than the other, amounts to approximately $76,000" (Miller, 2010). This discrepancy is attributed to teachers with more experience, and therefore higher pay, moving from high-poverty schools to low-poverty schools. This statistic should be easier to find beginning in 2011, as the U.S. Department of Education plans to collect and release the data on a national level for the first time.

Statistical Sources on the Web

This selective list of websites provides a wide range of education-related statistics. A particular website may focus on finance, achievement, demographic, or higher education statistics, but most contain a combination of these elements. All of the federal sources contain statistics for the states; some also have statistics for smaller geographic areas including school districts.

National Center for Education Statistics (NCES)
http://nces.ed.gov/

NCES is the primary federal entity for collecting and analyzing data related to education, located within the U.S. Department of Education and the Institute of Education Sciences. NCES publishes numerous reports and datasets each year. Some the NCES databases are individually covered in more depth within this list.

Digest of Education Statistics
http://nces.ed.gov/programs/digest/

A good starting place, the *Digest*, from the NCES, covers a wide variety of subjects including the number of schools and colleges, teachers, enrollments, graduates, educational attainment, finances, federal funds for education, libraries, and international education. All material is nationwide in scope, and spans from prekindergarten through graduate school. The *Digest*, like the *Statistical Abstract of the United States* covered in Chapter 8, also provides helpful information on the source of each of the statistics in the tables.

American FactFinder
http://factfinder.census.gov/

American FactFinder (from the U.S. Census Bureau and covered in Chapter 14), provides access to education-related statistics for the country as a whole, as well as for specific geographic areas, based on answers to questions from recent decennial censuses and the American Community Survey. For a quick start, select People (under Topics on the left navigation panel), and then expand Education to see which statistics are available on a subtopic such as educational attainment or school enrollment.

The American Community Survey (ACS), also covered in Chapter 14, offers a vast array of education-related data for states, cities and even school districts. The current ACS tables under the subject of Education: School Enrollment and Educational Attainment are listed here. You can enter the table number (the alphanumeric code on the left) into FactFinder for a quick look up.

B06009   Place of Birth by Educational Attainment in the United States
B07009   Geographical Mobility in the Past Year by Educational Attainment for Current Residence in the U.S.
B07409   Geographical Mobility in the Past Year by Educational Attainment for Residence 1 Year Ago in the U.S.

B13014 Women 15 to 50 Years Who Had a Birth in the Past 12 Months by Marital Status and Educational Attainment

B14001 School Enrollment by Level of School for the Population 3 Years and Over (Note: Tables B14002 and B14003 further break this down by Type of School and Level of School.)

B14004 Sex by College or Graduate School Enrollment by Type of School by Age for the Population 15+

B14005 Sex by School Enrollment by Educational Attainment by Employment Status for the Population 15+

B14006 Poverty Status in the Past 12 Months by School Enrollment by Level of School for the Population 3 Years and Over

B15001 Sex by Age by Educational Attainment for the Population 18 Years and Over

B15002 Sex by Educational Attainment for the Population 25 Years and Over (Note: this table is further broken down by Race/Ethnicity in tables C15002A–C150021.)

B15004 Poverty Status in the Past 12 Months by Sex by Educational Attainment for the Population 25 Years and Over

B16010 Educational Attainment and Employment Status by Language Spoken at Home for the Population 25 Years and Over

B17003 Poverty Status in the Past 12 Months of Individuals by Sex and Educational Attainment

---

Hispanic Classification

When using current census-based data, remember that White Alone includes Hispanics. By Office of Management and Budget definitions (see Chapter 7), Hispanic is not a race—Hispanics can be any race, including white, black, or some other race. Most users working with race/ethnicity will want to use White, Not Hispanic or Latino instead of simply White Alone.

School District Demographics System (SDDS)
http://nces.ed.gov/surveys/sdds/index.aspx

SDDS is a user-friendly version of some of the ACS data, plus some additional surveys and Census 2000 data, tailored to the school district level. However, SDDS doesn't have access to all the data elements in ACS and has one major drawback: for questions involving race and ethnicity, it currently uses the racial category of White Alone, which includes Hispanics who are white.

Public School Finance Data
http://www.census.gov/govs/school/

Since 1977, this Census Bureau survey includes financial data for all public school systems that provide elementary or secondary education. The data include revenue by source (local property tax, monies from other school systems, private tuition and transportation payments, school lunch charges, direct state aid, and federal aid passed through the state government), and expenditure by function and object. Since 1992, it also includes direct state aid for 11 different programs;

federal aid for Title I of the Elementary and Secondary Education Act, Children with Disabilities, and Impact Aid programs; salaries and employee benefits by function; maintenance, transportation, and business activities; and spending for instructional equipment. From 1957 to 1977, school expenditure data were collected and published as part of the Annual Government Finance Survey.

National Assessment of Educational Progress (NAEP, also known as The Nation's Report Card)
http://nces.ed.gov/nationsreportcard/

NAEP is the only national assessment of America's students in mathematics, reading, science, writing, the arts, civics, economics, geography, and U.S. history. NAEP provides results for populations of students (e.g., all fourth-graders) and groups within those populations (e.g., female students or Hispanic students). NAEP does not provide scores for individual students or schools, although state NAEP can report results by selected large urban districts.

State Education Data Profiles
http://nces.ed.gov/programs/stateprofiles/

The Profiles provide easy access to elementary and secondary education characteristics and statistics on finance, postsecondary education, public libraries, assessments, and selected demographics for all states. Via dropdown box or a map of the United States, users can select up to four states for comparison, or view U.S. averages as a whole.

Common Core of Data (CCD)
http://nces.ed.gov/ccd/

CCD annually collects fiscal and non-fiscal data about all public schools, public school districts, and state education agencies in the United States. The data are supplied by state education agency officials and include information for schools and school districts, including name, address, and phone number; descriptive information and demographics about students and staff; and fiscal data, including revenues and current expenditures. (This database is challenging; most users will need some help!)

State Contacts and Information
http://www2.ed.gov/about/contacts/state/index.html

This site provides a quick place to look for key statistics and additional information (such as Recovery Act Funding and Accountability Plans) and ED press releases by state. It also includes a useful list of contact information (phone numbers, e-mail, address, and website) for state education agencies and education-related organizations.

IPEDS: Integrated Postsecondary Education Data System
http://nces.ed.gov/ipeds/

This is the place to go for answers to in-depth questions requiring higher education statistics. IPEDS gathers information from every college, university, and technical and vocational institution that participates in the federal student financial aid programs. It includes data on student characteristics (race/ethnicity, gender, and age); institutional characteristics; institutional prices; enrollment; student financial aid; degrees and certificates conferred; graduation rates; and the institution's human and fiscal resources.

Historical Statistics

The first education statistics for the United States as a whole come from the 1840 decennial census. Slavery in the United States was legally sanctioned at that point, and free white men and women were asked whether they were literate. In 1850 and 1860 all free inhabitants, regardless of race or gender, were asked about literacy. In 1850 the census added a question about school attendance, but not until 1940 did it ask about the highest grade completed (York, 2002).

> **Contacting Agencies Directly**
>
> Sometimes the state education agency (or even the school or school district) has additional data that are not included in the published national or state sources. Personal contact may turn up that extremely elusive statistic that a patron needs. When calling or e-mailing, let the agency representatives know they are speaking with a librarian, and list the resources already searched. It establishes the librarian's appreciation for their expert knowledge and respect for their time. A handy list of state contacts is available at http://www2.ed.gov/about/contacts/state/index.html.

In 1867 the Bureau of Education (precursor to the cabinet-level Department of Education) was established, and the *Report of the Commissioner of Education* (title varies, also called *Annual Reports of the Commissioner of Education*) was published from 1869–1870 through 1916–1917 (Goldin, 2006). The original *Reports* may be difficult to find, but fortunately for librarians and researchers, these *Reports* were included in the U.S. *Congressional Serial Set*, which is also commercially available online. The *Reports* were continued by the *Biennial Survey of Education in the United States* through 1957–1958, followed by the *Digest of Education Statistics* from 1962 to the present. Selected statistics from these series are also included in the *Historical Statistics of the United States* as discussed in Chapter 8.

For those who want a bit less detail with their statistics, the National Center for Education Statistics published *120 Years of American Education: A Statistical Portrait*. It is also available on the web (http://nces.ed.gov/pubs93/93442.pdf) and lists historical sources, a brief history of education statistics, and statistical tables.

Some states (and even some school districts) have collected and published a variety of education-related reports including statistics on school finance, student demographics, and student achievement. In many cases these reports provide much more detailed information than the national compilations, and may even predate them. Many of these statistics are not found online; they exist only on paper and can be difficult to locate through the library catalog. As discussed in Chapter 8, it's important to think about who might have collected the data, and then to be creative with searching for agencies as authors in the catalog. For example, a patron is interested in education in Oakland, California, in the late nineteenth and early twentieth centuries. Searching the library catalog with simple keywords of education, California, and Oakland retrieves *Rules and Regulations of the Board of Education of the city of Oakland, California* from 1897. The full record leads us to the corporate author entry of "Oakland (Calif.). Board of Education." Finding this access point allows us to retrieve many relevant titles, including the *Annual Report* of the Board of Education from 1872 to 1918. Note that the corporate author is a very useful access point for historical government documents; it frequently retrieves more titles than searching by subject heading.

Since many education questions have a local focus, it's helpful to familiarize yourself with the sources available for your state and local area, as well as with how your library has cataloged them.

Emerging Trends in Education Research

Evidence-based practice is "a new educational and practice paradigm for closing the gaps between research and practice to maximize opportunities to help clients and avoid harm" (Gambrill 2006, 339). Evidence-based policy initiatives in education such as the 2001 No Child Left Behind legislation emphasize research as a necessary prerequisite for program support. In 2002, Congress created the Institute of Education Sciences (http://ies.ed.gov) to conduct and disseminate scientifically valid education research using methods from science and medicine such as randomized controlled trials and meta-analysis of the literature. As the IES website states:

> Our mission is to provide rigorous and relevant evidence on which to ground education practice and policy and share this information broadly. By identifying what works, what doesn't, and why, we aim to improve educational outcomes for all students, particularly those at risk of failure.

The implementation of these initiatives in education has not been without controversy. Some of the definitions of "what works" used by the What Works Clearinghouse have been criticized, and some have questioned whether test scores might rise as a result of "teaching to the test" rather than increasing the literacy and/or math skills of the students. There are concerns that standardized tests and accountability measures don't adequately take into account the impact of our long history of racial and socioeconomic disenfranchisement in education, and the difficulty of hiring and retaining skilled teachers in poorer school districts (Willinsky, forthcoming, also noting research of Banks and Darling-Hammond). More fundamentally, there is a sense that some of the emerging research is itself methodologically flawed, and that teachers are expected to improve student performance even though rigorous studies have exposed major deficits in the curricula that they are required to use (Begley, 2010). These criticisms are not a condemnation of using research to inform educational policy, but a plea to generate and disseminate more high-quality educational research.

Resources for evidence-based practice in education include the following:

- ERIC (http://www.eric.ed.gov/) indexes research based on evidence-based practice as well as information produced and disseminated by the What Works Clearinghouse (http://ies.ed.gov/ncee/wwc/), the ten Regional Educational Laboratories (http://ies.ed.gov/ncee/edlabs/), and the Research and Development Centers (http://ies.ed.gov/ncer/randd/).
- Best Evidence Encyclopedia: Empowering Educators with Evidence on Proven Programs (http://www.bestevidence.org/), from Johns Hopkins University School of Education's Center for Data-Driven Reform in Education, provides reviews of evidence-based programs.
- Doing What Works (http://dww.ed.gov/) offers research-based education practices online from the U.S. Department of Education.
- The Wing Institute (http://www.winginstitute.org/) is an independent, nonprofit organization promoting evidence-based education policies and practices.
- The Campbell Collaboration (http://www.campbellcollaboration.org/) provides a library of systematic reviews on the effects of interventions in education.

Open Access

As discussed in Chapter 1, open access is a growing movement to remove price barriers to information by making it freely available online. While the movement has found some resonance in the field of education, most academic education research is not freely available on the web. Remember our parent looking for information about how to help her child with cerebral palsy get the best education possible? Although the citations indexed in ERIC are freely available to anyone with access to the web, almost none of the actual articles she located are freely available online. Without open access, the work of educational researchers remains isolated within the academy (Willinsky, forthcoming).

Conclusion

As librarians, we have an important role in helping to ensure that educators, researchers, parents, and policy makers have meaningful access to the information they need. Education research is particularly challenging, because it frequently requires federal, state, and local government sources, as well as scholarly publications and the extensive grey literature produced by think tanks, nonprofits, and government agencies. As government documents librarians, we are fortunate to have some very powerful research tools available to us—and once we learn to use them, we can help parents, students, and researchers find the information they need.

Exercises

1. Using your library catalog (or WorldCat, if that's appropriate), what is the earliest government education source for your state?

2. Using American FactFinder (http://factfinder2.census.gov/), select People from the left-hand column and then Education. Using American Community Survey (ACS) 5-year estimates for your state, find:
   - What percent of the population ages 18–24 has less than a high school degree?
   - What is the percentage for males? For females?
   - What is the percentage for your county? Is it higher or lower than the state?

3. Using NAEP State Profiles (http://nces.ed.gov/nationsreportcard/states/), take a look at the report for your state. Did your state test higher or lower than the national average for eighth-grade math? Navigate to http://nces.ed .gov/nationsreportcard/statecomparisons. Select eighth-grade math and the latest year available, which lets you also select different student groups. Was there a gap in achievement based on gender? On race?

4. A student is interested in quantitatively based articles on the black-white achievement gap in high school. In ERIC, should you use Blacks or African Americans as a descriptor? (Hint: look at the Thesaurus for the terms and read the scope notes.) How would you restrict the search to articles with a quantitative focus?

Sources Mentioned in This Chapter

Sources mentioned in this section do not duplicate the References that follow.

Legislation and Court Cases (Chronological Order)

Agricultural and Mechanical Colleges Acts (Morrill Acts), (July 2, 1862, 12 Stat. 503).
Second Morrill Act (August 30, 1890, 26 Stat. 417).
Plessy v. Ferguson, 163 U.S. 537 (1896).
West Virginia Board of Education v. Barnette, 319 U.S. 624 (1943).
Brown v. Board of Education, 347 U.S. 483 (1954).
National Defense Education Act, P.L. 85-864, 72 Stat. 1580 (1958).
Engel v. Vitale, 370 U.S. 421 (1962).
Elementary and Secondary Education Act, P.L. 89-10, 79 Stat. 27 (1965).
Higher Education Act of 1965, P.L. 89-329, 79 Stat. 1219 (1965).

Education Amendments of 1972 (includes Title IX), P.L. 92-318, 86 Stat. 235 (1972).

To amend the Education Amendments of 1972... (Pell Grants, also known as Basic Educational Opportunity Grants), P.L. 93-35, 87 Stat. 72 (1973).

Rehabilitation Act of 1973, P.L. 93-112; 87 Stat. 355 (1973).

Education for all Handicapped Children Act, P.L. 94-142, 89 Stat. 773 (1975); the name was changed by P.L. 101-476 to the Individuals with Disabilities Education Act (104 Stat. 1103, 1990).

University of California Regents v. Bakke, 438 U.S. 265 (1978).

Plyler v. Doe, 457 U.S. 202 (1982).

Taxpayer Relief Act of 1997, P.L. 105-34, 111 Stat. 788 (1997).

No Child Left Behind Act, P.L. 107-110, 115 Stat. 1425 (2002); overview at http://www2 .ed.gov/nclb/overview/intro/execsumm.html.

Department of Education

120 Years of American Education: A Statistical Portrait, http://nces.ed.gov/pubs93/ 93442.pdf.

Common Core of Data (CCD), http://nces.ed.gov/ccd/.

Condition of Education, http://nces.ed.gov/programs/coe/.

Department of Education, http://www.ed.gov/.

Digest of Education Statistics, http://nces.ed.gov/programs/digest/.

Doing What Works: Research Based Education Practices Online, http://dww.ed.gov/.

Education Resources Information Clearinghouse, http:// www.eric.ed.gov/.

Individuals with Disabilities Education Act, http://idea.ed.gov/.

IPEDS: Integrated Postsecondary Education Data System, http://nces.ed.gov/ipeds/.

National Assessment of Educational Progress (The Nation's Report Card), http://nces .ed.gov/nationsreportcard.

National Center for Education Statistics (NCES), http://nces.ed.gov.

School District Demographics System (SDSS), http://nces.ed.gov/surveys/sdds/index .aspx.

State Contacts and Information, http://www2.ed.gov/about/contacts/state/index.html.

State Education Data Profiles, http://nces.ed.gov/programs/stateprofiles/.

Regional Educational Laboratories, http://ies.ed.gov/ncee/edlabs/.

Research and Development Centers, http://ies.ed.gov/ncer/randd/.

What Works Clearinghouse, http://ies.ed.gov/ncee/wwc/.

Other Sources

American Community Survey, http://www.census.gov/acs/.

American FactFinder, http://factfinder.census.gov/.

Best Evidence Encyclopedia: Empowering Educators with Evidence on Proven Programs, http://www.bestevidence.org/.

Campbell Collaboration, http://www.campbellcollaboration.org/.

Common Core State Standards Initiative, http://www.corestandards.org/.

Public School Finance Data, http://www.census.gov/govs/school/.

Wing Institute: Evidence-Based Education, http://www.winginstitute.org/.

References

Alire, Camila A. 2010. "Letter from the American Library Association to the Texas State Board of Education." American Library Association. May 13. http://www.ala.org/ala/aboutala/offices/oif/ifissues/texas_curriculum_sta.pdf.

Associated Press. 2010. "State Report Pegs Dropout Rate at 9.4%." *Education Week*, July 16. http://www.edweek.org/ew/articles/2010/07/16/366028txdropoutratetexas_ap.html.

Begley, Sharon. 2010. "Second Class Science: Education Research Gets an F." *Newsweek*, May 10. http://www.newsweek.com/2010/04/30/second-class-science.html.

Bureau of the Census. 2010. *Public Education Finances 2008*. June. http://www2.census.gov/govs/school/08f33pub.pdf.

Bureau of Education. 1874. *Report of the Commissioner of Education for the Year 1873*. Washington, DC: Government Printing Office.

Department of Education. 2010. "The Federal Role in Education." Accessed August 20. http://www2.ed.gov/about/overview/fed/role.html.

Department of Veterans Affairs. 2010. "GI Bill History." Accessed August 2. http://www.gibill.va.gov/gi_bill_info/history.htm.

Gambrill, Eileen. 2006. "Evidence-Based Practice and Policy: Choices Ahead." *Research on Social Work Practice* 16, no. 3: 338–357.

Goldin, Claudia. 2006. "Education." In *Historical Statistics of the United States (online)*, Susan B. Carter, Scott Sigmund Gartner, Michael R. Haines, Alan L. Olmstead, Richard Sutch, and Gavin Wright, eds. Millennial ed., vol. 2: 387. Cambridge, England; New York: Cambridge University Press.

McKinley, James C., Jr. 2010. "Texas Conservatives Win Curriculum Change." *New York Times*, March 13. http://www.nytimes.com/2010/03/13/education/13texas.html.

Miller, Raegen T. 2010. "Comparable, Schmomparable: Evidence of Inequity in the Allocation of Funds for Teacher Salary within California's Public School Districts." May. Washington, DC: Center for American Progress. http://www.americanprogress.org/issues/2010/05/pdf/comparable_schmomparable.pdf.

Strayer, Jean-Jacques. 2008. "ERIC Database Alternatives and Strategies for Education Researchers." *Reference Services Review* 36, no. 1: 86–96.

Weiner, Sharon A. 2009. "Tale of Two Databases: The History of Federally Funded Information Systems for Education and Medicine." *Government Information Quarterly* 26, no. 3: 450–458.

Willinsky, John. Forthcoming. "The New Openness in Educational Research." In *The SAGE Companion to Research in Education*, Paul Hart, Alan Reid, and Constance Russell, eds. London: Sage Publications. Preprint. Accessed July 19, 2010. http://pkp.sfu.ca/files/Sage%20Companion.pdf.

Wolfe, Christine O. 2009. *The Great Graduation-Rate Debate*. Washington, DC: Thomas B. Fordham Institute. July. http://www.eric.ed.gov/PDFS/ED508051.pdf.

York, Grace. 2002. "Population and Housing Items on the General Census Schedules, 1790–2000." University of Michigan Library. March. http://guides.lib.umich.edu/data/files3/102838/Historic%20Population%20and%20Housing%20Items.xls.

Chapter 11

Scientific and Technical Information

Margaret M. Jobe

Introduction

The United States government is one of the most prolific producers and publishers of scientific and technical information in the world—so prolific that it can be difficult to know where to start. The material produced, published, or distributed by the government ties directly to the legislatively mandated responsibilities of individual executive branch agencies such as the Department of the Interior and independent agencies such as the Environmental Protection Agency and NASA. The content ranges from fact sheets geared to a general audience to technical publications aimed at specialists in science disciplines. While some publications are written by employees of individual agencies, a significant number are written under contracts between the federal government and state agencies, universities, or other for-profit and not-for-profit organizations.

Why should a general librarian care about access to scientific and technical information? Because scientific and technical advances affect every aspect of our lives and form the basis of many of the policy and procedural decisions of the government. For example, we take tap water for granted with the understanding that regulations are in effect which prevent exposure to damaging amounts of toxic substances. How are those levels set? The Environmental Protection Agency uses basic science to determine nontoxic levels of harmful substances and writes regulations that help limit exposure. We tend to take other scientific developments such as the Internet for granted. In a comparatively short period of time, the Internet has transformed the way we access and look for information. Whether you think about it consciously or not, scientific and technical information profoundly affects our daily lives. Since the Internet has greatly increased our knowledge of and access to scientific information, it makes sense to understand the best sources to better serve our users.

Multiple Distribution Methods

Although the federal government has multiple channels for distribution of information, there are three main distribution methods relevant to this discussion:

sale and distribution to depository libraries by the Government Printing Office; sale by the National Technical Information Service; and distribution through the Internet on agency websites. Publications for sale by NTIS are often called technical reports, although that term can be applied equally to much of the information distributed by GPO and NTIS and available on agency websites. Confusion about the nature of technical reports is compounded by the some-times multiple means of dissemination, including distribution in tangible or electronic formats. Let's look at one example. *The Apollo Spacecraft: A Chronology* was distributed to depository libraries in four volumes with the SuDocs number NAS 1.21:4009/V.1-4. Volumes 1–3 were also distributed by NTIS with separate order numbers for each volume in the set. Lastly, the four volumes of the report are available in HTML from the NASA website (http://www.nasa .gov/) and as PDF files from the NASA Technical Reports Server (http://ntrs .nasa.gov/). Strictly speaking, this is not a technical report, but you get the drift. *The Apollo Spacecraft* nicely illustrates the point that one publication can be associated with multiple identifiers including a SuDocs number, an NTIS order number, an agency technical report number, a contract number, a series number, and so on. In the pre-Internet days, unraveling the various numbers and access points presented significant challenges. Now that the web is a mature delivery platform, it is fairly easy to unravel and locate information about known items.

Most people have a general notion about what we mean when we use the word *science*, but what is a technical report? Ellen Calhoun defines a technical report as "an account of work done on a research project which a scientist com-piles to convey information to his employer or sponsor or to other scientists." She further observes that, while there is great variability in the quality of the writing or presentation, technical reports "usually represent the first appearance in print of current scientific investigations" (Calhoun, 1991: 163). Figure 11.1 shows the cover page of a typical technical report.

Figure 11.1. Sample Technical Report

RECEIVED

OCT 2 4 2000

OSTI   DOE/ID/13511

TITANIUM METAL POWDER PRODUCTION BY THE PLASMA QUENCH
PROCESS

FINAL REPORT
01/31/1997 – 12/31/1999

R. A. Cordes
A. Donaldson

September 2000

Government Printing Office

Materials published by the GPO are distributed to a network of depository libraries around the country. While not every library receives every publication, the library serving as the regional depository should have copies of all publications distributed by GPO through the program. Since 1976, many depository libraries have added records for government information to their catalogs. With a nationwide network of libraries and catalog records in local catalogs and bibliographic networks, most materials that are not available locally should be available through interlibrary loan. Some materials are available from sale from the GPO Bookstore (http://bookstore.gpo.gov/).

Access points for materials distributed to depository libraries by GPO:

- The Catalog of Government Publications or CGP (http://catalog.gpo.gov/) includes bibliographic records for current material and a growing selection of historical material published before 1976. The site has simple and advanced search options. Records include links to digital versions for those that are available online. A large and increasing amount of government information is only distributed online. For a recent search for air pollution limited to Internet Publications under Catalogs in the advanced search interface, results included *Promoting Good Prenatal Health: Air Pollution and Pregnancy*, a fact sheet with tips for avoiding indoor and outdoor sources of air pollution.
- The Federal Depository Library Directory (http://catalog.gpo.gov/fdlpdir/FDLPdir.jsp) provides contact information, links to depository websites, and library catalogs.

National Technical Information Service

The National Technical Information Service provides a separate distribution mechanism for scientific and technical information and has some overlap in coverage with the materials distributed by GPO. The organization now known as NTIS has gone through several name and mission changes since its founding shortly after World War II. The original purpose was to translate and disseminate captured German scientific and technical documents to speed the development of military technology. Over time that role expanded to include indexing and distribution of federal scientific and technical information. In 1970, Congress created NTIS as a self-supporting agency under the umbrella of the Department of Commerce. Scientific and technical information, because it can fuel innovation, fulfills the Department of Commerce's overall mission to promote economic growth. With its mandate to be self-supporting, NTIS relies on sales of reports, indexing tools, and specialized databases and services for its continued existence. This makes NTIS technical reports one of the few instances where taxpayer-funded publications are not necessarily available to citizens for free.

The research tool produced by NTIS is the NTIS Database. Before the Internet matured, NTIS was the first place to look for technical reports. While NTIS is still a rich tool for government-funded scientific and technical research, its status as the premier tool has been somewhat diminished by the availability of individual agency-developed publications databases. Furthermore, the scope of the database has changed: NTIS has greatly expanded the subject coverage of the database so that it is no longer limited strictly to technical reports. For example, the *Statistical Abstract of the United States*, a reference standard distributed to depository libraries and sold by GPO (discussed in Chapter 8), is available for sale from NTIS. Also for sale is *Women in Iraq: Background and Issues for U.S. Policy*, a publication of the Congressional Research Service, an agency whose publications, while not technical, are not distributed by GPO (and are covered in Chapter 3).

Access points for NTIS (1964–present) are:

- Complete database with all features: Licensed versions of the NTIS bibliographic database of scientific, technical, and related information are available from vendors such as Cambridge Scientific Abstracts, Ovid, EBSCO, Engineering Information, and others. The licensed version of the database, which includes basic publication and order information as well as abstracts and controlled and uncontrolled terms, and various numbers, such as report number and contract number, is preferred for sophisticated searching. While the database coverage began in 1964, it now includes some citations that precede that date.
- Limited version: A free but limited version of the NTIS Database is available from the NTIS homepage (http://www.ntis.gov/). Although an advanced search feature is available, search results are much less precise because the individual bibliographic records have been slimmed down into thin versions with only the most basic information. NTIS, ever mindful of its need to be self-sustaining, relies on this thin version to generate direct sales while avoiding competition with the vendors leasing the full-featured version of the database. Because NTIS indexes technical literature from a wide area of federal agencies, however, even the basic search can yield relevant information. Armed with a known title, one can easily search for full text.
- Full-text version: National Technical Reports Library (NTRL) (http://ntrl.ntis.gov) is a subscription-based version of the NTIS database that includes bibliographic citations and selected full text for the technical reports subset of the database. Citations to materials other than technical reports which are available from the licensed and free versions of NTIS have theoretically been excluded from NTRL. Exactly what constitutes a technical report, however, is a little fuzzy. The full text of *Women in Iraq* is also available in this database, as well as *Structural Design Aspects and Criteria for Military UAV*, which is truly a technical report. (A quick read of the abstract for the latter reveals that "UAV" stands for "unmanned air vehicle.")

Materials identified using all versions of the NTIS database can be ordered directly from the NTIS website. Although a number of institutions have standing orders to NTIS publications through NTIS's SRIM (Selected Research in Microfiche) program, lack of cataloging for the bulk of the material limits availability through normal interlibrary loan channels. NTIS, upon request, will create digital copies from its archival collections of print and microfiche. Since users are often reluctant to use microfiche, this may be an attractive option when electronic copies are not available directly from agency websites described later in this chapter.

Agency Websites

Most federal agencies have large and well-developed websites. Once found, they can be a virtual treasure trove of scientific and technical information. The content can range from datasets, maps, and publications to consumer-oriented publications and discovery tools. For more information on looking at agency websites, see Chapter 2.

Tips for Locating Agency Websites for Scientific and Technical Information

Use the tools such as USA.gov, described in Chapter 2, to locate the main agency websites. With scientific and technical information, a subject-based approach is often the most useful. For example, the National Biological Infrastructure is a multiagency collaborative program to provided increased access to data and information about the nation's biological resources that is managed by the Biological Informatics division within the U.S. Geological Survey. Because there is no obvious connection between biology and geology, only the most knowledgeable user might go directly to the U.S. Geological Survey website to look for information about biological resources.

Science.gov, which has tools to guide users to resources by topic, is probably more intuitive for users than an agency-driven approach to information. Although it lacks a directory of agencies by name or organizational structure, with searching of over 40 federal databases and 2,000 websites, this site provides one-stop shopping for scientific and technical information. It has been described as the "easiest and best way for beginners to locate science information created by federal agencies" (Robinson, 2006). In addition to simple and advanced search features, the site includes menus of scientific information arranged by topic and subtopic. For example, the Agriculture and Food category is further subdivided by 12 narrower topics such as Food Safety and Pest and Weed Control. The site map and index help lead users directly to the appropriate topic and subtopic. These are useful features for users not familiar with an area of study. For example, Climate Change is a subtopic under Environment and Environmental Quality. In addition to search and browse features, the site provides special search features for diversity education, federal regulations, federal research and development summaries, internships and fellowships, other science portals, science conferences, and taxonomies and subject thesauri. There is also a Science in the News feature.

Online Publication Warehouses and Bibliographic Databases

The U.S. government produces a number of bibliographic databases and full-text collections that are described in this section. Databases that began as bibliographic databases, such as Agricola, Energy Citations, and Transportation Research

Information Services, index a mix of governmental and commercially produced materials. This mixture of resources means that while some of the material indexed is freely available online, some of the information remains inaccessible to all but subscribers for individual titles. Some databases, such as DOE Information Bridge, NASA Technical Reports Server, and others, are organized solely with the purpose of exposing government-sponsored and authored research to the general public. Treesearch, a database of research from the Forest Service, follows another pattern. Because the material it indexes is authored by government employees, all of the material is available at no charge, regardless of whether or not it was published in a commercially produced journal. Users can expect the open access initiative to exert pressure for other federal agencies to follow the Treesearch model.

Agricola: The National Agricultural Library Catalog

Agricola (http://agricola.nal.usda.gov/) is a catalog of books and other materials held by the library as well as an index to journal articles in agriculture and related disciplines. While some of the material may be hidden behind subscription barriers, a significant number of publications are available in full-text format from AgSpace, the National Agricultural Library's digital repository. AgSpace (http://agspace.nal.usda.gov/) includes the full text of journal articles and book chapters written by government authors, images, and other information. A search for information about genetically modified crops in the article segment of Agricola leads to a number of articles, some available from publishers' websites and some available in AgSpace.

Defense Technical Information Center

The Defense Technical Information Center (DTIC) (http://www.dtic.mil/dtic/) provides access to defense-related scientific information for the defense community—the various agencies of the Department of Defense (DoD), contractors, and those seeking potential contracts with the DoD. Since the DoD needs information on everything from the readability of gauges on flight controls to the durability of uniforms to weapon systems, it maintains an interest in many scientific and technical disciplines. While some of the information is restricted to registered users who meet certain eligibility requirements, the site provides access to a wide array of nonclassified materials. If the full text is not available from DTIC, declassified materials can be ordered from NTIS using the accession number. The site also features a multisearch for other governmental and nongovernmental sources of information. A simple search for IED (improvised explosive device) in the technical reports search yields over 200 citations, many in full text, one example being *Traumatic Brain Injury Hospitalizations of U.S. Army Soldiers Deployed to Afghanistan and Iraq*.

DOE Information Bridge

DOE Information Bridge (http://www.osti.gov/bridge/) is the Department of Energy's (DOE) online database of technical reports written by the agency, contractors, and recipients of DOE grants; it covers material produced from

1991 to the present, with some exceptions. It contains "documents and citations in physics, chemistry, materials, biology, environmental sciences, energy technologies, engineering, computer and information science, renewable energy, and other topics of interest related to DOE's mission" (Department of Energy, 2011). As of January 2011, it contained over 259,000 full-text publications. The search results include facets for narrowing an existing search. Search results include bibliographic information. Reports that are not available in full-text can usually be ordered from NTIS. The site allows registered users to create alerts. Information Bridge is an excellent place to search for information on alternative fuels and other energy-related topics. Looking for an alternative for your gas guzzler? You might want to read *Hydrogen Commercialization: Transportation Fuel for the 21st Century*, a report available in Information Bridge.

Energy Citations Database

The Energy Citations Database (http://www.osti.gov/energycitations) provides access to over 2.6 million citations (1943–present) for research of interest to DOE. The research interests of DOE range from chemistry, physics, materials science, environmental science, geology, engineering, and mathematics, to environmental science, geology, climatology, oceanography, and computer science. The database includes citations to technical reports, conference papers, journal articles, books, dissertations, and patents. While the site provides the full text of selected government information, much of the material cited in the database may be hidden behind subscription barriers.

NASA and NACA

NASA and its predecessor agency, the National Advisory Committee for Aeronautics (NACA) have been publishing information relating to aeronautics, astronautics, space exploration, remote sensing, and other topics since 1915. The NASA Technical Reports Server (http://ntrs.nasa.gov/search.jsp) simultaneously searches multiple collections including the NACA collection (1915–1958), NASA collection (1958–present), and NIX (NASA Image Exchange). Search results can include bibliographic citations with order information, full text, images, and video. If the full text is not available online, the site provides information on how to order copies from NASA or other suppliers including NTIS. Besides obscurely titled technical reports such as *Experiments Out of the Solar System Ecliptic Plane*, the site provides sources geared to a more general audience. A search for Wright brothers resulted in a link to the full text of *Learning to Fly: The Wright Brothers' Adventure. A Guide for Educators and Students with Activities in Aeronautics.*

National Service Center for Environmental Publications

The Environmental Protection Agency, with a mission, "create a livable environment," has jurisdiction over many aspects of the air, water, and land of the United States. Its interests range from air and water pollution to solid waste and emergency response to toxic substances, especially with regard to the human health effects of exposure to pollution. EPA's National Service Center for Environmental Publications (1970–present) (http://www.epa.gov/nscep/) provides access to over 7,000 in-stock print titles and 35,000 digital publications. Materials in stock can be ordered at no charge. Digital copies of publications are available for download in PDF, TIFF, and plain text formats. A search for lead poisoning retrieved consumer-oriented publications such as *Lead in Your Home: A Parent's Reference Guide* with editions in English and Spanish, as well as more technical material such as *Urban Soil Lead Abatement Demonstration Project*.

Transportation Research Information Services

Transportation Research Information Services (TRIS) (1900–present) (http://tris.trb.org/) is produced by the Transportation Research Board of the National Academy of Sciences under the sponsorship of the U.S. Department of Transportation. TRIS contains over 750,000 bibliographic citations to books, technical reports, conference proceedings, and journal articles in the field of transportation research. Subject matter includes transportation-related environmental impact statements, highways, transit, railroads, maritime issues, aviation, pipelines, pedestrians, and bicycles. A limited amount of full text is available from the site. Since TRIS indexes both commercially produced and noncommercial information sources, some materials are hidden behind subscription barriers. While the emphasis is definitely technical information, some material, such as *Public Transportation's Role in Responding to Climate Change*, is accessible to a general audience.

Treesearch

Treesearch (http://www.treesearch.fs.fed.us/) provides access to publications written by scientists in the U.S. Forest Service. Their goal is to make available all books, chapters, and articles written since 2004 and to add older publications as rapidly as possible. The site offers the largest freely available collection of forestry research in the world. Since all publications in Treesearch were written by employees of the Forest Service, they are in the public domain. Whereas many government databases built on the open access concept post manuscript versions of articles, this public domain status allows the developers of Treesearch to include final published versions of journal articles from subscription-based journals. The key difference lies in the employment status of the author. While many journal articles arise from scientific research performed under contract with agencies of the federal government, the scientist authors are employees of universities, nonprofits, and commercial entities. At the present time, all material in Treesearch is authored by employees of the Forest Service. If there are any restrictions on the use of material, they are noted at the end of the article. Since the search results, which are powered by a custom Google search, are presented in Google format, it can be a little disconcerting when users move from the Treesearch interface to a Google interface and then back again. One nice feature of the Google search results page, however, is the inclusion of the number of times a publication has been cited in Google Scholar. The number of times an article has been cited in other publications (or "impact factor") is one indicator of the influence that the research has had on subsequent publications.

For example, the article "Climate Change and Forest Disturbances," which appeared in the journal *Bioscience* in 2001, had been cited over 300 times as of January 2011. Based on the number of citations, this article is having a significant impact on the field. Treesearch is a valuable resource for people seeking information on pine beetles, forest fires, the effects of climate change, and other topics.

USGS Publications Warehouse

The U.S. Geological Survey (USGS) has been a prolific publisher of scientific information since the 1880s, with an emphasis on geology, mapping, flora, fauna, water supply, coal, oil, and gas fields, minerals with economic potential, and other topics. The USGS Publications Warehouse (1880–present) (http://pubs.er.usgs.gov) provides bibliographic citations for all series publications, with full text available for over half of the publications. Series include titles such as *Professional Papers*, *Trace Elements Investigations*, and *Scientific Investigations Reports*. Format of the publications varies. Recently the USGS began adding citations to book and journal literature published by commercial publishers. Although it is represents a very small portion of the database, the number of non-USGS publications is likely to grow. At the present time the database does not contain links to full text from external sources. When full text is not available, the site provides information on how to obtain copies of USGS publications directly from the agency or from depository libraries. The Warehouse also provides information about purchase when copies are available for sale.

Agency Publication Warehouses and Citation Databases

Title	Web address	Dates of coverage
Agricola	http://agricola.nal.usda.gov/	Unknown
AgSpace	http://agspace.nal.usda.gov/	Unknown
Defense Technical Information Center (DTIC)	http://www.dtic.mil/dtic/	Unknown
DOE Information Bridge: DOE Scientific and Technical Information	http://www.osti.gov/bridge/	1991–present with exceptions
Energy Citations Database	http://www.osti.gov/energycitations/	1943–present
NASA Technical Reports Server	http://ntrs.nasa.gov/search.jsp	1915–present
National Service Center for Environmental Publications	http://www.epa.gov/nscep/	1970–present
Transportation Research Information Services (TRIS)	http://tris.trb.org/	1900–present
Treesearch	http://www.treesearch.fs.fed.us/	2004–present with exceptions
USGS Publications Warehouse	http://pubs.er.usgs.gov/	1880–present

Budding miners can read publications such as *Introduction to Geology and Resources of Gold, and Geochemistry of Gold.*

Gateways to Scientific and Technical Information

Discussed earlier in this chapter in the section on tips for finding federal websites, Science.gov is emerging as the premier website for scientific and technical information, due to its in-depth coverage of scientific information. It provides a single search interface for 42 databases and over 2,000 federal websites. According to the website, Science.gov is the gateway to 200 million pages of government information. In addition to simple and advanced searching, the site includes a site map and index which lead users to information by topic.

Developed by the government agency that created Science.gov, WorldWide Science.org: The Global Science Gateway (http://www.worldwidescience.org) uses federated search technology to locate geographically dispersed information from science databases and science portals from over 60 countries. WorldWide Science is overseen by an alliance representing government agencies from around the world, including the Canada Institute for Scientific and Technical Information, the Institute of Scientific and Technical Information of China, the British government, and others. Much of the material that can be retrieved from the site is invisible to conventional search engines. The site features both simple and advanced search features. Results screens include facets that can be used to narrow an existing search. It also provides the ability to narrow the results with additional keywords or terms. Search results can include a mix of full text and bibliographic citations.

Related Resources

The National Academies Press (NAP) (http://www.nap.edu) publishes reports issued by the National Academy of Sciences, the National Academy of Engineering, the Institute of Medicine, and the National Research Council, which serve in an advisory capacity to Congress. The site offers search and browse by topic features. Browse topics are subdivided by narrow topics. A Browse All Topics, similar to a site map, is available from the subtopics menus. Reports and publications can be read online, ordered, or, for a subset of publications, downloaded in their entirety at no charge. Free executive summaries are available for most titles. Free online reading is greatly facilitated by detailed tables of contents, and sophisticated page navigation, search, and skim features. In addition to pure science, the site provides analysis of current policy for some topics. For example, in 2009 the NAP released *America's Uninsured Crisis: Consequences for Health and Health Care.*

The Technical Report Archive and Image Library (TRAIL) (pre-1974) (http://www.technicalreports.org/), a project of the Greater Western Library Alliance and the Center for Research Libraries under the leadership of the University of Arizona, represents a large-scale effort to digitize federal technical reports published before 1975. As of January 2011, the site provided access to several reports series from the Atomic Energy Commission, the National Bureau of

Standards, and the U.S. Bureau of Mines. Additional series are currently in production mode.

Military Standards

Assistdocs.com (http://www.assistdocs.com) provides access to nonclassified information distributed by Defense Standardization Program Office. Although the site has a dot-com address, it is an official site of the Department of Defense. Businesses hoping to develop and sell products for the DoD must comply with standards established by the various agencies under the department. The Assistdocs site collects and provides one-stop access to these standards. Engineering and government publications libraries receive requests for this type of material on a regular basis.

Abbreviations Used in Military Standards and Handbooks

Standards and handbooks often start with MIL for military or DOD for Department of Defense. The middle section of a number usually contains STD for standard or HDBK for handbook. For example, if a company is hoping to sell combat vehicles to the Army, its design must comply with criteria for heating, ventilation, controls, displays, vibration, seating and a host of other factors laid out in MIL-STD-1472-F (1) (*Human Engineering*). Information in the introduction indicates that the standard should be used in conjunction with MIL-HDBK-759C (2) *(Human Engineering Design Guidelines)*. MIL-HDBK-759C (2) also refers to two related handbooks that are also available online from Assistdocs. While military standards and handbooks frequently reference standards from nongovernmental standards organizations such as the American Society for Testing and Materials and the Society of Automotive Engineers, Assistdocs includes only official government standards. This can be a source of confusion for some users, who should be referred to engineering libraries for nongovernmental standards.

Patents

The founders who drafted the Constitution recognized the need to "promote the progress of science and the useful arts" by granting inventors exclusive rights to their discoveries for a limited period of time (Article I, Sec. VIII of the United States Constitution). The first United States patent, signed by George Washington, was issued to Samuel Hopkins on July 31, 1790, for a process for making potash, an ingredient for fertilizer. Since 1952, the U.S. Patent and Trademark Office, an agency of the Department of Commerce, has been charged with examining and issuing patents. While the emphasis of this chapter is on scientific invention, it is also worth noting that the Patent and Trademark Office is also responsible for protecting trademarks: the word, name, symbol, or device that distinguishes the goods made by one company from those made by another. To understand trademarks, think of Coke and Pepsi. Both manufacture carbonated cola products and would not like to be confused with one another. To eliminate confusion in the minds of their customers, the names of their products and their product designs are covered by trademarks. The Patent and Trademark website (http://www.uspto.gov/) provides search features for existing patents and patent applications and for trademarks.

The first patents were limited to a process, machine, article of manufacture, composition of matter, or improvement of any of these. Over time, the scope of patent protection has been expanded to include design patents, which protect the look of a product; plant patents, which protect plants that have been produced asexually; and patents for life forms other than plants, which protect human-engineered microorganisms and animals. Patents are classified into broad technological categories which are further divided into narrower subclasses. Under the system of classification, a single patent may be assigned more than one classification number if it fits into more than one category.

In the past, patents, which contain a wealth of scientific and technical information, were available only at the Patent Office or in patent and trademark depository libraries. Once again, the Internet has enabled fundamental change. The Patent and Trademark website now provides search features for both existing patents and patent applications. Patents and patent applications issued from 1976 to the present are available as plain text or as TIFF images, and may be discovered by a number of search points including patent number, inventor, title, words in the abstract, claims, and others. Claims "point out and distinctly claim the subject matter which the applicant regards as the invention... " To view the TIFF images, users need to download and install a browser plugin. Patents issued from 1790 to 1975, which are available only as TIFF images, can be searched by issue date, patent number, or current U.S. patent classification. While the Patent Office is the definitive site, issues with format (TIFF) and search points for the older material somewhat limit the usability of the site. Fortunately, a couple of sites help alleviate these problems. Enter a patent number at PAT2PDF (http://www.pat2pdf.org) and the site will download all of the TIFF images and fold them into one PDF for easy printing.

Google, in its Google Patents database (http://patents.google.com), has processed the image files to create additional search points including title, inventor, issue date, filing date, status, or text string. At the Google site, patents can be read online, downloaded in their entirety as PDF files, or viewed via the Patent and Trademark Office database. Because of the limitations that come with automatic processing of millions of images, however, Google patent searches are not completely reliable. For example, remember Samuel Hopkins, recipient of the first patent? That first patent was beautifully written by hand. Search as you might, you will be unable to find it in Google Patents because of the inherent difficulties of converting handwriting to text. The database also lags behind the Patent and Trademark versions of the patents and patent applications databases. Although PAT2PDF and Google Patents offer functional improvements for patents, the official U.S. Patent and Trademark site remains the mother lode. In addition to search tools for patents, patent applications, and trademarks, the site also provides extensive information for independent inventors seeking to patent their work. A step-by-step flowchart takes the budding inventor through the process of applying for and maintaining a patent. For fun, look for the patent for the Slinky toy (U.S. Patent 2415012).

Subject Search Strategies

As mentioned earlier in this chapter, Science.gov is the recommended starting point for subject-based searches. Use the Science.gov index to find a list of the agency and research projects by topic. For those instances when a subject is not included in the list of topics, use the simple or advanced search tools to locate information. The Catalog of Government Publications is also a useful tool. A recent search in both Science.gov and the Catalog of Government Publications for information on the use of bioremediation in the cleanup of marine oil spills yielded different, yet equally useful results. The top result on Science.gov was *Development of Bioremediation for Oil Spill Cleanup in Coastal Wetlands*. The top result from CGP was *Guidelines for the Biomediation of Oil-Contaminated Salt Marshes*. The tips for finding and navigating federal websites (Chapter 2) are also recommended for a subject-based search.

Finding a Known Item

Although the various report numbers quickly start to look like alphabet soup, if your patron has a citation to a known item, you are halfway to finding the information he or she needs. Many of the agencies that produce significant numbers of scientific and technical reports also have well-organized digital collections.

Step 1: Search by title using a standard search engine, or one of the specialized ones with a government information emphasis such as USA.gov (http://www.usa.gov/) or Google U.S. Government (http://www.google .com/unclesam/).

Step 2: If step 1 is unsuccessful, check the publications warehouses listed in this chapter. This is the best approach if you can attribute a publication to the publishing agency with some degree of confidence. On occasion you can find a PDF version of a publication that was overlooked by a general search engine. The scanned versions of publications tend to get buried in search results from a general search engine when a publication is also available in HTML format. Also, search engines are not always able to pull out reports from within databases.

Step 3: If steps 1 and 2 are unsuccessful, but your search results suggest that the publication was once available on the Internet, search for an earlier version of an agency website at the Wayback Machine at the Internet Archive (http://www.archive.org/).

Conclusion

Equipped with a few simple concepts and a basic understanding of the best ways to track down government information, any librarian can provide scientific and technical information to patrons. While some of the terminology may be daunting, the fundamentals of information gathering remain the same. When a user asks for information about the use of titanium in aircraft, take a deep breath and break the question down into its component parts: 1) which agencies of the government might be interested in this topic? 2) how do I find their websites? and 3) what keywords should I use for the search? Having read the information in this chapter, you should have some ideas on where to start. In this particular case, Science.gov is a good place to start. The top search result for the keywords titanium and aircraft at Science.gov was *Titanium Alloys and Processing for High Speed Aircraft*, a report from the NASA Technical Reports Server. *Survey of Ultrasonic Properties of Aircraft Engine Titanium Forgings*, a report from DTIC, was also included on the first page of results. While a librarian with experience in science and technology might have gone straight to NASA or DTIC, Science.gov proves to be a good source for this kind of information. Also on the first page of results were reports from NTIS and the Energy Citations database, demonstrating that Science.gov is a good place to begin research on scientific and technical topics.

Exercises

1. The Colorado River serves an extensive population and is heavily used for irrigation and recreation. What is the effect of drought on the river?
2. A patron is interested in selling helmet covers to the military. Where would you find the standard?
3. What safety improvements did NASA make after the Challenger disaster?
4. How often is drinking water tested? What do the tests look for?
5. How many patents are there relating to the iPod?
6. I'd like to learn more about that incident a couple of years ago when they thought that salmonella bacteria were in tomatoes.

Sources Mentioned in This Chapter

Sources mentioned in this section do not duplicate the References that follow.

Agricola, http://agricola.nal.usda.gov/.
AgSpace, NAL's Digital Repository, http://agspace.nal.usda.gov/.
Assistdocs.com, http://www.assistdocs.com/.

Catalog of Government Publications (CGP), http://catalog.gpo.gov/.

Defense Technical Information Center (DTIC), http://www.dtic.mil/dtic/.

Energy Citations Database, http://www.osti.gov/energycitations/.

EPA's NSCEP/NEPIS, http://www.epa.gov/nscep/.

Federal Depository Library Directory, http://catalog.gpo.gov/fdlpdir/FDLPdir.jsp.

Google Patents Database, http://patents.google.com/.

Google U.S. Government, http://www.google.com/unclesam/.

GPO Bookstore, http://bookstore.gpo.gov/.

NASA Technical Reports Server (NTRS), http://ntrs.nasa.gov/search.jsp.

National Academies Press (NAP), http://www.nap.edu/.

National Technical Reports Library (NTRL), http://ntrl.ntis.gov/.

NTIS Homepage, http://www.ntis.gov/.

Patent and Trademark, http://www.uspto.gov/.

PAT2PDF, http://www.pat2pdf.org/.

Science.gov, http://www.science.gov/.

Technical Report Archive and Image Library (TRAIL), http://www.technicalreports.org/.

Transportation Research Information Services (TRIS), http://tris.trb.org/.

Treesearch, http://www.treesearch.fs.fed.us/.

USA.gov, http://www.usa.gov/.

USGS Publications Warehouse, http://pubs.er.usgs.gov/.

Wayback Machine, Internet Archive, http://www.archive.org/.

WorldWideScience.org: The Global Science Gateway, http://www.worldwidescience.org/.

References

Calhoun, Ellen. 1991. "Technical Reports De-Mystified." *Reference Librarian*, no. 32: 163–175.

Department of Energy. 2011. "Information Bridge: DOE Science and Technical Documents." Accessed January 10. http://www.osti.gov/bridge/.

Robinson, William C. 2006. "IS 534: Federal Government Scientific and Technical Information." The University of Tennessee Knoxville. Last revised February. http://web.utk.edu/~wrobinso/534_lec_STM.html.

Chapter 12

Environment and Energy Information

JENNIE GERKE

Introduction

The April 2010 Deepwater Horizon oil spill incident in the Gulf of Mexico demonstrates the ties between environment and energy issues and government information. Long before the spill ever happened, growing energy needs drove new exploration into offshore waters. In the United States, this development is regulated and leased by the Bureau of Ocean Energy Management, Regulation, and Enforcement. Once the explosion and spill occurred, the Department of Defense and National Oceanic and Atmospheric Administration (NOAA) were called in to coordinate the spill abatement and recovery effort, and the Environmental Protection Agency (EPA) examined and permitted the various dispersants (chemicals used to dissipate oil) used to contain the spill.

As with many areas of government today, multiple agencies have an interest in the same issue—but each one has a different perspective through which it considers the issue, be it oil spills, power plants, or climate change. This chapter examines the governmental groups involved in environment and energy issues and will discuss pertinent agencies and key resources and strategies for researching the issues and the agencies. Each section will contain brief histories of the major agencies involved.

Energy Sources

Before getting to work in the morning, the average person uses two or three different energy sources—electricity, oil, and gas, for example: the alarm clock is powered by electricity, the gas or electric stove heats the water, and the car most likely uses gas to get down the road. These different energy sources fit seamlessly into the life of Americans. Indeed, it is hard to imagine that until the twentieth century the major source of energy was wood (Energy Information Administration, 2010).

The Department of Energy (DOE) oversees the majority of energy issues within the United States. The formation of DOE came about in 1977 with the consolidation of several existing agencies dealing with energy issues. The mission of

DOE "is to advance the national, economic, and energy security of the United States; to promote scientific and technological innovation in support of that mission; and to ensure the environmental cleanup of the national nuclear weapons complex" (Department of Energy, 2010). Therefore, DOE is the place to start when researching energy, whether seeking statistics about energy, information about alternative energies, or research related to energy production.

Other important energy research sources are the Federal Energy Regulatory Commission, which regulates the interstate transmission of natural gas, oil, and electricity, and state agencies that regulate energy issues and companies within their boundaries. For example, the Colorado Public Utilities Commission regulates the costs utility companies may charge the state's citizens.

Brief History of the Department of Energy

The agencies that were the precursors to the Department of Energy came into existence during World War II, when the Manhattan Engineer District (more commonly known as the Manhattan Project) was created in 1942 under the U.S. Army Corps of Engineers. Debate about postwar applications of atomic power led to the founding of the Atomic Energy Commission (through the Atomic Energy Act of 1946; P.L. 79-585, 60 Stat. 755). It wasn't too long before government interest went well beyond just atomic energy, especially during the energy crisis of the 1970s. The Energy Reorganization Act of 1974 (P.L. 93-280, 88 Stat. 123) reorganized federal involvement in energy into a nuclear (the Nuclear Regulatory Commission, successor to the Atomic Energy Commission) and research and development side (the Energy Research and Development Administration). Soon thereafter, Congress passed the Department of Energy Organization Act of 1977 (P.L. 95-565, 91 Stat. 565), which brought nearly all energy agencies under a single, cabinet-level department. The current Department of Energy covers all aspects of energy in the United States.

In addition to these executive departments, both Congress and the White House can change the direction of these agencies through legislation or executive orders, respectively (see Chapter 3, Congress, and Chapter 6, The President). In addition, for information on scientific and technical research in energy and the environment, see Chapter 11, Scientific and Technical Information.

Statistics

As noted in Chapter 8, many questions involving government information are statistical in nature. This is true of energy resources, and there are numerous tools that make finding energy statistics and creating tables and graphs easy. The Energy Information Administration (EIA) within DOE produces the majority of statistics on energy production and use. EIA's output includes statistics on both domestic and international energy. EIA analyzes and disseminates energy information to assist in the work of the United States government. EIA writes reports on energy outlooks, profiles energy use and production in states and countries, and compiles the raw data that inform these reports. EIA arranges this information on its website (http://www.eia.gov) by energy source, topic, and geography, providing quick access to reports and tables with links to historical data. For example, Figure 12.1 shows the cost of gasoline by month in the Rocky Mountain region, with links to the historic data. Every table on EIA's

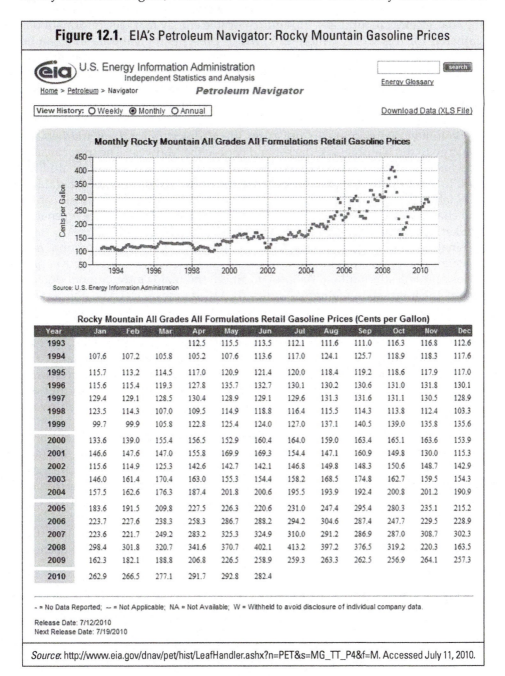

Figure 12.1. EIA's Petroleum Navigator: Rocky Mountain Gasoline Prices

Rocky Mountain All Grades All Formulations Retail Gasoline Prices (Cents per Gallon)

Year	Jan	Feb	Mar	Apr	May	Jun	Jul	Aug	Sep	Oct	Nov	Dec
1993				112.5	115.5	113.5	112.1	111.6	111.0	116.3	116.8	112.6
1994	107.6	107.2	105.8	105.2	107.6	113.6	117.0	124.1	125.7	118.9	118.3	117.6
1995	115.7	113.2	114.5	117.0	120.9	121.4	120.0	118.4	119.2	118.6	117.9	117.0
1996	115.6	115.4	119.3	127.8	135.7	132.7	130.1	130.2	130.6	131.0	131.8	130.1
1997	129.4	129.1	128.5	130.4	128.9	129.1	129.6	131.3	131.6	131.1	130.5	128.9
1998	123.5	114.3	107.0	109.5	114.9	118.8	116.4	115.5	114.3	113.8	112.4	103.3
1999	99.7	99.9	105.8	122.8	125.4	124.0	127.0	137.1	140.5	139.0	135.8	135.6
2000	133.6	139.0	155.4	156.5	152.9	160.4	164.0	159.0	163.4	165.1	163.6	153.9
2001	146.6	147.6	147.0	155.8	169.9	169.3	154.4	147.1	160.9	149.8	130.0	115.3
2002	115.6	114.9	125.3	142.6	142.7	142.1	146.8	149.8	148.3	150.6	148.7	142.9
2003	146.0	161.4	170.4	163.0	155.3	154.4	158.2	168.5	174.8	162.7	159.5	154.3
2004	157.5	162.6	176.3	187.4	201.8	200.6	195.5	193.9	192.4	200.8	201.2	190.9
2005	183.6	191.5	209.8	227.5	226.3	220.6	231.0	247.4	295.4	280.3	235.1	215.2
2006	223.7	227.6	238.3	258.3	286.7	288.2	294.2	304.6	287.4	247.7	229.5	228.9
2007	223.6	221.7	249.2	283.2	325.3	324.9	310.0	291.2	286.9	287.0	308.7	302.3
2008	298.4	301.8	320.7	341.6	370.7	402.1	413.2	397.2	376.5	319.2	220.3	163.5
2009	162.3	182.1	188.8	206.8	226.5	258.9	259.3	263.3	262.5	256.9	264.1	257.3
2010	262.9	266.5	277.1	291.7	292.8	282.4						

- = No Data Reported; -- = Not Applicable; NA = Not Available; W = Withheld to avoid disclosure of individual company data.

Release Date: 7/12/2010
Next Release Date: 7/19/2010

Source: http://www.eia.gov/dnav/pet/hist/LeafHandler.ashx?n=PET&s=MG_TT_P4&f=M. Accessed July 11, 2010.

website may be downloaded as a spreadsheet, enabling patrons to take the information and create graphics and run their own mathematical analyses.

While EIA discusses energy resources and use, the Federal Energy Regulatory Commission (FERC) examines energy market trends (this is not the gas station, but the energy commodities market). Since FERC is the regulatory agency for the coal, electric, natural gas, oil, and renewable energy markets, information is gathered for this work. Unlike EIA, which presents topical data that can be used to create tables covering different time periods, FERC provides the majority of its data in report form. The best way to access market data on the website is through the Market Oversight section (http://www.ferc.gov/market-oversight/market-oversight.asp). This area looks at each of the markets regulated by FERC and provides reports. For instance, if the user wanted to know the trading volume, consumption, or prices for the Midwest natural gas market, she could go to the Natural Gas Market and choose the Midwest. The user can also find links to the various external data sources (some free, most not) that FERC uses to compile the data tables. Because the FERC's site presents the data as PDF tables, users must manually reenter the data if they wish to create tables and charts. Despite this issue, this is the best place to go for free data on energy market research.

Finally, while energy use may be local, the development, production, and consumption often cross international borders. EIA, as mentioned above, provides selected international data. In addition, the major international organization, the International Energy Agency (IEA), provides select data and reports online; basic country information is free, but to create tables and access larger data sets, the user needs access to the OECD iLibrary. IEA, as a part of the Organisation for Economic Co-operation and Development (OECD), focuses its attention on the 31 member countries, providing only basic data for the other countries of the world. For a free set of data covering the entire world, the United Nations Statistics Division provides energy data on consumption, exports, stockpiles, and production by product and country in the freely available UNdata.

The final statistical resource to examine is not a fixed data set found on a website, but rather an interactive tool: energy calculators. For example, if a user wants to buy a new television, the Energy Star website (discussed in the next section) has a section on calculating cost savings over the life of a product. There is no comprehensive list of these resources, but the Department of Energy Efficiency and Renewable Energy (more in the next section) provides a directory of the calculators from the Department of Energy. In addition, the Environmental Protection Agency, a major topic in the environment section, also offers a number of energy calculators.

Renewable Energy/Energy Efficiency

Energy efficiency has taken on ever greater importance in recent years. Terms such as Energy Star and hybrid are used to describe products, and the government has an impact on both the development and regulation of such products. Energy Star, a joint program of the U.S. Department of Energy and the Environmental Protection Agency, provides information on energy efficient products. The program began in 1992 with EPA evaluating computers and monitors; it now covers over 60 product categories and attempts to make it easier for people to purchase energy efficient products (Energy Star, 2010). The Energy Star website (http://www.energystar.gov/) acts as an example of government information aimed at consumers. For example, the user can find information on tax credits, rebates, and which products have Energy Star ratings. The rebate finder can be of particular use since it is customized to the local area of the user, so that only applicable rebates appear.

Another extremely popular government energy resource is http://www.fuel economy.gov/, providing consumer information on energy efficiency of automobiles featuring official estimates of gas mileage. This website allows side-by-side comparison of fuel efficiency, air pollution, and the carbon footprint of cars, including both current and older models. In addition to this abundantly practical information for car shopping, FuelEconomy.gov also provides useful information such as information on hybrids and how they work and tips on driving more efficiently.

Finally, when researching energy efficiency, DOE's Office of Energy Efficiency and Renewable Energy (EERE) provides additional consumer information, as well as data and technical information on renewable energy and energy efficiency. EERE (http://www.eere.energy.gov/) focuses on ten energy programs that deal with energy efficiency and how these programs work within the government and private sector. Businesses seeking to invest in renewable energy technologies have the opportunity to apply for funding through DOE's e-Center (http://e-center.doe.gov/). While the focus of EERE may be on investing "in clean energy technologies that strengthen the economy, protect the environment, and reduce dependence on foreign oil" (Office of Energy Efficiency and Renewable Energy, 2010), it also provides information on these technologies to consumers in the form of energy calculators, maps (see Figure 12.2), and tips on using renewable energy technologies.

Environmental Sources

While energy covers a broad spectrum of resources, most energy information from the federal government originates in the Department of Energy. The study of the government and environmental issues, however, spans many more agencies, as environmental issues are notoriously complex, not confined to a single topic. For example, when studying environmental regulation, the majority of the resources may live within the Environmental Protection Agency. Researching air pollution and how it travels across the United States may lead one to consult both EPA and the National Oceanic and Atmospheric Administration, while an issue such as drilling for resources on public lands may have useful information from EPA, the Department of the Interior, and, from a policy

Figure 12.2. Geothermal Resources of the United States

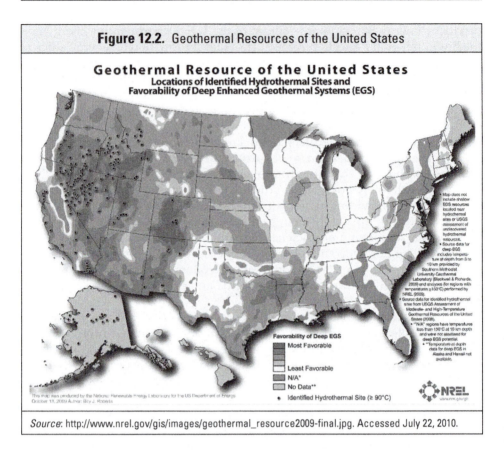

Source: http://www.nrel.gov/gis/images/geothermal_resource2009-final.jpg. Accessed July 22, 2010.

standpoint, DOE. This section explores EPA, discusses climate and weather resources (with special attention to climate change, including international governmental information), and covers public lands.

Brief History of EPA and NOAA

Attention to environmental issues in the United States is frequently traced back to the publication in 1962 of Rachel Carson's *Silent Spring*. Through this book's focus on pesticides, the book (which first appeared as a serial in the *New Yorker*) brought environmental issues and environmental health concerns to prominence. Nothing happens quickly in politics, but the National Environmental Protection Act of 1969 (P.L. 91-190, 83 Stat. 852) established the Council of Environmental Quality, which was meant to advise the president on environmental matters. Within another year there was a large oil spill (off the coast of Santa Barbara, California), the first Earth Day, and mention of environmental issues in the State of the Union address.

In 1970, these issues helped lead to the creation of two agencies that make up the primary bodies focused on the environment in the United States government, EPA and NOAA. The agencies were established via Richard Nixon's

Reorganization Plans 3 and 4 of 1970. On July 9, 1970, President Nixon transmitted a message to Congress stating:

> As concern with the condition of our physical environment has intensified, it has become increasingly clear that we need to know more about the total environment—land, water and air. It has also become increasingly clear that only by reorganizing our Federal efforts can we develop that knowledge, and effectively ensure the protection, development and enhancement of the total environment itself.
>
> The Government's environmentally-related activities have grown up piecemeal over the years. The time has come to organize them rationally and systematically. As a major step in that direction I am transmitting today two reorganization plans: one to establish the Environmental Protection Agency, and one to establish, within the Department of Commerce, a National Oceanic and Atmospheric Administration. (Nixon, 1970: 1)

EPA quickly began working with laws such as the Clean Air Act (P.L. 88-206, 77 Stat. 392) and the Clean Water Act (P.L. 80-845, 62 Stat. 1155) to protect human health, and manages related issues such as hazardous wastes and cleanup, chemicals and pesticides, and fuel economy. NOAA is largely concerned with weather, natural disasters, and marine health.

Environmental Protection Agency

EPA researches three primary areas: water, air, and waste and pollution, and how these areas affect human health, the ecosystem, and the climate. Due to the long and varied reaches of these issues, EPA can often be an intimidating agency to explore, but its website (http://www.epa.gov) provides numerous features to help navigate available resources. Using the website's A–Z index, one can browse by topic such as asbestos, radon, air pollution, and carbon footprints, to many useful reports, portals, and other resources.

While the A–Z directory leads to a mostly comprehensive collection of resources, there are a few other tools worth examining in depth. "My Environment" connects citizens and researchers to a variety of environmental data on a particular community. One can enter, for instance, a ZIP code and find information on air, land, water, and health indicators, integrated into one interactive map (see Figure 12.3, a sample for St. Louis). In the map, the user can see current air quality and streamflow data; data on health conditions related to the local environment; nearby hazardous waste sites and facilities that must report pollutants; water quality data; and more. Using this map and data service, the user can link to the different EPA databases for more in-depth analysis, eliminating the need for the patron to know which database to choose for toxic releases and hazardous waste sites (TOXMAP, http://toxmap.nlm.nih.gov/toxmap/main/index.jsp).

While Chapter 3 covers legislation and Chapter 4 covers regulations, the EPA website has some resources in this area due to the importance of environmental rule and regulations. The Rulemaking Gateway (http://www.epa.gov/

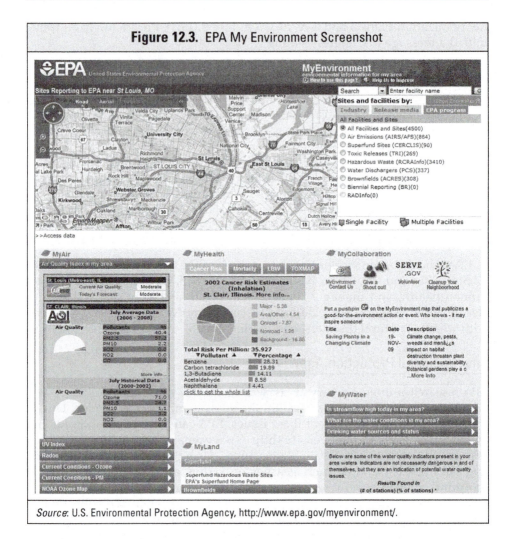

Figure 12.3. EPA My Environment Screenshot

Source: U.S. Environmental Protection Agency, http://www.epa.gov/myenvironment/.

lawsregs/rule making/index.html), a new site, provides easy access to the rules from EPA. While Regulations.gov has functionality that allows easy searching across new regulations, EPA's Rulemaking Gateway has some additional features, allowing more nuanced searching for only environmental regulations and topics, and also by phase (what step in the process is the rule at), topic, or effect of the rule, such as Children's Health, Environmental Justice, Local Governments, or Unfunded Mandates. In addition, this website links directly to Regulations.gov for the ability to comment and view other public comments on active or passed rules.

Finally, when looking for publications or reports from EPA, the best source is NSCEP, which covers their output from the formation of the agency. For more in-depth coverage of this topic, see Chapter 11, Scientific and Technical Information.

Climate and Weather

Created concurrently with EPA, NOAA produces popular government information on climate and weather, among other resources. While NOAA is the agency that tracks climate and weather, growing attention to climate change and global warming has increased collaboration between NOAA and EPA. The biggest difference between NOAA and EPA is the regulatory work. NOAA is primarily a research arm of the government, gathering and sharing, with its regulatory work focused primarily on oceanic topics, such as fisheries. While all government regulation has an impact, EPA often gathers just as much attention for its regulations as its research, whereas NOAA gathers more attention for its research work.

Weather forecast and weather data are a prime example of NOAA's reach to citizens. Weather forecasts, whether presented on the radio, TV, or web, are based on data provided by an arm of NOAA, the National Weather Service (NWS). Weather forecasts are relatively easy to find and weather data represents some of NOAA's most useful resources. The highest-use weather-related resource from this agency is historical weather information. Historical weather data presents a unique situation where an in-person visit to a local federal depository library is required: the National Climatic Data Center (NCDC) provides historic data back to the 1800s, but access to this data—while available via the web—is not free (except for a few sets) unless accessed in a depository library (Government Printing Office, 2009). This website (http://www.ncdc.noaa.gov/) allows the discovery of precipitation, temperature, and wind speeds for locations across the United States, and some select locations outside the country. Each data set name gives a hint of its contents; for example, "Surface Data, Daily U.S.," contains data on the minimum and maximum temperature, wind gusts, and other pertinent information at the surface each day, and there is a corresponding data set for the month. Annual summary data can also be generated looking at the temperature and precipitation using the "Annual Climatological Summary" data set (as seen in Figure 12.4 for New York, NY).

On February 8, 2010, NOAA and its parent agency, the U.S. Department of Commerce, proposed the creation of a NOAA climate service (National Oceanic and Atmospheric Administration, 2008). This service maintains the new Climate.gov (http://www.climate.gov), whose interface makes browsing for data much easier than NCDC's site. This site will be very useful for recurrent class assignments, such as "find the weather conditions the day you were born." Climate.gov has a feature on the homepage (called "past weather") that allows the discovery of the temperature, wind, and dew point across the United States. Again, while this data is free, it is available only for places where the information was collected, so if the patron was born in the first half of the twentieth century in a small town, the data may be unavailable.

Climate Change

Among the countless topics and many reports and resources related to energy and environment, one topic is increasingly prominent: climate change. This

Figure 12.4. Annual Climatological Summary: New York John F Kennedy International Airport, 2009

U.S. Department of Commerce
National Oceanic & Atmospheric Administration

National Climatic Data Center
Federal Building
151 Patton Avenue
Asheville, North Carolina 28801

ANNUAL CLIMATOLOGICAL SUMMARY (2009)

Station: 305803/94789, NEW YORK JFK INTL AP, New York Elev. 11 ft. above sea level Lat. 40°38N, Lon. 73°46W

Temperature (°F)

2009 Month	MMXT Mean Max	MMNT Mean Min	MNTM Mean	DPNT Depart. from Normal	HTDD Heating Degree Days	CLDD Cooling Degree Days	EMXT Highest	High Date	EMNP Lowest	Low Date	DT90 Max>=90	DX32 Max<=32	DT32 Min<=32	DT00 Min<=0
1	34.6	22.7	28.7	-3.1	1119	0	45	7	7	17	0	12	29	0
2	44.1	27.9	36.0	2.5	803	0	62	11	12	5	0	3	23	0
3	48.5	33.3	40.9	0.0	740	0	68	7	13	3	0	2	12	0
4	60.7	44.8	52.8	2.7	377	16	80	26	35	13	0	0	0	0
5	67.6	53.4	60.5	0.8	148	18	80	31	44	19	0	0	0	0
6	73.8	61.0	67.4	-1.4	33	113	83	29	50	1	0	0	0	0
7	81.1	66.3	73.7	-1.1	0	276	90	30	58	10	1	0	0	0
8	83.2	66.8	76.5	2.4	0	364	92	10	60	31	5	0	0	0
9	74.2	59.5	66.9	-0.3	30	94	86	5	50	30	0	0	0	0
10	62.4	48.9	55.7	-0.8	286	2	73	7	39	19	0	0	0	0
11	57.2	44.9	51.1	4.3	415	0	67	15	33	7	0	0	0	0
12	42.6	29.8	36.2	-1.0	885	0	66	3	18	29	0	7	18	0
Annual	60.8	48.9	53.9	0.4	4836	883	92	Aug	7	Jan	6	24	82	0

Precipitation (inches)

2009 Month	TPCP Total	DPNP Depart. from Normal	EMXP Greatest Observed Day	EMXP Date	TSNW Total Fall	MXSD Max Depth	MXSD Max Date	DPO1 >= .10	DPO5 >= .50	DPO10 >= 1.0
1	2.85	-0.77	1.52	7	6.4	2	28	3	2	1
2	0.98	-1.72	0.38	3	4.0	7	7	3	0	0
3	1.92	-1.87	0.55	29	7.0	3	29	6	2	0
4	4.24	0.49	1.22	20	0.0T	0T		7	4	1
5	4.39	0.28	1.03	29	0.0	0		11	3	1
6	7.74	4.15	2.25	18	0.0	0		10	6	3
7	3.57	-0.35	0.76	21	0.0T	0T		7	7	0
8	3.50	-0.14	1.47	28	0.0	0		5	4	1
9	3.16	-0.34	1.41	27	0.0	0		4	3	1
10	5.87	2.84	1.80	3	0.0	0		7	4	3
11	1.41	-2.07	0.67	20	0.0	0		3	1	0
12	6.25	2.94	1.51	9	18.2	14	14	11	6	1
Annual	45.88	3.42	2.25	Jun	33.6	14	Dec	77	39	12

Notes

(blank) Not reported.

+ Occurred on one or more previous dates during the month. The date in the Date field is the last day of occurrence. Used through December 1983 only.

A Accumulated amount. This value is a total that may include data from a previous month or months or year (for annual value).

B Adjusted Total. Monthly value totals based on proportional available data across the entire month.

E An estimated monthly or annual total.

X Monthly means or totals based on incomplete time series. 1 to 9 days are missing. Annual means or totals include one or more months which had 1 to 9 days that were missing.

M Used to indicate data element missing.

T Trace of precipitation, snowfall, or snowdepth. The precipitation data value will = zero.

Elem-> Element Types are included to provide cross-reference for users of the NCDC CDO System. Station Station is identified by: CoopID/WBAN, Station Name, State.

S Precipitation amount is continuing to be accumulated. Total will be included in a subsequent monthly or yearly value. Example: Days 1-20 had 1.35 inches of precipitation, then a period of accumulation began. The element TPCP would then be 0013S and the total accumulated amount value appears in a subsequent monthly value. If TPCP = "M" there was no precipitation measured during the month. Flag is set to "S" and the total accumulated amount appears in a subsequent monthly value.

Dynamically generated Thu Jul 22 14:11:48 EDT 2010 via http://cdo.ncdc.noaa.gov/ancsum/ACS
Data provided from the NCDC CDO System
Additional documentation can be found at http://cdo.ncdc.noaa.gov/cdo/3220doc.txt

Source: U.S. National Climatic Data Center, http://cdo.ncdc.noaa.gov/ancsum/ACS. Accessed July 22, 2010.

topic has come to special prominence in environmental research; no longer is it just a scientific discussion, it has spilled into politics and the development of environmental policy. When polar bears were considered for inclusion on the endangered species list, the topic of climate change was part of the debate. Note that this category of research in government information has special terminology. When referred to in the media, the concept is often dubbed global warming; in the government, the terms are generally climate change or global change. In either case, science suggests a general warming of Earth's temperatures (although some areas are predicted to get colder). This broad, pervasive, and sometimes controversial issue does not fit neatly into one particular agency, so there is a program that integrates the work of 13 interested departments and agencies, the U.S. Global Change Research Program (USGCRP). Through evolving from climate change to the broader global change, the program more completely assesses all environmental changes which have the potential to affect Earth's capacity to support life. USGCRP's website, http://www.global change.gov (formerly http://www.climatechange.gov), leads to the major government reports on this topic, listed under Publications. The list of agencies participating in USGCRP provides a nice list of agencies one might explore further, not only for resources about global change, but about environment and energy in general. USGCRP is evolving rapidly, and new publications and changes to the website are sure to continue, but it remains a central location for government-wide reports and knowing which 13 agencies are involved.

EPA and NOAA are two of the most prominent agencies that provide research and resources related to climate change. EPA has adopted the terminology *climate change* and has a special page on the topic that can be discovered from the A–Z list. On this page you can find links to relevant EPA reports on climate change, regulations, statistics, science on the causes and effects of climate change, and information on what individuals can do to fight climate change. NOAA's work on climate change is evolving. The previously mentioned Climate.gov site already contains data and reports on climate change and the developer of this site, NOAA Climate Service Agency, will coordinate the work done by the various groups in NOAA on this topic.

Climate change is a seminal global issue; therefore, there is a large body of work done in the international arena. The Intergovernmental Panel on Climate Change (IPCC) is the international scientific body that studies climate change and attempts to coordinate a global response. The other primary international agency known for work on climate change is the United Nations Framework Convention on Climate Change (UNFCCC). The best way to determine the difference between these two bodies is that the UNFCCC focuses on the policy and IPCC focuses on the science. UNFCCC led the Bonn climate talks held in June of 2010 and coordinated the Kyoto Protocol of 1997, to date the largest international treaty addressing climate change. IPCC allows governments to nominate experts to write its scientific reports, to guarantee a diverse group that covers different views, expertise, and geographies, so that the findings should be nonpartisan. IPCC has released its fifth set of reports and the majority of its publications are freely available on its website. UNFCCC has useful data and reports on global warming, as well as data on each nation's success in meeting climate targets and signing and ratifying environmental treaties. The primary example of this is the inventory review reports, which are issued as a part of the Kyoto protocol for developed countries. These reports provide data on the greenhouse gas emissions by general source on an annual basis.

Public Lands

Another prominent area of government environment and energy resources relates to public lands. These lands—which make up anywhere from one quarter to some three quarters of most of the western states (and significantly less east of the Rocky Mountains)—are owned and managed by the federal government, which plays a vital role in timber, ranching, mineral extraction, and recreation in the United States. Four agencies provide the primary management of public lands in the United States: the National Park Service (NPS), Bureau of Land Management (BLM), U.S. Fish and Wildlife Service (FWS), and U.S. Forest Service (USFS). Each of these agencies has a slightly different mission, but the easiest way to describe the difference is as a focus on preservation versus management. NPS and FWS have a focus on preservation. BLM and USFS—while they do not ignore the question of conservation in their work with public lands—focus on use, which includes drilling for resources, grazing, and logging.

Brief History of Public Lands

With the purchase of additional government territory, such as the Louisiana Purchase and the Northwest Ordinance, the young United States government of the early nineteenth century needed to determine how to manage these large tracts of land. Congress directed that the lands be surveyed and made available for settlement, and in 1812 the General Land Office was formed within the Department of Treasury to manage such settlement, popularly known as homesteading. This practice continued until just before the turn of the twentieth century. By then, with most desirable lands already homesteaded, the remaining public land in the United States switched from being handled for settlement to use for the public good. The first act of preservation of public land can be traced to President Ulysses Grant, who set aside the Pribilof Islands in Alaska as a reserve for the northern fur seal (done by executive order in 1868). The first official national park was Yellowstone, also set aside by President Grant, in 1872. In 1903, the first official wildlife refuge, Florida's Pelican Island, was created under Teddy Roosevelt. Soon thereafter, in 1905, the Forest Service was established within the Department of Agriculture, tasked with providing quality water (as timber extraction has a major effect on runoff and stream flows) and timber for the nation's benefit. And in 1916, the National Park Service was formed within the Department of the Interior, bringing together the various groups that had managed the national parks, including the Secretary of War.

Public land management continued to evolve; in 1934 the refuge system came under the coordination of the Fish and Wildlife Service, also in the Department of the Interior, and in 1946 the Bureau of Land Management was formed to manage remaining public lands, merging the Grazing Service and General Land Office. Interestingly, BLM had no unified legislative mandate until the passage of the Federal Land Policy and Management Act of 1976 (P.L. 94-579, 90 Stat. 2743), which states that all such land will remain property of the United States and instructs BLM to manage the lands "in a manner that will protect the quality of scientific, scenic, historical, ecological, environmental, air and atmospheric, water resource, and archeological values; that, where appropriate, will preserve and protect certain public lands in their natural condition; that will provide food and habitat for fish and wildlife and domestic animals; and that will provide for outdoor recreation and human occupancy and use" (Federal Land Policy and Management Act, 1976).

Public Lands Resources

A large portion of the resources related to work on public lands can be discovered in Environmental Impact Statements (EIS). These statements have their origins in the National Environmental Policy Act (NEPA), enacted on January 1, 1970 (P.L. 91-190, 83 Stat. 852). There have been numerous revisions to this law since its passage, but one of the requirements of NEPA is that federal agencies "integrate environmental values into their decision making processes by considering the environmental impacts of their proposed actions and reasonable alternatives to those actions" (Environmental Protection Agency, 2010). The primary means for accomplishing this is through the required creation of Environmental Impact Statements. EISs must be written for any activity having an impact on federal lands and the "federal Government owns nearly 650 million acres of land—almost 30 percent of the land area of the United States" (Department of Interior, 2010). So, for example, when the Federal Highway Administration wanted to build a bridge to expand the I-69 highway in Mississippi, it had to file an EIS and go through an evaluative process, which cumulated with a final EIS issued July 9, 2010. These EISs are announced each week in the *Federal Register*, but can also be found in EPA's Environmental Impact Statement Database. Further, public lands are split into some type of geographic division, be it a specific national forest, or the boundaries of particular BLM field office. Each of these public land entities goes through a periodic planning process, through which documents are created, be they EISs, land use plans, or management plans. Each of these documents takes into account current and proposed activities on the land, and their impact.

A main concern with EPA's Environmental Impact Statement Database and with EIS searching in general is that these materials are not always distributed through the depository program. In addition, with the advent of e-government, many are often not published in print at all, and while there is a requirement that these statements be published, there is no requirement that they be preserved.

Most national forests and other public lands divisions have websites that have copies of EISs and other planning documents. Other times, a call or visit to a specific office might be necessary. When looking for historical reports, keep a few strategies in mind. First, check WorldCat to see if a local library has managed to collect the EIS in question. Second, the largest privately held collection of EISs is at Northwestern University, which claims to hold every EIS issued by federal agencies from 1969 to the present, whereas EPA's library covers only 1970 to 1990 (Northwestern University, 2007). Finally, *Environmental Impact Statements*, a commercial subscription from Cambridge Scientific Abstracts, provides full-text EISs from 2003 to the present.

Recreation

One aspect of the study of the environment involves the enjoyment of public lands. When exploring these areas, the most comprehensive resource will be the website of each national park or wildlife refuge (see Figure 12.5 for an example). This works only if the user knows the place to explore, so to that end the government has developed a portal to all federal recreation activities: Recreation.gov. Note that the site is focused mainly on fee activities, and reservations for facilities such as campsites. So while it appears that the user can search for hiking opportunities, the results will be only those campsites, picnic tables, etc., that are next to hiking trails. Despite this caveat, this site provides assistance in discovering which government agency manages the land in a particular area.

Conclusion

Environmental and energy issues impact the daily lives of American citizens through a variety of means. Energy issues influence the economy through factors such as prices at the gas pump or the complex interaction of energy needs and their impact on the environment. Environmental issues affect the quality of the air, water, and climate. This chapter has given an introduction to these resources and how to find them by examining the governmental bodies that work in these areas.

Exercises

1. Starting with the Energy Information Administration website at http://www.eia.doe.gov/, find historical data for the average amount of gasoline consumed in the month of November in the United States. How easy

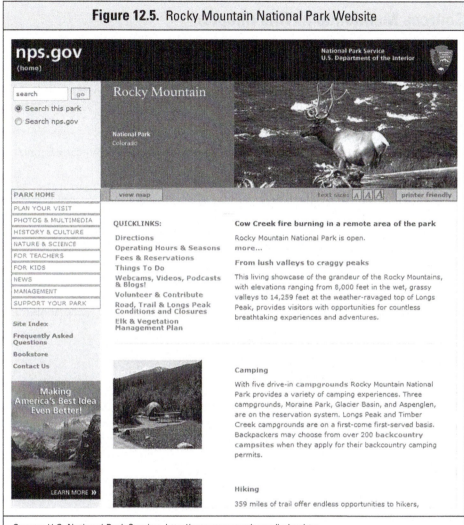

Figure 12.5. Rocky Mountain National Park Website

Source: U.S. National Park Service, http://www.nps.gov/romo/index.htm.

or difficult is it to determine this number, and how far back do the statistics go?

2. Using http://www.fueleconomy.gov/, compare the fuel efficiency and carbon footprint of the Ford Escape Hybrid, Chevy Tahoe Hybrid, and Ford Edge. Which is the most eco-friendly vehicle, for the most current year?

3. Using tools at http://www.epa.gov/, find out all that you can about environmental concerns in Commerce City, Colorado. A patron has inquired about air pollution emitted by the gas refineries there.

4. Find weather data for Denver, Colorado, for the day you were born.

5. How can you track the cruises of a NOAA ship, the *Nancy Foster*, for the past year?

Sources Mentioned in This Chapter

Sources mentioned in this section do not duplicate the References that follow.

U.S. Sources

Bureau of Land Management, http://www.blm.gov/.
Climate.gov, http://www.climate.gov/.
Department of Energy, http://www.doe.gov/.
EERE Energy Calculators and Software, http://www1.eere.energy.gov/calculators/.
Energy Information Administration, http://www.eia.doe.gov/.
Energy Star, http://www.energystar.gov/.
Energy Star: Rebate Finder, http://www.energystar.gov/index.cfm?fuseaction=rebate
    .rebate_locator.
Environmental Impact Statements, http://www.epa.gov/compliance/nepa/eisdata.html.
Environmental Protection Agency, http://www.epa.gov/.
EPA—Climate Change, http://www.epa.gov/climatechange/index.html.
EPA—My Environment, http://www.epa.gov/myenvironment/.
EPA—Rulemaking Gateway, http://yosemite.epa.gov/opei/RuleGate.nsf/.
EPA—Tools (calculators), http://www.epa.gov/climatechange/wycd/waste/tools.html.
Federal Energy Regulatory Commission, http://www.ferc.gov/.
Fish and Wildlife Service, http://www.fws.gov/.
Forest Service, http://www.fs.fed.us/.
Fueleconomy.gov, http://fueleconomy.gov/.
Global Change Research Program, http://www.globalchange.gov/.
National Climatic Data Center, http://www.ncdc.noaa.gov/oa/ncdc.html.
National Environmental Protection Act, http://www.epa.gov/oecaerth/basics/nepa.html.
National Oceanic and Atmospheric Administration, http://www.noaa.gov/.
National Park Service, http://www.nps.gov/.
National Weather Service, http://www.nws.noaa.gov/.
Recreation.gov, http://recreation.gov/.

International Resources

Intergovernmental Panel on Climate Change, http://www.ipcc.ch/.
International Energy Agency, http://www.iea.org/.
Organisation for Economic Co-operation and Development, http://www.oecd.org/.
UNdata, http://data.un.org/.
United Nations, http://www.un.org/.
United Nations Framework Convention on Climate Change, http://unfccc.int/.

References

Department of Energy. "Department of Energy—About DOE." Accessed May 26.
    http://www.energy.gov/about/index.htm.

Department of Interior. 2010. "Printable Maps." Accessed May 26. http://www.national atlas.gov/printable/fedlands.html.

Energy Information Administration. 2010. "History of Energy in the United States 1635–2000." Accessed May 4. http://www.eia.doe.gov/emeu/aer/eh/frame.html.

Energy Star. 2010. "History of Energy Star." Accessed July 15. http://www.energystar .gov/index.cfm?c=about.ab_history.

Environmental Protection Agency. 2010. "National Environmental Policy Act (NEPA)." Accessed May 4. http://www.epa.gov/compliance/nepa/index.html.

Federal Land Policy and Management Act of 1976, P.L. 94-579, 90 Stat. 2743 (1976).

Government Printing Office. 2009. "Setting up National Climatic Data Center Access in a Depository Library." Last revised December 8. http://www.fdlp.gov/component/ content/article/55-partnerships/419-ncdc-faqs.

National Oceanic and Atmospheric Administration. 2008. "Commerce Department Proposes Establishment of NOAA Climate Service." February 8. http://www .noaanews.noaa.gov/stories2010/20100208_climate.html.

Nixon, Richard. "Reorganization Plans Nos. 3 and 4 of 1970. Message from the President of the United States Relative to Reorganization Plans nos. 3 and 4 of 1970." July 9, 1970. 91st Cong., 2nd sess., 1970. H. Doc 366.

Northwestern University. 2011. "How to Search for Environmental Impact Statements (EIS)." Accessed January 10. http://www.library.northwestern.edu/libraries-collections/evanston-campus/transportation-library/services/reference-services/ search-eis.

Office of Energy Efficiency and Renewable Energy. 2010. "Home Page." Accessed July 19. http://www.eere.energy.gov/.

Chapter 13

Business, Economic, and Consumer Information

Introduction

The business of America is business.

President Calvin Coolidge's famous misquote—he actually said, "After all, the chief business of the American people is business" (Coolidge, 1925)—rings true when considering the amount of government effort and government information that exist to support business enterprise. It's impossible to imagine the study and analysis of U.S. economics, business, and industry without the use of data collected, processed, and disseminated by governments, especially the U.S. federal government.

> The federal government is a friend of business when it comes to producing information. Most economic indicators, forecasts, and other macroeconomic data are the result of long-standing cooperation among the companies that fill out forms, the government that collects and tabulates the data, and private and government economists who interpret the results. (Boettcher, 2005, 19)

Look at the broad contents of the 2010 edition of the *Statistical Abstract of the United States* (that most popular of government documents, covered in Chapter 8) in terms of business and economics coverage: among the 30 browsable sections, as many as 14—nearly half—are directly focused on economics, business, and industry:

- Accommodations, Food, and Other Services
- Arts, Recreation, and Travel
- Banking, Finance, and Insurance
- Business Enterprise
- Construction and Housing
- Energy and Utilities
- Foreign Commerce and Aid
- Forestry, Fishing, and Mining
- Income, Expenditures, Poverty, and Wealth
- Information and Communications
- Labor Force, Employment, and Earnings
- Manufactures
- Prices
- Wholesale and Retail Trade

Another eight of these categories (at least) are also contexts for key information about U.S. business and economics:

- Agriculture (think of the business of agriculture—even the U.S. Department of Agriculture produces scores of market research reports)
- Federal Government Finance and Employment (think of the U.S. budget and federal income tax data)
- Geography and Environment (think of the interplay between industry and the environment)
- Health and Nutrition (health care use and expenditures, health insurance, and even disease incidence all figure prominently in the ever-more interdisciplinary world of the business reference librarian)
- Population (think of marketing and demographic data)
- Science and Technology (think of R&D expenditures and other measures of the entrepreneurial environment)
- Social Insurance and Human Services (think of philanthropy and the activities of nonprofit organizations)
- State and Local Government Finances and Employment

Governments serve numerous functions related to business and commerce:

- Measure business and economic activity
- Define and classify business ventures via systems (the Standard Industrial Classification [SIC] Code and North American Industry Classification System [NAICS]) widely adopted by major private business information products
- Measure and support the nation's labor force (U.S. Bureau of Labor)
- Regulate everything from certain operations of small businesses, to accounting practices of public corporations, to Wall Street, to food and drugs, to foreign trade
- Support U.S. business productivity and success (U.S. Department of Commerce and the Small Business Administration)

While the government produces all of this business, economic, and consumer data, it is not always easy to find, and packaging the data for easy public consumption is not necessarily government's first priority. Note that many fee-based business information products analyze or expand upon government information, making it more usable. "Proprietary business-resource databases distinguish their services by providing value-added analysis, organization, and one-stop convenience. As a general rule, one should expect to consult a variety of government sources to obtain equivalent information supplied in commercial databases" (Scott, 2009).

This chapter will address the source of much of this data: the major business, economic, and consumer information available from governments, primarily the U.S. federal government. (Note that Business.gov was formerly known as the "official business link to U.S. government." It was actually primarily aimed at those starting and running their own businesses, information now found through SBA.gov, discussed in this chapter. As of this writing, plans for the Business.gov domain are unknown.)

Types of Business and Economic Information

Much of the government-produced business information relates to categories spelled out by the most famous of economic inspirations for the United States, economist and father of capitalism Adam Smith. In Book V, Chapter 1 of *The Wealth of Nations* (Smith, 1819), Smith discusses public goods and government duties in some detail. These duties include, for Smith, things such as national defense, police, and the justice system; protecting intellectual property such as patents and trademarks; enforcing contracts; building infrastructure; and regulating banking. Generally, these government functions are those which Smith did not think that free markets could adequately perform.

In addition, as particularly seen in the next chapter about the decennial census, governments in the United States quickly saw the benefit in measuring economic and business enterprise data alongside gathering population counts. Much government information about business, then, is data and statistics measuring the economy. This includes famous economic statistics—those widely reported in the media—such as inflation, unemployment, and retail spending, to less known but much more detailed measures, such as business activity by industry, types of business, and geography.

Several government surveys collect data about people, such as about their occupations and wages, and publish compilations of this data. Remember that in no instance is any individual's personal data revealed; law ensures privacy. In some instances the government publishes information about specific companies, such as public company financials (to inform investors), or specifics about company operations related to oversight in the more regulated industries, such as utilities, airlines, and communications.

The government collects and publishes much useful market research information via surveys such as the decennial census. It also publishes and manages patents and other intellectual property, and handles business bankruptcies and antitrust actions.

Governments support businesses and consumers, providing help for new and existing businesses, protecting and educating its citizens as consumers, and regulating industries for the safety and benefit of citizens when the free market might not provide such protections.

Finally, the U.S. government is particularly supportive of U.S. businesses operating abroad, and publishes quite a bit of information in support of exporting and selling abroad. Other international data, such as foreign trade and exchange rates, are also popular, and published by various international government bodies.

This chapter will look at each of these categories.

Economic Indicators

One of the most prominent types of government business information is the indicators of various economic and business activities in the country. These indicators, often produced monthly, frequently end up as lead stories in not just business news sources, but general news sources as well. Watch the *New York Times* for a month and count how often economic data releases are covered on the front page. Depending on the news cycle and the content of the information, stories about economic data produced by the government may appear in a dozen top headlines in that month. The implications of these indicators can drive government policy in many ways. Unemployment data can influence government policy and funding of unemployment benefits; price and inflation data are key to actions of the Federal Reserve and its management of money supply; exchange rates and trade balances influence government policies related to international trade; occupational measures influence vocational and higher education priorities. In any case, understanding this data and identifying its sources—reports and statistical data sets—is a frequent task in using government information.

Depending on how one defines an economic indicator, there could be hundreds of them. There is not currently a single compilation of all such releases from the government. However, a significant subset of the nation's most important economic indicators is compiled into the monthly *Economic Indicators*, transmitted to Congress from the President's Council of Economic Advisors. Although *Economic Indicators'* (Figure 13.1) paper and PDF format may not be extremely friendly to more robust statistical extraction, it does provide a consistent platform for this data, as its publication dates back to the 1940s. Among the 46 currently compiled statistics here are popularly reported data such as gross domestic product, unemployment, inflation and prices, interest rates, and foreign trade. All tables in each monthly issue generally include annual data for the last ten years, and quarterly data for the last two years. The Federal Reserve also archives the data from *Economic Indicators* via its FRASER (Federal Reserve Archival System for Economic Research) system (http://fraser.stlouisfed.org/publications/ei/).

Most of the popular data releases from *Economic Indicators* come from three primary agencies: the Department of Commerce, the Bureau of Labor Statistics (BLS, under the Department of Labor), and the Federal Reserve (the Fed). Each of these agencies provides a portal to their popular releases, which many will consider easier to use than *Economic Indicators*, if not as complete. The Department of Commerce (specifically, its subagency the Economics and Statistics Administration or ESA), produces EconomicIndicators.gov (http://www.economicindicators.gov/); the BLS produces Economy at a Glance (http://www.bls.gov/eag/eag.us.htm); and the Board of Governors of the Federal Reserve System features a webpage of its statistical data (http://www.federalreserve.gov/econresdata/releases/statisticsdata.htm).

EconomicIndicators.gov (not to be confused with the monthly *Economic Indicators* report) compiles the most key releases from the two Department of

---

Figure 13.1 Table of Contents from the August 2010 *Economic Indicators*

Contents

Commerce agencies, the Census Bureau and the ESA (and its subagency the Bureau of Economic Analysis, or BEA), which compile economic data. Prominent among these are retail sales, which is often reported on in media as consumer spending (think of news stories discussing how people are spending more, or less, and how that affects the economy), sales and construction of new and existing homes, GDP (Gross Domestic Product, the most basic, complete indicator of the output of the nation's economy), and foreign trade (think of discussions of trade deficits).

BLS produces several prominent economic indicators as well, all available from its Economy at a Glance (http://www.bls.gov/eag/eag.us.htm). Unemployment is possibly its most cited indicator. The agency's mission also includes measurement of a less intuitive statistic when one considers labor: prices. BLS's Consumer Price Index and Producer Price Index are the source for news articles about prices and inflation. Another popular indicator available from Economy at a Glance is productivity, a measure of how productive the nation's workers are. Also noteworthy is the fact that BLS unemployment indicators are also available for states and metropolitan areas at Economy at a Glance. This is the source of unemployment rates frequently reported for states and cities. Several other BLS data items are available for smaller geographies as well. The map interface at Economy at a Glance helps users to navigate to this data.

The third most prominent agency producing popular economic indicators is the Federal Reserve, whose mission is largely to manage the nation's money supply. As economic and monetary theory surrounding money supply has grown in prominence in recent decades, the Fed, and especially its chair, have become economic rock stars. While key indicators from the Fed, such as those measuring consumer credit and money stocks, may not have quite the broad popularity of unemployment, prices, and home sales, markets and the financial industry pay very close attention to this data from the Fed. The most popular Fed action is its control of the interest rate (popularly known as the prime rate or the federal funds rate), which may change after a meeting of the Fed's Open Market Committee, and always makes front page news. Announcements of changes to the prime rate garner rapt attention from economists, politicians, bureaucrats, and nation and world markets.

A classic compilation of economic indicators and statistics across government is the annual *Economic Report of the President* (*ERP*). Published annually by the Council of Economic Advisors (an agency within the president's office established by Congress in 1946), the *ERP* is the best and easiest place to find time-series of economic data about the nation. Nearly all of the categories mentioned above—prices, employment and unemployment, GDP and output by sector or industry, foreign trade, government spending, interest rates, and over 100 more items—are included in the *ERP*, with most data available here annually for 40, 50, and 60 years or more. The *ERP* is transmitted to Congress each February. Prior to its statistics section, it includes a prose description and analysis of the current economy, with chapters on various current issues. For instance, the 2010 volume includes essays on topics such as "Rescuing the Economy from the Great Recession," "Reforming Health Care," and "Transforming the Energy Sector and Addressing Climate Change." The *ERP* then concludes each year with the statistical tables. The *ERP* is available via FDsys, and is also archived on FRASER.

An excellent compilation of economic indicators for states is the Regional Economic Conditions database (RECON, http://www2.fdic.gov/recon/index .asp/) from the Federal Deposit Insurance Corporation (FDIC). FDIC, an independent federal agency that regulates banking, created RECON in order to assess financial risk of banks (think of a bank with many outstanding business loans—one wants to know how the local business economy is doing in order to assess the risk of those loans defaulting). For each state, RECON collects data on industry output, housing and real estate, employment, wages, and spending. All of the data compiled in RECON is derived from the other sources discussed in this section.

Economic data for states is largely derived from federal statistical efforts. For instance, the BEA measures economic output for states, while the BLS measures employment and prices for states. But states do usually have their own economic and/or commerce-related agencies, which may conduct some research on their own to supplement the federal data. Become familiar with appropriate state resources for relevant states. City and local data follows the same pattern, except only a few of these classic economic indicators cover smaller geographies, and when they do, it's generally only for larger metropolitan areas. But many cities and counties are the subject of more in-depth local economic analysis, sponsored by local governments, or perhaps by a university or research center nearby.

Government Finance

Finances of governments have large implications for government programs, as well as being important to the investment community. Governments take in revenue in the form of taxes and fees, and expend monies to fund programs and services. Governments often borrow to meet expenditure needs, whether in the short term to cover expenses for which the tax revenues have not yet come in, or to cover longer-term expenses that go beyond budgeted projections of revenue (deficit spending). In each case, governments issue bonds to cover shortages.

Federal government finance begins with the federal budget. As covered in the Chapter 7 section about the Office of Management and Budget, the president's office and the OMB transmit a proposed budget to Congress each February. While the proposed figures are just that—proposals—this multivolume set also includes historical data that does reflect actual spending. Data is very detailed for the past two years, and the *Historical Perspectives* volumes contain historical budget data, in most cases back to 1940. These budget documents are all available via FDsys.

Congress actually sets the budgets for programs and agencies through the appropriations process, as mentioned in Chapter 3 on Congress. Like other legislation, appropriations bills (also called spending bills) must go through the committee and floor process, are debated, may produce reports and hearings, and are eventually passed and signed into law. Generally speaking, it can be easier to get actual budget numbers from the OMB documents rather than finding and looking through spending laws. But if one wants the current year budget, one must consult the legislation. Of course the documented work of Congress during the process is enlightening as well. The hearings, reports, and debate about spending priorities give plenty of insight into the goals of government programs.

While Congress sets the budget, the Department of the Treasury ultimately manages the actual federal monies. The agency's primary publication is an annual report of the U.S. government, known as the *Combined Statement* (officially, the *Combined Statement of Receipts, Outlays, and Balances of the United States Government*). The *Combined Statement*, perhaps a document that only a government

Figure 13.2. Page from the *Daily Treasury Statement*, August 27, 2010

TABLE II—Deposits and Withdrawals of Operating Cash

Deposits	Today	This month to date	Fiscal year to date
Federal Reserve Account:			
Agriculture Loan Repayments (misc)	$ 53	$ 611	$ 7,866
Air Transport Security Fees	3	25	1,911
Commodity Credit Corporation programs	59	697	8,377
Customs and Certain Excise Taxes	110	3,011	29,738
Deposits by States:			
Supplemental Security Income	4	82	3,488
Unemployment	22	6,106	37,684
Education Department programs	60	2,347	24,091
Energy Department programs	12	684	6,550
Estate and Gift Taxes	35	1,177	16,717
Federal Reserve Earnings	0	7,412	88,422
Foreign Deposits, Military Sales	6	1,470	16,943
FTD's Received (Table IV)	2,399	42,055	534,064
Housing and Urban Development programs	2	251	2,331
Individual Income and Employment			
Taxes, Not Withheld	174	4,120	263,948
Interest recd from T&L Depositaries	0	0	0
Justice Department programs	4	712	6,568
Postal Service	278	6,594	81,618
Public Debt Cash Issues (Table III-B)	694	754,093	7,718,972
Other Deposits:			
TARP	142	2,993	141,650
Thrift Savings Plan Transfer	131	741	9,294

Withdrawals	Today	This month to date	Fiscal year to date
Federal Reserve Account:			
Commodity Credit Corporation programs	$ 19	$ 482	17,972
Defense Vendor Payments (EFT)	1,947	30,064	357,783
Education Department programs	5,721	29,072	213,545
Energy Department programs	237	3,081	32,980
Federal Employees Insurance Payments	172	5,099	57,482
Fed. Highway Administration programs	394	4,284	37,543
Federal Salaries (EFT)	118	14,216	161,688
Food and Nutrition Service (misc)	155	6,565	80,207
GSA programs	44	1,610	17,407
Health and Human Services Grants (misc)	517	6,968	89,426
Housing and Urban Development programs	192	11,080	70,538
Interest on Treasury Securities	2	34,226	173,534
Justice Department programs	64	1,268	15,031
Labor Dept. prgms (excl. unemployment)	134	1,219	14,565
Medicaid	482	20,996	243,915
Medicare	1,391	27,542	487,813
NASA programs	96	1,458	15,308
Postal Service Money Orders and Other	121	2,993	38,178
Public Debt Cash Redemp. (Table III-B)	735	609,446	6,447,697
Social Security Benefits (EFT)	3	48,296	522,863
Supple. Nutrition Assist. Program (SNAP)	12	395	4,684
Temporary Assistance for Needy Families (HHS)	72	2,133	18,852

accountant can truly love, details all receipts and outlays of the federal government for the fiscal year. It is one of a triad of publications that also includes the *Daily Treasury Statement* and the *Monthly Treasury Statement*. For instance, the *Daily Treasury Statement* details how much money came in to the federal government each day, and how much went out, by function. Figure 13.2 (see facing page) shows the *Daily Treasury Statement* for August 27, 2010. One can see that on this day, the largest sources of revenue were FTDs (federal tax deposits, such as those withheld from paychecks), income from public bonds (Public Debt Cash Issuances, such as when someone buys a T-bill), and the Postal Service. The biggest expenditures for the day were education programs, Medicare, payments to defense contractors, and repayments on bonds.

So this group of publications also contains useful and very current information on government spending and receipts, and details spending by agencies and on specific programs.

Of particular interest in Department of Treasury information are the details related to these government receipts; specifically, information about tax receipts from the Internal Revenue Service (a subagency of Treasury), and information about public bonds. The IRS, in addition to providing access to federal tax forms and instructions for individuals and businesses, compiles and publishes a remarkable wealth of compiled data related to income taxes. Whether for individuals, business, or corporations, data is available. For instance, one can find the number of returns, and the percentage of returns, that use various deductions, such as an IRA; breakdowns of adjusted income by age, marital status, and income; and, for corporate and business returns, tax data by industry or sector. Traditionally, this data was made available via the Statistics of Income (SOI) series. While SOI still exists, the IRS statistics site is the place to begin to find data related to tax collection (http://www.irs.gov/taxstats/index.html).

The TreasuryDirect website (http://www.treasurydirect.gov/), meanwhile, is the government portal for buying federal bonds and securities. When you buy a treasury bond, you are loaning the government money in order to pay its bills—not unlike what you would do when you buy a school bond, a municipal bond (generally for funding a municipal government), or a corporate bond. There are several different types of bonds and securities, from classic U.S. savings bonds to treasury notes and bills. Often considered among the safest investments, treasury bonds may be purchased and tracked right from TreasuryDirect.

Business and Industry Data

The federal government produces quite a bit of information about the state of particular industries and business enterprises. Some of this data has been referred to already: the BEA, for instance, tracks overall production by sectors of the economy (sectors are broad categories such as retail trade, manufacturing, mining, and services); the IRS publishes tax return data by sector.

The Census Bureau has several survey programs that produce more robust business and industry data. Also, various government services produce intelligence about specific companies. This section addresses industry and specific company information available from the government.

Surveys of Business and Industry

Census Bureau surveys of business highlight this category, and their major survey is the economic census. The economic census is similar to the regular census (covered in Chapter 14), but instead of surveying people, it surveys businesses. With some exceptions, nearly every business in the country that has employees receives an economic census questionnaire, and is required by law to complete it. Just as the regular decennial census gathers key data such as population, age, race, and sex, all by location, the economic census, currently taken every five years, asks every business questions so as to gather key data: type of business (what industry; for example, there are companies who manufacture car parts, companies that sell car parts, and companies that perform car repairs: all are in different industries); a measure of size, such as number of employees and payroll; a measure of output, such as value of shipments or services, or retail sales; and location, to allow all of this data to be available for states, counties, cities, and ZIP codes. The economic census yields a rich picture of the U.S. economy, with data by industry and location.

History of the Economic Census

As Micarelli (1998) summarizes, the first economic census took place as part of the 1810 decennial census after Congress passed a law specifically calling for it. At this time, the economic census consisted of counting manufacturers by broad types of products (25 categories), with an estimate of their output. Results were compiled into a single volume as part of the 1810 census results: *A Series of Tables of Several Branches of American Manufacturers of Every County in the Union so far as they are returned in the reports of the Marshals, and of the secretaries and of their respective assistants, in the autumn of the year 1810: Together with returns of certain doubtful Goods, Productions of the Soil and agricultural stock, so far as they have been received.* These measures of economic activity continued as part of the regular census at the behest of Congress. Over the years, more and more data was compiled. In 1850, it was expanded beyond manufacturing to include mining and fishing. In 1880, transportation and communication industry information was gathered in response to the burgeoning railroad, steamer, and telephone industries.

The twentieth century saw a continued expansion of the economic census, and it began to be staggered in time from the regular census. For a time it was taken every two years. There was no 1945 census—the nation was busy at war—but the 1947 census of manufactures was notable for the introduction of standard classification codes for industries (up until this time, the Census Bureau created its own industry categories). This happened because in 1941, a predecessor to OMB created the *Standard Industrial Classification (SIC) Manual,* which became a standard classification of industries that, in revised form, is still sometimes used today. So the 1947 economic census classified each business according to categories defined in the *SIC Manual*.

The rest of the twentieth century saw the modern economic census take shape: held every five years (in years ending in 2 and 7), covering all industries except for agriculture (which now has a separate census of agriculture), and with data available alongside population census data via the American FactFinder platform.

Finding and Using Economic Census Data

American FactFinder has a section for Business and Government that presents the latest data from the economic census—currently, that data is for 2007. The survey takes place during 2008, and businesses provide data on the previous year, 2007. Data tabulation and publishing of results occurs during 2009 and 2010. The Economic Fact Sheet in Figure 13.3 presents summary information

Figure 13.3. Economic Fact Sheet Summary for the Entire Nation, from the 2007 Economic Census

Selected Statistics from the 2007 Economic Census — Reference Map
2007 Economic Sectors

2007 NAICS code and description	Number of establishments	Sales, shipments, receipts ($1,000)	Annual payroll ($1,000)	Number of employees	
21 Mining, quarrying, and oil and gas extraction	22,667	413,524,731	40,687,472	730,433	
22 Utilities	16,578	584,192,658	51,653,618	637,247	more »
23 Construction	729,345	1,731,841,830	331,002,718	7,316,240	
31-33 Manufacturing	293,919	5,339,345,058	612,474,100	13,333,390	
42 Wholesale trade	434,983	6,515,708,554	336,206,776	6,227,389	more »
44-45 Retail trade	1,128,112	3,917,663,456	362,818,687	15,515,396	more »
48-49 Transportation and warehousing	219,706	639,916,407	173,183,073	4,454,383	more »
51 Information	141,566	1,072,342,856	228,836,587	3,496,773	more »
52 Finance and insurance	(r)501,713	(r)3,669,302,691	(r)502,416,670	(r)6,607,511	more »
53 Real estate and rental and leasing	384,297	485,058,597	84,764,864	2,188,479	more »
54 Professional, scientific, and technical services	847,492	1,251,003,504	502,074,331	7,870,414	more »
55 Management of companies and enterprises	51,451	104,442,966	249,510,832	2,664,203	more »
56 Administrative and Support and Waste Mang and Remediation Srvs	395,292	630,771,091	301,450,047	10,250,955	more »
61 Educational services	61,385	44,980,656	14,259,109	539,951	more »
62 Health care and social assistance	784,626	1,668,276,808	662,719,938	16,792,074	more »
71 Arts, entertainment, and recreation	124,620	189,416,942	58,359,104	2,061,348	more »
72 Accommodation and food services	634,361	613,795,732	170,826,847	11,600,751	more »
81 Other services (except public administration)	540,148	405,284,048	99,123,269	3,479,011	more »

Source: U.S. Census Bureau, 2007 Economic Census

for the entire nation, by major industry. An Economic Fact Sheet for an industry, meanwhile, is much more precise, offering the same data for thousands of industries classified by NAICS codes (see sidebar), such as sporting goods stores, barber shops, law firms or offices, or sandals or rubber and plastics footwear manufacturing. One can further access this industry information for specific geographies. Figure 13.4 shows a breakdown for the city of Santa Barbara, CA, for sporting goods stores. Note that if a geography only has one or a few types of any particular establishment, data will likely be suppressed, so as to prevent publication of data that might be easy to attribute to a particular business.

Other Business and Economic Surveys

The Census Bureau conducts a number of other related surveys of business and industry. A popular data set is the *County Business Patterns* (CBP)/*ZIP Code Business Patterns* (ZBP)/*Metro Business Patterns* (MBP) series. These series are similar to the economic census in that they count number of establishments by NAICS code and location. For each entry, there is also data on the size of the establishments (by number of employees and payroll). CBP/ZBP/MBP is published annually. The key item that this series lacks when compared to the economic census is the all-important measure of output, whether that be sales, shipments, or receipts. The key advantage of this data is that it is annual.

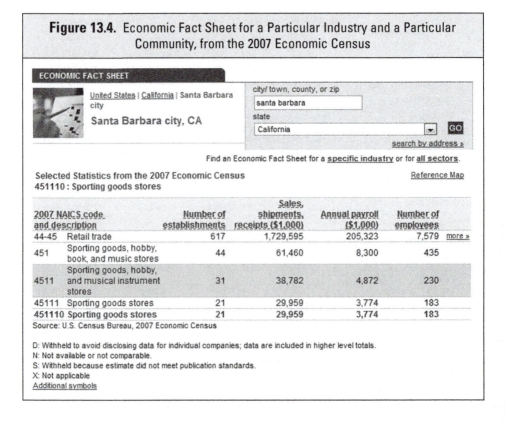

Figure 13.4. Economic Fact Sheet for a Particular Industry and a Particular Community, from the 2007 Economic Census

ECONOMIC FACT SHEET

United States | California | Santa Barbara city

Santa Barbara city, CA

city/ town, county, or zip
santa barbara

state
California

search by address »

Find an Economic Fact Sheet for a **specific industry** or for **all sectors**.

Selected Statistics from the 2007 Economic Census   Reference Map
451110 : Sporting goods stores

2007 NAICS code and description		Number of establishments	Sales, shipments, receipts ($1,000)	Annual payroll ($1,000)	Number of employees	
44-45	Retail trade	617	1,729,595	205,323	7,579	more »
451	Sporting goods, hobby, book, and music stores	44	61,460	8,300	435	
4511	Sporting goods, hobby, and musical instrument stores	31	38,782	4,872	230	
45111	Sporting goods stores	21	29,959	3,774	183	
451110	Sporting goods stores	21	29,959	3,774	183	

Source: U.S. Census Bureau, 2007 Economic Census

D: Withheld to avoid disclosing data for individual companies; data are included in higher level totals.
N: Not available or not comparable.
S: Withheld because estimate did not meet publication standards.
X: Not applicable
Additional symbols

NAICS and SIC Codes

As noted above, the *SIC* (the letters are pronounced, S I C) *Manual* was first used by the Economic Census in 1947. In its most recent form it is divided into ten broad categories:

- Agriculture, Forestry, and Fishing
- Mining
- Construction
- Manufacturing
- Transportation, Communications, Electric, Gas, and Sanitary Services
- Wholesale Trade
- Retail Trade
- Finance, Insurance, and Real Estate
- Services
- Public Administration

These ten broad categories are then broken down into several dozen smaller categories designated by the first two digits of the SIC code, with further digits delineating the industries in more detail.

For example, the Services category includes two-digit industries, such as 75 Automotive Repair, 80 Health Services, and 83 Social Services. A tiny piece of the Services category looks like this:

73 Business Services
    734 Services to Dwellings and Other Buildings
        7342 Disinfecting and Pest Control Services

With this breakdown, data is then available for pest control businesses.

NAICS (the North American Industry Classification System, pronounced "nakes") was developed in the 1980s and 1990s and both updated the SIC system and implemented a system more in line with standards. NAICS was first used in the economic census in 1997. It is similar to the SIC system in that it has broad and then more specific categories denoted by numbers. Unlike SIC, NAICS goes down to six digits. For example:

56 Administrative and Support and Waste Management and Remediation Services
    561 Administrative and Support Services
        5617 Services to Buildings and Dwellings
            56171 Exterminating and Pest Control Services

While the NAICS system has now been widely adopted to classify industries both by governments and private market research products, the SIC system is still sometimes used.

Current Industrial Reports is another long-standing Census Bureau product. It produces quarterly reports on manufacturing activity by product. For instance, the report on socks details the number of socks manufactured in the United States by year and quarter, and by type of sock, such as by material (e.g., cotton or wool) and audience (e.g., women's socks, infant socks). CIRs cover only the entire nation; no smaller geography is available.

Several other Census Bureau surveys supplement the economic census. The Census Bureau's Business and Industry website (http://www.census.gov/econ/) leads to surveys and data by topic. And the BEA's Industry Economic Accounts data (http://www.bea.gov/industry/) features broad measure of output (such as GDP) by industry. Occasionally, another agency has specific oversight of an industry and produces useful data about that industry. For example, the FDIC produces data about the banking industry, available at http://www.fdic.gov/bank/statistical/index.html.

Company Information

Just like information about citizens, information about companies gathered by federal and state governments is nearly always confidential. One can no sooner access the tax returns of the business down the street than could one see a neighbor's tax forms, census forms, or Medicaid application. There are exceptions, however, which are noteworthy. As Boettcher points out, the notion that there is no company-specific information is a "long-standing myth" (2005, 19).

While company information is indeed generally confidential, there are several laws and regulatory actions for which making company information collected by the government public is a byproduct. Perhaps the most noteworthy are the company financial reports from publicly traded companies. This information is gathered by the Securities and Exchange Commission (SEC) for the explicit purpose of making basic company financial information public for companies that are traded on a stock market. This effort began through laws passed after the 1929 market crash (see the Securities Act of 1933, 48 Stat. 74, and the Securities Exchange Act of 1934, 48 Stat. 881), and is intended to insure that investors have accurate financials about companies they may choose to invest in.

While these SEC company reports have been available for years, until the Internet era they were not widely available outside of investment circles, and generally required a fee to acquire. Public information advocate Carl Malamud led efforts to put these reports online, for free, available to the public (Markoff, 1993). These reports are now published in the SEC's free EDGAR database (http://www.sec.gov/edgar.shtml). Different reports are published at various stages in the year and based on company actions affecting shareholders, but the most famous EDGAR report is the annual 10-K (Figure 13.5), which features much of the same data that companies share with shareholders via annual reports. EDGAR reports are key government information for investors and others researching companies.

Another relatively obvious source of government information about individual companies is patents. Covered in Chapter 11, patents are frequently scoured by competitors and the media for clues to new products and services. For instance, in 2009 Apple, Inc. filed an application for a patent (patent application number 2010/0207721) about security related to using an electronic device, like a cell phone. According to the application, the device could match a voice, heartbeat, or some other authentication method, and upon receiving suspicious results, could lock the device, automatically take a photo tagged with GPS coordinates of the device, or take another action. Upon Apple's filing the application, the media and other technology companies began speculating on new iPhone security measures that might be in development. Note that this patent, like Nike's self-lacing, lighted sneakers (patent application number 2009/0272013, Figure 13.6) is an application only. Both patent applications and actual

Figure 13.5. The Header and Beginning of Data from IBM's 2009 10-K Report on EDGAR

UNITED STATES
SECURITIES AND EXCHANGE COMMISSION
WASHINGTON, D.C. 20549

FORM 10-K
ANNUAL REPORT
pursuant to Section 13 or 15 (d) of the
Securities Exchange Act of 1934
FOR THE YEAR ENDED DECEMBER 31, 2009

1-2360
(Commission file number)

INTERNATIONAL BUSINESS MACHINES CORPORATION
(Exact name of registrant as specified in its charter)

NEW YORK	13-0871985
(State of Incorporation)	(IRS Employer Identification Number)
ARMONK, NEW YORK	10504
(Address of principal executive offices)	(Zip Code)

914-499-1900
(Registrant's telephone number)

Securities registered pursuant to Section 12(b) of the Act:

Title of each class	Voting shares outstanding at February 10, 2010	Name of each exchange on which registered
Capital stock, par value $.20 per share	1,299,003,390	New York Stock Exchange Chicago Stock Exchange
4.00% Notes due 2011		New York Stock Exchange
4.95% Notes due 2011		New York Stock Exchange
6.625% Notes due 2014		New York Stock Exchange
7.50% Debentures due 2013		New York Stock Exchange
8.375% Debentures due 2019		New York Stock Exchange
7.00% Debentures due 2025		New York Stock Exchange
6.22% Debentures due 2027		New York Stock Exchange
6.50% Debentures due 2028		New York Stock Exchange
7.00% Debentures due 2045		New York Stock Exchange
7.125% Debentures due 2096		New York Stock Exchange

Indicate by check mark if the registrant is a well-known seasoned issuer as defined in Rule 405 of the Securities Act. Yes ☒ No ☐

Indicate by check mark if the registrant is not required to file reports pursuant to Section 13 or Section 15(d) of the Act. Yes ☐ No ☒

granted patents are public. Industries watch the patent space for new inventions, hoping to find clues as to future product development of competitors.

Businesses that are contracting with, or doing business with, government generally have that relationship made public. While the process for vendors to bid for, and win, government contracts and sales is complicated and beyond the goals of this chapter, it is notable that the primary portal for advertising opportunities for doing business with the government over $25,000, FedBiz Opps.gov, allows one to search for award recipients by many criteria, including agency for which the work is to be done, industry (the nature of the work), and location. Figure 13.7 shows the winner of an award to provide paint for roads in Utah's Canyonlands National Park. Another website, USAspending.gov, was specifically created to provide transparency on recipients of government contracts (it was created by the Federal Funding Accountability and Transparency Act of 2006, P.L. 109-282, cosponsored by Senators Obama and McCain). It allows

Figure 13.6. Sneaker Diagram from Nike Patent Application

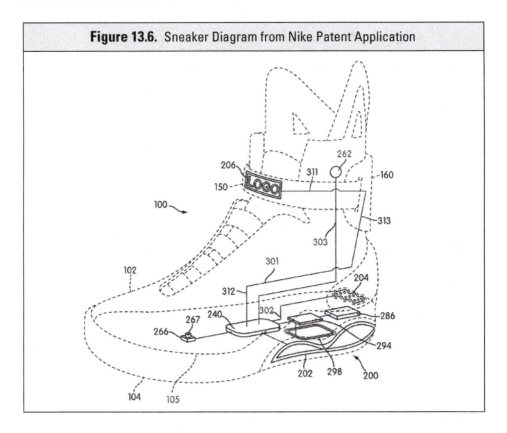

searching by various criteria. For instance, one can see government contracts awarded by agency, company, type of award, or product. Listed are awards to companies such as Halliburton, or Lockheed Martin and its 23.2 billion dollars in federal contracts awarded in FY2010 (see Figure 13.8).

Another public database containing company information is Federal Election Commission (FEC) campaign finance data. Law requires political donations to be public; the FEC provides a database to search such information at http://www.fec.gov/disclosure.shtml. For instance, one can search Microsoft and find some $5 million in various political contributions in the last 15 years, including the candidates, parties, and political organizations contributed to. An alternative, privately produced interface to this data that is extremely useful is http://www.opensecrets.org/.

Many other government agencies gather and publish some company information when the company operates in an industry that is regulated so as to allow such information to be public. A classic example is the My Environment database from EPA, discussed in Chapter 12. Companies that produce products and byproducts of various environmental effects—such as those that produce air pollutants, or who may have material run off into water sources—are monitored and required to report to EPA certain data, which is then made public via My Environment. Enter a location here to see a list of companies or

Figure 13.7. Sample Federal Contract Award from USAspending.gov

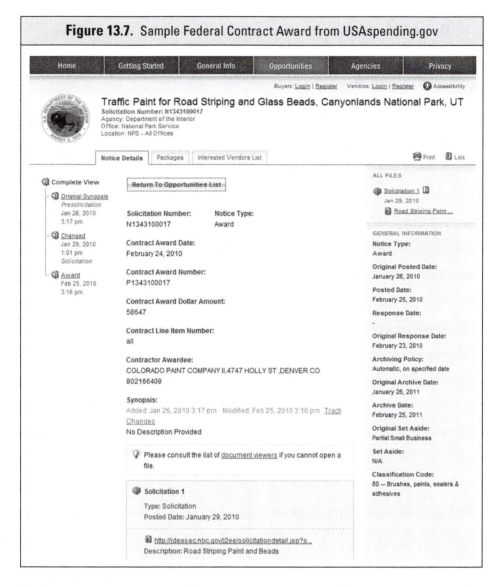

facilities in your location that produce emissions that are required to be reported to the government.

Various other government regulation efforts lead to company data. Airlines are regulated by the federal government, and airline data is published by the Bureau of Transportation Statistics (BTS) at http://www.bts.gov/press_releases/airline_financial_data.html. Want to see what airlines take in the most in baggage fees? Check the releases here. Fuel costs, profits/loss, and many other tables are available for U.S. airlines. This company-specific data is only a fraction of the data available from the BTS at http://www.bts.gov/programs/airline_information/. Also available here are statistics like causes of flight

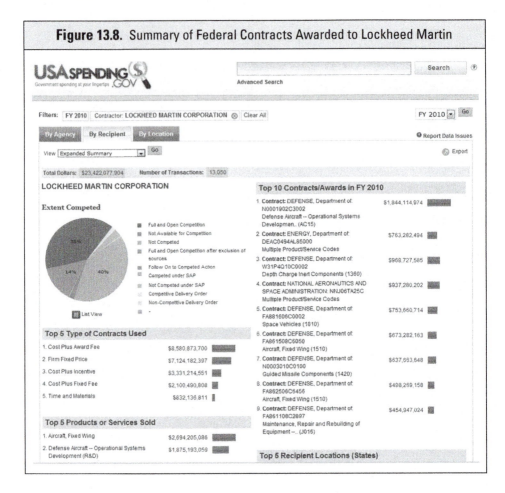

Figure 13.8. Summary of Federal Contracts Awarded to Lockheed Martin

delays, airline hub volume, tarmac times, chronically delayed flights, and rankings of airports by flight delays (hint: Salt Lake City, Portland, and Seattle are safer bets for non-delayed flights).

Another useful site with some company information is ClinicalTrials.gov (http://www.clinicaltrials.gov/), which lists clinical trials for medical drugs and products. One can see which companies are conducting trials with which drugs, and where, and for what purpose. Several other sources from the government list company information (see Scott, 2009 for additional resources).

Market Research

Market research is generally any information about consumers and competitors that provides intelligence about a particular market, whether that market be widgets, food, or some service such as medicine. We've just seen government information which provides information about industries and sectors, and even sometimes about specific companies. But most useful market research data gathered by governments is about its citizens, the nation's consumers. The federal government is the single biggest compiler of this market research in the country, and this is primarily for one reason: it conducts the decennial census (and its companion the American Community Survey), discussed in depth in the next chapter. These comprehensive surveys provide social, demographic, and economic information about the entire population, in such detail that data is available for even very small geographies, such as ZIP codes and smaller census-defined places such as census tracts and blocks.

So the details of the decennial census and the ACS are covered in the next chapter; what is important here is simply that the data gathered by these surveys provides the basic information about the population of the nation that forms the basis of most market research done by private market research firms. From these surveys, one can tell the population, age and sex characteristics, income, occupation, and much more information, about every place in the country. Private market research firms take this census data and repackage it, supplement it with other data, and make it more usable for business planners and marketers. Understanding how to use the census data covered in the next chapter allows anyone to understand the most core market research product in the country.

There are several other government surveys which provide information about the population that also acts as market research. The joint Census Bureau/Bureau of Labor Statistics monthly Current Population Survey (CPS), while it primarily gathers data related to the labor market, also asks enough economic and social questions beyond the decennial census and ACS to make it useful as market research. Data on income and poverty, occupations, and health insurance are among its highlights. The CPS table generator (http://www.census.gov/hhes/www/cpstc/cps_table_creator.html) allows access to much of this data. Note that unlike decennial census and ACS data, CPS data is not available for smaller geographies such as cities and towns: the sample just isn't big enough.

Perhaps the single most core piece of data that marketers seek is details about how people spend their money. This is what market research is all about, and the decennial census doesn't really provide any clues as to spending. The Bureau of Labor Statistics conducts a survey called the Consumer Expenditure Survey (CES, http://www.bls.gov/cex/). As the title says, it surveys people as to how they spend their money. It covers over twenty categories of spending: housing, such as mortgages, home repairs, and utilities; transportation expenses such as automobiles, gasoline, and mass transit; personal expenditures such as apparel, healthcare, and personal products; and entertainment and recreation expenditures (see Figure 13.9). Like the census, the CES can form the basis of more in-depth, private market research products. Unlike the census, the CES does not provide data for even states, much less smaller geographies. So while a useful portrait of the nation's spending, it is of lesser use to local business planners. It does break data down by some market segments, including age, race, region, broad occupation, and family type (e.g., single, dual earner, married with children).

Market research is a very broad topic, and much data is potentially useful. In addition to those just covered, statistical products such as those discussed earlier from the IRS are also useful. Surveys such as the BLS's American Time Use

Figure 13.9. Core Data from the Consumer Expenditure Survey

Table A. Average annual expenditures of all consumer units and percent changes, Consumer Expenditure Survey, 2006–08

Item	2006	2007	2008	Percent change 2006–07	Percent change 2007–08
Number of consumer units (in thousands)	118,843	120,171	120,770	...	...
Income before taxes	$60,533	$63,091	$63,563	...	...
Averages:				...	...
Age of reference person	48.7	48.8	49.1	...	...
Number of persons in consumer unit	2.5	2.5	2.5	...	...
Number of earners	1.3	1.3	1.3	...	...
Number of vehicles	1.9	1.9	2.0	...	...
Percent homeowner	67	67	66	...	...
Average annual expenditures	$48,398	$49,638	$50,486	2.6	1.7
Food	6,111	6,133	6,443	.4	5.1
Food at home	3,417	3,465	3,744	1.4	8.1
Cereals and bakery products	446	460	507	3.1	10.2
Meats, poultry, fish, and eggs	797	777	846	−2.5	8.9
Dairy products	368	387	430	5.2	11.1
Fruits and vegetables	592	600	657	1.4	9.5
Other food at home	1,212	1,241	1,305	2.4	5.2
Food away from home	2,694	2,668	2,698	−1.0	1.1
Alcoholic beverages	497	457	444	−8.0	−2.8
Housing	16,366	16,920	17,109	3.4	1.1
Shelter	9,673	10,023	10,183	3.6	1.6
Utilities, fuels, and public services	3,397	3,477	3,649	2.4	4.9
Household operations	948	984	998	3.8	1.4
Housekeeping supplies	640	639	654	−.2	2.3
Household furnishings and equipment	1,708	1,797	1,624	5.2	−9.6
Apparel and services	1,874	1,881	1,801	.4	−4.3
Transportation	8,508	8,758	8,604	2.9	−1.8
Vehicle purchases (net outlay)	3,421	3,244	2,755	−5.2	−15.1
Gasoline and motor oil	2,227	2,384	2,715	7.0	13.9
Other vehicle expenses	2,355	2,592	2,621	10.1	1.1
Public transportation	505	538	513	6.5	−4.6
Healthcare	2,766	2,853	2,976	3.1	4.3
Entertainment	2,376	2,698	2,835	13.6	5.1
Personal care products and services	585	588	616	.5	4.8
Reading	117	118	116	.9	−1.7
Education	888	945	1,046	6.4	10.7
Tobacco products and smoking supplies	327	323	317	−1.2	−1.9
Miscellaneous	846	808	840	−4.5	4.0
Cash contributions	1,869	1,821	1,737	−2.6	−4.6
Personal insurance and pensions	5,270	5,336	5,605	1.3	5.0
Life and other personal insurance	322	309	317	−4.0	2.6
Pensions and Social Security	4,948	5,027	5,288	1.6	5.2

Survey (http://www.bls.gov/tus/), which asks people to measure how much time they spend on activities such as work, housework, entertainment, and education, can be useful to market researchers. Many other statistical programs and products covered elsewhere in this book (such as health data that can inform the market for health products and services, or education data that informs the market for educational products and services), can also be useful as market research, since they all provide intelligence about the nation and its citizens. So one seeking market research data from the government should creatively apply lessons from throughout this book in order to maximize the possibilities.

Labor

There is ample government information related to labor and employment. The government gathers data on occupations and wages, productivity, earnings, and more. This section will briefly summarize key information from the

Department of Labor (and its subagency the Bureau of Labor Statistics) beyond the key data on employment and unemployment and prices covered in the earlier Economic Indicators section.

Some of the most popular government business information is related to occupations. BLS produces a classic, annual survey of occupations called the *Occupational Outlook Handbook (OOH)*. The *OOH* looks at hundreds of occupations, and provides several types of information for each one:

- The nature of the work
- The qualifications, schooling, training, and professional certificates necessary for the occupation
- The occupation's salaries and wages
- The outlook for the occupation: is it in demand? Will more people be needed in these jobs in the future, or is there a glut of trained people already?

The *OOH* is a staple of any library that provides information about careers.

A related product is BLS's compensations surveys. Wages by Occupation (http://www.bls.gov/bls/blswage.htm) provides median and average salaries and wages for over 800 occupations, and includes breakdowns for states and metropolitan areas. Are you a dietician looking to relocate? Figure 13.10 shows the top five metro areas with the highest salaries for dieticians. It further shows how many dieticians are employed in each metro area, and what percentage dieticians make up of the area's workforce. Similar, comparative data is available for occupations and locations nationwide.

BLS compiles numerous other data related to occupations, employment, and prices. Its parent agency, the Department of Labor, serves labor broadly. It features much information helpful to workers, including data from the Occupational Safety and Health Administration (OSHA, discussed in the following section on law and regulations), information and support of employment for people with disabilities, information about job discrimination, rules about union activities, employer health insurance, workers compensation, and more.

Figure 13.10. BLS Table of Highest-Paying Markets for Dieticians

MSA	Employment	Hourly mean wage	Annual mean wage	Employment per thousand workers
San Jose-Sunnyvale-Santa Clara, CA	300	$38.69	$80,470	0.339
Bethesda-Frederick-Gaithersburg, MD Metropolitan Division	150	$38.27	$79,610	0.274
Modesto, CA	70	$33.55	$69,780	0.439
San Francisco-San Mateo-Redwood City, CA Metropolitan Division	300	$33.37	$69,410	0.307
Santa Rosa-Petaluma, CA	60	$33.13	$68,910	0.347

Laws and Regulations

A classic intersection of business and government is in the regulation of business to insure fair markets and to balance the needs of business with the needs of citizens and consumers. As noted earlier, none other than Adam Smith, the father of free market capitalism, discussed some of the instances where government needed to be involved in order to insure a functioning free market (Smith, 1819). Debate about government's role in regulating business remains lively.

Government regulation of business is rooted in laws passed by Congress and the regulations promulgated by executive agencies in order to enforce these laws. Chapters 3 and 4 discuss the process of making laws, and of making regulations, while Chapter 5 discusses finding laws already on the books. Sources covered in those chapters are used to find instances of regulation of business.

Suppose you are interested in starting a small organic produce business. The Small Business Administration website (http://www.sba.gov) includes a section on Business Laws & Regulations that summarizes the legal steps necessary to start and register a business, as well as the basics for complying with tax and finance, labor, and environmental laws. While these steps are necessary and apply to starting any business, there are also laws and regulations pertaining to specific industries. In this example, for instance, using the skills and tools for finding laws and regulations discussed earlier in the book—and also the skills about finding executive branch information in Chapters 2 and 7—one can find information about laws and regulations related to organic farming from the Department of Agriculture. For instance, see the National Organic Program at http://www.ams.usda.gov/AMSv1.0/nop, and related information at http://www.ers.usda.gov/Briefing/Organic/, as well as information from the EPA (http://www.epa.gov/agriculture/torg.html), specifically the Organic Foods Production Act of 1990 (P.L. 101-624; current law after subsequent amendments at 7 U.S.C. 6501) and the regulations at 7 CFR 205. There are countless other laws and regulations related to specific products, businesses, and business practices. While starting at the SBA.gov page noted above is helpful, it can still be daunting to figure out all applicable laws related to one's business without additional legal advice and support.

There are several other government sites that do help, however. EPA's Laws and Regulations section (http://www.epa.gov/lawsregs/) provides detailed information about environmental regulations, and makes finding environmental regulations a bit easier than using the *CFR*. The Department of Labor has a similar Compliance portal (http://www.dol.gov/compliance/) that leads users to laws and regulations regarding employees and the workplace, including those from the Occupational Safety and Health Administration.

Another agency involved in regulating commerce is the Federal Trade Commission (FTC). Much of the FTC's activity is related to antitrust, as it works to "ban unfair business practices and prevent mergers that harm consumers," which are prohibited by law (FTC, http://www.ftc.gov/opa/2008/07/bcwebfyi .shtm). While one might associate FTC with only antitrust issues, and its work related to companies such as IBM, Microsoft, and now Google, FTC provides a variety of research and information materials aimed at business owners and consumers, everything from economic research reports on health care economics to "How to Avoid Bamboozling Your Customers," which addresses the use of bamboo in products. Business owners and consumers can both profit by concise, clear explanations in numerous publications, such as information about buying a home, getting a credit card, dealing with identity theft and business fraud, and complying with telemarketing rules such as the Do Not Call list.

A less savory aspect of business and the law is bankruptcy. Many people and businesses seek bankruptcy protection when they can no longer pay their debts and they seek some relief or a structured response. All bankruptcy cases are handled by special federal bankruptcy courts. There is information on the laws and processes for bankruptcy at http://www.uscourts.gov/Federal Courts/Bankruptcy.aspx. Also useful are bankruptcy statistics available at http://www.uscourts.gov/Statistics/BankruptcyStatistics.aspx.

Support for Business

Governments at all levels in the United States offer support for businesses. The federal government and each state government all have offices that give advice and information on starting and operating a business, including the legal basics such as how to register a business; practical tips on how to manage, grow, research, and document business activities; and how to access market research and other business intelligence sources available from the government.

The U.S. Small Business Administration (SBA), and especially its website, http://www.sba.gov/ (Figure 13.11), is the starting point for business planning and is useful to any business or prospective business. The "Starting and Managing a Business" section features information and instructions on how to legally start and register a business, with information by state and even ZIP code; how to write a business plan; determining type of business (sole proprietorship, partnership, or some form of corporation); finding local zoning and real estate information; finding financing; and getting expert help. It is a must-use portal for anyone starting a business, as it pulls together information from across all appropriate levels of government—everything from the IRS to the EPA.

The SBA, as an independent agency that exists solely to help, nurture, and guide small businesses in the United States, meant to connect small businesses to intelligence, advice, and financial help. Sections on the website include information about contracting opportunities, finding loans and grants, and tools to connect potential lenders and investors to startups in need of financial backing. Also notable from SBA are some of its expert help services. SCORE (Service Corps of Retired Executives) is an SBA program that has provided expert advisory services to small business owners for decades. There are hundreds of SCORE offices around the nation, covering most cities. SBA also administers Small Business Development Centers and Women's Business Centers, which also

Figure 13.11. SBA.gov Screenshot

offer counseling to prospective small business owners and have physical offices throughout the nation.

The U.S. Department of Commerce is another agency that provides key support for businesses, especially to U.S. business looking to export or operate abroad. This will be covered under Exporting and Doing Business Abroad, p. 321.

Support for Consumers

Another key role of government involvement in business is to support citizens' and consumers' rights. Largely, this role is fulfilled via the law and rulemaking process already discussed. For instance, the Credit Card Accountability, Responsibility, and Disclosure (CARD) Act of 2009 (P.L. 111-24) included numerous provisions to protect consumers with credit cards from certain card-issuer practices that Congress deemed worthy of attention. Appropriate executive agencies are writing regulations to aid in implementation and enforcement of this law. In this sense, laws and regulations are the key source for information about consumer and citizen protections, whether they be financial, environmental, aimed at workers, etc.

As noted, executive agencies often have plain language summaries and compilations of laws and regulations. EPA and OSHA are two good examples. Similarly for consumer information, there are two particular agencies that provide information relating to protection of consumers and summaries of applicable laws. The Federal Trade Commission, discussed earlier as a source to aid business owners, is also very useful to citizens. For instance, instead of finding and reading through all of the appropriate laws and regulations related to credit cards, one can navigate to the consumer protection portion of the FTC website and find the concise document *Credit and Your Consumer Rights* (http://www.ftc.gov/bcp/edu/pubs/consumer/credit/cre01.shtm). This is one of dozens of documents available online from the FTC aimed at protecting consumers, on topics such as credit, identity theft, health and the environment, buying a car or a house, getting an education or a job, and shopping online and avoiding online scams.

The other prominent agency supporting consumers is the Consumer Product Safety Commission (CPSC). While FTC protects consumers broadly, CPSC is more narrowly focused on preventing injury caused by consumer products. The CPSC website lists recalls and safety warnings, but also provides publications to aid consumer safety, such as those on creating a safe baby nursery; keeping pools and playgrounds safe; preventing fire, electrical, and carbon monoxide hazards; and dangerous toys.

Exports and International and Foreign Business Information

The global economy is a large and complicated entity. While the U.S. federal government is unparalleled in its support for, and breadth of information about, its own business climate, there are nonetheless some key government and international organization resources which provide key global information. This section provides a brief, selective guide to major sources.

International Sources

The comprehensive sources of country statistics covered in Chapter 8—UNdata, *World Development Indicators*, and the comparative international statistics section of the *Statistical Abstract of the United States*—all provide international economic and business data. UNdata links to a number of useful databases compiled by various international organizations, which work with countries to standardize and share data on economic topics.

Databases available via UNdata include:

- Energy Statistics Database—country by country data on production, imports, and exports of energy resources.
- FAO Data—from the Food and Agriculture Organization, country-by-country data on production and yield of crops, livestock, fertilizers, and land related to agriculture.
- INDSTAT—from the United Nations Industrial Development Organization, a rich database of data resembling that of the U.S. Economic Census: country-by-country estimates of the number of establishments, employees, payroll, and output by industry.

- International Financial Statistics—from the International Monetary Fund, the premier compilation of country-by-country financials, not unlike the data for the U.S. available from the U.S. Treasury Department.
- National Accounts databases—output and consumption for the world's nations, similar to data from the U.S. BEA.
- LABORSTA—from the International Labor Organization, with prices and employment by economic activity, country-by-country, similar to the U.S. BLS.

There are several other large, key databases of international economic activity, available from http://data.un.org/Explorer.aspx.

Trade

There are several sources for foreign trade statistics. For the United States, data on both exports and imports is gathered at ports of entry by Customs and Border Protection, a subagency of the Department of Homeland Security (until 2003, known as the U.S. Customs Service, a sister agency of Census in the Department of Commerce). The Census Bureau compiles and publishes United States trade data. Robust data is available via a cost-recovery database (so not free), USA Trade Online (http://www.usatradeonline.gov). USA Trade Online features data on the type of goods, the destination country (or origin for imports), the amount of goods, and the port. Trade data is also available from the International Trade Administration (ITA), also in the Department of Commerce, although it's not as robust as USA Trade Online. ITA's primary trade statistics product is TradeStats Express (http://www.export.gov/trade data/index.asp), which provides total volume of U.S. imports and exports by foreign nation. TradeStats Express also shows imports and exports by product, both for the nation as a whole, and for states. U.S. foreign trade data is also available via databases at the Census Bureau (http://www.census.gov/foreign-trade/) and the International Trade Commission (http://dataweb.usitc.gov/). Note that trade data uses its own systems for product classification, different than the industry classifications in NAICS or the SIC Manual. For imports, it is the *Harmonized Tariff Schedule* of the United States. For exports, it is *Schedule B: Statistical Classification of Domestic and Foreign Commodities Exported from the United States.*

For trade between two *foreign* countries not including the United States (such as between England and Argentina), there are several sources. Consult the *Direction of Trade Statistics*, from the International Monetary Fund (in print and as an online subscription database), for data on the value of trade between any two countries (but not data about the product or commodities involved). The World Trade Organization, meanwhile, compiles and publishes data (http://www.wto.org/english/res_e/statis_e/statis_e.htm) about exports and imports of a country by commodity and product, but does not have this data specifically between any two countries. And the UN Comtrade database (http://comtrade.un.org/) further compiles trade data from several UN sources.

Exporting and Doing Business Abroad

The ITA's Export.gov compiles information to help U.S. businesses export and succeed in foreign markets. Export.gov is one of the more important government resources for business, and is highlighted by materials in the Market Research Library (http://www.export.gov/mrktresearch/), from the U.S. Commercial Service. The Market Research Library provides access to several key series:

- Country Commercial Guides (CCG). Prepared by U.S. embassies, these annual guides for most of the world's countries are invaluable in their descriptions of the commercial climate of the country, as well as political and economic factors that affect American businesses' operations. CCGs describe characteristics of the labor force (will the American firm be able to find and hire qualified employees?), infrastructure (not just roads, but communications, such as the Internet), the law and justice system (is theft rampant, or piracy of intellectual property?), government regulation (is there corruption?), and banking and finance (is it safe to use a local bank?). There are usually extensive descriptions of good products and markets to enter, as well as details on exporting, whether about tariffs, shipping concerns, or legal considerations. CCGs also discuss strategies for entering the market, including franchising, finding a local distributor for your product, and how to make sales in the local climate. Finally, CCGs describe business customs and etiquette, such as prevalence of long lunches or appropriateness of electronic communication. CCGs also include extensive lists of local contacts.
- Market Research Reports. Market research reports, which are in-depth reports containing intelligence about a particular product or business type (and often in a specific location), are usually very expensive. But the U.S. government, in order to support U.S. business abroad, does produce or acquire a number of market research reports about foreign markets. While not comprehensive for any sector or country, one lucky enough to find an on-target market research report here has much of their research already done. Examples of titles are *Ecuador: Medical Equipment*; *Serbia: Green Industries*; *Germany: Consumer Electronics*; and *Taiwan: Apparel Market*.

Export.gov provides various other information for the international American businessperson. This is highlighted by extensive information describing business opportunities by region.

State and Local Business and Economic Information

Most state and local business information is derived from the many federal government surveys and programs covered in this chapter. This local information includes decennial census data, economic census and the *County/ZIP Code/Metro Business Patterns*, unemployment and prices from the BLS, and more.

Yet states generally have a state agency or office that produces some business and economic information. For instance, the Florida Legislature's Office of Demographic and Economic Research (http://edr.state.fl.us/) prepares economic information for the state (many other states have similar research offices associated with their legislative branches). In Arkansas, the biggest producer of state data is the Institute of Economic Advancement out of the University of Arkansas Little Rock (http://www.aiea.ualr.edu/default.html). Nebraska has a Department of Economic Development state agency whose Research Library features state economic data (http://info.neded.org/). Familiarize yourself with your appropriate state agencies or related institutions and their outputs.

Probably most important is the state and local information to help businesses. Much of this information is linked from the SBA website, and includes state data on registering a business, securing proper licenses, and complying with state and local regulations. All states have portals to such information. Idaho's business portal (http://www.idaho.gov/business/), for instance, features the Idaho Business Wizard (http://www.idahobizhelp.org/bizwiz.htm), which allows one to enter a type of business and see regulatory and licensing requirements. Texas has a similar service called MyTexasBiz (https://business.texas.gov/oog/bizq/), found as part of the rich information on starting and maintaining a Texas business at http://www.texas.gov. Every state has some information designed to support new and existing businesses. Use the SBA website and an exploration of state websites to find these portals for your own state.

Local information is likewise sometimes available from federal and state sources. Beyond those, check your local city and county government sources; also check for research about your local economy wherever it might be published.

Conclusion

With a nation founded on a capitalist market economic system, business is very important to the American people and their government. Numerous government agencies produce information about the economy and business situation, aid business growth and success, and support the nation's consumers. An earlier chapter encouraged you to think like a government documents librarian. To find and use business information from governments, continue to use these civics skills—and also think like a businessperson.

Exercises

1. What is the current discount rate? What is the logic from the Fed regarding the latest discount rate?

2. What is the SIC Code and the NAICS code for law offices? What is the total value of services from law offices in the United States for 2007? How many law office establishments were there in Chicago in 2008?
3. What federal or state agency handles child care center licensing in Missouri?
4. According to official SEC filings, what is Google's net income for the first two quarters of 2010?
5. What are the top five destinations for exports from the state of Tennessee (in 2009)?

Sources Mentioned in This Chapter

Sources mentioned in this section do not duplicate the References that follow.

American Community Survey, http://www.census.gov/acs/www/.

American FactFinder, http://factfinder.census.gov/.

American Time Use Survey, http://www.bls.gov/tus/.

Bankruptcy (United States Courts), http://www.uscourts.gov/FederalCourts/Bankruptcy .aspx.

Bankruptcy Statistics (United States Courts), http://www.uscourts.gov/Statistics/Bank ruptcyStatistics.aspx.

Budget of the United States (*Historical Perspectives*), http://www.gpoaccess .gov/usbudget/ index.html.

Bureau of Economic Analysis Industry Economic Accounts, http://www.bea.gov/ industry/.

Bureau of Transportation Statistics, Data and Statistics, http://www.bts.gov/data_and_ statistics/.

Census Bureau Business and Industry, http://www.census.gov/econ/.

Census Bureau Foreign Trade, http://www.census.gov/foreign-trade/.

ClinicalTrials.gov, http://www.clinicaltrials.gov/.

Combined Statement of Receipts, Outlays, and Balances of the United States Government, http://www.fms.treas.gov/annualreport/index.html.

Consumer Expenditure Survey, http://www.bls.gov/cex/.

Consumer Price Index, http://www.bls.gov/cpi/.

County Business Patterns, http://www.census.gov/econ/cbp/index.html.

Credit and Your Consumer Rights, http://www.ftc.gov/bcp/edu/pubs/consumer/ credit/cre01.shtm.

Current Industrial Reports, http://www.census.gov/manufacturing/cir/index.html.

Current Population Survey table generator, http://www.census.gov/hhes/www/ cpstc/cps_table_creator.html.

Daily Treasury Statement, http://www.fms.treas.gov/dts/index.html.

Decennial Census, http://www.census.gov/population/www/.

Department of Labor compliance portal, http://www.dol.gov/compliance.

Direction of Trade Statistics, http://www2.imfstatistics.org/DOT/.

Economic Census, http://www.census.gov/econ/census07/.

Economic Indicators, http://www.gpoaccess.gov/indicators/index.html.

Economic Indicators.gov, http://www.economicindicators.gov/.

Economic Report of the President, http://www.gpoaccess.gov/eop/.

Economy at a Glance, http://www.bls.gov/eag/eag.us.htm.

EDGAR, http://www.sec.gov/edgar.shtml.

Energy Statistics Database, http://unstats.un.org/unsd/energy/edbase.htm; http://data.un.org/Explorer.aspx.

EPA's Laws and Regulations, http://www.epa.gov/lawsregs/.

Export.gov, http://www.export.gov/.

FAO Data, http://faostat.fao.org/; http://data.un.org/Explorer.aspx.

FDIC banking data, http://www.fdic.gov/bank/statistical/index.html.

FedBizOpps.gov, http://www.fedbizopps.gov/.

Federal Election Commission campaign finance data, http://www.fec.gov/disclosure.shtml.

Federal Reserve System statistical data, http://www.federalreserve.gov/econresdata/releases/statisticsdata.htm.

FRASER (Federal Reserve Archival System for Economic Research) system, http://http://fraser.stlouisfed.org/publications/ei/.

Harmonized Tariff Schedule of the United States, http://hts.usitc.gov/.

INDSTAT, http://data.un.org/Explorer.aspx.

International Financial Statistics, http://www.imfstatistics.org/imf/; http://data.un.org/Explorer.aspx.

International Trade Commission, http://dataweb.usitc.gov/.

LABORSTA, http://laborsta.ilo.org/; http://data.un.org/Explorer.aspx.

Metro Business Patterns, http://www.census.gov/econ/cbp/index.html.

Monthly Treasury Statement, http://www.fms.treas.gov/mts/index.html.

My Environment, http://www.epa.gov/myenvironment/.

NAICS (the North American Industry Classification System), http://www.census.gov/eos/www/naics/.

Occupational Outlook Handbook, http://www.bls.gov/oco/.

OpenSecrets.org, http://www.opensecrets.org/.

Producer Price Index, http://www.bls.gov/ppi/.

Regional Economic Conditions database, http://www2.fdic.gov/recon/index.asp.

Schedule B: Statistical Classification of Domestic and Foreign Commodities Exported from the United States, http://www.census.gov/foreign-trade/schedules/b/.

SCORE (Service Corps of Retired Executives), http://www.score.org.

Small Business Administration, http://www.sba.gov/.

Small Business Administration, Business Law & Regulations, http://www.sba.gov/category/navigation-structure/starting-managing-business/starting-business/business-law-regulations.

Small Business Planner portal, http://www.sba.gov/smallbusinessplanner/index.html.

Standard Industrial Classification (SIC) Manual, http://www.osha.gov/pls/imis/sicsearch.html.

Statistical Abstract of the United States, http://www.census.gov/compendia/statab/.

Statistics of Income; IRS statistics, http://www.irs.gov/taxstats/index.html.

TradeStats Express, http://tse.export.gov/.

TreasuryDirect, http://www.treasurydirect.gov/.
UN Comtrade, http://comtrade.un.org/.
UNdata, http://data.un.org/.
U.S. Patent and Trademark Office, http://www.uspto.gov/.
USAspending.gov, http://www.usaspending.gov/.
USAtrade.gov, http://www.usatrade.gov.
Wages by Occupation, http://www.bls.gov/bls/blswage.htm.
World Development Indicators, http://data.worldbank.org/.
World Trade Organization data, http://www.wto.org/english/res_e/statis_e/statis_e.htm.
ZIP Code Business Patterns, http://www.census.gov/econ/cbp/index.html.

References

Boettcher, Jennifer C. 2005. "Company Research Using U.S. Federal Government Sources." *Online* 29, no. 2: 19–24.

Coolidge, Calvin. 1925. "Address to the American Society of Newspaper Editors" (speech), January 17. http://www.presidency.ucsb.edu/ws/index.php?pid=24180.

Markoff, John. 1993. "Plan Opens More Data to Public." *New York Times*, October 22. http://www.nytimes.com/1993/10/22/business/plan-opens-more-data-to-public.html.

Micarelli, William F. 1998. "Evolution of the United States Economic Censuses: The Nineteenth and Twentieth Centuries." *Government Information Quarterly* 15, no. 3: 335–377.

Scott, Kerry, and Lucia Orlando. 2009. "Government Resources: Worth a Hard Look in Hard Times." *BRASS Business Reference in Academic Libraries Committee* 4, no. 2. http://www.ala.org/ala/mgrps/divs/rusa/sections/brass/brasspubs/academic brass/acadarchives/vol4no2/vol4no2.cfm.

Smith, Adam. 1819. *An Inquiry into the Nature and Causes of the Wealth of Nations*. Edinburgh: Stirling and Slade. http://catalog.hathitrust.org/api/volumes/oclc/2340521.html.

Chapter 14
Census

Introduction

The decennial census and the United States Census Bureau were introduced in Chapter 8, but these resources are of such importance that they merit their own chapter. In many libraries, statistics are the most heavily requested genre of government information, and the decennial census is far and away the largest single statistical undertaking in the nation.

Think about the scale of the decennial census. Or better yet, think of the *second* largest statistical effort in the United States, the related American Community Survey (ACS)—which will also be covered in this chapter. The ACS surveys a whopping 250,000 households each month, and so reaches some three million households annually. This is much larger than any other government statistical survey, or any other regular statistical survey, for that matter. Yet the decennial census—by counting each and every person in the entire United States—counted some 310 million people in the year 2010, making it more than *100 times* bigger than the ACS.

The decennial census's core constitutional function is to determine the apportionment of representatives in the House of Representatives. But the census (especially now in combination with the American Community Survey) also provides the basic demographic and social statistics about our nation. It is the only nationwide statistical effort of sufficient scale to result in usable statistical data about even small cities and towns. In fact, this ability to access uniform, comparative data for these small geographies cannot be stressed enough. The size of the census, the data for small geographies, and the fact that it has been taken consistently for over 200 years all make the census a singular and vital source of statistics.

Scientists, economists, and public policy makers use decennial census data heavily in research about the nation's populace. But perhaps the most important purpose beyond apportionment, and the one stressed in marketing campaigns designed to maximize voluntary census compliance, is census data's role in determining shares of billions of dollars in federal funds to states, cities, and communities. For instance, when Medicaid funds are distributed to states by the federal government, they are distributed based on population figures and characteristics taken from the census. Census figures helped determine shares of redevelopment money after Hurricane Katrina. The same goes for dozens of other government programs. In short, the communities that most completely answer the census stand to win the most federal monies. In other words: when it comes to filling out the census, compliance literally pays.

The Census in the Constitution

While the Latin word *censere* more closely means estimate rather than count, the idea of a census has generally been associated with counting and especially counting people. Babylonians, Egyptians, Chinese, and indigenous Peruvians all appeared to conduct some type of census in ancient times (Halacy, 1980). In the Roman Empire, a census was often associated with either determining the numbers of men to potentially conscript for the purposes of war, or to count people for the purposes of taxing them. Neither reason is likely to have made a census a popular undertaking amongst citizens. Further, "the penalty for refusing to reveal how many people were in your household, how many slaves, how much livestock, was forfeiting it all and becoming a slave yourself" (Gibbs, 2010:56). A census also appears several times in the Bible. Moses was told to conduct censuses of the Israelites, while King David is "said to have been punished for ordering a census—though the punishment was inflicted on the very people being counted (2 Samuel 24:15)," because it was Satan who tempted David into taking the census ("Census," Browning, 2009). One gospel, Luke, says that Joseph and Mary's compliance with the taxing purposes of a census was the reason they went to Bethlehem (Luke 2:1–6). While citizen concerns about participating in a census remain and will be discussed later, such concerns are now more likely to be for reasons related to privacy and accuracy rather than fear of conscription, taxes, or a vengeful god.

The United States' decennial census has a completely different mission than these ancient efforts, and its fascinating history goes far in explaining how we arrived at our modern decennial census. As introduced in Chapter 8, the decennial census is the original statistical program of the nation, drawing its statutory authority ultimately from Article I, Section 2 of the Constitution:

> Representatives and direct taxes shall be apportioned among the several states which may be included within this union, according to their respective numbers, which shall be determined by adding to the whole number of free persons, including those bound to service for a term of years, and excluding Indians not taxed, three fifths of all other Persons. The actual Enumeration shall be made within three years after the first meeting of the Congress of the United States, and within every subsequent term of ten years, in such manner as they shall by law direct. (U.S. Constitution, art. I, sec. 2)

Debate in drafting this particular clause included various suggestions related to whether race or even wealth was a factor in whether or not a citizen was even counted (Halacy, 1980). The framers eventually intended slaves to be counted as only three-fifths of a person, which in addition to its shameful sentiment cost certain states representation. This lasted through 1860, when the Fourteenth Amendment took away the right to count any *male* person for apportionment purposes unless they had the right to vote, essentially insuring that all inhabitants would be counted (although women were still counted in the census, it wasn't until the Nineteenth Amendment in 1920 that they were guaranteed the right to vote).

The three-fifths clause was not the only portion of the founders' census article that was soon discarded. "Indians not taxed" referred to American Indians living free, a category that was largely gone by the end of the nineteenth century, and was officially retired in the 1940s. Indentured servants "bound to service for a term of years" similarly ceased to exist. The "direct taxes" line, meanwhile, was originally inserted to reduce temptation for a state to inflate its population in order to gain an unequal share of representation (for the greater the population, the greater the potential tax paid by the state). In practice, however, taxes were very rarely billed on the basis of census counts, only occasionally during early periods of wartime, although in the 1830s the federal government did distribute an *excess* of federal funds to states on the basis on census counts. The Sixteenth Amendment, in 1909, removed the concept of direct taxes entirely from the census, meaning that all in all, four facets of the founders' original census clause eventually disappeared from the law.

Census Privacy

All census data is confidential for 72 years, although it was not until 1840 that census takers were specifically instructed to treat all information with confidentiality (Halacy, 1980). By 1880, confidential returns became law (13 U.S.C. 9). Census data may only be used for statistical purposes (so no taxation or conscription will result from filling out a census form). An individual or household's census answers are even protected from subpoenas or search warrants—they cannot be used as legal evidence. This privacy requirement applies to workers in the field, those working with data at the census, and the published public data, meaning that what you fill out about the census will be nothing more than anonymous numbers for most if not all of your lifetime. On a related note, citizens who do not answer the census can be fined, although in practice this has almost never happened.

Conducting the Census

The first census, taken in August of 1790, was conducted by U.S. marshals, who traveled the nation on horseback and simply went looking for people. With citizens not always expecting or wanting to be found, the enterprise carried some danger. While these marshals received instructions in how to conduct the count, there were no official forms, and marshals were responsible for procuring paper and organizing it in such a way as to facilitate a count. It was a labor-intensive process (see Figure 14.1).

Figure 14.1. Excerpt from 1790 Census Schedules Showing Name of Head of Household and Tick Marks for Each Resident of the Home

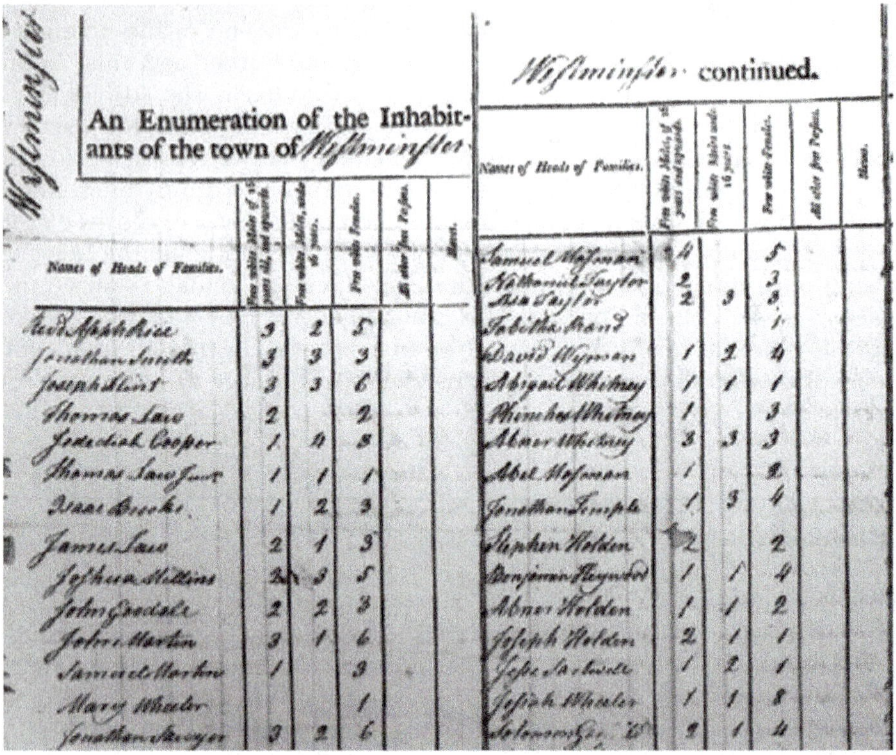

With an ever-exploding population, taking the census remained a massive undertaking, especially as it continued to be taken by hand, in person. Although population growth made the census increasingly difficult to conduct with each passing decade, improved methods somewhat mitigated the increase in volume. In 1840, the government finally instituted an official form for the marshals to use. The census of 1870 saw the introduction of the first rudimentary counting machines. In 1871, the census contracted with a young scientist to devise a better tabulation machine in time for the 1880 census. The scientist, Herman Hollerith, famously succeeded in building a machine that could rapidly read encoded punch cards (Figure 14.2). Hollerith and his invention later became the basis for the company IBM. The 1880 census also saw the U.S. marshals finally replaced by workers specifically dedicated and trained to conduct the census, creating the first large, once-a-decade class of temporary census workers. Counting was further eased in 1950 by the first use of an electronic computer to aid in tabulation. The 1960 census, meanwhile, saw the census recorded by the use of blackened dots which were microfilmed, and then read and tabulated by cameras and computers.

Figure 14.2. Punchcard from 1910 Census Used to Encode Each Household's Answers, Which Were Then Tabulated by Machine

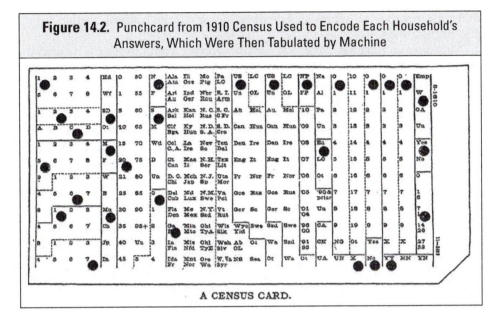

A CENSUS CARD.

Modern-day census data is tabulated in the manner discussed in Chapter 8, with very large microdata files from which are made various specific reports and tables. Parts of contemporary decennial census microdata are available to the public, allowing researchers to create their own tables and reports out of the original data. See the section on Decennial Census Microdata later in this chapter for more information.

Amazingly, all of these censuses were still conducted in person—a huge undertaking with the now extremely large population. The 1910 census saw the first effort at a mail-in census; response was abysmal, and the effort was abandoned. The 1960 census again saw forms mailed to households. Households could not mail them back, but at least the forms would be filled out and ready to share when the census worker came knocking, saving time and expense. Finally, in 1970, the government stopped sending workers to every household; citizens were able to mail back census forms, and only nonrespondents received a personal visit.

It's natural to wonder about the viability of taking an online census, but like online voting, fears about the integrity and security of such an effort have kept an online census from occurring. In 2010, census forms were once again sent and returned via U.S. mail, with nonrespondents receiving a personal visit or phone call.

Census Content

The content of the questions is the single most important aspect of the census. If a question was asked as part of a decennial census, a wealth of data exists on that topic for the entire nation. The questions form the basis of available data and publications.

Almost from the beginning, the census evolved from the simple headcount called for by the Constitution. As early as 1790, James Madison proposed using the opportunity of the census effort to gather further information and despite some opposition—these early efforts were denounced by some as "a waste of trouble and supplying materials for idle people to make a book" (Cassedy, 1969: 216)—Congress soon acted on the potential to learn more about the nation via the census effort. Questions related to age, sex, ancestry, schooling, and wages presented a broader demographic portrait of the nation, while questions about the economic structure helped Congress understand the fast-evolving state of the nation's industry and agriculture. Over the ensuing years, these extra questions have come and gone. In addition to many economic and demographic questions, the census has made some unique and interesting inquiries. For many years, people were asked about their place of religious worship, which aroused suspicion and some controversy in a nation built on religious freedom and individual privacy (law now forbids any government survey of religious worship, practice, or beliefs). Citizens were asked how many and what type of bathroom facilities they had (i.e., indoor vs. outdoor). People were asked to record how many insane or "idiotic" persons lived in the household (presumably, the insane were not the ones filling out the forms) and they were asked about habitual drunkards and tramps (Halacy, 1980). Regardless of whether the questions make sense today, what had begun as a simple census had grown over a century to a census of hundreds of questions, about health, education, housing, ancestry, with even further separate questionnaires for American Indians, the recently deceased (filled out by surviving family members), and soldiers, among others.

The invaluable census publication *Measuring America: The Decennial Census from 1790 to 2000* includes a history of the census along with copies of every question asked and every form used in each census. Especially useful is a grid (excerpted in Figure 14.3) that summarizes the subjects asked over each census, making it easy to see, census by census, if a particular piece of data was gathered.

While the specific questions asked shifted over the years, extra questions have remained a staple of the census in one manner or another up through the 2000 census. The 2010 census, for reasons discussed shortly, has seen these extra questions largely jettisoned and a return to what is the shortest and simplest census since the very first one in 1790.

Statistical Sampling

Asking these extra questions, as important as they were, did eventually begin taking a toll, as the more expansive census was becoming both harder for the citizens to answer and more expensive for the nation to conduct. Picture a census worker sitting in a household and asking over 100 questions. And then going next door. And so on, through the entire nation.

The mid-twentieth century saw two changes to address these issues. First, much of the extra data that the census had been gathering began to be covered

---

Figure 14.3. Excerpt of Grid Summarizing All Questions Asked in the Decennial Census from 1790 to 2000

Population Items on Principal Census Questionnaires: 1790 to 1890

(Excludes identification items, screening questions, and other information collected, but not intended for tabulation)

Demographic characteristics	1790	1800	1810	1820	1830	1840	1850	1860	1870	1880	1890
Age	-	¹X	¹X	X	X	X	X	X	X	X	X
Sex	¹X	¹X	¹X	X	X	X	X	X	X	X	X
Color or Race	X	X	X	X	X	X	X	X	X	X	X
Ancestry/Ethnic Origin	-	-	-	-	-	-	-	-	-	-	-
If American Indian, proportions of Indian or other blood	-	-	-	-	-	-	-	-	-	-	-
If American Indian, name of Tribe	-	-	-	-	-	-	-	-	-	-	-
Relationship to head of family or household	-	-	-	-	-	-	-	-	-	X	X
Married in the past year	-	-	-	-	-	-	²X	²X	X	X	X
Marital status	-	-	-	-	-	-	-	-	-	X	X
Number of years married	-	-	-	-	-	-	-	-	-	-	-
Age at or date of first marriage	-	-	-	-	-	-	-	-	-	-	-
Married more than once	-	-	-	-	-	-	-	-	-	-	-
If remarried, was first marriage terminated by death?	-	-	-	-	-	-	-	-	-	-	-
Number of years widowed, divorced, or separated	-	-	-	-	-	-	-	-	-	-	-
Social Characteristics											
Free or slave	X	X	X	X	X	X	X	X	-	-	-
Per slave owner, number of fugitives	-	-	-	-	-	-	X	X	-	-	-
Per slave owner, number of manumitted	-	-	-	-	-	-	X	X	-	-	-
Physical and mental handicaps and infirmities:											
Deaf or deaf mutes	-	-	-	-	X	X	X	X	X	X	X
Blind	-	-	-	-	X	X	X	X	X	X	X
Insane	-	-	-	-	-	X	X	X	X	X	X

Source: Measuring America: The Decennial Census from 1790 to 2000.

by other surveys. For instance, a great deal of health and education data are now gathered by much smaller surveys (see Chapter 8). Economic questions—which made up many of the extra questions—were spun off into their own economic census, covered in Chapter 13. Finally, the extra questions that remained—and there were still dozens not related to the basic headcount used for apportionment—began to be asked of only a sample of the population, taken concurrently and as part of the census. In this scenario, 100 percent of households were still counted and asked basic questions such as age and sex; however, a smaller sample of the population would answer a census that added these extra questions. Since this extra data was not used for the constitutional apportionment, a statistical sample was and remains sufficient to gather this data, as modern statistical techniques ensure an accurate count of these questions.

Beginning in 1940 and continuing through Census 2000 (changes for the 2010 census are discussed below), approximately one in five to one in six of all households received the longer sample form, which included the basic questions and also the extra questions. This became known as the census long form. Everyone else received the census short form. The data from those who filled out the short form (plus the short form elements of those who filled out the long form) is referred to as 100 percent data, to make clear that this data is from all respondents to the census, unadjusted by sampling. The actual percentage of people receiving the long form varied by geography. Part of what makes the census so invaluable is its ability to provide data for even small geographies such as small towns. To gather enough data via the sample to provide good data for smaller geographies, a larger portion of the population in smaller places and rural areas were given the long form in order to make the results statistically significant for those smaller geographies. In a big city, one in six is still a massive sample and very statistically accurate; in a small city, asking only one in six does not yield enough data, so as many as one in every two households were given the longer survey.

The content of these extra questions is always subject to debate and sometimes controversy. The Census Bureau receives thousands of suggestions for questions to include on the census, most of them related to a specific interest of a researcher or organization. For instance, if one is selling shoes, what better way to collect data about shoe usage or preferences than through the census—it's paid for by taxes and gathers data for even small geographies, so a shoe company could easily see which cities and towns bought which types of shoes. There is nearly no end to what people hope could be asked in the census, from the serious to the silly: "As long as we're spending all this money to reach so many people, imagine what we could find out. Which do you favor, Leno or Letterman? Smooth or chunky? Faith or works? Liberty or equality?" (Gibbs, 2010: 56). The Census Bureau, however, rejects nearly all such requests as outside the scope of the decennial census.

Census Controversies

The census has been central to numerous formative political and social controversies in American history. Simply figuring out how to use the population data to determine the size of the House of Representatives was contentious right from the first census effort. How big should the House be, and most importantly, what is the population threshold for a new representative? Disagreement over how to determine the allotment of representatives led to the very first presidential veto in the nation's history when George Washington vetoed the Apportionment Act on April 5, 1792.

The years leading up to the Civil War saw the census at the center of a number of very divisive arguments related to the balance of power between slaveholding and free states. In the published reports of 1860, the Census Bureau editorialized about what the numbers meant with regard to slaves and their potential freedom, suggesting that some combination of morality, barbarianism, and genetics would see the black population soon become either extinct altogether or totally absorbed into the white population—an example of official government racism (Kennedy, 1864). Less controversial but more famous, in 1890 the Census Bureau declared the closing of the frontier as shown in the latest census figures.

Contemporary census controversies are both familiar and novel: familiar in that the census still scares some part of the population, who fear it as an intrusion into their privacy and a manifestation of a big brother government; novel in that the census's consistent inability to accurately count every person has raised the idea of using more sophisticated statistical means to make a more accurate census.

Privacy advocates have long resisted the extra questions on the census, arguing for keeping the census to only its strict constitutional role of counting inhabitants and apportioning representatives. Even the 2010 census—one of the shortest in history—had its detractors. Minnesota Representative Michele Bachmann claimed at the time to be "leaving most of its form blank except for the question that asks directly how many people reside in her home. 'We won't be answering any information beyond that,' she says. She complains that the remaining nine questions are 'very intricate, very personal' and argues that 'the Constitution doesn't require any information beyond that'" (Colvin, 2010: 41). Despite such resistance (which is technically illegal, as returning the census is the law, albeit one that has not been enforced punitively), voluntary census response rates have remained steady over recent decades, with over 70 percent of households returning the form via mail, and the rest receiving personal visits.

While the law suggests that these privacy concerns are unfounded, census data has been abused in the past. The most notable instance was during World War II, when the Census Bureau provided the War Department names and addresses of Japanese Americans, information which aided efforts to identify Japanese Americans for internment (Holmes, 2000). Scholars Margo Anderson and William Seltzer, who discovered and reported this abuse of census data, have done extensive work related to government statistics and confidentiality (see https://pantherfile.uwm.edu/margo/www/govstat/integrity.htm).

The other great contemporary census controversy surrounds the problem of undercounting the population. Poor areas and racial minorities are especially prone to being undercounted, a phenomenon first truly noted when more blacks registered for the World War II draft than were even thought to be in the country based on census data. As Holden summarizes, statisticians have long advocated for using statistical sampling to adjust the results to more accurate figures (2009). While sampling has been used for the extra questions, it had never been the basis for the apportionment data, which is taken from 100 percent results only. To address this in time for Census 2000, the Census Bureau proposed a plan to use limited statistical sampling to make population numbers more accurate, arguing that such methods were sound and fair and would represent a more accurate count. Before such a plan could be instituted, however, the Supreme Court, in the 5–4 decision *Department of Commerce v. U.S.*

House of Representatives (525 U.S. 326), ruled sampling for apportionment purposes to be unconstitutional. So to make the census as accurate as possible, the Census Bureau relies on vigilance, education, and outreach rather than statistical methods. It tries hard to make people understand that by not responding to the census, they only hurt themselves and their communities, and they are essentially going unrepresented in the House of Representatives. To maximize an accurate count, the census even has a large-scale marketing campaign, which in 2010 saw the first ever census Super Bowl commercial.

Another often contentious issue in the decennial census surrounds race. The first time that respondents were able to identify themselves as part of more than one race was in the 2000 census. O'Hare (1998) provides background and summary of federal statistical classification of race categories, including the change for Census 2000. This move has been both welcomed and criticized, indicative of ongoing sensitivity in the nation to issues of race. This new method of asking about race also impacted the ability to accurately compare race data over time. Ancestry questions (which ask respondents to identify their country of origin), meanwhile, are consistently dogged by claims of undercounts, and concerns that respondents do not always willingly identify their ancestry.

Census Geography

Geography is key to the decennial census. Obviously, the census must count the people in each state in order to apportion representatives by state. But in order to distribute federal funds—not to mention for the benefit of research about the nation—the census also presents data that can describe smaller geographies, such as cities and towns. The census does that and more, providing data for states, counties, cities and townships, and smaller geographies known as census tracts, block numbering areas, block groups, and blocks. This last geography is more or less akin to an actual city block. All of these smaller geographies, from census tracts on down, began in the twentieth century, and it was not until the 2000 census that every place in the country was assigned a census tract. Previous decennial censuses, then, do not feature census tract (or equivalent) data for all places.

Figure 8.2 (see Chapter 8, p. 197) showed major census geographic entities; Figure 14.4 shows the census geographies that a particular address belongs to.

Census Geography, Major Divisions, Values for Address Shown in Figure 14.4

1. Census Region (of four regions: Northeast, Midwest, South, West): West
2. State: California
3. County or equivalent: Santa Barbara County
4. County subdivisions: n/a
5. Place (city or equivalent): Santa Barbara city
6. Census Tract (within a county, between 1,200–8,000 people; ideally 4,000): 5.02
7. Block group (within census tract, a cluster of blocks of 600–3,000 people): 4
8. Census Block (within block group, much like an actual city block): 4,000

Figure 14.4. On the Top, Census Map of Santa Barbara, CA; on the Bottom, Inset Showing Census Tract 5.02; Block Group 4; and Block 4000

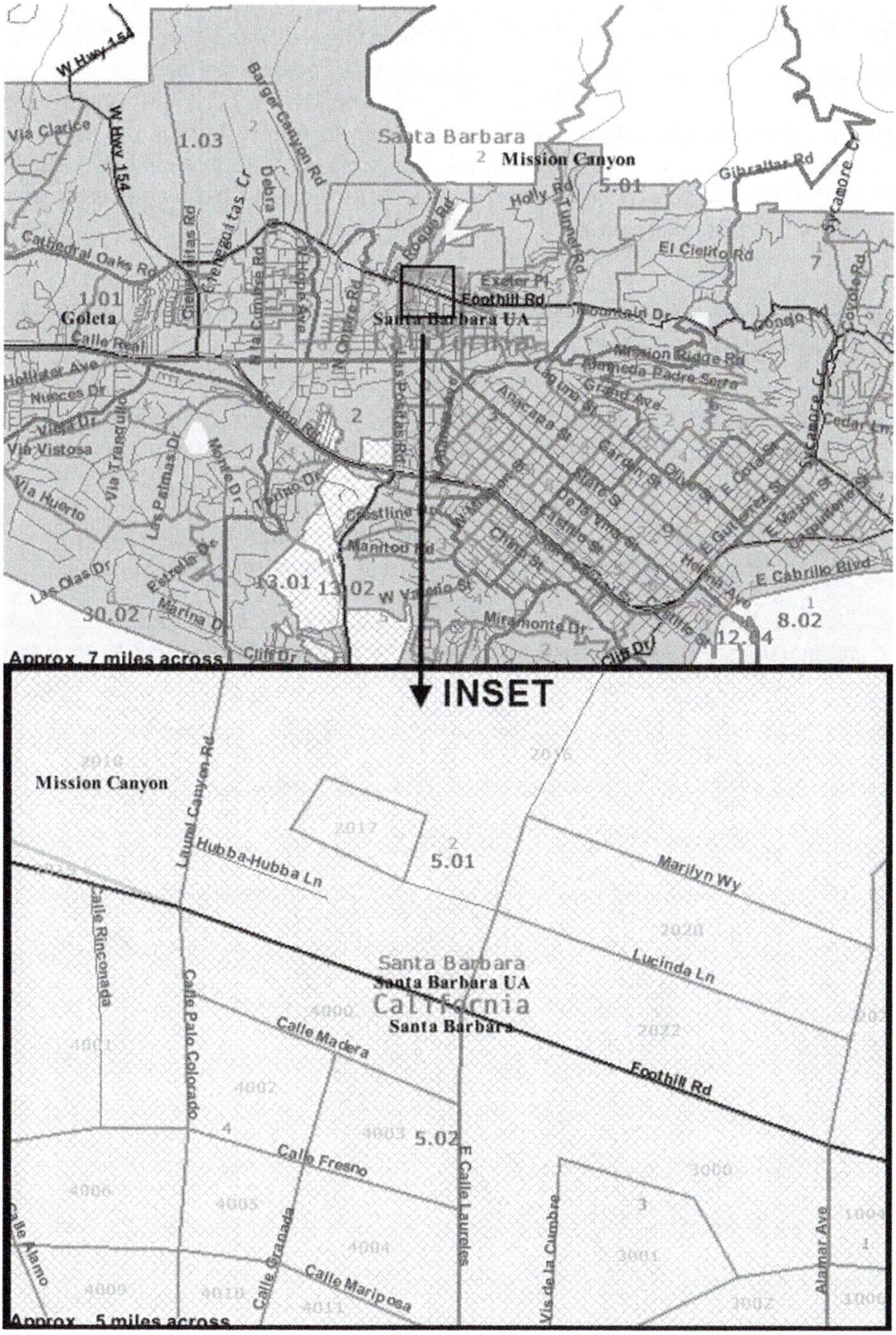

While beyond the scope of this chapter, the Census Bureau also developed the TIGER (Topologically Integrated Geographic Encoding and Referencing) system, geographic reference files that, in addition to their use in census geography, helped spur the development of the world of GIS data and software. These TIGER files were created by combining United States Geological Survey topographical maps with Census Bureau maps of addresses used by decennial census takers in the field. When used with GIS software, TIGER files combined with decennial census data enable creation of sophisticated maps, including features such as roads, rivers, elevation data, and legal and census boundaries, all mapped with demographic and socioeconomic data from the census (see Figure 14.5 for an example).

Census Publications

Although neither the constitution nor later action by Congress called for publication of census results, publications (thankfully for librarians and for this

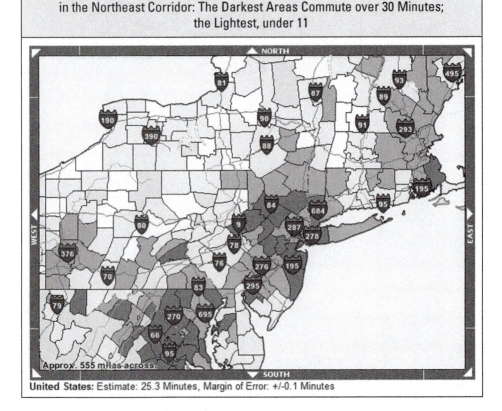

Figure 14.5. Map Showing Average Commute-to-Work Times, by County, in the Northeast Corridor: The Darkest Areas Commute over 30 Minutes; the Lightest, under 11

United States: Estimate: 25.3 Minutes, Margin of Error: +/-0.1 Minutes chapter) did start with the first census, with a single 56-page report. In 1800, another single report was produced, of 74 pages. By 1840, there were well over 1,000 pages of decennial census reports; by 1880, 20,000; by 1960, over 100,000 pages (Eckler, 1972). That's hundreds of times bigger than *War and Peace*. And the 1970, 1980, and 1990 censuses were much bigger than that, with hundreds of published volumes. As of 2000, most data and publications began to be available via the web as part of the same rapid transition to web access that has transformed so much government information. Within one ten-year decennial census period, access evolved from these hundreds of printed reports (with limited and difficult-to-use electronic access via CD-ROMs and primitive online systems) to a full point-and-click web interface.

Early Census Reports: 1790–1840

Using the earliest decennial census reports is straightforward. As published in print or scanned online by the Census Bureau (http://www.census.gov/prod/ www/abs/decennial), these historical census reports usually contain a summary table or two, and then have several pages of data per state. The state data is further broken down by smaller geographies, namely, by county and city/town/place, and occasionally, a subdivision of a place, such as Harlem Division in Figure 14.6.

The published data depend on the questions asked. For each relatively simple decennial census in this early period, there is only a volume or two of results: one volume of the basic population data by geography, and sometimes a second volume or two for extra data such as the economic or pensioner data. From 1790 to 1840, the census generally just took a count and gathered data by sex and a few basic age categories, and for free citizens versus slaves. The 1810 census saw a concurrent effort to count manufacturers, the result being some data on the number, volume, and type of manufacturing done, in the nation, states, and for each county. Separate volumes were published to share this data. The 1820 census was the first to add an economic question as part of the census itself, with citizens noting whether they were employed in agriculture, commerce, or manufacturing. Again, a second volume was published to present this data. The 1830 and 1840 censuses, meanwhile, more closely resembled the early censuses, although 1840 included some extra questions asked of military pensioners.

Accessing the data in these volumes is pretty straightforward. There is usually a summary page with general population data for each state, and then a chapter for each state with further breakdowns by county and town. This is important as it mirrors—in a simpler form—all census data throughout history, namely, with data gathered by geography.

Not all reports are online at the historical census reports website. The invaluable *Catalog of United States Census Publications 1790–1972* lists and describes every report in each census. Getting one's hands on these volumes is not always easy. While historical census reports have sometimes been republished by private publishers, it is mostly larger libraries that own significant runs of historical decennial census reports. The Census Bureau also has a

---

Figure 14.6. 1790 Census Summary Results for the Nation (Left) and Part of New York (Right)

The Return for SOUTH CAROLINA having been made fince the foregoing Schedule was originally printed, the whole Enumeration is here given complete, except for the N. Weftern Territory, of which no Return has yet been publifhed.

DISTICTS	Free white Males of 16 years and upwards, including heads of families	Free white Males under fixteen years	Free white Females, including heads of families	All other free perfons	Slaves.	Total.
Vermont	22435	22328	40505	255	16	85539
N. Hampfhire	36086	34851	70160	630	158	141885
Maine	24384	24748	46870	538	NONE	96540
Maffachufetts	95453	87289	190582	5463	NONE	378787
Rhode Ifland	16019	15799	32652	3407	948	68825
Connecticut	60523	54403	117448	2808	2764	237946
New York	83700	78122	152320	4654	21324	340120
New Jerfey	45251	41616	83287	2762	11423	184139
Pennfylvania	110788	106948	206363	6537	3737	434373
Delaware	11783	12143	22384	3899	8887	59094
Maryland	55915	51339	101395	8043	103036	319728
Virginia	110936	116135	215046	12866	292627	747610
Kentucky	15154	17057	28922	114	12430	73677
N. Carolina	69988	77506	140710	4975	100572	393751
S. Carolina	35576	37722	66880	1801	107094	249073
Georgia	13103	14044	25739	398	29264	82548
	807094	791850	1541263	59150	694280	3893635

	Free white Males of 21 years and upwards.	Free Males under 21 years of age.	Free white Females.	All other Perfons.	Slaves.	Total
Total number of Inhabitants of the United States exclufive of S. Weftern and N. Territory.						
S.W. territory	6271	10277	15365	361	3417	35691
N. Ditto	—	—	—	—	—	—

NEW-YORK.

NEW-YORK. CITY and COUNTY.	Free white Males of 16 years and upwards, including heads of families.	Free white Males under 16 years.	Free white Females, including heads of families.	All other free Perfons.	Slaves.	Aggregate total.	Mary Females above 16.	Mary Males above 16.
City of New York } Harlem Divifion	8328	5797	14963	1061	2180	31328	838	
	171	110	291	41	189	803	9	
Total,	8500	5907	15254	1101	1369	33131	847	
WEST CHESTER COUNTY.								
Morrifina	41	17	41	2	30	133		19
Weft Chefter	217	218	411	46	142	1203		70
Eaft Chefter	174	160	320	11	75	740		14
Pelham	43	31	84	3	38	199	8	
Yonkers	265	220	458	12	170	1135		27
Greenburgh	330	323	616	9	122	1400		37
New Rochelle	170	130	277	26	89	692		23
Scarfdale	73	53	123	14	18	281		11
Momaroneck	108	98	171	18	57	452		35
Rye	258	164	427	14	123	986	5	
Harrifon	242	120	451	35	54	1004		9
White Plains	131	100	218	8	46	505		12
Mt. Pleafant	501	421	909	8	84	1924		14
North Caftle	608	593	1203	43	19	2470	4	
Bedford	610	612	1182	1C	38	1470		58
Poundridge	247	270	538	7		1062	11	
Salem	396	316	728	14	19	1452	36	
North Salem	266	239	509	16	18	1058	4	
Stephen	343	297	612	7	38	1297		
York	380	381	771	18	40	1609	1	18
Courtlandt	484	452	905	25	66	1932		31
Total,	5939	5330	10958	157	1419	24003	79	390
DUTCHESS COUNTY.								
Frederickftown	1437	1540	2851	41	63	5932		126
Phillipstown	517	593	942	31	22	2079		163
Southeaft Town	231	242	433	3	13	921		39
Pawling	1031	1068	2098	01	42	4130		1
Beekman	847	951	1682	31	106	3597		116
Fifhkill	1366	1290	2643	41	601	5941		13
Poughkeepfie	617	573	1092	48	190	2529		98
Clinton	1173	1112	2115	31	176	4607		17
Amenia	763	782	1449	29	52	3078		95

print-on-demand program for reports that it has scanned. Finally, each state is home to a State Data Center (http://www.census.gov/sdc) that coordinates access to census data. Each of these sources can aid users in actually laying hands on the appropriate decennial census volume.

Multivolume Reports: 1850–1930

Beginning in 1850 the amount of data gathered in the decennial census grew quickly and steadily. This was partly because more extra questions were asked, and partly because of the nation's rapidly expanding population. The year 1850 was notable in that it was the first census to ask additional questions not only related to manufacturing and industry but also about education, literacy, and real estate, among others (Figure 14.7). Meanwhile, 1880 was notable for the first census questions related to health and health conditions. And 1910 saw the first use of census tracts and smaller geographic designations, for the first time allowing users to access data about particular parts of towns. Use of census tracts expanded over the following decades, mainly in metropolitan areas, but eventually the Census Bureau expanded the program to include the entire county by 2000.

Figure 14.7. Page from 1850 Census Volume on North Carolina Showing Literacy Data by City and Occupations by State

STATISTICS OF NORTH CAROLINA. 317

TABLE IX.—ADULTS IN THE STATE WHO CANNOT READ AND WRITE—Continued.

COUNTIES.	WHITES.			FREE COLORED.			Native.	Foreign.	Aggregate.
	M.	F.	Total.	M.	F.	Total.			
Hertford	215	320	535	144	181	325	860	....	860
Hyde	250	436	686	3	5	8	694	....	694
Iredell	172	305	477	5	6	11	487	1	488
Johnson	510	937	1,447	30	17	47	1,494	....	1,494
Jones	114	183	297	28	37	65	362	....	362
Lenoir	222	389	611	18	26	44	655	....	655
Lincoln	68	103	171	4	4	8	179	....	179
McDowell	230	450	680	34	35	69	749	....	749
Macon	335	609	944	14	13	27	971	....	971
Martin	133	7	140	1	....	1	141	....	141
Mecklenburgh	63	62	125	23	41	64	187	2	189
Montgomery	175	366	541	7	10	17	552	6	558
Moore	287	703	990	23	16	39	980	40	1,020
Nash	433	875	1,308	99	107	206	1,514	....	1,514
New Hanover	172	284	456	1	....	1	452	5	457
Northampton	504	860	1,364	148	162	310	1,674	....	1,674
Onslow	392	613	1,005	1	....	1	1,002	4	1,006
Orange	440	830	1,270	95	114	209	1,425		1,475

TABLE X.—PROFESSIONS, OCCUPATIONS, AND TRADES OF THE MALE POPULATION.*

Agents	52	Brewers and distillers	124	Cotton manufacturers	15
Agricultural implement makers	10	Brick makers	10	Daguerreotypists	8
Apothecaries and druggists	31	Butchers	37	Dentists	34
Architects	5	Cabinet and chair makers	424	Drivers	131
Artists	10	Carpenters	2,474	Drovers	5
Auctioneers	5	Carriers	5	Editors	37
Authors	1	Cartors	33	Engineers	40
Bakers	13	City, county, and town officers	412	Factory hands	41
Bankers	1	Civil engineers	6	Farmers	81,808
Bank officers	31	Clergymen	747	Fishermen	434
Barbers	39	Clerks	1,298	Foundry men	14
Barkeepers	29	Clock makers	5	Gardeners and florists	21
Basket makers	12	Coach makers	393	Gate keepers	6
Black and white smiths	2,036	Collectors	7	Gold and silver smiths	47
Block and pump makers	4	Colliers	27	Gold miners	91
Boat builders	16	Confectioners	23	Grocers	88
Boatmen	329	Contractors	13	Gunsmiths	152
Bone-black makers	4	Coopers	1,326	Hat and cap manufacturers	175
Bookbinders	5	Coppersmiths	19	Inn keepers	147
Booksellers and stationers	9	Cordwainers	1,587	Inspectors	46

By 1880, the decennial census had become undeniably long, and the number of published reports numbered into the dozens. Extended social and demographic questions were asked, as well as many questions about agriculture, industry, and manufacturing. By this time finding the desired data becomes more complicated. Different volumes cover different geographies, and different topics. Data for a particular place might appear in many different volumes, depending on the subject; similarly, data for a particular subject might appear in many different volumes, depending on geography.

To find specific data, consult the *Catalog of United States Census Publications, 1790–1972*, mentioned in the previous section. Like census reports from earlier eras, some of the reports from this period will be a part of the Census Bureau's historical census reports website; others will be owned by depository libraries, and perhaps State Data Centers.

Era of the Statistical Sample: 1940–2000

As noted, the 1940 census was notable for the introduction of statistical sampling. Census workers—still on foot, remember—asked an extended set of questions to every twentieth household. Sampling continued to be refined over the coming decades. With the growth of the nation and the census—data was also being tabulated for thousands of smaller geographic units, such as census tracts—published reports by this time number in the hundreds for each census, and finding the desired data can still take some digging. In 1970, published reports also began to be broken out by whether the data was from the 100 percent questions or the sample questions, which is occasionally helpful in identifying the right volumes. For instance, there are single volumes of the basic 100 percent data for each state (covering places and smaller geographies within the state, too); there are also single volumes for each state with the sample data results, and volumes containing data by census tract for metropolitan areas. Many subject-based reports have been produced, too. In addition to the listing of all reports in the *Catalog of United States Census Publications, 1790–1972*, each recent census has a separate guidebook. And to get a sense of the scale of decennial census publishing, there is also the (now discontinued) annual *Census Catalog and Guide*, which lists the available reports from each recent census (see Figure 14.8)—for 1990, just the *listing* of decennial census publications spanned over 30 pages.

Once in a volume, the Table Finding Guides (Figure 14.9), which are just after the table of contents, are quite useful. With their grids of subjects by geographies, these guides allow users to quickly find the right table.

Schulze's three-volume set (1983, 1985, 1988) is also very useful in navigating the library of decennial census volumes from the first decennial census through 1980, using handy grids to identify years, volumes, subjects, and geographies, and lead to detailed listings of data by volume.

The 1990 and especially the 2000 census data are best—and increasingly only—accessed online via the American FactFinder, which allows for easier discovery of data by subject and geography. Print volumes may be found using the same method as for various older volumes: online as part of the historical census reports website; in local depository libraries; and at State Data Centers.

End of the Long Form and Birth of the American Community Survey: Census 2010

The 2010 census is the shortest and simplest census since the very first one. There is no long form and nearly no extra questions: nothing about education, earnings, occupation, transportation, physical characteristics of the dwelling, ancestry, languages, and other detailed socioeconomic and demographic statistics. There is no sample of the population answering more questions. Everyone gets only the short form, which counts the population, asks about relationships in

Figure 14.8. First Page of 30 Listing Reports and Data Products of Census '90, from the *Census Catalog and Guide*, 1995

1990 Census of Population and Housing

Contents

Title (and Series)	*Abstract No.*
Introduction	
Data Products Issued October-December 1994	
Reports	
Population and Housing	
Population and Housing Unit Counts (1990 CPH-2)	1602
Population and Housing Characteristics for Census Tracts and Block Numbering Areas (1990 CPH-3) and Census Tract/Block Numbering Area Outline Maps (1990 CPH-3)	1603
Population and Housing Characteristics for Congressional Districts of the 103rd Congress (1990 CPH-4)	1604
Selected Population and Housing Data Paper Listings (1990 CPH-L)	1608.5
Metropolitan Areas as Defined by OMB, June 30, 1993 (1990 CPH-S-1-1)	1610
Urbanized Areas of the United States and Puerto Rico (1990 CPH-S-1-2)	1611
We Asked . . . You Told Us. Census Questionnaire Content, 1990 (1990 CQC)	1624
Population	
Social and Economic Characteristics (1990 CP-2)	1626
The Foreign-Born Population in the United States (1990 CP-3-1)	1630
Ancestry of the Population in the United States (1990 CP-3-2)	1631
Persons of Hispanic Origin in the United States (1990 CP-3-3)	1632
Education in the United States (1990 CP-3-4)	1633
Asians and Pacific Islanders in the United States (1990 CP-3-5)	1635
Metropolitan Area Housing Characteristics (1990 CH-3-1)	1647
Evaluation and Research	
Content Reinterview Survey: Accuracy of Data for Selected Population and Housing Characteristics as Measured by Reinterview (1990 CPH-E-1)	1648
Effectiveness of Quality Assurance (1990 CPH-E-2)	1649
Programs to Improve Coverage in the 1990 Census (1990 CPH-E-3)	1651
General and Reference	
Population and Housing Reference Reports	
Guide (1990 CPH-R-1)	1653.6
History (1990 CPH-R-2)	1653.8
Alphabetical Index of Industries and Occupations (1990 CPH-R-3)	1654
Classified Index of Industries and Occupations (1990 CPH-R-4)	1655
1990 Census Questionnaires and Other Public-Use Forms (1990 CPH-R-5)	1656
Other General and Reference Reports	
Census ABC's—Applications in Business and Community	1658
Census '90 Basics	1658.5
Counting for Representation: The Census and the Constitution	1659.2
Informational Brochures (Titles Vary) (1990 CPH-I)	1659.7
Introduction to 1990 Census Products	1660
1990 Census of Population and Housing: Special Tabulations Program Brochure	1661.3
1990 Census of Population and Housing: Tabulation and Publication Program	1661.5
Official 1990 U.S. Census Form	1663
Profiles of America's Elderly	1663.2
Strength in Numbers	1664
Computer Files	
Summary Tape Files	
Summary Tape File 1B Extract on CD-ROM—Puerto Rico	1673.7
Summary Tape File 1B—Puerto Rico	1674
Summary Tape File 1D	1678
Summary Tape File 1D and 3D, Congressional Districts of the United States, 103rd Congress, on CD-ROM	1679
Summary Tape File 3D	1688
Summary Tape File 3 on CD-ROM—Puerto Rico	1689.5
Summary Tape File 3—Puerto Rico	1690
Summary Tape File 4C	1693.2
Summary Tape File 420—Place of Work 20 Destinations File (Puerto Rico)	1694
Subject Summary Tape Files	
The Foreign-Born Population in the United States (SSTF 1)	1695
Ancestry of the Population in the United States (SSTF 2)	1695.2
Persons of Hispanic Origin in the United States (SSTF 3)	1695.4
Characteristics of Adults With Work Disabilities, Mobility Limitations, or Self-Care Limitations (SSTF 4)	1695.6
The Asian and Pacific Islander Population in the United States (SSTF 5)	1695.8
Education in the United States (SSTF 6)	1696
Metropolitan Housing Characteristics (SSTF 7)	1696.2
Housing Characteristics of New Units (SSTF 9)	1696.6
Mobile Homes (SSTF 10)	1696.8
Employment Status, Work Experience, and Veteran Status (SSTF 12)	1697.2
Fertility (SSTF 16)	1698
Condominium Housing (SSTF 18)	1698.4
Journey to Work in the United States	

each household, and gathers data about race and age. The results will form the basis of reapportioning Congress; be used to distribute shares of billions of federal dollars; and allow researchers, policy makers, and the public to access basic statistics about the populations of states, cities, counties, and smaller census geographies such as census tracts, block groups, and blocks.

The shift to this throwback census is due to the emergence of the American Community Survey (ACS). Because recent decennial census efforts saw increased difficulty in getting households to fill out the long and cumbersome long form, the census—after years of planning and testing—instituted the ACS

Figure 14.9. Table Finding Guide from a Volume of the 1990 Census

Subjects by Type of Geographic Area and Table Number

Subjects covered in this report are shown on the left side, and types of geographic areas are shown at the top. For definitions of area classifications, see appendix A. For definitions and explanations of subject characteristics, see appendix B. Race and Hispanic origin are indicated with reference letters in parentheses after the table numbers. When a range of table numbers is shown together with a reference letter, there is one table for each race and Hispanic group. Reference letters for population counts and characteristics by race and Hispanic origin are:

- (A) White; Black; American Indian, Eskimo, or Aleut; Asian or Pacific Islander; Hispanic origin; White, not of Hispanic origin
- (B) American Indian, Eskimo, Aleut, All Asian, Chinese, Filipino, Japanese, Asian Indian, Korean, Vietnamese, Cambodian, Hmong, Laotian, Thai; All Pacific Islander, Hawaiian, Samoan, Guamanian
- (C) Mexican, Puerto Rican, Cuban, Other Hispanic origin, Dominican, Central American, Costa Rican, Guatemalan, Honduran, Nicaraguan, Panamanian, Salvadoran, South American, Argentinean, Chilean, Colombian, Ecuadorian, Peruvian, Venezuelan, All other Hispanic origin
- (D) Race by Hispanic origin

Subject	The State			County		Place and (in selected States) county subdivision[1]		American Indian and Alaska Native area[2]
	Total	Urban, rural, size of place, and rural farm	Inside and outside metropolitan area	Total	Rural or rural farm	10,000 or more	2,500 to 9,999	
SUMMARY CHARACTERISTICS	1-3, 8-13(A)	1-3, 8-13(A)	1-3, 8-13(A)	1-3, 8-13(A)	...	1-3, 8-13(A)	1-3, 8-13(A)	14-16
POPULATION COUNTS BY RACE AND HISPANIC ORIGIN	4-5(A-D)	4(A-D)	5(A-D)	6(A-D)	214(A), 218(A)	7(A-D)	7(A-D)	...
SOCIAL CHARACTERISTICS								
Age	20, 34, 45(A), 110(B), 119(C), 128(D)	20, 56-61(A)	34, 56-61(A)	140, 151(A)	215, 219	169, 180(A)	196	222
Ancestry	17, 31	17	31	137	...	166	195	...
Disability	20, 34, 45(A), 111(B), 120(C), 129(D)	20, 62-67(A)	34, 62-67(A)	140, 152(A)	216, 220	169, 181(A)	197	223
Education:								
School enrollment and type of school, educational attainment	22, 36, 47(A), 111(B), 120(C), 129(D)	22, 62-67(A)	36, 62-67(A)	142, 152(A), 160(B), 163(C)	215, 219	171, 181(A), 189(B), 192(C)	197, 205(A), 208(B), 211(C)	223
Fertility (children ever born)	21, 35, 46(A), 110(B), 119(C), 128(D)	21, 56-61(A)	35, 56-61(A)	141, 151(A), 160(B), 163(C)	215, 219	170, 180(A), 189(B), 192(C)	196, 205(A), 208(B), 211(C)	222
Household and family characteristics:								
Household type and relationship	21, 35, 46(A), 110(B), 119(C), 128(D)	21, 56-61(A)	35, 56-61(A)	141, 151(A)	215, 219	170, 180(A)	196	222
Selected living arrangements, unmarried partner households	21, 35, 46(A), 110(B), 119(C), 128(D)	21, 56-61(A)	35, 56-61(A)	141, 151(A)	...	170, 180(A)	196	222
Family type by presence of own children	21, 35, 46(A), 110(B), 119(C), 128(D)	21, 56-61(A)	35, 56-61(A)	141, 151(A), 160(B), 163(C)	215, 219	170, 180(A), 189(B), 192(C)	196, 205(A), 208(B), 211(C)	222
Language:								
Language spoken at home (detailed list)	18, 32	18	32	138	...	167	...	...

---

to replace the long form. The goal of the ACS isn't only to make the decennial census easier to gather, but also to provide ongoing current data.

The ACS gathers demographic, social, and economic data similar to that included on the census long form. Age, race, sex, family relationships, housing characteristics, education and literacy, health and health insurance, employment and income, language, and transportation are all among the subjects of questions asked. And since the ACS is ongoing instead of once a decade, it provides more current data than the census long form did.

In the ACS, approximately 250,000 households are sampled each month across the nation. This sample is large enough to provide estimates for larger geographies—states, cities, and counties with a population of 65,000 or more— every year instead of every ten years, as the three million or so total surveys per year will get enough responses from these larger cities to yield statistically valid results. As such, the ACS produces three distinct data sets each year: one-year data sets, three-year data sets, and five-year data sets. This is because the ACS needs three years of surveys before it can compile statistically sound data for places with 20,000 to 65,000 people; and five years to gather enough responses for places with less than 20,000 residents.

This process—taking multiple years to gather enough data for smaller places—makes the ACS different than the long form in one significant way. Except for those places with over 65,000 people, which yield yearly data, ACS data is based on moving averages (also known as period averages). This means that if one is looking for data about Gunnison, Colorado, whose population is under 20,000, ACS will have data for the 2005–2009 period, because it takes five years of surveys to gather enough responses for an adequate survey of Gunnison. It will also have data for 2006–2010; 2007–2011; and so on. It will not have data for any single year because not enough residents of Gunnison will receive an ACS in a year to yield useful data. It is, therefore, important to understand that the resulting data is for a period of time, unlike data from the decennial census, which is for a single point in time.

These moving averages do occasionally present confusing options when using the ACS. All places with over 20,000 people will have multiple ACS figures available. For instance, Syracuse, New York (with a population well over 100,000), will have ACS data for the year 2007, the years 2007–2009, and the years 2005–2009. Each figure will be slightly different. All three are legitimate and useful, one just needs to understand the peculiarities of these moving averages—which is especially tricky when measuring something like prices, which can fluctuate over even short periods (the Census Bureau is using inflation data to attempt to normalize such statistics). Herman (2008) offers an excellent overview of the issues surrounding the ACS in general and moving averages in particular.

Online Census Data and American FactFinder: 2000–2010

As seen, the Census Bureau has scanned many of its historical census reports, although nowhere near comprehensively, and made them available online at http://www.census.gov/prod/www/abs/decennial/. Also worth noting is the Historical Census Browser (http://mapserver.lib.virginia.edu/), a grant-funded project of the University of Virginia Geospatial and Statistical Data Center which uses an online interface to present a huge amount of historical census data, all the way back to 1790, although only for counties and larger geographies. And the National Historical Geographic Information System (http://www.nhgis.org/) provides a similarly interesting compilation of historical census data with advanced geographic capabilities.

Census 2000 was the first census that used the web as the primary and original distribution method, via a portal called American FactFinder (see Figure 14.10).

American FactFinder (http://factfinder.census.gov) is the primary method of accessing contemporary census data. The American FactFinder, newly redesigned to coincide with the release of Census 2010 data, presents data

Figure 14.10. American FactFinder Screenshot

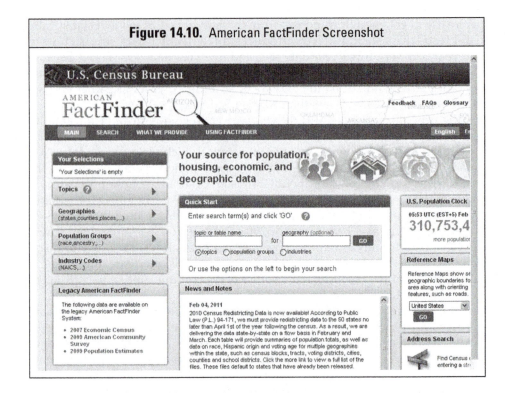

about the population and economy of the United States and places within; it's simple to enter in a state, city, county, place, or even type in an address to get data for smaller geographic areas (census tracts, etc.).

The three largest data sources found in American FactFinder are the decennial census, the ACS, and the economic censuses. Most data is presented as coming from one of these sources. If one seeks population or demographic data for a particular state, county, or place, data is available from both decennial censuses and the ACS. For instance, in Figure 14.11, data may be accessed for a particular

---

Census 2010

This chapter was written after the 2010 census was conducted, but before any demographic data were released. The website http://2010.census.gov is the gateway to Census 2010 information and data, and will link to the data in American FactFinder. The first data release—termed the apportionment data, as it is used to apportion representation in the U.S. House of Representatives for the next decade—was released at the end of 2010, with the rest of the data following in the ensuing months and years.

While American FactFinder remains the source for recent census data, Census 2000 and Census 1990 also have their own gateway pages, pointing to the data and relevant documentation:

http://www.census.gov/main/www/cen2000.html
http://www.census.gov/main/www/cen1990.html

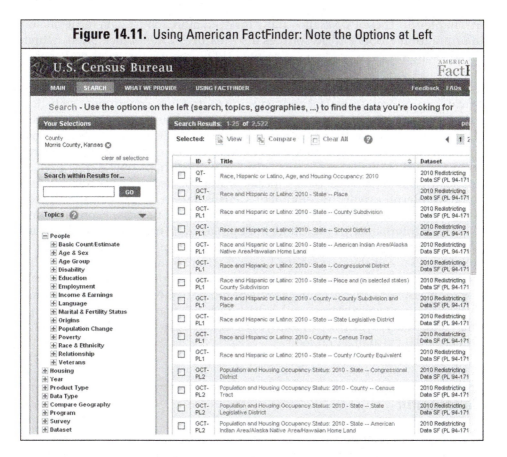

Figure 14.11. Using American FactFinder: Note the Options at Left

place for either decennial census data or from the Population Estimates program. As of this writing, 2010 census data is still slowly being released, and ACS data is being added into the new FactFinder. Options on the left allow for easy access of data by other demographic and socioeconomic characteristics, surveys, topics, and more.

Decennial Census Microdata and Enhanced Census Data-Based Products

Larger amounts of data are available via the Download Center in American FactFinder. For instance, one can download a file with specific data for all states, or all places in the nation, or all census tracts in a county, among other powerful options. These files are of particular use to more serious researchers who need cross-sectional data. The Tools and Resources page, meanwhile, is highlighted by Public-Use Microdata Samples (PUMS), which are extracts of the actual decennial census microdata (microdata was introduced in Chapter 8). These PUMS files allow for even more robust data retrieval and manipulation. Tools and Resources also features a Reference Shelf, which includes hundreds of on-demand printed (PDF) reports for states and special subjects.

Decennial census data is also among the most fertile basis for enhanced, privately produced statistical and mapping tools. Since government statistical data is—within the limits of privacy law—public, third-party developers are able to use the data as the basis of new products. While sometimes such reuse is somewhat disingenuous—some publishers simply take government documents and reprint them under their own imprint, with perhaps only a new preface as added value—statistical data, especially from the decennial census, has seen some wonderful private development. Census data is behind countless products designed for market research (see Chapter 13, Business, Economic, and Consumer Information), or for more in-depth research use, companies like SimplyMap (http://www.geographicresearch.com/simplymap) use the data to create specialized thematic maps beyond what is possible using American FactFinder's mapping options. Among other noteworthy products that create maps, charts, and other graphical analysis tools are those from Social Explorer (http://www.socialexplorer.com), which uses all available historical census data, and Many Eyes (http://manyeyes.alphaworks.ibm.com), which adds attractive data visualization tools.

Conclusion

The unmatched size and scope of the decennial census, and the related American Community Survey, make it the most important statistical repository from the government, and the most popular single statistical undertaking in the nation. The decennial census continues to evolve, and understanding and finding data sources for any particular decennial census requires some research—even when the reports and data are online, it is necessary to know the nature of the statistical effort in order to interpret the results. From American FactFinder to census microdata to printed reports, the Census Bureau houses an astonishing amount of statistical data about the nation, available to use in methods designed for the novice user through the statistician. The ACS, meanwhile, is a groundbreaking new effort to provide updated demographic information even for small geographies, which will also prove important, but one must understand its nature in order to properly locate pertinent data.

Exercises

1. Explore the 1830 census. What statistics are available on race and slavery? Are there statistics by state? By city?

2. Find the population of Phoenix, Arizona, in every census from 1920 to 1980. What further geographic breakdowns exist by decade? When were census tracts introduced?

3. Generate a list of the commuting times to work for all cities in California from Census 2000.

4. For your current address, identify the census tract, block group, and block. What streets or geographic features form the boundaries for your block? What is the population, by age and sex, for your block?

5. What is the most recent median household income for the county you currently reside in? The one you grew up in? For each, what is the specific source of the data?

Sources Mentioned in This Chapter

Sources mentioned in this section do not duplicate the References that follow.

1990 Census, http://www.census.gov/main/www/cen1990.html.

2000 Census, http://www.census.gov/main/www/cen2000.html.

2010 Census, http://2010.census.gov/.

American Community Survey, http://www.census.gov/acs/www/.

American FactFinder, http://factfinder.census.gov/.

Bureau of the Census. 1974. *Catalog of United States Census Publications, 1790–1972.* Washington, DC: Government Printing Office. http://catalog.hathitrust.org/Record/000732965.

Bureau of the Census. *Census Catalog and Guide.* Annual, 1946–1998. http://www.census.gov/prod/www/abs/catalogs.html.

Historical Census Browser, http://mapserver.lib.virginia.edu/.

Historical Census Reports, http://www.census.gov/prod/www/abs/decennial/.

National Historical Geographic Information System, http://www.nhgis.org/.

References

Anderson, Margo J. 1988. *The American Census: A Social History.* New Haven: Yale University Press.

Browning, W. R. F. 2009. *A Dictionary of the Bible.* New York: Oxford University Press. Oxford Reference Online.

Bureau of the Census. 2002. *Measuring America: The Decennial Census from 1790 to 2000.* Washington, DC: Government Printing Office.

Cassedy, James. 1969. *Demography in Early America: Beginnings of the Statistical Mind.* Cambridge: Harvard University Press.

Colvin, Jill. 2010. "Down for the Count." *First Things*, 202: 39–42.

Eckler, A. Ross. 1972. *The Bureau of the Census.* New York: Praeger.

Gibbs, Nancy. 2010. "Count Me In." *Time* 175, no. 13 (April 5): 56.

Halacy, Dan. 1980. *Census: 190 Years of Counting America*. New York: Elsevier/Nelson.

Herman, Edward. 2008. "The American Community Survey: An Introduction to the Basics." *Government Information Quarterly* 25, no. 3: 504–519.

Holden, Constance. 2009. "The 2010 Census: America's Uncounted Millions." *Science* 324, no. 5930 (May 22): 1008–1009.

Holmes, Steven. 2000. "Report Says Census Bureau Helped Relocate Japanese." *New York Times*, March 17. http://www.nytimes.com/2000/03/17/us/report-says-census-bureau-helped-relocate-japanese.html.

Kennedy, J. C. G. 1864. *Population of the United States in 1860: Compiled from the Original Returns of the Eighth Census under the Direction of the Secretary of the Interior*. Washington: GPO.

O'Hare, William. 1998. "Managing Multiple-Race Data." *American Demographics* 20, no. 4 (April): 42–45.

Schulze, Suzanne. 1983. *Population Information in Nineteenth Century Census Volumes*. Phoenix: Oryx Press.

Schulze, Suzanne. 1985. *Population Information in Twentieth Century Census Volumes, 1900–1940*. Phoenix: Oryx Press.

Schulze, Suzanne. 1988. *Population Information in Twentieth Century Census Volumes, 1950–1980*. Phoenix: Oryx Press.

Chapter 15

Historical and Archival Information

Introduction

As stewards of collections containing mostly the *published* record of government, librarians recognize those times when our users are really seeking another kind of government content: the inner workings of an agency or the papers of important government figures. Primary sources are documentary evidence of an event or moment in time: actual accounts (letters, diaries, news articles, speeches and more), photographs, artwork, and every manner of records in their original form. Understanding where to find, and how to think about, archival primary sources generated by the activities of the federal government is critical to providing reference and managing government documents collections for the long term. This chapter explores research possibilities using archives, museums, and two important laws: the Freedom of Information Act and the Privacy Act.

Archives, Museums, Libraries: Distinctions Are Fading

In our digital age, many have noted that cultural heritage institutions (see sidebar) are working less and less in isolation (Marty, 2010). Technology as an access tool for exhibits and collections has democratized and helped demystify archives, special collections, and museums—research destinations no longer the exclusive domain of academic scholars. The web has afforded these institutions exposure in ways unimaginable a decade ago. Libraries, archives, and museums, especially those that charge no entrance fees, report an increase in patrons despite the current economic downturn (American Library Association, 2009).

With their treasures more accessible to the general public via the web, libraries, archives, and museums are pulling down other barriers for the benefit of their users and their collections. They are sharing resources (technical infrastructure, storage facilities, costs for traveling exhibits); partnering for grants; and venturing into collaborative policy development. This convergence, comparatively recent and very fluid, signals an increased readiness to look beyond individual repositories. Many archives and museums have developed outreach programs and customized curricula for teachers and middle or high school students, yet another way of revealing their collections. The convergence

---

Cultural Heritage Organizations

What are cultural heritage organizations and why should libraries and archives work with them? The phrase *cultural heritage* refers to both the tangible components of a society (such as buildings and monuments) as well as intangibles (the dramatic arts, languages, traditional music, and informational, spiritual, and philosophical components) meaningful to a particular people's history and identity. Many institutions manage and preserve cultural heritage resources, including museums, antiquities departments, community cultural centers, and park services. Both government and nongovernmental organizations are involved with cultural heritage management and preservation, from the intergovernmental level—such as the United Nations Educational, Scientific, and Cultural Organization (UNESCO), which designates World Heritage sites—to the smallest local community group (Corbey, 2008).

---

is good news for librarians, who should not hesitate to contact their often invisible colleagues working behind closed doors in archives and museums. For government documents librarians, collaboration and the art of intelligent referrals are not new. With more practice, librarians are starting to overcome the myths and preconceptions of noncirculating, tightly secured archival materials.

Archives

In considering the role of archives, one must start with basic assumptions. We live with the hope that institutions, including governments, keep good records, and that these records are eventually archived and kept accessible for future researchers and historians. As with the preservation of historical artifacts from any era, there is wide variation in practice and circumstances; sometimes records are lost or irrevocably damaged. In the case of the federal government, the agencies themselves are responsible for keeping good records, but their records are (after a time, and on very specific schedules and according to very specific rules) destroyed or transferred to the National Archives and Records Administration (NARA). If one considers an institution—such as one's workplace—one sees that many types of resources are generated as records of activities of the organization (calendars, committee reports, meeting minutes, photos, memos, video and audio recordings, personal notes, letters and e-mail, posters, announcements, and more); these will one day be winnowed down to just the most relevant representative examples. There are also legal, administrative files (personnel files, account statements and transaction logs, etc.), referred to as administrative records; these will be retained at the agency while still in active use, then transferred to a records center for a certain number of years according to law, and ultimately disposed of—either sent to the archives or destroyed (see Figure 15.1 for a records management example from the Department of State). The retaining, transferring, and disposing is not done haphazardly but is based on a records schedule, monitored by records managers within each agency. The idea is to keep only active records at the agency, whether physical or virtual, and place other materials in a Federal Records Center (FRC) for a predetermined number of years. Seventeen such centers are maintained by NARA throughout the country, a low-cost, organized alternative

Figure 15.1. The *U.S. Department of State Records Manual* Lists Retention and Disposition Practices for Different Types of Files

U.S. Department of State Records Schedule

Chapter 15: Overseas Citizens Services Records

A-15-001- 07c	Property Claims Case Files - Consists of correspondence regarding the protection of property and other interests owned by U.S. nationals abroad, and claims of U.S. nationals against foreign governments.
Description:	c. Claims actions involving foreign government restitution or compensation.
Disposition:	Destroy 3 years after case is closed.
DispAuthNo:	NC1-59-77-28, item 7c Date Edited: 4/1/1999

A-15-001-08	Death Case Files - Consists of communications pertaining to the notification of interested parties in the United States of the deaths abroad of non-official U.S. nationals.
Description:	Report of Death of an American Citizen (Form DS-2060).
Disposition:	Permanent. Retire to RSC 3 years after the case is closed. Transfer to WNRC after 2 years. Transfer to NARA when 30 years old.
DispAuthNo:	NC1-59-77-28, item 8b Date Edited: 4/1/1999

Source: http://www.state.gov/documents/organization/128461.pdf.

to storage at the agency. The federal records management system is described in detail in the "Records Managers" portal at http://www.archives.gov/records -mgmt/. Further examples of records retention guidance pages at federal agencies include "What Is a Records Schedule?" from the Environmental Protection Agency (http://www.epa.gov/records/what/quest6.htm) and "Geology Discipline Research Records Schedule" from the U.S. Geological Survey (http://www.usgs.gov/usgs-manual/schedule/432-1-s5/gd.html).

How Archives Differ from Libraries

One easy-to-see difference between government information libraries and archives is that archives tend to be closed-stack collections, allowing visitors access to only a public reading room. In an out-of-sight stack area, print-on-paper materials are housed in acid-free folders and archival boxes, sometimes referred to by the trade name of a predominant manufacturer: Hollinger Metal Edge boxes or simply Hollinger boxes. Electronic media, photographs, and all other imaginable artifacts are stored with care according to preservation standards for that medium. Archivists (over 50 percent of whom are also librarians) often see access and long-term preservation as competing first principles. The more use, the more wear and tear on materials, and the greater chance of theft, loss, or damage. An archivist's challenge is to keep collections intact for as many researchers and for as many years as possible. The idea of "permanence" is no longer part of the archival vocabulary. Unlike most libraries, archives rely heavily on deeds of gift, legal contracts with donors of collections, which may come with restrictions to access or specific preservation requirements. This is less of a concern for governmental archives, as materials tend to be transferred into them based on a regular release schedule. A notable exception: political archives (see later in this chapter), which may contain large amounts of privately donated material. With the archival mission to preserve the historical record, it is important to understand that archives, even government archives, do not and cannot collect everything. Collecting policies are usually made transparent on repository websites. As in libraries, weeding of collections is an accepted archival practice determined by institutional criteria. For more information on specific practices in the government sphere, including the tremendous challenges of managing electronic records, consult the National Association of Government Archives and Records Administrators (http://www.nagara.org/), whose members are practitioners at the local, state, and federal levels.

Archives: Give Me Everything That Happened

At a university library, a college senior recently requested access to "all the secret Oval Office audiotapes from the Reagan administration." After hearing the excerpts from the Johnson tapes, he assumed that all White House conversations were secretly audio recorded and that the recordings and their transcripts became available to a waiting public. The question is an example of expectations versus reality. The student had not considered pre- and post-Nixon information practices. Since the Watergate hearings established that recordings are not the president's personal property but could be brought forth as evidence in investigations, it appears that presidents since Nixon have assiduously avoided similar covert taping. Subsequent presidents have made selective use of open audio- and videotaping and still photography in the Oval Office, have sometimes employed stenographers to transcribe important meetings, or have kept audio or video diaries, but this is different from undercover recordings. Because secret recordings have now been declassified from the Kennedy, Johnson, and Nixon administrations, the student had an expectation of access—though unbeknownst to him, his task would have been gargantuan: if the Reagan Oval Office were audiotaped for as little as two hours a day for approximately 300 working days per year for eight years, the result would be 4,800 hours of recordings. Whether recordings exist or not, what the patron wanted was the unpublished record of government, what went on behind the scenes. He wanted the riches that government archives can offer. But was he prepared to put in the extra effort that archival research involves?

From a user's point of view, archives and libraries represent a very different kind of experience. Today's users are accustomed to remote digital access to library resources. Using archives (with the obvious exception of purely digital archives) means traveling to a specific facility with limited hours of operation, requiring a level of preplanning and effort now increasingly unfamiliar to young researchers. Completely digitized online archival collections are very rare. Personal visits to a repository remain the order of the day. Microforms librarian Glenda J. Pearson used the term "captive researchers" to describe individuals whose research compels them to visit a specific facility, such as those with microforms or archives (1988: 288). The benefit of the captive research environment is that it forces the user into an interaction, however minor, with the specialist on hand who may be able to offer significant assistance.

Some of the best advice librarians can give their users is to make contact with an archive before going there for research, confirm that relevant material is available (order it from storage if need be), and prepare as much as possible before making the trip. Archivists Linda Whitaker and Michael Lotstein describe the differences between archives/special collections and libraries.

> Archives are distinguished from libraries by their rare, unique, original, unpublished materials that require security measures such as signing in, showing identification, removing back packs, prohibiting food and beverages, and viewing items under supervision in a reading room. Nothing is allowed to be checked out and most archives do not participate in interlibrary loans. How this material is described bears no resemblance to the standard, publication format found in library catalogs. The archives call numbers are unique to the repository and reflect many items aggregated together. The descriptions are variable and dependent on an archivist to create them. Archives have rituals, customs and a language all their own. If you cannot speak the language, you cannot ask the right questions. Understanding the rules of engagement and the basic differences between a library and an archive are fundamental to navigating the system. (Whitaker and Lotstein, 2010)

Print-on-paper archives tend to be organized by numbered record group (RG numbers), within which are numbered boxes containing folders of materials. Keeping materials grouped by source and preserving original order are of utmost importance. How are materials cataloged? Just as the dawn of MARC cataloging standardized bibliographic description, and Dublin Core set standards for metadata, encoded archival description, or EAD, has set an XML protocol for archival description. An increasing amount of material in archives is described today with online finding guides, developed using EAD. Online finding guides may also be linked to bibliographic records in library online catalogs or WorldCat, a useful bridging of the archival and library worlds. Frequently, refining a search by archival materials as the format, or even combining a keyword search with the term *papers*, is enough to locate such materials in a library catalog. A WorldCat subject search on subversive activities—United States, limited to archival materials, includes a record for the papers of Elmer Charles Kistler, a Washington State veteran, labor union activist, and Communist Party member, leading to an online finding aid at http://www.lib.washington.edu/specialcoll/findaids/docs/papersrecords/KistlerElmer5347.xml.

Library users expect every individual article or book to be described in an online catalog or database (piece-level holdings information); archival researchers can expect only to see groups of materials described. In the Kistler papers, Box 1, File 29 contains "miscellaneous ephemera, correspondence, and clippings"—one would need to open the folder to see exactly how many or what they are.

NARA: A Pivotal Agency

Archives and the archival profession as we know them today had their beginnings with NARA.

When the National Archives was founded in 1934 there was no archival profession in the United States. The Archives relied on historians and a small cadre of archivists trained in the small number of state archives that had been founded since the first state archives, in Alabama, in 1901. Within two years, led in large part by National Archives staff, the Society of American Archivists was founded in 1936. The growing number of archivists in the US needed a common forum to develop both theory and practice for this new line of work. (Jimerson, 2005: 1)

NARA describes itself to the general public this way:

The National Archives and Records Administration (NARA) is the nation's record keeper. Of all documents and materials created in the course of business conducted by the United States Federal government, only 1%–3% are so important for legal or historical reasons that they are kept by us forever. Those valuable records are preserved and are available to you, whether you want to see if they contain clues about your family's history, need to prove a veteran's military service, or are researching an historical topic that interests you. (National Archives and Records Administration, 2010a)

NARA works directly with agencies to ensure that the entire life cycle of federal record-keeping is done according to legal requirements (think of a group of important memos and their creation, use, and disposition, remembering that relatively few—up to 3 percent—are actually transferred to the Archives). For these (hypothetical) memos or papers, if their disposition involves transfer to the Archives, the remainder of their life cycle at Archives includes arrangement and description, preservation, reference, and continuing use by the public (National Archives and Records Administration, 2010b). All of this activity takes place according to federal laws, many of which are codified in 44 U.S.C., and regulations (for details, see http://www.archives.gov/about/laws/).

NARA has two impressive research facilities in the Washington, DC area: the neoclassical National Archives Building, also known as Archives 1, adjacent to the National Mall (a marble palace holding originals of the Constitution and Declaration, complete with its own Metro stop: Archives/Navy Memorial); and the National Archives at College Park, Maryland, dubbed by users Archives 2, a modern facility that opened in 1994. NARA has about 20 other facilities across the United States in locations as diverse as Long Island and Anchorage, Alaska—all with original material. These geographically dispersed collections contain records of federal agencies in their multistate area (see sidebar) and can help users order reproductions of materials from other NARA facilities. The NARA website continually adds finding aids and newly digitized content, providing users with more and more of an educated stab at what they might be likely to find deep in NARA's collections. A standard reference work, the three-volume *Guide to Federal Records in the National Archives of the United States*, provides a master list of record groups. The resource has been converted into a simplified online format at http://www.archives.gov/research/guide-fed-records. Entries include historical notes on each agency or activity (such as inclusive dates) and brief descriptive notes (type and extent of records available).

NARA departments specialize in still pictures (images like Lewis Hine's documentation of child labor, the National Parks photos of Ansel Adams, and much more—see Figure 15.2); motion pictures, sound and video recordings; and cartographic and architectural records. NARA's Access to Archival Databases (http://aad .archives.gov) allows direct searching of federally compiled records databases. Examples include databases like *Records for Passengers Who Arrived at the Port of New York During the Irish Famine... 1/12/1846–12/31/1851* (similar files exist

> **NARA Gems May Be Found Locally**
>
> The NARA facility in Seattle contains original records from federal agencies in Washington, Oregon, Idaho, and parts of Montana, with microfilm holdings from other areas. For example, the holdings from the Bureau of Prisons include over 100 years of records from Washington State's federal penitentiary (on remote McNeil Island), with such items as prisoner and staff publications, staff journals, expense records, inmate case files, and mug shots.
>
> *Source*: Guide to Archival Holdings at NARA's Pacific Alaska Region (Seattle), http://www .archives.gov/pacific-alaska/seattle/holdings/ rg-100-199 .html#129.

for those arriving from Germany, Russia, and Italy) and *Records About Worker-Initiated Strikes and Employer-Initiated Lockouts... 1953–1981*. One of the most exciting NARA databases is simply the Archival Research Catalog or ARC (http://www.archives.gov/research/arc). Although a disclaimer points out that only a fraction of NARA's holdings are represented here, just searching the ARC and using its search help screens is an education. A search on military science yielded thousands of results, including one for *Record Group 385: Records of the Naval Facilities Engineering Command, 1948–1999* that included Operation Safe Haven Photographs ca. 1994,

> a disassembled album of photographs documenting construction of housing for Cuban refugees at the Rodman Naval Station in Panama during Operation Safe Haven. The photographs show construction battalion personnel (Seabees) erecting tents and fencing and putting cots together at Navy Camp Number Three on Empire Range Six. Also pictured are volunteers, camp staff, the arrival of Cubans, refugees being greeted by General Barry McCaffrey, and recreational activities. (National Archives and Records Administration, 2010c)

From the ARC homepage, one can use different navigational tools for What's New?, Family Historians, and Teachers and Students, as well as an attractive array of ARC galleries (topical groupings) for both national and regional holdings.

The growing search capabilities of the ARC are already evident. If one were searching for materials from the Yokohama War Crimes Trials, as one example, either the *Guide to Federal Records* or the ARC would be a logical starting place. A search in the *Guide* for Yokohama brings five results, each representing different record groups (RGs). The identical search in the ARC brings 1,060 results; refining the search to Yokohama AND "war crimes" reduces the results

---

Figure 15.2. Women Welders During World War II, Washington State

```
1893-42. Puget Sound Navy Yard. 7 September 1942.
Miss Margaret A. Christenson making weld on keel of BDE 40.
Fire Watch Mrs. Ruth E. Hafta.
```

Source: Commandant's Central Subject Files, 1936–1961; Puget Sound Navy Yard; Records of Naval District and Shore Establishments (RG 181), http://www.archives.gov/pacific-alaska/picturing-the-century/wwii-era.html.

---

to a more manageable 28, including a cache of materials within RG 338: *Yokohama War Crimes Trials Case Dockets, compiled 1946–1949*. With the archival description for this item, the "Archived Copies" tab describes the exact physical extent of the material, where it is located (College Park, MD), and how users can order reproductions. A prominent link on the NARA homepage also instructs users how to obtain copies of records for purchase: http://www.archives.gov/research/order.

Political Archives

There are many different archives across the United States holding the papers of those who have served in national elective offices (see http://www.archives.gov/legislative/repository-collections). NARA administers the national system of presidential libraries, addressed in Chapter 6. Congress has its own historians (the Senate Historical Office and U.S. House of Representatives Office of the Historian), but what happens to the papers of former members of Congress once they leave office? The story is not entirely straightforward, so consider the life cycle of congressional archival material, starting at the opening of a member's office. Both the Secretary of the Senate and the Clerk of the House are busy managing the records of Congress, including materials from committees and reports required to and from Congress. Members and their office staffs are supplied with the Records Management Manual for Members (Office of the Clerk, 2010).

In 2008, the passage of House Concurrent Resolution 110-307 was a tremendous leap forward, welcomed by congressional papers archivists, as it spells out the importance of members' papers, makes it clear that their maintenance and organization is every member's responsibility, and encourages members to "arrange for the deposit or donation of the Member's own noncurrent Congressional papers with a research institution that is properly equipped to care for them, and to make these papers available for educational purposes at a time the Member considers appropriate" (H. Con. Res. 110-307, 2008: 1). It is important to note that this resolution supports voluntary donations of papers. A member may retain his or her papers or donate them at will. Time will tell the effectiveness of this new law, but archivists are hopeful for this movement in the right direction.

So the answer to the question "Where do members' papers end up?" is actually the last item on the to-do lists of federal legislators as they leave office. Sometimes a member woos an institution, sometime an institution woos a member—but in either case, with few exceptions, the member or the repository must raise a sufficient amount of money to allow for the accessioning and processing of his or her papers. Congressional papers collections, especially those of senators, are notoriously large and difficult to process. Former Speaker Thomas "Tip" O'Neill's papers are at Boston College; Senator Barry Goldwater's are at the Arizona Historical Foundation, and the late Senator Robert Byrd's (the longest-serving senator in U.S. history) are at Shepherd University in Shepherdstown, West Virginia. For those members who do not designate a specific institution for their papers, their materials can go to NARA's Center for Legislative Archives, which preserves members' materials as well as committee, caucus, and oversight records. Congressional materials stored here are generally opened to the public after 30 years, unless an earlier waiting period is specified by the member. Two excellent guides are available for any librarian interested in legislative archives: *Managing Congressional Collections* (Miller, 2008) and *An American Political Archives Reader* (Paul et al., 2009), both published in conjunction with the Society of American Archivists.

Museums

The federal government is home to an array of museums, starting with 15 listed on USA.gov. The list is deceptively short, however, as both the Smithsonian Institution and the National Park Museums represent groupings of museums. The National Park Service's "History" page is a reminder that our nation's history can be found in the almost 400 national parks as well as every American town, with sites ranging from the evidence of ancient civilizations, to U.S. presidents' childhood homes, to battlefields, to civil rights memorials

(National Park Service, 2010). The USA.gov portal also links to numerous state museums. Museum collections are one important means for scholars to supplement the resources they might find in a library or archive. Museums, notes Jennifer Trant,

> are most often subject-based collections of exceptional objects or specimens. For all but the most senior scholar, an encounter with a museum collection is a highly mediated experience. Unique artifacts are presented in an exhibition space, assembled according to a curatorial thesis and sequenced to support an argument or illustrate a theme. (Trant, 2009: 371)

Federally Affiliated Museums Listed at USA.gov

American Art Museum
Cooper-Hewitt, National Design Museum
Freer Gallery of Art and Arthur M. Sackler Gallery
Hirshhorn Museum and Sculpture Garden
Holocaust Museum
National Arboretum
National Gallery of Art
National Museum of African Art
National Museum of American History
National Museum of Natural History
National Museum of the American Indian
National Park Museums
National Portrait Gallery
National Postal Museum
Smithsonian Institution

(*Source*: http://www.usa.gov/Citizen/Topics/History_Museums.shtml.)

Curators and other museum professionals collect not only artifacts but information resources. Most museums, especially the larger ones, maintain libraries and archives to support their collections and the research of curators, docents, and visitors. These may be open to the public or may require special permission to use. Seattle's Wing Luke Museum of the Asian Pacific American Experience includes the Governor Gary Locke Library and Community Heritage Center (http://db.wingluke.org/), a repository that goes beyond traditional boundaries of museum collections and libraries by combining the two. Government documents may show up in unexpected places: Kansas City's renowned Nelson-Atkins Museum of Art houses the 155,000-volume Spencer Art Reference Library (http://www.nelson-atkins.org/education/Library.cfm). A quick online catalog search finds six volumes from the Missouri Division of Energy, including a copy of a 1980 report entitled *Missouri Coal Data*. The McCracken Research Library at the Buffalo Bill Historical Center in Cody, Wyoming (http://www.bbhc.org/mccracken/), collects materials about the American West, including *Concessions in National Parks: Hearings before the Sub-Committee on Public Lands* (1948).

The digital convergence of libraries, archives, and museums has created a buzz in the professional literature, resulting in collaborative theme issues on this topic in *Library Quarterly 80, no. 1* (2010), *Archival Science 8, no. 4* (2008) and *Museum Management and Curatorship 24, no. 4* (2009). Librarians interested in honing their government information skills must learn to get out of the house and learn more about other kinds of heritage organizations. Making a regular practice of visiting archives and museums—or better yet, performing research there to get a feel for the user experience—is a commonsense way to start.

National Libraries

Since this chapter mostly explores primary resources in museums and archives, why mention libraries? The United States is unique in supporting five national libraries: The Library of Congress, the National Agricultural Library, the National Library of Education, the National Transportation Library, and the National Library of Medicine (addressed in Chapter 9). Most of these libraries also serve archival and museum roles, acquiring and preserving thousands of unique and rare materials, creating internationally respected exhibits, and using their webpages to promote their holdings.

The Library of Congress (LC) is in a league of its own, containing 144 million items as of 2009, including 21 million books, 63 million manuscript items, "the largest rare book collection in North America; and the world's largest collection of legal materials, films, maps, sheet music, and sound recordings" (Library of Congress, 2010). If ever there were an institution meaning different things to different people, it would be LC. In the minds of many Americans, it is the national collection of last resort, containing "every book that has ever been published"—both myths! To cataloging librarians, it is the authoritative body setting standards like name authorities, subject headings, and more. To Congress, it contains the Congressional Research Service, a highly skilled team of scholars preparing reports in support of the legislative process (see Chapter 3). To old-time music lovers, it is home of the American Folklife Center, where one can listen online to hours of traditional music or hear examples of American dialects. To educators, students, and anyone interested in history, it contains American Memory, the prototypical digital archive, piloted in 1990, allowing users to explore many different kinds of primary sources online, all documenting the American experience. American Memory is a public-private collaboration, with content contributed from many different museums.

The National Agricultural Library (http://www.nal.usda.gov/) has two facilities, one in Beltsville, Maryland, and one in Washington, DC. It is the nation's premier agricultural library, a coordinative body for the agricultural collections at land grant university libraries and USDA field libraries. Its extensive website has a History, Art, and Biography section pointing to much primary source material. The National Library of Education (http://ies .ed.gov/ncee/projects/nat_ed_library.asp) serves the public, the federal government, and the education community, housing a collection of 60,000 volumes and 800 journal subscriptions, primarily government literature. Reference assistance is available on site, via phone or e-mail, but the library does not offer a portal-style website at the time of this writing. The National Transportation Library (NTL) (http://ntl.bts.gov/) was founded to collect materials in support of government decision making on transportation matters. In 2008 it merged with the U.S. Department of Transportation Library. Its fastest area of collection growth is in digital material (statistical, policy, and technical) deposited by government agencies from the federal, state, local, and tribal levels.

Historical Biographical Information

Any documents librarian working in a medium-to-large library should work collaboratively with the institution's history librarian, archivist, and/or special collections librarian(s). Such colleagues have much to teach us about effectively researching time periods, local and regional culture, and historical events. We can reciprocate by bringing our special government lens to studies of the past and present: our orientation to agencies, government processes, and publication patterns. In the next section, we consider a topic area that is increasingly finding its way into every librarian, archivist, and curator's day-to-day work.

The Mainstreaming of Genealogy

One clear trend in archives and special collections is the growth of a large, enthusiastic user group: genealogists (Hedegaard, 2008). Information useful for family histories can be found in both published and unpublished government documents. Historically, genealogical collections and services in libraries tend to be segregated from mainstream services. Most academic libraries do not usually offer deep resources for searching family history; this has typically fallen to public libraries, state and local historical societies, church organizations, state and regional archives, and the private sector. Technology has disrupted this configuration, as the digitization of government resources, newspapers, and archival sources has led to some rich new sources for searching personal history and new interconnectedness between different kinds of primary resources. Academic librarians, including government documents librarians, are starting to acknowledge that the same skills used to research family history are good for general biographical and historical research and vice versa. And the medical information field overlaps with genealogy: a recent study of family historians showed that over half of the responding households collect some kind of ancestral medical data. These data typically come from death certificates, obituaries, and word-of-mouth or family records and might be useful in promoting increased awareness and surveillance of health risks, both individual and societal (Case, 2008).

A very selective sample of government information useful for genealogical research would include:

- Congressional publications, such as the *Serial Set* (as stated in Chapter 3, it is worth traveling to use a library that subscribes to the commercially digitized *Serial Set*, congressional hearings, or *Congressional Record*): a family member may have been cited by Congress, testified, been under investigation, or filed a claim against the federal government, or may be listed in one of the military directories.
- General Land Office patents: a family member may have purchased or homesteaded land from the federal government; see http://www.glorecords .blm.gov/ or http://www.archives.gov/genealogy/land/.
- NARA offers immigration records, military service records, and an ARC Guide for Genealogists and Family Historians: http://www.archives .gov/research/arc/topics/genealogy/.
- The Social Security Administration death index (http://www.ntis.gov/ products/ssa-dmf.aspx) allows fee-based searching; various commercial sites allow free searching, such as http://ssdi.rootsweb.ancestry.com/, which provides full name, birth date, death date, Social Security number, state of birth and last residence of the deceased.
- Patent and Trademark Office: a family member may hold a patent (http:// www.uspto.gov/patft/index.html).
- Copyright Office: a family member may have copyrighted an original work (http://cocatalog.loc.gov/).
- After 72 years census questionnaires become available on microfilm at NARA facilities and large centers for genealogy; digital editions (fee based) are available through Ancestry.com, HeritageQuest.com, and others.
- Citizenship and Immigration Services: users may write to obtain immigration and naturalization records of deceased family members, for a reasonable fee (https://genealogy.uscis.dhs.gov).
- Birth, death, marriage, and divorce certificates are available via state and/or county vital records offices, county clerks, or county courts. See Where to Write for Vital Records, http://www.cdc.gov/nchs/w2w.htm.

More detailed lists may be found in Constance Reik's *Bibliography for Farmers, Soldiers and Sailors for Family Research and Historical Research* (Reik, 2008) and in a 48-page bibliography from the Oklahoma Department of Libraries entitled *Genealogical Resources in U.S. Federal Depository Libraries* (Oklahoma Department of Libraries, 2006).

Ancestry.com and HeritageQuest.com are two subscription services that have managed to prevail in the genealogical research marketplace. Both are available as individual or institutional subscriptions, and all types of libraries are now subscribing to one or the other. In a recent Reference Backtalk column in *Library Journal*, aptly titled "Why I Love Ancestry.com," the author answers her question with two simple replies: because it works and because we need it (Kundanis, 2008). Kundanis attributes its success in the library market to Ancestry's inclusion of U.S. and U.K. census, birth, marriage, death, immigration, and military records, as well as school yearbooks, ancestral charts, and family group sheets, all at an affordable rate. HeritageQuest (http://www.heritage questonline.com/hqoweb/library/do/index), produced by ProQuest, allows the searching of U.S. federal census materials; a sizable genealogy article database; Revolutionary War pension and warrant files; and memorials, petitions, and private relief actions culled from the *Serial Set*. It would be hard to argue that these commercial products have not significantly increased the usefulness and discovery of historical government data.

Directories

Knowing who worked in a government agency and when can provide significant context for historical research. Those seeking a deeper look inside a federal agency, such as detailed staff and office listings, should consult a commercially produced guide or directory. Once a staple in many kinds of libraries, these directories today seem most apt to be held by law, corporate, archival, and government collections. Librarians who have managed to collect and retain copies of the *Federal Yellow Book* have a valuable historical resource at their fingertips. Produced by Leadership Directories, Inc., it is an annual subscription (with new editions delivered quarterly) that allows users to search for tens of thousands of federal employees by name, organization, or subject, even annotating entries by type of political appointment (Leadership Directories, 2010). Print directories offer a fixed, permanent record for a sequence of years, with more detail than one might find with constantly updated agency directory databases on the web. Greenwood Press offers *The United States Executive Branch: a Biographical Directory of Heads of State and Cabinet Officials* covering 1789–2000. From 1816 to 1959, the government itself issued the *Official Register of the United States* (http://catalog.hathitrust.org/Record/002137439), the directory of choice for finding federal employees in the days when the government workforce, now referred to as the civil service sector, was appreciably smaller. Additionally, many agencies published their own directories, such as the Department of Health and Human Services *Telephone Directory* (HE 1.28:) and while these are valuable, they generally lack advanced indexing features. The hefty *Biographical Directory of Congress* (http://bioguide.congress.gov/) provides authoritative summaries of congressional careers and notes the holding institution for members' papers when known. The biennial *Congressional Pictorial Directory* (http://catalog.hathitrust.org/Record/000535814 and http://catalog.hathitrust.org/Record/000535816) offers photos of House and Senate members in volumes going back as far as 1951.

Requesting Government Records Using FOIA and the Privacy Act

Congress passed the Freedom of Information Act or FOIA (P.L. 89-554, 80 Stat. 378) in 1966; it went into effect the following year, and has been amended in

1974 (P.L. 93-502, 88 Stat. 1561), 1996 (P.L. 104-231, 110 Stat. 3048), 2002 (P.L. 107-306, 116 Stat. 2383), and 2004 (P.L. 108-136, 117 Stat. 1392). This groundbreaking law gives any individual or group the opportunity to request previously unreleased records from executive branch agencies. Citizens' rights under FOIA are frequently mentioned along with rights under the Privacy Act (P.L. 93-579, 88 Stat. 1896), a 1974 act outlining how executive branch agencies gather, maintain, and release personal information about citizens and legal permanent residents. The Privacy Act protects individuals against other members of the public accessing their government files, and allows individuals to correct information appearing in their own government files.

Journalists, researchers, activists, investigators, people seeking to clear their names, and others use FOIA and the Privacy Act to request files, including files on themselves. Agencies must release the requested information unless it falls into one of nine exemptions and three exclusions (see sidebar). The agency has 20 working days to acknowledge a request in writing, and may extend that for an additional 10 working days, with notification to the requestor. The Department of Justice oversees FOIA compliance, and OMB oversees Privacy Act compliance. The best source of FOIA information on the government web is http://www.justice.gov/oip/index.html, which provides reference materials

---

What Information Is Available under the FOIA?

The Freedom of Information Act provides public access to all federal agency records except for those records (or portions of those records) that are protected from disclosure by any of nine exemptions or three exclusions (reasons for which an agency may withhold records from a requester). The exemptions cover:

1. Classified national defense and foreign relations information
2. Internal agency rules and practices
3. Information that is prohibited from disclosure by another law
4. Trade secrets and other confidential business information
5. Inter-agency or intra-agency communications that are protected by legal privileges
6. Information involving matters of personal privacy
7. Certain information compiled for law enforcement purposes
8. Information relating to the supervision of financial institutions
9. Geological information on wells

The three exclusions, which are rarely used, pertain to especially sensitive law enforcement and national security matters. The FOIA does not apply to Congress, the courts, or the central offices of the White House, nor does it apply to records in the custody of state or local governments. However, all state governments have their own FOIA-type statutes (a list is available through the National Freedom of Information Coalition, http://www.nfoic.org/state-foi-laws). "...The FOIA does not require a state or local government or a private organization or business to release any information directly to the public, whether it has been submitted to the federal government or not. However, information submitted to the federal government by such organizations or companies may be available through a FOIA request if it is not protected by a FOIA exemption, such as the one covering trade secrets and confidential business information."

(*Source*: United States General Services Administration, 2009: 2.)

and serves as a directory of other agencies' FOIA sites. OMB brings together a complicated set of Privacy Act guidelines at http://www.whitehouse.gov/omb/privacy_default/.

Fulfilling requests may take months or even years. The person making the request must pay for all research (15 to 40 dollars per hour) and photocopying fees involved (minimally ten cents per page) (General Services Administration, 2009). Every agency is required to maintain a public FOIA reading room (so that requestors may view materials in person); a link on its agency webpage providing FOIA contacts; instructions; and an electronic reading room displaying materials already released. The FBI's electronic reading room is the most famous, with many celebrity files and historically significant cases available for perusal. One random foray into a file mentioning illegal drugs and the Grateful Dead (http://foia.fbi.gov/foiaindex/gratefuldead.htm) also turns up a reference to the Shelter Half, a 1970s-era Tacoma, Washington, coffeehouse geared toward GIs opposed to the Vietnam War—see Figure 15.3. Exempt information is blacked out, or redacted, and numbers along the side provide the reason for the redaction: b7c in Fig. 15.3 means that names were withheld because of "records or information compiled for law enforcement purposes . . .

Figure 15.3. Sample Page, Concerning a Tacoma (WA) Coffeehouse, from a 14-Page FBI File on the Grateful Dead

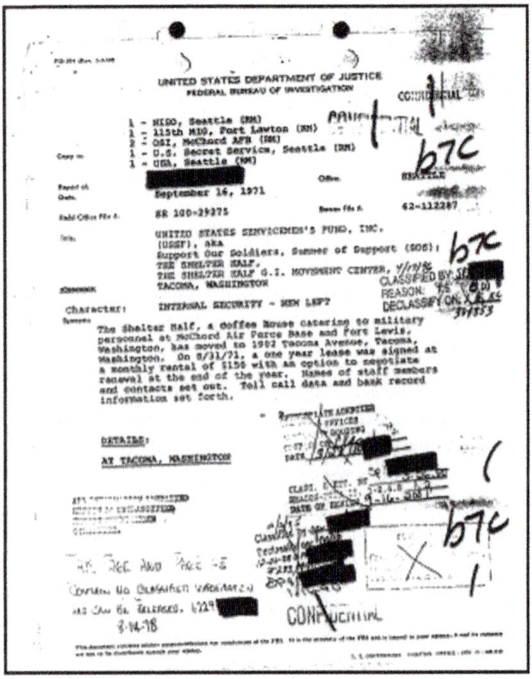

Source: http://foia.fbi.gov/grateful_dead_the/grateful_dead_the_part01.pdf

[that] could reasonably be expected to constitute an unwarranted invasion of personal privacy" (5 U.S.C. 552).

The National Security Archive, a project of George Washington University, offers an outstanding set of FOIA guides at http://www.gwu.edu/~nsarchiv/nsa/foia/guide.html. Here are detailed ways to make FOIA work for you; follow a sample request through the process; understand the related areas of classification, declassification, reclassification, and redeclassification; and learn about FOIA guidance, history, and news. A newly created Office of Government Information Services (OGIS) within NARA opened its doors in September 2009 (http://www.archives.gov/ogis). The office will mediate FOIA disputes, review policies, and recommend policy changes as appropriate, serving as a government-wide FOIA ombudsperson.

Feast or Famine in the World of FOIA

Professor David H. Price of St. Martin's University filed over six hundred FOIA requests during the course of his research on the intelligence community and anthropologists. In an appendix to *Threatening Anthropology: McCarthyism and the FBI's Surveillance of Activist Anthropologists*, Price offers specific advice from his years of filing requests and appealing FOIA denials. He points out that some agencies, such as the National Security Agency, denied all of his requests (by law, such denials must be based on exemptions). The Department of Energy gets high marks for requests fulfilled within weeks, whereas the FBI frequently takes six or more years to send records or denials of records (Price, 2004).

Conclusion

This chapter examined diverse sources for primary source material from the government. Special attention has been paid to the convergence of libraries, archives, and museums as trusted repositories in the digital age. NARA is a particular focus, with its central role in preserving the unpublished record of the federal government. As with other chapters, the structures and services explored on the federal level have local parallels in the form of state, county, and municipal archives and museums. The role of museums and national libraries has been considered, along with the blossoming field of genealogy and its relationship to government documents. We concluded our review by considering FOIA and Privacy Act requests as a further line of inquiry into the riches of the federal government.

Exercises

1. Spend some time in a congressional papers collection, an archive holding the unpublished (manuscript) materials of members of Congress. Such collections are dispersed throughout the United States—your own institution

may very well serve as one. The Center for Legislative Studies has a directory by archival institution, by state, or by member of Congress (http://www .archives.gov/legislative/repository-collections). Visit an archive and see firsthand how members of Congress participated in the decision making of their era. As one possible place to start your exploration, ask to see constituent correspondence for one member of Congress. If you cannot visit a collection in person, locate one with a well-established collection of digitized material on its website.

2. Using a library-licensed version of Ancestry.com or HeritageQuest.com, or your own personal or trial account, look for historic census questionnaires filled out a) by someone with your own last name or a similar last name or b) a family member. How did the census code this individual's race? His or her occupation? Who else lived in the same household?

3. What is your own nearest NARA facility? Name three agencies whose materials are housed there.

4. Pick a federal agency and find its FOIA electronic reading room. What kinds of materials are there, and is it well organized? What happens when you look for FOIA information from a similar agency on the state level?

5. Can you find historical (more than 25 years old) government-produced films available for viewing on the open web? Are you able to view them, and what are some of the topics?

Sources Mentioned in This Chapter

Sources mentioned in this section do not duplicate the references that follow.

Access to Archival Databases (AAD), http://aad.archives.gov/.

An American Political Archives Reader. 2009. Paul, Karen Dawley, Glenn Gray, L. Rebecca Johnson Melvin, and Congressional Papers Roundtable (Society of American Archivists). Lanham, MD: Scarecrow.

Ancestry.com, http://www.ancestry.com/.

ARC Guide for Genealogists and Family Historians, http://www.archives.gov/research/arc/topics/genealogy/.

Archival Research Catalog, http://www.archives.gov/research/arc/.

Bibliography for Famers [sic], Soldiers and Sailors for Family Research and Historical Research, http://www.fdlp.gov/home/repository/doc_download/157-bibliography-for-famers-soldiers-and-sailors-for-family-research-a-historical-research.

Biographical Directory of Congress, http://bioguide.congress.gov/.

Center for Legislative Archives, http://www.archives.gov/legislative/.

Citizenship and Immigration Service Genealogy Page, https://genealogy.uscis.dhs .gov/.

Congressional Pictorial Directory, http://purl.access.gpo.gov/GPO/LPS11679.

Congressional Record. 1873–. Washington, DC: Government Printing Office.

Copyright Office, http://cocatalog.loc.gov/.

Federal Staff Directory. 2009. Mt. Vernon, VA: Staff Directories.

Federal Yellow Book. 2010. New York and Washington, DC: Leadership Directories.

Freedom of Information Act (Department of Justice), http://www.justice.gov/oip/.

Genealogical Resources in U.S. Federal Depository Libraries, http://www.odl.state.ok
.us/usinfo/GenealogicalResources/.

General Land Office Patents, http://www.glorecords.blm.gov/.

Guide to Federal Records in the National Archives of the United States, http://www.archives
.gov/research/guide-fed-records/.

HeritageQuest.com, http://www.heritagequest.com/.

Library of Congress, http://www.loc.gov/.

Miller, Cynthia. *Managing Congressional Collections*. 2008. Chicago: Society of American
Archivists.

National Agricultural Library, http://www.nal.usda.gov/.

National Archives and Records Administration, http://www.archives.gov/.

National Association of Government Archives and Records Administrators (NAGARA),
http://www.nagara.org/.

National Freedom of Information Coalition, http://www.nfoic.org/index.cfm.

National Library of Education, http://ies.ed.gov/ncee/projects/nat_ed_library.asp.

National Security Archives FOIA Guide, http://www.gwu.edu/~nsarchiv/nsa/foia/
guide.html.

National Transportation Library (NTL), http://ntl.bts.gov/.

Office of Government Information Services, http://www.archives.gov/ogis/.

Official Register, http://catalog.hathitrust.org/Record/002137439.

Patent & Trademark Office, http://www.uspto.gov/patft/index.html.

Privacy Act Guidance, http://www.whitehouse.gov/omb/privacy_default/.

Sobel, Robert, and David B. Sicilia. 2003. *The United States Executive Branch: A Biographical
Directory of Heads of State and Cabinet Officials*. Westport, CT: Greenwood.

Social Security Administration Death Index, http://ssdi.rootsweb.ancestry.com or
http://www.ntis.gov/products/ssa-dmf.aspx (fee-based).

Society of American Archivists, http://www.archivists.org/.

U.S. *Congressional Serial Set*. 1817–. Washington, DC: Government Printing Office.

Where to Write for Vital Records, http://www.cdc.gov/nchs/w2w.htm.

References

American Library Association. 2009. "Comments of the American Library Association in
Response to NBP Public Notice # 18 *District Dispatch*." December 4. http://www
.wo.ala.org/districtdispatch/wp-content/uploads/2009/12/Libraries-Economy-
FCC.pdf.

Case, Donald O. 2008. "Collection of Family Health Histories: The Link Between
Genealogy and Public Health." *Journal of the American Society for Information Science
and Technology* 59, no. 14: 2312–2319.

Corbey, Raymond. 2008. "Cultural Heritage." In *New Encyclopedia of Africa*, John Middleton
and Joseph C. Miller, eds. 2nd ed., vol. 2. Detroit: Thompson, Gale, 550–555.

Department of State. 2010. *U.S. Department of State Records Schedule*. Chapter 15: Overseas Citizens Services Records. Accessed September 23. http://www.state.gov/documents/organization/128461.pdf.

Fisher, Steven. 2004. *Archival Information: How to Find It, How to Use It*. Westport, CT: Greenwood Press.

General Services Administration. 2009. Your Right to Federal Records: Questions and Answers on the Freedom of Information Act and the Privacy Act. November. http://www.pueblo.gsa.gov/cic_text/fed_prog/foia/foia.htm.

H. Con. Res. 307, 110th Cong., 2d sess. 2008. Expressing the Sense of Congress that Members' Congressional Papers Should Be Properly Maintained and Encouraging Members to Take All Necessary Measures to Manage and Preserve These Papers.

Hedegaard, Ruth, and Elizabeth Anne Melrose. 2008. *International Genealogy and Local History: Papers Presented by the Genealogy and Local History Section at IFLA General Conferences 2001–2005*. IFLA publications series, 130. Munchen: K G Saur.

Jimerson, Randall. 2005. "Notes from the 20th Anniversary of the National Archives and Records Administration Panel Discussion." May 20. http://www.archives.gov/about/history/anniversary/panel/randall-jimerson.html.

Kundanis, Barb. 2008. "Why I Love Ancestry.com." *Library Journal* 133, no. 17: 98. http://www.libraryjournal.com/article/CA6602853.html.

Library of Congress. 2010. "About the Library." Last revised April 8. http://www.loc.gov/about/generalinfo.html#2007_at_a_glance.

Marty, Paul. 2010. "An Introduction to Digital Convergence: Libraries, Archives, and Museums in the Digital Age." *Library Quarterly* 80, no. 1 (January): 15.

National Archives and Records Administration. 2009. *The National Archives in the Nation's Capital: Information for Researchers*. Washington, DC: National Archives and Records Administration.

National Archives and Records Administration. 2010a. "About the National Archives." Accessed August 1. http://www.archives.gov/about/.

National Archives and Records Administration. 2010b. "What's a Record?" Accessed August 1. http://www.archives.gov/about/info/whats-a-record.html.

National Archives and Records Administration. 2010c. "Operation Safe Haven Photographs, compiled ca. 1994–ca. 1994" (Archival Description, Scope & Content Note). ARC Identifier 637550/Local Identifier 385-SH. Accessed November 30. http://www.archives.gov/research/arc/.

National Park Service. 2010. "National Park Service: Discover History." Last revised June 16. http://www.nps.gov/history/.

Office of the Clerk, House of Representatives. 2010. *Records Management Manual for Members*. Publication M-1. Accessed August 28. http://www.archivists.org/saagroups/cpr/publications/Manual%20for%20Members.pdf.

Oklahoma Department of Libraries, U.S. Government Information Division. 2006. *Genealogical Resources in U.S. Federal Depository Libraries*. Last revised July 23. http://www.odl.state.ok.us/usinfo/GenealogicalResources.pdf.

Pearson, Glenda J. 1988. "Government Publications on Microform: Integrating Reference Services." *Microform Review* 15, no. 5, 286–291.

Price, David H. 2004. *Threatening Anthropology: McCarthyism and the FBI's Surveillance of Activist Anthropologists*. Durham: Duke University Press.

Reik, Constance. 2008. *Bibliography for Famers* [*sic*], *Soldiers and Sailors for Family Research and Historical Research*. http://www.fdlp.gov/home/repository/doc_download/157-bibliography-for-famers-soldiers-and-sailors-for-family-research-a-historical-research.

Trant, Jennifer. 2009. "Emerging Convergence? Thoughts on Museums, Archives, Libraries, and Professional Training." *Museum Management and Curatorship* 24, no. 4: 369–387.

USA.gov. 2010. "Museums." Accessed August 28. http://www.usa.gov/Citizen/Topics/History_Museums.shtml.

Whitaker, Linda, and Michael Lotstein. 2010. "Pulling Back the Curtain: Archives and Archivists Revealed." Unpublished essay.

Zorich, Diane, Günter Waibel, Ricky Erway, and OCLC Programs and Research Division. 2008. *Beyond the Silos of the LAMs : Collaboration Among Libraries, Archives and Museums in OCLC Programs and Research*. Dublin, OH: OCLC.

Index

Page numbers followed by the letter "f" indicate figures.

T

About the Authors

Eric J. Forte began his library career as an undergraduate student, writing SuDoc call numbers on congressional documents for the regional federal depository at the Texas State Library in Austin. He holds a Masters in Library and Information Science from the University of Illinois at Urbana-Champaign, and has worked as a librarian with government information at the University of Illinois, Western State College of Colorado, the University of California at Santa Barbara, and Boise State University. He has taught, presented, and written about government information in various venues. He is currently a Member Services Consultant with OCLC.

Cassandra J. Hartnett began her career shelving fiction books at the Platts-burgh Public Library. She received her Master of Library and Information Studies from the University of Michigan. She has been employed at the University of Michigan Library (Research Library Residency Program), the University of Michigan School of Information, and Detroit Public Library. She currently serves as U.S. documents librarian, University of Washington Libraries. She has served as an adjunct lecturer at the University of Washington Information School, teaching LIS 526 (Government Publications). She is a cofounder of the Northwest Government Information Network (NGIN) and served as 2008–2009 chair of the American Library Association's Government Documents Round Table.

Andrea L. Sevetson began her library career checking in periodicals at Macalester College. She received her Master of Arts in Library and Information Studies from the University of Wisconsin-Madison, and has since been employed as a government documents librarian at the University of California, Berkeley; the U.S. Census Bureau; and LexisNexis. She is currently employed as a trainer with ProQuest. She has served as the chair of the American Library Association's Government Documents Round Table, and was appointed to the U.S. Depository Library Council to the Public Printer and served as its chair. She is the recipient of the CIS/GODORT/ALA "Documents to the People" Award and the James Bennett Childs Award for distinguished contributions to documents librarianship.

■ ■ ■

Susan Edwards, author of Chapter 10, received her Master of Library and Information Science degree from the University of California, Berkeley. She has worked at Golden Gate Law Library and Amherst College Library and is currently Head of the Education Psychology & Social Welfare Libraries at the University of California, Berkeley.

Jennifer Gerke, author of Chapter 12, is the electronic government information librarian at the University of Colorado at Boulder. She provides general reference services in Norlin Library, as well as bibliographic instruction for classes related to political science, international area studies, and government publications. She is also responsible for collection development in political science and international area studies. Her research interests lie in how to effectively provide services both on and off desk as well as the crossroads between electronic and print provision of materials.

Ann Glusker, author of Chapter 9, is the medical librarian at Group Health Cooperative in Seattle, WA, and has also worked as an epidemiologist at Public Health—Seattle & King County, answering data requests. She has a PhD in Sociology/Demography, a Master's degree in Public Health, and a Master's degree in Library and Information Science, all from the University of Washington. Her dissertation was published as a book entitled *Fertility Patterns of Native- and Foreign-Born Women: Assimilating to Diversity*. She has worked in academic, medical, public, and special library settings. She loves to work with data and is a government publications aficionado; one of her favorite events of the year is the release of the latest American Community Survey data from the U.S. Census Bureau.

Margaret M. Jobe, author of Chapter 11, is the director of the Government Information Library at the University of Colorado at Boulder. She has also served as the head of its Engineering and Math Physics Libraries. She has written on topics relating to government information and collection analysis.

CPSIA information can be obtained at www.ICGtesting.com
Printed in the USA
BVOW06s1402200116

433630BV00019B/145/P